The South African
AID

By the same author:

The Six Language Picture Aid (Protea Book House, 2008)
Feitegids (Pharos, 2006)
The Macro English Aid (J.L. van Schaik, 2000)
Die Afrikaanse Makro Gids (Queillerie, 1998)
The English Afrikaans Xhosa Zulu Aid (Queillerie, 1996)
The English Aid, later *The Macro English Aid* (J.L. van Schaik, 1994)

The South African
AID
Facts and tips

ISABEL UYS

Protea Book House
Pretoria
2009

The South African Aid – Isabel Uys
First edition, first impression in 2009 by Protea Boekhuis
PO Box 35110, Menlo Park, 0102
1067 Burnett Street, Hatfield, Pretoria
8 Minni Street, Clydesdale, Pretoria
protea@intekom.co.za
www.proteaboekhuis.com
Translators: Amanda Tremeer and Iolandi Pool
Proof reader: Iolandi Pool
Cover design: Hanli Deysel
Typography: 10 on 12 pt Helvetica Neue by Etienne van Duyker
Printed and bound: Craft Print, Singapore

© 2009 Isabel Uys
ISBN 978-1-86919-325-6

All rights reserved. No part of this book may be reproduced or transmitted in any form or by any electronic or mechanical means, including photocopying and recording, or by any other information storage or retrieval system, without written permission from the publisher.

CONTENTS

PART I: SOUTH AFRICA

General

Official name, area, oceans, time zones, capital cities, motto   4
The National Anthem   5
Die Stem van Suid-Afrika   7
The Call of South Africa   7
Nkosi sikelel' iAfrika   8
The Constitution   8
The National Flag   11
Former South African flags   11
National symbols   12
The coat of arms   14
Former coat of arms   14
Official languages   15
Public holidays   15
National Orders   16
Population and most important home languages of each province   17

Geography

The provinces of South Africa   20
Most important cities and towns: founding dates and origin of names   22
"Firsts" in Kimberley   33
Place names after 1994   33
Regional names in South Africa   34
Important mountain ranges   37
Highest mountain peaks   38
Well-known mountain passes   39
Well-known caves   42
Most important rivers   42
Important dams   45
Largest ports   47
Important islands   48
Important lighthouses   49
Neighbouring countries   58
Border posts   59

Conservation and Ecotourism

National parks   64
National botanical gardens   87
World Heritage Sites   88
Well-known provincial and private reserves   89
Well-known hiking trails   95
Tips for hikers   101

Well-known monuments, churches and other places of interest

Monuments   106
Certain Historic Churches   112
Interesting towns, places, attractions, events, phenomena
   and legends   122

People

Commanders and governors of the Cape Colony   138
Prime ministers of the Union and the Republic of
   South Africa (1910–1984)   141
(State) presidents of the Republic of South Africa
   (1961–present)   141
Presidents and secretaries-general of the
   African National Congress (ANC)   142
Speakers of Parliament (1910–present)   143
Economists of the year   144
Business leaders of the year   144
Nobel Prize winners   145
Some famous South Africans   146
Interesting South Africans   156
Well-known South African heroes and heroines   159

Literature

The Dewey system   164
South African literary awards   166
   Alan Paton Award   166
   Alba Bouwer Prize   167
   Eugène Marais Prize   168
   Herman Charles Bosman Prize   170
   Hertzog Prize   171
   Ingrid Jonker Prize   174
   MER Prize   176
   Olive Schreiner Prize   178

Recht Malan Prize   179
Sunday Times Fiction Award   180
Tienie Holloway Medal   181
W.A. Hofmeyr Prize   181

Transport

South Africa's national roads   184
South Africa's cars of the year   185
Tips for purchasing a second-hand car   186
Tips for a safe journey   188
The correct conduct at a vehicle accident   189
Tips for saving fuel   190
The development of trains and railways in South Africa   192
South Africa's trains   194
South African airlines   197
New names of South African airports   197
Inkwazi, the South African presidential jet   198
Luggage allowances on flights   198
Animals on aeroplanes   200
South Africa's submarines   201
Notable shipping disasters   202

Economy and finances

The South African currency and previous monetary units   208
Personal budgets   210
Financial tips   210
Children and finances   211
Bank costs   212

Plants and animals

Common weeds and alien plants   214
Popular indigenous trees, shrubs, flowers and climbers   216
South Africa's trees of the year   225
The gestation of animals   227
The feeding of small kittens and puppies   229
The biggest mammals in the world   230
Remarkable animals of South Africa   231
Extinct and endangered mammals of South Africa   234
Illnesses spread by pets   235
South Africa's most poisonous snakes   239

Sport

South African Olympic winners   244
The Comrades Marathon   245
Rugby   250
Cricket   258
Soccer   261
Tennis   264
Golf   265
Horse races   268
Athletics   269
Swimming   272
Highlights of South Africa's sports calendar   273

History

Highlights of South African history and interesting events in South Africa   276
Important South African inventions   316

PART 2: GENERAL

Lifestyle

Tips for happiness   320
Developing a good self-image and self-confidence   321
Friendships   322
Stress   324
How to support someone during a crisis   327
Tips for public speaking   328
Good table manners   329

The school and workplace

Study tips   332
CVs   334
The personal interview   340
Success in the workplace   344
Tips for success for entrepreneurs   349

Marriages

Types of marriages and the wedding ceremony   352
People who may not marry   353

Permission for marriages between minors   354
Marriage contracts   354
Duties of the wedding party   355
Guidelines on who pays for what   356
Tips for lowering expenses   357
Timeline for wedding planning   357
Seating arrangements at the reception   359
Speeches and toasts   360
Traditional etiquette for thank-you notes   360
Wedding etiquette   361
Divorces   361

Wills

General information about wills   364
Criteria for a valid will   365
Division of assets if a person dies intestate   365
Circumstances in which a person may not inherit   365
Example of a simple will   366
A living will   367
Example of a living will   368

Safety and security

Home security   370
Safety in the street and in shops   372
Safety in a vehicle   372
Vehicle hijackings   373
Banking safety   374
Internet shopping   376
Cellphones   377
Identity documents, passports and driver's licences   378
Safety for children   378

Houses

Advantages of buying a house   382
Disadvantages of buying a house   382
Tips for buying a house   383
Home loans and the new Credit Act of 2007   383
Advantages of renting a house   384
Tips for tenants   385
Tips for landlords   385
Example of a simple rental contract   387
Tips on selling a house quickly   389
Building and renovating a house   392

Important regulations and contracts for domestic workers

Workers to whom regulations apply   394
Minimum wages   394
Example of a simple service contract   395
The payment of wages   397
Leave and sick leave   398
Termination of service   398

Food and drink

Traditional recipes   400
Herbs and spices used in food   407
Wine   409
Toast etiquette   412
Wine and food   413

Household tips

Stain removal   416
Cleaning tips   420
Cooking tips   423
General   428

Medical

Traditional remedies and natural remedies   432
Important medicinal herbs   438
Programme of immunisation of children   442
First aid   443
Depression   448
HIV/Aids   451
Organ donation   452
Cot death   453
Abortion   453
Medical specialists   455
Operations and procedures   456
Medical emergency numbers   458

Useful information

Greetings and useful words and phrases in English, Afrikaans, Xhosa, Zulu, Northern Sotho and Tswana   462
Change of name   467
Adoptions   467
The Small Claims Court   468
Tips for saving water   470
Tips for saving electricity   471
Firearms   475
Tips for consumers   477
Contracts   478
Complaint procedure   478
Contacts for complaints   479

Part 1
SOUTH AFRICA

1. GENERAL

Republic of South Africa

Official name: Republic of South Africa

Area:
1 219 090km²

Oceans:
South Africa has the longest coastline of any African country – 2 954km.
The Atlantic Ocean, with the cold Benguela current, is on the west coast.
The Indian Ocean, with the warm Mozambican current, is on the east coast.
The Indian and Atlantic Oceans meet at Cape Agulhas, the southernmost point of Africa.

Time zone:
Greenwich Mean Time (GMT) + 2

Total population:
44,8 million (2001 census), 48,7 million (2008 estimate)

Capitals:
Cape Town (legislative capital)
Pretoria (administrative capital)
Bloemfontein (judicial capital)

Motto on the coat of arms:
Unity in Diversity (!ke e: /xarra //ke, from the Khoisan language /Xam, which died out between 1860 and 1900.)

South Africa's name in the eleven official languages (alphabetically)
Afrikaans: *Republiek van Suid-Afrika*
English: *Republic of South Africa*
Ndebele: *IRiphabliki yeSewula Afrika*
Northern Sotho: *Rephaboliki ya Afrika-Borwa*
Southern Sotho: *Rephaboliki ya Afrika Borwa*
Swazi: *IRiphabhulikhi yeNigizimu Afrika*
Tsonga: *Riphabliki ra Afrika Dzonga*
Tswana: *Rephaboliki ya Aforika Borwa*
Venda: *Riphabu'iki ya Afurika Tshipembe*
Xhosa: *IRiphabliki yaseMzantsi Afrika*
Zulu: *IRiphabliki yaseNingizimu Afrika*

The National Anthem of South Africa

Xhosa and Zulu

Nkosi sikelel' iAfrika,
Maluphakanyisw' uphondo lwayo,
Yizwa imithandazo yethu,
Nkosi sikelela, thina lusapho lwayo.

Sesotho

Morena boloka setjhaba sa heso,
O fedise dintwa le matshwenyeho,
O se boloke, O se boloke setjhaba sa heso,
Setjhaba sa South Africa – South Africa

Afrikaans

Uit the blou van onse hemel,
Uit the diepte van ons see,
Oor ons ewige gebergtes,
Waar the kranse antwoord gee,

English

Sounds the call to come together,
And united we shall stand,
Let us live and strive for freedom,
In South Africa our land.

- The official national anthem is a combination of "Nkosi sikelel' iAfrika" ("God Bless Africa"), "Die Stem van Suid-Afrika" and "The Call of South Africa".
- The words of "Die Stem van Suid-Afrika" were written in 1918 by C.J. Langenhoven, and the music was composed in 1921 by Reverend M.L. de Villiers.
- "Die Stem" was sung in public for the first time on 31 May 1928, at the official raising of the national flag.
- In the 1920s it was played along with "God Save the Queen" at the beginning and end of the SABC's daily transmission.
- "Die Stem" was translated into English in 1952.
- On 2 May 1957, "Die Stem" was accepted as the official national anthem.
- Between 1994 and 1996, "Die Stem" and "Nkosi sikelel' iAfrika" both served as national anthems.
- In 1996, a combination of "Nkosi sikelel' iAfrika", "Die Stem van Suid-Afrika" and "The Call of South Africa" was accepted as the national anthem of South Africa.

C.J. Langenhoven   Enoch Sontonga

- "Nkosi sikelel' iAfrika" was written and composed in 1897 by Enoch Sontonga, a teacher at a Methodist mission school. He wrote the first verse in Xhosa. Later, seven verses were added by the poet Samuel Mqhayi. In 1942 it was translated into Sotho by Moses Mphahlele. The last two lines of the first verse are in Zulu.
- The lyrics of the national anthem encompass five of the eleven official languages of South Africa (Xhosa, Zulu, Sesotho, Afrikaans and English).
- "Nkosi sikelel' iAfrika" was a popular song in church and was also sung at political meetings and rallies of the ANC.
- There are no standard versions or translations of "Nkosi sikelel' iAfrika", so the words may vary.
- Solomon Plaatje, a writer and founding member of the ANC, had the first recording of "Nkosi sikelel' iAfrika" made in 1923 in London.
- Translations of "Nkosi sikelel' iAfrika" also serve as the national anthems of Tanzania and Zambia.

Die Stem van Suid-Afrika

Uit die blou van onse hemel,
uit die diepte van ons see,
oor ons ewige gebergtes
waar die kranse antwoord gee.
Deur ons ver verlate vlaktes
met die kreun van ossewa –
ruis die stem van ons geliefde,
van ons land Suid-Afrika.
Ons sal antwoord op jou roepstem,
ons sal offer wat jy vra:
ons sal lewe, ons sal sterwe –
ons vir jou, Suid-Afrika.

In die merg van ons gebeente,
in ons hart en siel en gees,
in ons roem op ons verlede,
in ons hoop op wat sal wees,
in ons wil en werk en wandel,
van ons wieg tot aan ons graf –
deel geen ander land ons liefde,
trek geen ander trou ons af.
Vaderland! Ons sal die adel
van jou naam met ere dra:
waar en trou as Afrikaners –
kinders van Suid-Afrika.

In die songloed van ons somer,
in ons winternag se kou,
in die lente van ons liefde,
in die lanfer van ons rou,
by die klink van huweliksklokkies,
by die kluitklap op die kis –
streel jou stem ons nooit verniet nie,
weet jy waar jou kinders is.
Op jou roepstem sê ons nooit nee nie,
sê ons altyd, altyd ja:
Om te lewe, om te sterwe –
ja, ons kom Suid-Afrika.

Op U almag vas vertrouend,
het ons vadere gebou:
Skenk ook ons die krag, o Here!
Om te handhaaf en te hou –
dat die erwe van ons vaad're,
vir ons kinders erwe bly:
knegte van die Allerhoogste
teen die hele wêreld vry
Soos ons vadere vertrou het,
leer ook ons vertrou, o Heer –
met ons land en met ons nasie,
sal dit wel wees, God regeer.

The Call of South Africa

Ringing out from our blue heavens,
from our deep seas breaking round;
over everlasting mountains,
where the echoing crags resound;
from our plains where creaking wagons,
cut their trails into the earth –
calls the spirit of our country,
of the land that gave us birth.
At thy call we shall not falter,
firm and streadfast we shall stand,
at thy will to live or perish,
O South Africa, dear land.

In our body and our spirit,
in our inmost heart held fast;
in the promise of our future,
and the glory of our past;
in our will, our work, our striving,
from the cradle to the grave –
there's no land that shares our loving,
and no bond that can enslave.
Thou hast borne us and we know thee.
May our deeds to all proclaim,
our enduring love and service,
to thy honour and thy name.

In the golden warmth of summer,
in the chill of winter's air,
in the surging life of springtime,
in the autumn of despair;
when the wedding bells are chiming,
or when those we love do depart;
thou dost know us for thy children,
and dost take us to thy heart.
Loudly peals the answering chorus;
we are thine, and we shall stand,
be it life or death, to answer,
to thy call, beloved land.

In thy power, Almighty, trusting,
did our fathers build of old;
strenghten then, O Lord, their children,
to defend, to love, to hold –
that the heritage they gave us,
for our children yet may be;
bondsmen only of the Highest
and before the whole world free.
As our fathers trusted humbly,
teach us, Lord to trust Thee still;
guard our land and guide our people.
in Thy way to do Thy will.

Nkosi Sikelel' iAfrika

(Current Xhosa version)
Nkosi sikelel' iAfrika
Maluphakanyisw' uphondo lwayo
Yiva imathandazo yethu
Nkosi sikelela Nkosi sekelela

Nkosi sikelel' iAfrika
Maluphakanyisw' uphondo lwayo
Yiva imathandazo yethu
Nkosi sikelela

Koor:

Yihla moya, yihla moya
Yihla moya oyingcwele
Nkosi sikelela
Thina lusapho lwayo
(repeat)

The Constitution of South Africa

- The Constitution of South Africa is the supreme law of South Africa and no other law or act of government can overrule it.
- The current constitution was ratified on 4 December 1996. Since then it has been amended a few times.
- The Constitution took effect on 4 February 1997.
- The Constitution is based on the values of human dignity, freedom and equality.
- The Constitution consists of an introduction, 14 chapters and seven addenda.
- Each chapter and addendum deals with a specific subject.

Preamble of the Constitution of South Africa

Act 108 of 1996

We, the people of South Africa,
Recognise the injustices of our past;
Honour those who suffered for justice and freedom in our land;
Respect those who have worked to build and develop our country; and
Believe that South Africa belongs to all who live in it, united in our diversity.
We therefore, through our freely elected representatives, adopt this Constitution as the supreme law of the Republic so as to
Heal the divisions of the past and establish a society based on democratic values, social justice and fundamental human rights;
Lay the foundations for a democratic and open society in which government is based on the will of the people and every citizen is equally protected by law;
Improve the quality of life of all citizens and free the potential of each person; and

Build a united and democratic South Africa able to take its rightful place as a sovereign state in the family of nations.
May God protect our people.
Nkosi Sikelel' iAfrika. Morena boloka setjhaba sa heso.
God seën Suid-Afrika. God bless South Africa.
Mudzimu fhatutshedza Afurika. Hosi katekisa Afrika.

Highlights from the Bill of Rights of the Constitution

For more information: www.info.gov.za

The Rights of Adults

- Everyone is equal before the law and has the right to equal protection and benefit of the law.
- The state or any person may not unfairly discriminate directly or indirectly against anyone.
- Everyone has inherent dignity and the right to have their dignity respected and protected.
- Everyone has the right to life.
- Everyone has the right to freedom and may not be detained without trial; they have the right not be exposed to violence, not to be tortured and not to be treated or punished in a cruel, inhuman or degrading way.
- Everyone has the right to bodily and psychological integrity and has the right to make decisions concerning reproduction and their own body.
- No one may be subjected to medical or scientific experiments without informed consent.
- No one may be subjected to slavery, servitude or forced labour.
- Everyone has the right to privacy. Their person, property or home may not be searched, their possessions may not be seized and the privacy of their communications may not be infringed.
- Everyone has the right to freedom of conscience, religion, thought, belief and opinion.
- Everyone has the right to freedom of expression, which includes freedom of the press and other media; freedom to receive or impart information or ideas; freedom of artistic creativity and academic freedom and freedom of scientific research.
- Everyone has the right, peacefully and unarmed, to assemble, to demonstrate, to picket and to present petitions.
- Every citizen has the right to free, fair and regular elections for any legislative body established in terms of the Constitution.
- No citizen may be deprived of citizenship.
  Every citizen has the right to a passport, freedom of movement, the right to leave the country, to enter, to remain in and to reside anywhere in the country.
- Every citizen has the right to choose their trade, occupation or profession freely and a right to fair labour practices.

- Everyone has the right to an environment that is not harmful to their health or well-being.
- Everyone has the right to have access to adequate housing.
- Everyone has the right to have access to health care services, sufficient food and water; and social security, if they are unable to support themselves and their dependants.
- No one may be refused emergency medical treatment.

The rights of children (persons under 18)

- Every child has the right to a name and a nationality from birth.
- Every child has the right to family care or parental care, or to appropriate alternative care.
- Every child has the right to basic nutrition, shelter, basic health care services and social services.
- Every child has the right to be protected from maltreatment, neglect, abuse or degradation.
- Every child has the right to be protected from exploitative labour practices, and to not be required or permitted to perform work or provide services that are inappropriate for a person of that child's age; or place at risk the child's well-being, education, physical or mental health or spiritual, moral or social development.
- Children have the right not be detained except as a measure of last resort, and then separately from detained persons over the age of 18 years and only for the shortest appropriate period of time.
- Every child has the right not to be used directly in armed conflict, and to be protected in such times.
- Children have the right to basic education in the official language of their choice where that education is reasonably practicable.

The National Flag

Current South African flag

The colours of the national flag are black, yellow, green, white, blue and red. The two green bands that merge symbolise reconciliation and the future unity of the diverse population of South Africa. The flag was designed by a state herald, Fred Brownell. It was raised for the first time at midnight on 26 April 1994.

- The South African flag is the only one in the world with six colours.
- When the flag flies, the red stripe must always be on top, and the black triangle must be on the left.
- If the flag is displayed next to an important person, it should always be on the person's right hand side.
- In times of emergency or a national disaster, the flag can only be flown at half mast on the instruction of the president.

British flag (Union Jack)

Union Flag

From 1910 to 1928, the British flag, the Union Jack, was the official flag of the Union of South Africa. From 1928 to 1957 South Africa had two flags: the Union Jack and the then-new South African flag (the Union flag). The new South African flag consisted of three bands of equal width in orange, white and blue with the Union Jack, the flag of the Orange Free State and the Transvaal *Vierkleur* (literally "four-colour") in the middle of the white band. In 1957 the National Party government decided that the Union Jack would no longer be used and that there would only be one official South African flag.

National symbols

Flower: King protea (*Protea cynaroides*)

Tree: Real yellowwood (*Podocarpus latifolius*)

Animal: Springbok (*Antidorcas marsupialis*)

Fish: Galjoen (*Coracinus capensis*)

Bird: Blue crane (*Anthropoides paradisia*)

The coat of arms

The new coat of arms was designed by Ian Bekker and was unveiled on 27 April 2000, Freedom Day, by President Thabo Mbeki in Bloemfontein. The motto on the coat of arms is Unity in Diversity (*!ke e: /xarra //ke*, from the Khoisan language /Xam, which died out between 1860 and 1900).

Symbols on the national coat of arms

Sun: The promise of rebirth and the faculties of reflection, knowledge, good judgement and willpower.

Secretary bird: The ascendency of the nation and the protection of the nation against its enemies.

Protea: South Africa's plants and the potential of the country that must "blossom".

Spear and knobkierie: Defence, authority and peace (the latter because the spear and knobkerrie have been laid down).

Shield and human figures: The origins all South Africans have in common. The two figures greeting each other symbolise unity and solidarity. (The Khoisan figure is derived from figures on the Linton Rock, which is world famous as an example of South African rock art. This rock, along with its drawings, is on display and conserved in the South African Museum in Cape Town.)

Elephant tusks: Wisdom, strength, moderation and eternity.

The ears of wheat: Fertility, growth, the development of potential, the nourishment of people and the agricultural aspects of the land.

South Africa's former coat of arms

South Africa's previous coat of arms was adopted in 1910. The country's motto was "Unity is Strength" (*Ex unitate vires*).

Official languages (2001 census)

The words in parentheses are the terms used in the Constitution of South Africa.

Language	First language speakers
Zulu (isiZulu)	10 677 305
Xhosa (isiXhosa)	7 907 153
Afrikaans	5 983 426
Northern Sotho/Pedi (Sesotho sa Leboa/Sepedi)	4 208 980
Tswana (Setswana)	3 677 016
English	3 673 203
Southern Sotho (Sesotho)	3 555 186
Tsonga (Xitsonga)	1 992 207
Swazi (siSwati)	1 194 430
Venda (Tshivenda)	1 021 757
Ndebele (isiNdebele)	711 821

- Although English is the mother tongue of only 8,2% of the population, it is the language understood by most South Africans and the most commonly used as a second language.
- The following unofficial languages are also acknowledged: sign language, Nama, San, Fanagalo, Phuthi, Khoe, Lobedu and North Ndebele.
- South Africa is, after India, the country with the most official languages.

Public Holidays

1 January	New Year's Day
21 March	Human Rights Day
Friday before Easter Sunday	Good Friday
Monday after Easter Sunday	Family Day
27 April	Freedom Day
1 May	Workers' Day
16 June	Youth Day
9 August	National Women's Day
24 September	Heritage Day
16 December	Day of Reconciliation
25 December	Christmas Day
26 December	Day of Goodwill

National Orders

A national order is the highest honour that the president can bestow on a South African or foreigner who has made an important contribution to the country. Three national orders were announced in 2002 and two more orders in 2003.

Order of Mapungubwe*
This is awarded to South African citizens for outstanding achievement and excellence.

Order of the Baobab**
This is award to South Africans for outstanding and exceptional contributions in the following categories:
- Nation-building
- Freedom and security
- Democracy (struggle)
- Democracy and human rights (advancement of)
- Journalism, literature, art, culture, sport and music
- Business world and economy
- Science, medicine and technical innovation
- Community Service

**The massive baobab *(Adansonia digitata)* is a familiar face in the bushveld of Africa. This tree, known for its vitality, toughness and tenacity, is linked to many of Africa's legends and secrets.

Order of the Companions of O.R. Tambo**
This is awarded to foreign heads of state, heads of government and dignitaries for goodwill shown towards South Africa.

---

* The Kingdom of Mapungubwe flourished a thousand years ago in the north-west of the area now known as Limpopo.
** Oliver Reginald Tambo led the ANC while he was in exile (1960–1990).

Order of Luthuli*
This is awarded to South Africans who have made an outstanding contribution to the advancement of democracy, human rights, nation-building, justice, freedom and peace, and the resolution of conflict in Africa.

Order of Ikhamanga**
This is awarded to South Africans who have contributed outstanding achievements in the arts, literature, culture, music, journalism and sport.

Order of Mendi° for Bravery
The Wolraad Woltemade decoration for gallantry was replaced in 2003 with the Mendi decoration. It was later changed to the Order of Mendi for Bravery.

Population and most important home languages of the provinces (2001 census)

Province	Population	Most important languages
Gauteng	8 837 million	Zulu 21,5% Afrikaans 16,7% English 12,5% Southern Sotho 13,1% Northern Sotho 10,7% Tswana 8,4% Xhosa 7,6% Tsonga 5,7%
KwaZulu-Natal	9 426 million	Zulu 80,9% English 15,6% Afrikaans 1,6%
Limpopo	5 273 million	Northern Sotho 52,7% Tsonga 22,6% Venda 15,5% Afrikaans 2,3%
Mpumalanga	3 122 million	Swazi 30% Zulu 25,4% Ndebele 12,5% Northern Sotho 10,8% Afrikaans 6,2%

* Albert John Mavubi Luthuli was a leader in the freedom struggle and was awarded the Nobel Peace Prize in 1960.
** *Ikhamanga* is the Xhosa name for the strelitzia.
° The *Mendi*, a ship with a group of multi-racial South African soldiers on board, was sunk in the First World War. It is also the name of a South African Navy patrol corvette that has been in use since 2004.

Province	Population	Most important languages
Northern Cape	822 million	Afrikaans 69,3% Tswana 19,9% Xhosa 6,3%
North-West	3 669 million	Tswana 67,2% Afrikaans 7,5% Xhosa 5,8% Southern Sotho 5,7%
Eastern Cape	6 436 million	Xhosa 83,4% Afrikaans 9,3% English 3,6%
Free State	2 706 million	Southern Sotho 64,4% Afrikaans 11,9% Xhosa 9,1% Zulu 5,1%
Western Cape	4 524 million	Afrikaans 55,3% Xhosa 23,7% English 19,3%

- Moloko Temo of Limpopo was the oldest South African until 2009. She was born on 4 July 1984. According to her identity document (issued in 1988), she was 134 years old at the time of her death in June 2009. She still voted in the 2009 election. She was confined to a wheelchair for 56 years and was blind. Her age was never recognised by *Guinness World Records*.
- Madge Bester of Bloemfontein is the world's smallest woman – she is 65cm tall.

2. GEOGRAPHY

Full moon at L'Agulhas

The provinces of South Africa

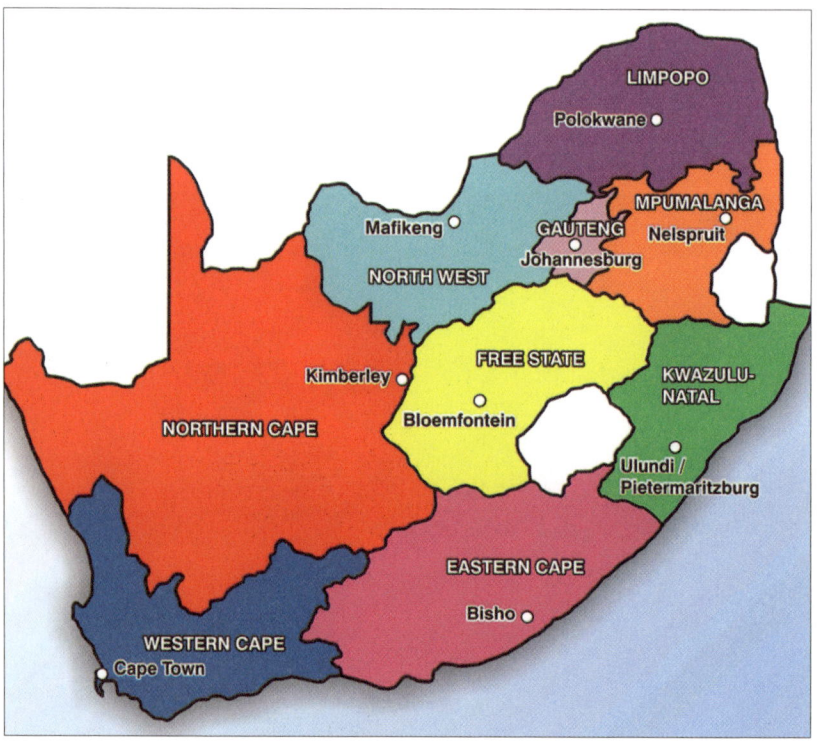

Current Provinces (after 1994)

Province	Area	Capital
Gauteng*	18 810 km²	Johannesburg
KwaZulu-Natal	92 180 km²	Ulundi/Pietermaritzburg
Limpopo (formely Northern Province)	123 280 km²	Polokwane (formely Pietersburg)
Mpumalanga**	78 370 km²	Nelspruit
Northern Cape	361 800 km²	Kimberley
North-West	116 190 km²	Mafikeng
Eastern Cape	169 600 km²	Bisho
Free State	129 480 km²	Bloemfontein
Western Cape	129 370 km²	Cape Town

* *Gauteng* is a Sotho word meaning "place of gold".
** *Mpumalanga* is a Swazi word meaning "place where the sun rises".

Former provinces

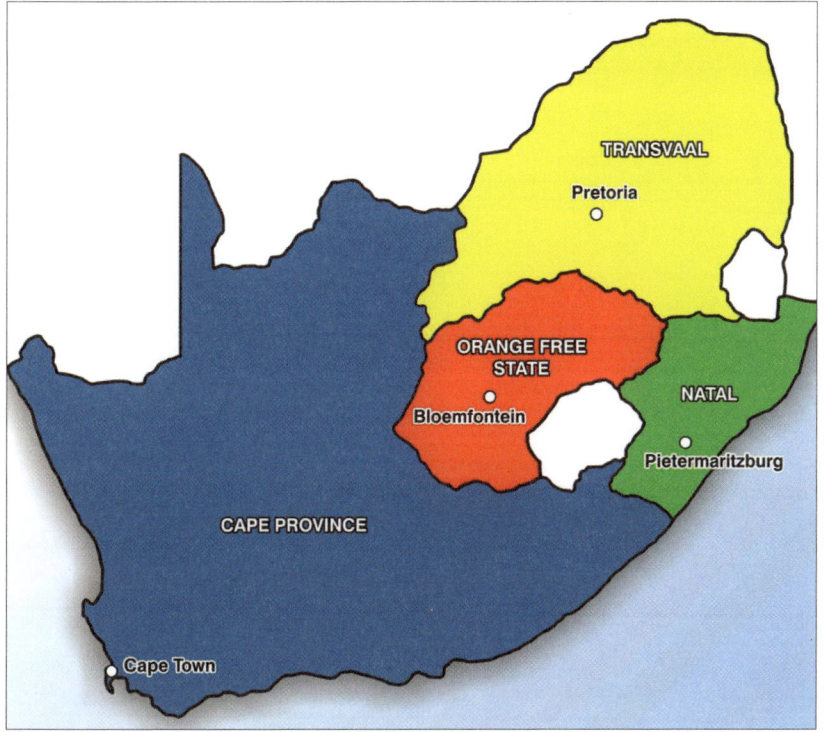

From 1910 to 1994 South Africa had only four provinces, namely:

Province	Capital
Cape Province	Cape Town
Natal	Pietermaritzburg
Orange Free State	Bloemfontein
Transvaal	Pretoria

Important cities and towns: founding dates and origin of names

Place	Date established	Named after whom/what
Aberdeen	1855	Aberdeen, Scotland
Adelaide	1834	Queen Adelaide (wife of William IV of England)
Alberton	1904	General Hendrik Abraham Alberts
Barberton	1902	Graham Hoare Barber, who discovered gold there in 1884
Beaufort West	1818	The Duke of Beaufort, father of the governor of the Cape, Lord Charles Somerset
Bethlehem	1860	Biblical Bethlehem
Bloemfontein	1846	Probably after the Dutch word *bloem* ("flower")
Boksburg	1887	Secretary of State Willem Eduard Bok of the ZAR
Bredasdorp	1838	Michiel van Breda, who dedicated himself to the establishment of the church and town
Brits	1924	Gert Brits, owner of the farm on which the town developed
Calitzdorp	1821	The Calitz family, owners of the farm on which the town developed
Calvinia	1851	John Calvin, the church reformer
Carnarvon	1860	Henry Howard Molyneux Herbert, the Earl of Carnarvon, the then British minister of colonies
Citrusdal	1916	After the citrus fruit grown there
Clanwilliam	1814	The Earl of Clanwilliam, the father-in-law of Governor John Cradock
Colesberg	1830	Sir Galbraith Lowry Cole, a British governor of the Cape
Cradock	1813	Sir John Cradock
Darling	1853	Sir Charles Henry Darling, a British governor of the Cape
De Aar	1902	Underground channel of water (*aar*)

Place	Date established	Named after whom/what
Douglas	1838	Sir Robert Percy Douglas, a British lieutenant-governor of the Cape
Dundee	1882	Dundee in Scotland
Durban	1835	Sir Benjamin D'Urban, Cape governor
Durbanville	1806	Sir Benjamin D'Urban, Cape governor
Fort Beaufort	1837	The Duke of Beaufort (see Beaufort West)
George	1806	King George III of England
Grahamstad	1812	Colonel John Graham, who commanded British troops in the Eastern Cape
Heidelberg (Kaap)	1855	Heidelberg in Germany
Heidelberg (Gauteng)	1866	Heidelberg in Germany
Hermanus (formely Hermanuspietersfontein)	1855	Hermanus Pieters, a Dutch teacher who always took his sheep there
Hoopstad (formerly Hauptstad)	1876	A.P. Haupt, surveyor who surveyed the town
Hopefield	1852	Major William Hope, auditor-general of the Cape, and a certain Mr Field who planned the town
Hopetown	1853–1854	Major William Hope (see Hopefield)
Humansdorp	1849	Matthys Gerhardus Human, who made his farm available for the establishment of a new congregation
Johannesburg	1886	Johann Rissik and Christiaan Johannes Joubert, who were involved with the surveying and proclamation of the new city
Joubertina	1907	Reverend W.A. Joubert of Uniondale
Kaapstad (formely Cabo de Goede Hoop, Het Vlek van de Caap)	1652	The word *cape*, which means a strip of land or high land that projects into the sea
Kakamas	1898	The Khoi word for "place to drink water"
Kimberley	1873	The Duke of Kimberley, who was then the British minister of colonies
King William's Town	1835	King William IV of England

Place	Date established	Named after whom/what
Kirkwood (formely Bayville)	1885	James Somers Kirkwood, who worked to improve irrigation in the area
Klerksdorp	1837	Jacob de Clerq, first magistrate of the town
Knysna	1882	The Khoi word for "ferns"
Kokstad	1871	The Griqua leader Adam Kok III
Krugersdorp	1887	President Paul Kruger
Kuruman	1887	Possibly the Tswana word *kurwana* ("calabash") or *kludu* ("tortoise")
Ladismith (Kaap)	1852	Lady Smith, wife of Governor Sir Harry Smith
Lady Grey	1858	Lady Grey, wife of Governor Sir George Grey
Ladybrand	1867	Lady Brand, wife of Sir Christoffel Brand, the father of President J.H. Brand of the Orange Free State
Ladysmith (Natal)	1847	Originally known as Windsor, later renamed in honour of Lady Smith, wife of Governor Sir Harry Smith
Laingsburg	1881	John Laing, commissioner of Kroongrond at the end of the nineteenth century
Lichtenburg	1886	The Dutch word *lichten* ("lights")
Loxton	1889	A.E. Loxton, on whose farm the town was developed
Lydenburg	1850	The Dutch word for suffering
Machadodorp	1895	General Joachim Jose Machado, who played a major role in the construction of the railway line between Delagoa Bay and Pretoria
Malmesbury	1829	Sir James Harris, the Earl of Malmesbury and father-in-law of the Cape governor Sir Lowry Cole
Middelburg (Eastern Cape)	1852	The word *middel* ("middle"), because of the area between Cradock, Colesberg and Graaff-Reinet, among others
Middelburg (Mpumalanga) (formerly Nazareth)	1866	Possibly after Middelburg in the Netherlands

Place	Date established	Named after whom/what
Montagu	1851	John Montagu, the colonial secretary of the Cape between 1843 and 1853
Moorreesburg	1879	Reverend J.C. le Febre Moorrees, minister of the Swartland congregation for nearly 50 years (1833–1881)
Mosselbaai (formely Aliwal)	1848	Mussel (mollusc)
Murraysburg	1856	Andrew Murray snr., minister of Graaff-Reinet
Nababeep	1860	Khoi word meaning "place of the rhinoceros"
Nigel	1909	The surveyor was apparently reading the novel *The Fortunes of Nigel* by Sir Walter Scott when he discovered gold there. According to another explanation, the name comes from Nigel MacLeish, who developed the Nigel gold mine
Noupoort	1937	A pass through the Carlton Hills near the town
Okiep (formely O'okiep)	1862	The Khoi word meaning "large brackish place"
East London (formely Port Rex)	1845	The British city of London
Orkney	1940	Orkney gold mine, which in turn was named after the islands of Orkney
Paarl	1690	Paarl rock; *paarl* is Dutch for "pearl"
Parow	1901	Johann Parow, German ship's captain whose ship was wrecked and who later became the owner of the land on which the suburb lies
Parys	1876	Paris in France
Pietermaritzburg	1884	The Voortrekker leaders Piet(er) Retief and Maritz
Pietersburg	1884	Commandant General Piet Joubert of the ZAR
Pinetown	1848	Sir Benjamin Pine, lieutenant governor of Natal (1873–1875)
Port Elizabeth	1799	Elizabeth Francis, wife of Sir Rufane Donkin, Cape governor
Porterville	1863	William Porter, attorney-general of the Cape Colony in that year

Place	Date established	Named after whom/what
Postmasburg (formely Sibiling and Blinkklip)	1890	Rev. Dirk Postma, the founder of the Dutch Reformed Church
Potchefstroom	1838	Voortrekker leader Andries Hendrik Potgieter, who was titled *chef* (Dutch "leader") by the town residents
Pretoria	1855	Voortrekker leader Andries Pretorius
Queenstown	1853	Queen Victoria
Reitz (formely Singer's Post and Amsterdam)	1889	President F.W. Reitz of the Republic of the Orange Free State
Richmond Northern Cape)	1844	The Earl of Richmond, the father-in-law of the Cape governor Sir Peregrine Maitland
Richmond (KwaZulu-Natal) (formely Beaulieu)	1850	The Earl of Richmond, the father-in-law of the Cape governor Sir Peregrine Maitland
Riversdal	1838	Harry Rivers, a magistrate of Swellendam that year
Robertson	1853	Dr William Robertson, Dutch Reformed minister in Clanwilliam and Swellendam
Sabie	1895	Sabie River
Sasolburg	1950	Acronym of the "Suid-Afrikaanse Steenkool, Olie and Gaskorporasie" *
Simonstad	1743	Simon van der Stel
Somerset East	1825	Lord Charles Somerset, the well-known Cape governor
Somerset West	1822	Lord Charles Somerset, Cape governor
Springbok (formely Springfontein)	1862	Afrikaans version of the Khoi term *guchas*, meaning "springbok"
Standerton	1878	Commandant Adriaan H. Stander of the ZAR, on whose farm the town was laid out
Stellenbosch	1685	Simon van der Stel
Sutherland	1858	Rev. Henry Sutherland, Dutch Reformed minister in Worcester who established the congregation there

* Afrikaans for the South African Coal, Oil and Gas Corporation

Place	Date established	Named after whom/what
Swellendam	1747	The Cape governor Hendrik Swellengrebel and his wife Helena ten Damme
Tulbagh	1795	The Cape governor Ryk Tulbagh
Tzaneen	1919	Possibly derived from the Karanga word *dzana* ("dance") – thus the place where people dance – or the Sotho word *tsana* ("small basket")
Uitenhage	1804	J.A. Uitenhage de Mist, commissioner-general of the Batavian Republic of the Cape from 1803 to 1804
Umtata	1882	Mthatha River
Uniondale	1865	The villages of Lyon and Hopedale, which were joined to become Uniondale
Upington (formely Olijvenhoutsdrift)	1871	Sir Thomas Upington, first minister of the Cape Colony (1884–1886)
Vanrhynsdorp	1887	Petrus Benjamin van Rhyn, on whose farm the town was laid out
Vanwyksdorp	1882	Van Wyk family, on whose farm the town was apparently laid out
Victoria-Wes (formely Victoria)	1844	Queen Victoria
Villiersdorp	1844	Pieter Hendrik de Villiers, owner of the farm on which the town was apparently laid out
Vredenburg	1883	The word *vrede*, meaning "peace", after the town founded there was formerly known as Processfontein
Vryburg	1883	The word *vryburger* – "free citizen"
Vryheid	1884	The word *vryheid*, meaning "freedom". It was the capital of the short-lived Boer Republic of Stellaland, where the residents called themselves "free citizens"
Warden	1912	Charles Frederick Warden, magistrate of Harrismith
Warrenton	1884	Sir Charles Warren, British officer who, in the late nineteenth century, was involved in the awarding of property and mineral rights in the area

Place	Date established	Named after whom/what
Weenen	1838	The word *ween*, meaning "weep", a reference to the sorrow at the death of 182 Voortrekkers in the area in 1838
Welkom	1948	The word *welkom*, meaning "welcome"
Wellington (formely Wagenmakersvallei)	1840	The Duke of Wellington, a British general who defeated Napoleon at the Battle of Waterloo in 1815
Wepener	1875	Commander Louw Wepener, Free State Boer commanding officer who died a hero's death at Thaba Bosigo
Willowmore	1862	Possibly the farm Willows on which the town was laid out, or after the owner's wife Petronella Mooreen and the willow tree that grew near the house
Witbank	1903	White rocks found there
Wolmaransstad	1888	Jacobus M.A. Wolmarans, member of the Executive Committee of the ZAR
Wolseley (formely Ceres Road)	1875	Sir Garnet Joseph Wolseley, of the British forces in the Zulu war of 1879
Worcester	1820	The Marquis of Worcester, brother of the governor Lord Charles Somerset
Zastron	1876	Johanna Zastron, wife of President J.H. Brand of the Republic of the Orange Free State

- **Beaufort West** was the first town in the Cape Colony to become a municipality (1837).
- **Bloemfontein** is also known as the City of Roses.
- Western Deep Levels at **Carletonville** is the deepest mine in the world – 4,2km.
- **Darling** was put on the map when the satirist Pieter-Dirk Uys converted Darling's old station into a cabaret theatre and restaurant. He often performs at "Evita se Perron".

Evita se Perron

- Its subtropical climate makes **Durban** a popular holiday destination with rows of hotels along the beachfront.
- **Graaff-Reinet** has the most national monuments in the country (220).

Zolile Baleni, whale crier

- **Hermanus** is the only town in the world to have a whale crier. In August 1992, Pieter Claasen, who worked at the old harbour, became the first whale crier. He became famous and was even a guest of honour at the annual Town Crier's Competition in Topsham, England. He retired in 1998 and was succeeded by Wilson Salukazana. The current whale crier is Zolile Baleni. The duty of a whale crier is to let tourists know when there are whales nearby by blowing on his sea bamboo horn.

Johannesburg from the Hillbrow Tower   Uppermost part of the Hillbrow Tower

- The Carlton Centre in **Johannesburg** is the tallest office building in Africa (50 floors).
- The Hillbrow Tower in **Johannesburg** is the highest tower in South Africa (270 m).
- **Johannesburg** is also known as Egoli or the City of Gold.
- **Johannesburg** is the town with the most trees in the world – around six million.
- There is also a **Johannesburg** in Suriname and in the American states of California, Wisconsin and Michigan.

Parliament Buildings, Cape Town   Cape Town from Table Mountain

- **Cape Town** is the southernmost city in Africa.
- **Cape Town** is also known as the Mother City.

Ostriches

Feather Palace

- **Oudtshoorn** is situated near the Cango Caves **(see page 42 &126)** and is also known for ostrich farming. The ostrich industry boomed before the First World War and farmers became extremely wealthy. Beautiful "Feather Palaces" were built in this time. With the outbreak of war, demand for the feathers suddenly dropped and many farmers went bankrupt. Today, the feathers, meat and skin of ostriches are used. Bone meal is made from the bones.
- **Port Elizabeth** is also known as the Windy City or the Friendly City.

Union Buildings, Pretoria

- Church Street in **Pretoria** is the longest urban street in South Africa – 24km.
- **Pretoria** has the largest zoo in Africa.
- **Pretoria** is also known as the Jacaranda City.

Squatters' shacks in Soweto

A new house in Soweto

- **Soweto**, south-west of Johannesburg, is the biggest township in South Africa.
- The **Chris Hani-Baragwanath Hospital** in **Soweto** near Johannesburg is the biggest hospital in the southern hemisphere.

- Near **Sutherland** is the South African Astronomical Observatory (SAAO), the largest observatory in the southern hemisphere. The SALT telescope (South African Large Telescope) was completed in 2005. It is the largest telescope in the southern hemisphere.
- This life-sized bronze sculpture of a donkey stands on the premises of the Kalahari-Orange Museum in **Upington**. It was made by the sculptor Hennie Potgieter and serves to remind people of the important role donkeys played in the development of the lower Orange River valley.

"Firsts" in Kimberley

Many events in South Africa took place for the first time in Kimberley

1871	A private postal delivery service begins
1881	Stock exchange opens
1882	Electric streetlights come into use
1883	A strike
1892	An electric tram comes into use
1904	Conference of the Poultry Association
1912	Marie Bocciarelli, the first female pilot, is trained
1913	A flight school is established and a fatal plane crash in South Africa occurs
1919	Daniel Walter Smith sells a dummy in a rugby game
1928	A diamond cutting works begins to operate
1931	An aeroplane lands at night
1940	Female traffic officers are appointed
1958	A state school for paraplegics is opened
1977	Remote-controlled ore trains are used

Place names after 1994

Former name	New name
Almansdrift	Mbhongo
Buffelspruit	Mhlambanyatsi
Ellisras	Lephalale
Lydenburg	Mashishing
Messina	Musina
Naboomspruit	Mookgophong
Nylstroom	Modimolle
Pietersburg	Polokwane
Potgietersrus	Mokopane
Skilpadfontein	Marapyane
Warmbad	Bela-Bela
Witbank	Emalahleni
Witsieshoek	Phuthaditjhaba

Louis Trichardt's name was changed to Makhado, but in 2007, after a court case lasting three years, it was changed back to Louis Trichardt.

Regional names in South Africa

These regions do not have official borders and the descriptions supplied here are just a general indication of the location of the area.

Boesmanland:
The area from Calvinia in the south to Namaqualand in the west, with the Orange River in the north and east.

Boland:
This region is usually defined to include the Berg and Breede river valley from Stellenbosch, Franschhoek and Worcester to Tulbagh in the north of the Western Cape.

Boland

Bosveld:
The region north of the Soutpansberg to the Zimbabwean border.

Great Karoo:
The vast dry area north of the Swartberg in the Western and Eastern Cape.

Hantam:
The plateau that stretches from Calvinia in the Northern Cape to around Loeriesfontein.

Highveld:
The area from Volksrust and Wakkerstroom in the south to Belfast and Machadodorp in the north.

Kalahari:
The great sandveld that stretches from the Orange River in the Northern Cape into Botswana and the east of Namibia.

Kamdeboo: The districts of Graaff-Reinet, Pearston, Somerset East, Jansenville, Willowmore and Aberdeen in the Eastern Cape.

Kannaland:
The valley between Barrydale and Oudtshoorn in the Western Cape.

Little Karoo:
The valley between the Langeberg and Outeniqua mountains, in the south of the Western Cape, and the Swartberg in the north.

Karoo

Knersvlakte:
The dry plains between Vanrhynsdorp and Bitterfontein in the Northern Cape.

Koue Bokkeveld:
The area north of the Warm Bokkeveld in the Western Cape. The Gydo and Waboom mountains divide the two regions.

Koup:
The districts of Touwsrivier, Laingsburg, Prince Albert, Merweville, Beaufort West and Willowmore.

KwaZulu-Natal Midlands:
The area south of the Tugela River in KwaZulu-Natal past Pietermaritzburg in the south and westwards up to the Drakensberg; the coastal area is excluded.

Lowveld:
The fertile region of Mpumalanga and Limpopo east of the plateau.

Langkloof:
he valley north of the Outeniqua and Tsitsikamma mountains from Herold in the west to Kareedouw in the east.

Maputaland:
The coastal flats south of the Mfolozi River, which stretch northwards into Mozambique and westwards to the Lebombo and Ubombo mountains.

Moordenaars Karoo:
The western part of the Great Karoo that stretches from Lainsburg to Sutherland.

Namaqualand:
The area between the Olifants River in the south and the Orange River in the north; in the west the Atlantic Ocean forms the border and the eastern border is an imaginary line a few hundred kilometres from the sea where Boesmanland begins.

North Coast:
The stretch of coastline in KwaZulu-Natal north of Durban to Richards Bay.

Overberg: The whole area from the Hottentots Holland mountains to Mossel Bay in the east and the Langeberg mountains in the north.

Richtersveld: A desolate mountainous desert area that stretches from the Orange River to Port Nolloth on the Atlantic Ocean.

Richtersveld

Riemland:
The districts of Bethlehem, Reitz, Heilbron and Kroonstad in the Free State.

Rûens:
The hilly area around Caledon in the Western Cape.

Sandveld:
A narrow area between the Cape West Coast and the Swartland with a sparse population; it stretches from Hopefield in the south to Lutzville in the north.

Swartland

South Coast:
The stretch of coastline in KwaZulu-Natal between Port Edward and Durban.

Swartland:
The districts of Malmesbury and Moorreesburg to Piketberg.

Garden Route:
The narrow stretch of coastline between George and the easternmost point of the Tsitsikamma mountains.

Warm Bokkeveld:
A fertile valley between the Hex River Mountains in the south, the Witsenberg and Skurweberg in the west, and the Gydo and Waboom mountains in the north.

West Coast:
The Atlantic coastal area between Yzerfontein in the south and Strandfontein in the north.

Wild Coast:
The stretch of coastline of about 250km from the Great Kei River in the south to Port Edward, in KwaZulu-Natal, in the north.

Zululand:
A wide stretch in KwaZulu-Natal from the Tugela River in the south to Kosi Bay in the north; in the east it stretches to the Indian Ocean and in the west to Pongola and just north of Weenen.

Important mountain ranges

Du Toits Mountains

Maltese Cross, Cederberg

Mountain Range	Location	Highest Peak	Height
Amatola Mountains	Eastern Cape	Gaikaskop	1 970m
Cederberg	Western Cape	Sneeuberg	2 028m
Drakensberg (± 1 000km long)	Eastern Cape to Limpopo	Thabana Ntlenyana (Lesotho)	3 482m
Du Toits Mountains	Western Cape	Du Toits Peak	1 995m
Great Winterhoek Mountains	Western Cape	Great Winterhoek Peak	2 077m
Hex River Mountains	Western Cape	Matroosberg	2 249m
Langeberge	Western Cape	Misty Point	1 710m
Magaliesberg	Gauteng and North-West	Nooitgedacht West	1 805m
Maluti Mountains	Free State	Namahadi Peak	3 291m
Outeniqua Mountains	Western Cape	Cradock Peak	1 579m
Rooiberg Mountains	Free State	Ribbokkop	2 829m
Sneeuberg Mountains	Eastern Cape	Kompasberg	2 502m
Soutpansberg Mountains	Limpopo	Letjuma	1 748m
Swartberg Mountains	Western Cape	Seweweekspoort Peak	2 325m
Table Mountain	Western Cape	Maclear's Beacon	1 086m
Tsitsikamma Mountains	Eastern Cape	Formosa Peak	1 600m
Witteberg	Eastern Cape	Edge Hill	2 725m
Wolkberg	Limpopo	Ysterkroon	2 126m

Paarl Rock
Paarl Rock is the largest granite rock in South Africa and the second largest granite formation in the world.

The highest mountain peaks in the provinces of South Africa

Province	Peak	Location	Height
Gauteng	Toringkop	Suikerboschrand, Heidelberg	1 913m
KwaZulu-Natal	Mafadi	Injasuti, Drakensberg	3 451m
Limpopo	Ysterkroon	Wolkberg, Haenertsburg	2 126m
Mpumalanga	The Berg	Steenkampsberg, Lydenburg	2 331m
Northern Cape	Kriegersbaken	Sneeuberg, Richmond	2 156m
North-West	Nooitgedacht West	Magaliesberg, Hekpoort	1 805m
Eastern Cape	KwaDuma	Ongeluksnek, Drakensberg	3 019m
Free State	Namahadi Peak	QwaQwa, Drakensberg	3 291m
Western Cape	Seweweekspoort Peak	Little Swartberg, Ladismith	2 325m

Highest peaks in the Drakensberg

Most of the highest peaks are on the border between KwaZulu-Natal and Lesotho.

Thabana Ntlenyana	3 482m
Makheka	3 463m
Mafadi Peak	3 451m
Ubutsuane	3 434m
Champagne Castle	3 377m
Popple Peak	3 331m
Giant's Castle	3 315m
Mont-aux-Sources	3 299m
Monk's Cowl	3 261m
Cathkin Peak	3 182m
Devil's Tooth	3 028m
Cathedral Peak	3 004m

- The highest peak in the Drakensberg is Thaba Ntlenyana (3 482m) in Lesotho.
- The highest peak in South Africa is Mafadi Peak (3 451m) in the Injasuti area.
- Table Mountain was first climbed in 1503 by the Portuguese admiral Antonio de Saldanha, after whom Saldanha Bay was named.
- The Soutpansberg is the northernmost mountain range in South Africa.
- The oldest dinosaur footprints in South Africa can be seen in the lowest rock formations of the Stormberg, on the farm Oakleigh, north of Maclear. The footprints are 200 million years old.

Well-known mountain passes

Du Toitskloof

Sir Lowry's Pass

Pass	Location	Builder (Year completed)
Bainskloof	Between Wellington and Wolseley (Hawequas Mountains)	Andrew Bain (1853)
Du Toitskloof	Between the Paarl and Worcester (Klein Drakenstein Mountains)	Italian prisoners of-war (1949)
Garcia	Between Riversdal and the Little Karoo (Langeberg)	Andrew Bain (1877)
Gydo	Between Warm and Koue Bokkeveld (Gydoberg)	Andrew Bain
Kogmanskloof	Between Ashton and Montagu (Langeberg)	Thomas Bain (1877)
Long Tom	Between Lydenburg and Sabie (Drakensberg)	Abraham Espag (1953)
Meiringspoort	Between Klaarstroom and De Rust (Swartberg)	Thomas Bain (1858)
Mitchells	Between Ceres and Wolseley (Skurweberg)	Andrew Bain (1848)
Montagu	Between George and Herold (Outeniqua Mountains)	Henry Fancourt White (1847)
Outeniqua	Between George and Oudtshoorn (Outeniqua Mountains)	P.A. de Villiers (1945)
Pakhuis	Between Clanwilliam and Calvinia (Cederberg)	Thomas Bain (1870)

Pass	Location	Builder (Year completed)
Piekenierskloof	Between Piketberg and Citrusdal (Olifants River Mountains)	Thomas Bain (1858)
Prins Alfred	Between Knysna and Avontuur (Outeniqua Mountains)	Thomas Bain (1865)
Robinson	Between Mossel Bay and Oudtshoorn (Outeniqua Mountains)	M.R. Robinson (1869)
Sani	Between KwaZulu-Natal and Lesotho (Drakensberg)	Basotholand administration (1955)
Seweweekspoort	Between Laingsburg and Calitzdorp (Swartberg Mountains)	Thomas Bain (1862)
Sir Lowrys	Between Somerset West and Botrivier (Hottentots-Holland Mountains)	Charles Michell (1830)
Swartberg	Between the Little and Great Karoo (Swartberg)	Thomas Bain (1887)
Tradouw	Between Swellendam and the Little Karoo (Langeberg)	Thomas Bain (1873)
Van Reenens	Between the Highveld and KwaZulu-Natal (Drakensberg)	Frans van Reenen (1856)
Van Rhyns	Between Nieuwoudtville and Vanrhynsdorp (Bokkeveld Mountains)	Thomas Bain (±1882)

Tradouw Pass

Meiringspoort

- **Bainskloof's haunted house**
  A manor house was built for the jam factory pioneer of Wellington, P.J. Hugo, during the Second World War. It was built on the Bainskloof Pass, halfway up the mountain on the Wellington side. It was an impressive gabled house with a thatched roof and tall chimney stacks decorated with spirals, built by the master builder Charl Marais. Hugo bought the land in 1938 but died in 1941 and never lived in the house. Above the place where the house stood, a memorial slab to him and his son was erected. In 1949 the house burned down. The last remnants of the "haunted house" were only demolished in 1979 after a British student and his wife were murdered nearby and in the ruins respectively. Today just a section of stone wall between the bushes and trees can be seen.
- Bainskloof Pass is a national monument.
- The road through Meiringspoort crosses the Groot River 25 times.
- Naudé's Nek Pass, in the southern Drakensberg between Rhodes and Maclear, is the highest pass in South Africa – between 1 920m and 2 621m above sea level. This dirt road is dangerous in wet weather. It's often closed because of snow. It is also very long – along with the Pot River and Bell River Pass, it is 100km.
- The oldest unaltered pass is the Montagu Pass. It was completed in 1847.
- The grave of the writer C. Louis Leipoldt is under an overhanging rock at the foot of the Pakhuis Pass.

Huguenot Tunnel

- The Huguenot Tunnel in the Du Toits Kloof Pass is 4km long. The tunnel is constantly monitored by TV cameras.
- The Lootsberg Pass between Graaff-Reinet and Middelburg is the highest pass in the Karoo.
- Thomas Bain and his father, Andrew Geddes Bain, were both well-known road engineers. Andrew Bain built most of the roads and passes that today link the Western Cape with the interior.

Well-known caves

Cave	Location
Boomslang caves	Kalk Bay, Western Cape
Echo caves	Ohrigstad, Mpumalanga
Eland caves	Drakensberg, KwaZulu-Natal
Cango caves	Oudtshoorn, Western Cape
Makapansgat caves	Potgietersrus, Limpopo
Sterkfontein caves	Krugersdorp, Gauteng
Sudwala caves	Nelspruit, Mpumalanga
Wolkberg caves	Tzaneen, Limpopo

- The Sudwala Caves are the oldest in the world – excavations show that the caves were first inhabited about 2 000 million years ago. About 160 years ago it was the centre of a power struggle between two Swazi leaders (and stepbrothers), Somcumba and Mswati. After defeating Somcumba, Mswati became a strong and famed Swazi king. In 1967 and 1968 various new chambers were discovered in the caves. In front of the entrance to the caves is a dinosaur park.
- The Cango Caves are the longest underground caves in the world.
- In 1854, 1 500 of Chief Makapan's warriors died in the Makapansgat Caves of hunger and thirst. They sought shelter there from a Voortrekker commando under the leadership of Piet Potgieter and M.W. Pretorius who were seeking revenge for the murder by Makapan's people of 28 Voortrekker men, women and children under the leadership of Hermanus Potgieter.

Most important rivers

Orange River

River	Length	Source	Mouth
Orange (Gariep)	2 250km	Lesotho (Drakensberg)	Atlantic Ocean
Limpopo	1 600km	Witwatersrand	Indian Ocean
Vaal	1 160km	Highveld (vicinity of Breyten)	Merges near Douglas with the Orange River

- The Orange River (Gariep River) was named after the Prince of Orange in 1779 by Colonel Robert Gordon, commanding officer of the Cape garrison.
- The Orange River Project was initiated in the 1960s to better utilise the water of the Orange River. Until then the water was only used for large-scale irrigation in the vicinity of Upington. The goal of the project was to make more water available for irrigation in the Orange River Valley, Great Fish Valley and Sundays River Valley, to get more water to Bloemfontein and Port Elizabeth, and also to generate hydro-electric power. The Gariep and Vanderkloof dams, the Vanderkloof canals and the Orange-Fish River Tunnel were built. The Orange-Fish River Tunnel is 82,5km long and the second-longest water supply tunnel in the world.
- Cannon Island – one of many islands in the Orange River – is the largest inhabited island (2 570ha) in a South African river.
- There are hundreds of islands in the Vaal River; the biggest is Groot Island (154ha) near Parys.
- The Bloukrans Bridge over the Bloukrans River, between Nature's Valley and Coldstream, was completed in 1983. It is the highest single span arch bridge in the world – 448m long.
- The longest bridge in South Africa is the D.H. Steyn Bridge – 121m. It is a combined rail-road bridge over the Orange River (Gariep River) at Bethulie in the Free State.

Paul Sauer Bridge

Van Stadens Bridge

- The Van Stadens Bridge over the Van Stadens River between Jeffreys Bay and Port Elizabeth is one of the longest concrete arch bridges in South Africa. It is 350m long and 125m high, while the road on the bridge has four lanes. Because of the amount of people who have committed suicide there (by July 2008, 67 people had died there), the bridge has earned the nickname "Bridge of Death". The first suicide was in 1971, just twelve days after the bridge was opened to traffic. A cross was erected on the mountain next to the bridge to discourage suicide attempts. In 2003, it was decided to put six observation cameras on the bridge. The Golden Gate Bridge in San Francisco, USA, is regarded as the place where the most suicides in the world are committed – more than 1 000 people have committed suicide there in the past 142 years.

Malgas pontoon

- The only remaining inland pontoon on a public road in South Africa is at Malgas over the Breede River. The original wooden pontoon was first used in 1830. It was replaced in 1906 by a steel pontoon, which was later washed away in a flood. The current pontoon came into use in 1914, and is also made of steel. It is pulled by hand by two helpers. The maximum load is 10t. The pontoon is the only way to cross the Breede River south of Swellendam. Moxie Dunn pulled the Malgas pontoon across the river on his own for 25 years.

Important dams

Gariep Dam

Theewaterskloof Dam

Dam	Full Capacity (million cubic meters)	River in which dam is situated
Gariep	5 340	Orange
Vanderkloof	3 171	Orange
Sterkfontein	2 616	Nuwejaarspruit
Vaal	2 603	Vaal
Pongolapoort	2 445	Phongolo
Katse	1 518	Malibamatso
Bloemhof	1 240	Vaal
Theewaterskloof	480	Sonderend
Heyshope	451	Assegaai
Woodstock	380	Tugela
Loskop	361	Olifants
Grootdraai	354	Vaal
Kalkfontein	318	Riet
Goedertrouw	304	Mhlatuze
Albert Falls	288	Mgeni

Dam	Full Capacity (million cubic meters)	River in which dam is situated
Brandvlei	284	Smalblaar/Holsloot
Spioenkop	277	Tugela
Umtata	253	Mtata
Driekoppies	250	Lomati
Inanda	241	Mgeni
Hartbeespoort	212	Crocodile
Erfenis	207	Groot Vet
Rhenosterkop	204	Elands
Molatedi	200	Groot Marico
Ntshingwayo	198	Ngagane
Zaaihoek	192	Slang
Midmar	175	Mgeni

New names of dams

Old name	New name
Braam Raubenheimer	Kwena
Charlie Malan	Impofu
Chelmsford	Ntshingwayo
Fanie Botha	Tzaneen
Hans Strijdom	Mokolo
Hendrik Verwoerd	Gariep
Hudson Ntsanwisi	Nsami
Jan Wassenaar	Klaserie
J.G. Strijdom	Pongolapoort
Mentzmeer	Darlington
Mokgomo Matlala	Arabie
Paul Sauer	Kouga
P.K. le Roux	Vanderkloof

- The Gariep Dam, the biggest dam in South Africa, has a surface area of 36 500ha when full.
- The Sibayi Lake (7 750ha) in Maputaland is the biggest freshwater lake in South Africa.
- The Sarel Hayward Canal's name was changed to the Orange-Riet Canal.
- In 2008 the Berg River Dam near Franschhoek was completed. It has a surface area of 537ha and a full capacity of 130 million cubic metres. The dam wall is 68m high.

Largest ports

Cape Town

1. Richards Bay (designed for the handling of coal and oil)
2. Saldanha (export port for iron ore and other minerals)
3. Durban (busiest port in Africa)
4. Cape Town
5. Port Elizabeth
6. East London
7. Mossel Bay

- Saldanha is the deepest and safest port in South Africa.
- In 2001 construction began on the eighth commercial port in South Africa. The port of Ngqura is being built in the Coega River (Eastern Cape) by the National Harbour Authority. It will be the country's deepest terminus for container shipping. The nearby Coega Development Corporation industrial development zone will provide employment and promote international trade.

Saldanha

Important islands

Bird Island at Lambert's Bay

Robben Island

Island	Location	Area
Dassen Island	Near Yzerfontein	222ha
Dyer Island	Near Gansbaai	20ha
Geyser Island	Near Gansbaai	3ha
Jutten Island	In Saldanha Bay	43ha
Malgas Island	In Saldanha Bay	18ha
Marcus Island	In Saldanha Bay	17ha
Marion Island	2 300km south-east of Cape Town	29 000ha
Meeuwen Island	In Saldanha Bay	7ha
Prince Edward Island	South Atlantic Ocean	4 400ha
Robben Island	In Table Bay	574ha
Schaapen Island	In Saldanha Bay	29ha
St Croix Island	In Algoa Bay	16ha
Bird Island	In Lamberts Bay	19ha
Bird Island	East of Algoa Bay	11ha
Vondeling Island	Sea side of the Langebaan Lagoon	9ha

In the past so many ships were wrecked near Dassen Island that tortoises and rabbits were released on the island to provide food for the shipwrecked sailors.

Important lighthouses

Lighthouse and date erected	Location	Details
Agulhas (1849)	At Cape Agulhas, the southernmost point of Africa	Unmanned. Active. It was built after the model of the Pharos of Alexandria, one of the Seven Wonders of the Ancient World. In 1962 the sandstone began to erode and in 1968 a temporary aluminium lighthouse was erected. The lighthouse was declared a national monument in 1973. The original, restored lighthouse came into use in 1988. There is a museum and restaurant in the lighthouse.
Anglo American-Building (1986)	On top of the 26th floor of the Anglo American Building on the Durban waterfront	Unmanned. Active.
Bird Island (1852)	On the largest of four islands 58km north-east of Port Elizabeth	Unmanned. Active. The island was declared a protected marine reserve in 2004.
Cooper (1954), first lighthouse 1867	On the Bluff in Durban	Unmanned. Active. This lighthouse is named after the well-known lighthouse engineer H.C. Cooper. The first lighthouse was replaced by a second that was demolished in 1942, because it was in the way of coastal defence artillery. The current lighthouse is the third one.

Agulhas

Anglo-American building, Durban

Danger Point, near Gansbaai

Lighthouse and date erected	Location	Details
Danger Point (1895)	Tip of Walker Bay near Gansbaai	Unmanned. Active. A commemorative plaque in memory of those who drowned when the *Birkenhead* sank in 1852 is on the wall of the lighthouse. Accommodation is available for tourists.
Dassen Island (1893)	On Dassen Island 11km from Yzerfontein	Manned. Active. The lighthouse keeper and his family live on the island and are visited every six weeks by helicopter and taken to the mainland for a short visit.
Donkin (1861) (Also sometimes called The Hill)	In the Donkin reserve in Port Elizabeth	Unmanned. Inactive since 1973. The lighthouse was rebuilt in 1930 and currently houses a military museum. Near the lighthouse is a sandstone pyramid in memory of Sir Rufane Donkin's wife, after whom Port Elizabeth is named. The lighthouse keeper's house is now a tourism bureau.
Doring Bay (current) (1963)	At Doring Bay, a holiday resort and fishing village, about 8km south-east of Strandfontein	Unmanned. Active. The construction date of the previous lighthouse is unknown. It was destroyed during a wind storm in 1963.

Lighthouse and date erected	Location	Details
Durban South breakwater (date unknown)	On the southern breakwater at the mouth of the Umgeni River	Unmanned. Active. Can only be reached by boat.
Great Fish Point (1898)	At the mouth of the Great Fish River north-east of Port Alfred	Unmanned. Active. Accommodation in two self-catering units is available. There is also a tourism bureau, gift shop, swimming pool and a hall used for wedding and functions.
Green Point (Western Cape) (1823)	On the north-west point of Table Bay in Green Point, Cape Town	Unmanned. Active. It is the oldest built lighthouse in South Africa. In 1926 it was fitted with a foghorn and in 1928 it was electrified. It is used to train lighthouse keepers. These days there are offices, a gift shop and conference facilities.
Green Point (KwaZulu-Natal) (1905)	At Clansthal, a village between Scottburgh and Umkomaas, about 60km south-west of Durban	Unmanned. Active. In 1892 two iron towers were erected at Scottburgh and just south of Umkomaas respectively. It was ineffective and was replaced by this new lighthouse. Scottburgh's lighthouse was moved to Port Shepstone and the other one to St Lucia.

Green Point

Lighthouse and date erected	Location	Details
Groen River Mouth (1988)	About 30km north-west of Strandfontein at the mouth of the Groen River	Unmanned. Active. This is the most recently built lighthouse in South Africa.
(Cape) Hangklip (1960)	At Hangklip at the most easterly point of False Bay	Unmanned. Active. It is controlled from Green Point.
Hondeklip Bay (1956)	At Hondeklip Bay, a holiday town 104km from Springbok	Unmanned. Active. This is a metal tower with a red and white striped diamond-shaped day mark.
Hood Point (1895)	In East London	Unmanned. Active. Before this lighthouse was built, the Castle Point lighthouse served this area. There is a tourism bureau, a gift shop and a conference and wedding facility.
Jesser Point (1986)	South of Sodwana Bay	Unmanned. Active. This area has the southernmost coral reefs on the east coast of Africa. It is very popular with scuba divers.
Cape Columbine (1936)	At Cape Columbine about 3km from Paternoster	Unmanned. Active. This lighthouse is named after the ship *Columbine*, which sunk here in 1829. Three chalets provide accommodation. There are conference facilities, a swimming pool and a gift shop.
Cape Hermes (1905)	Near Port St Johns	Manned. Active.
Cape Morgan (1964)	About 5km east of Morgan Bay on the Wild Coast.	Unmanned. Active.
Cape Point (Current lighthouse at Dias Point) (1919)	At Cape Point, the southernmost point of the Cape Peninsula	Manned. Active. This is the only lighthouse in the country that is still manned 24 hours a day. The first tower was erected in 1860 at Cape Maclear. The new Cape Point lighthouse is the most powerful lighthouse in South Africa. Accommodation is available.

Lighthouse and date erected	Location	Details
Cape Point (First lighthouse at Cape Maclear) (1860)	At Cape Point, the southernmost point of the Cape Peninsula	Inactive. Unmanned. This lighthouse was too high and sometimes could not be seen in the mist. It is used as the central monitoring point for all the lighthouses in South Africa.
Cape Recife (1851)	About 20km south-east of Port Elizabeth, next to the Cape Recife Nature Reserve, at the entrance to Nelson Mandela Bay (formerly Algoa Bay)	Unmanned. Active. There is a gift shop.
Cape Town Breakwater (1930s)	On the breakwater at the north-western side of the Cape Town harbour	Unmanned. Active. This lighthouse replaced a light erected in 1916. Previously there was a light on a tramline bar.
Cape St Blaize (1864)	At Mossel Bay	Unmanned. Active. The lighthouse is automated but there are three personnel who carry out weather observations and radio communications. There is self-catering accommodation, a gift shop and a coffee shop.

Cape St Blaize, Mossel Bay

Milnerton

Lighthouse and date erected	Location	Details
Cape St Lucia (1892)	Erected here in 1915. On a sand dune 20km south of St Lucia	Unmanned. Inactive. Originally it was erected south of Umkomaas and was moved to the current location in 1915.
Cape Vidal (1985)	About 35km north-north-east of St Lucia	Unmanned. Active. The unusual yellow of the lighthouse creates a lovely contrast with the greenery behind it
Milnerton (1960)	At the north-eastern point of Table Bay in Milnerton, near Cape Town	Unmanned. Active. More ships have sunk in the short stretch of coast between Green Point and Milnerton than on the rest of the South African coast.
Mouille Point (1842)	Was at the north-eastern point of Table Bay at Granger Bay	This lighthouse was demolished in 1908. It was the second lighthouse to be erected in South Africa. The foundations can still be seen at the Cape Hotel School's restaurant.
North Sand Bluff (1999) (First lighthouse: 1968)	In Port Edward, the southernmost point of KwaZulu-Natal	Unmanned. Active. The previous aluminium tower has been replaced with a new concrete tower. Accommodation is available in two self-catering cottages. There is also a museum, coffee shop, swimming pool and playground.
Port Nolloth (1909)	At Port Nolloth on the Diamond Coast	Unmanned. Active.

Lighthouse and date erected	Location	Details
Port Shepstone (1986)	On the southern bank of the Umzimkulu River in Port Shepstone	Unmanned. Active. In 1906 this lighthouse was moved here from Scottburgh. There is a gift shop, tourism bureau and tea room.
Quoin Point (1955)	At Quoin Point between Danger Point and Cape Agulhas about 3km south of The Dam	Unmanned. Active.
Richards Bay (1979)	On a bluff about 3km north-east of Richards Bay	Unmanned. Active.
Richards Bay (northern breakwater) (date unknown)	On the tip of the northern breakwater in Richards Bay	Unmanned. Active.
Robben Island (1865)	On the highest point of Robben Island, Minto Hill	Unmanned. Active. In Jan van Riebeeck's time a primitive fire beacon was erected. It consisted of a pole with rings on top that were smeared with tar and lit. The light can be seen for 25km.
Roman Rock (1861)	On a rock in the sea at the entrance to Simon's Town harbour. The lighthouse was fully restored in 1992.	Unmanned. Active. At high tide the rock is completely submerged. It took ten years to complete the tower.
Seal Point (Cape St Francis) (1870)	At Cape St Francis, about 30km from Humansdorp	Unmanned. Active. It is the tallest wooden building in South Africa. The tower has a fog horn, a radio beacon and fog detector. There is a tea room and gift shop and a rehabilitation centre for penguins.
Simon's Town dockyard (1910)	At the turn of the breakwater at the Simon's Town dockyard	Unmanned. Active.
Slangkop (Point) (1919)	At Slangkop Point in Kommetjie on the Cape Peninsula	Manned. Active. It is the tallest metal tower in South Africa.

Lighthouse and date erected	Location	Details
Stompneus Point (1920s)	On the northern-most point of the Cape St Martins peninsula at the westerly entrance to St Helena bay	Unmanned. Active.
Umhlanga Rocks (1954)	On the beach at Umhlanga Rocks	Unmanned. Active. This lighthouse and the Cooper lighthouse replace the old one on the Bluff in Durban as they guide ships into Durban's harbour.
Ystervark (First lighthouse 1964)	At Ystervark Point about 80km south of Mossel Bay, between the Gouritz River mouth and Stilbaai	Unmanned. Active. In 2005 the old steel tower was replaced with a modern concrete tower.

On the beach at Umhlanga Rocks

Lighthouse records

Cape Columbine

Lighthouse	Details
Agulhas Lighthouse	Most southerly lighthouse in Africa (1848)
Dassen Island Lighthouse, 11km from coast	Most isolated manned lighthouse
Green Point Lighthouse, KwaZulu-Natal	First automated lighthouse (1961)
Groen River Mouth Lighthouse, Strandfontein	Newest (1988)
Green Point Lighthouse, Cape Town	Oldest (1824)
Jesser Point Lighthouse, KwaZulu-Natal	Most northern lighthouse
Cape Columbine Lighthouse, West Coast	Only diaphonic foghorn still being used and the most powerful lighthouse in the country
Roman Rock Lighthouse, False Bay	Only lighthouse on a rock
Seal Point Lighthouse, Cape St Francis	Tallest wooden building in South Africa
Slangkop Lighthouse, Cape Peninsula	Tallest lighthouse

Neighbouring countries

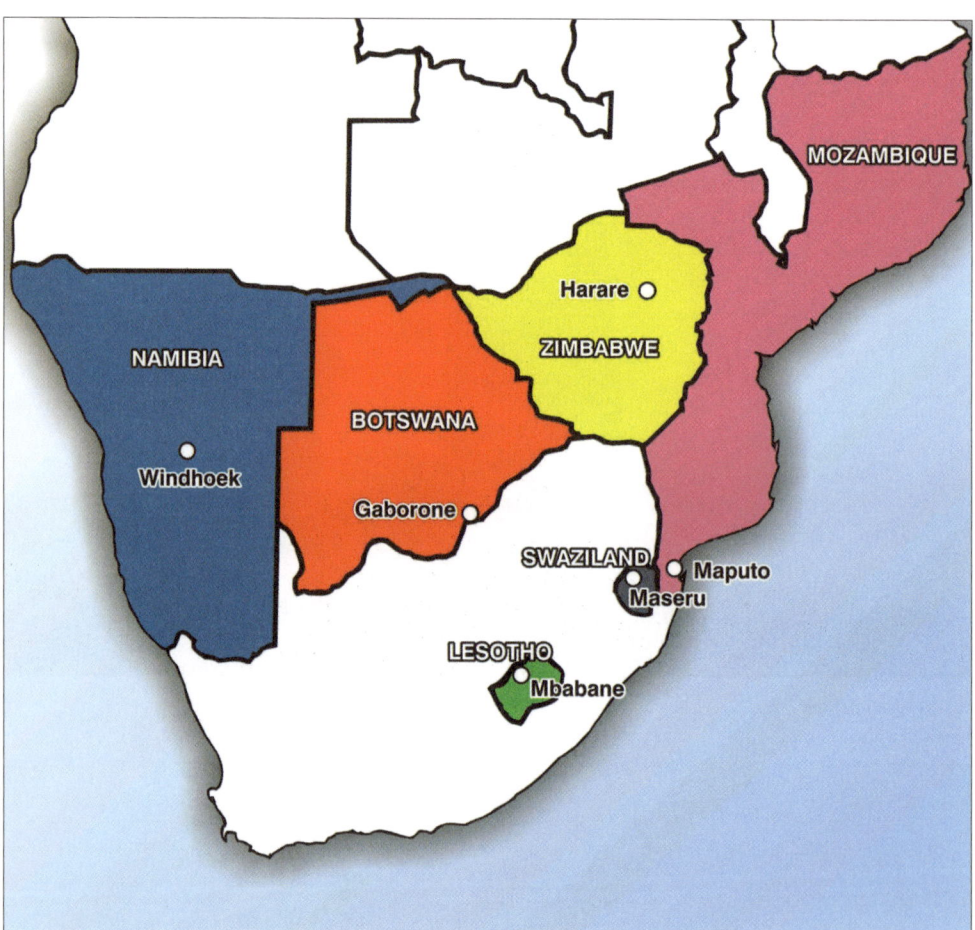

Country	Location	Capital	Head of State
Botswana	North	Gaborone	President Seretse Khama Ian Khama (2008–)
Lesotho	Surrounded by SA	Maseru	King Letsie III (1996–)
Mozambique	North-east	Maputo	President Armando Guebuza (2005–)
Namibia	North-west	Windhoek	President Hifikepunye Pohamba (2005–)
Swaziland	East	Mbabane	King Mswati III (1986–)
Zimbabwe	North	Harare	President Robert Mugabe (1980–)

- **Botswana** is, along with Australia, the world's biggest producer of diamonds.
- **Lesotho** is a small mountainous country that could fit more than three times into South Africa's smallest province, KwaZulu-Natal.
- **Mozambique** was, like Angola, a Portuguese colony until 1975.
- **Namibia**'s biggest tourist attraction is the Etosha National Park in the north of the country.
- **Swaziland** is the smallest country in Africa.
- **Zimbabwe**'s two best-known tourist attractions are the Victoria Falls and the Zimbabwe Ruins.

Victoria Falls

Border Posts

Botswana	Border Post	Opening hours
	Boshoek	08:00–16:00
	Bray	08:00–16:00
	Derdepoort	06:00–19:00
	Gemsbok	08:00–16:30
	Groblers Bridge	06:00–22:00
	Kopfontein	06:00–24:00
	Makgobistad	08:00–16:30
	McCarthy's Rest	08:00–16:30
	Middelputs	07:30–16:30
	Mokopong	08:00–16:00
	Platjan	08:00–16:00
	Pontdrif	08:00–16:00
	Ramatlabama	06:00–20:00
	Skilpads Gate	06:00–22:00
	Stockpoort	08:00–18:00
	Swartkopfontein	06:00–22:00
	Twee Rivieren	07:30–16:00
	Zanzibar	08:00–16:00

Lesotho	Border Post	Opening Hours
	Boesmansnek	08:00–16:00
	Caledonspoort	06:00–22:00
	Ficksburg Bridge	24 hours
	Makhaleng Bridge	08:00–16:00
	Maseru Bridge	24 hours
	Monantsa Pass	08:00–16:00
	Ongeluksnek	08:00–16:00
	Peka Bridge	08:00–16:00
	Quacha' s Nek	07:00–20:00
	Ramatsilitso	08:00–16:00
	Sani Pass	08:00–16:00
	Sepapus Gate	08:00–16:00
	Telle Bridge	06:00–22:00
	Van Rooyenshek	06:00–22:00

Vioolsdrift

Mozambique	Border Post	Opening Hours
	Kosibaai	08:00–18:00
	Lebombo	06:00–22:00
	Pafuri	08:00–16:00

Namibia	Border Post	Opening hours
	Alexander Bay	06:00–22:00
	Mata-Mata	07:30–16:00
	Nakop	24 hours
	Noenieput	08:00–16:30
	Onseepkans	08:00–16:30
	Rietfontein	08:00–16:30
	Sendelingsdrift	08:00–16:15
	Twee Rivieren	07:30–16:00
	Vioolsdrift	24 hours

Swaziland	Border Post	Opening hours
	Bothashoop	08:00–16:00
	Emahlathini	08:00–18:00
	Golela	07:00–22:00
	Jeppe's Reef	07:00–20:00
	Josephsdal	08:00–16:00
	Mahamba	07:00–22:00
	Mananga	07:00–18:00
	Nerston	08:00–18:00
	Onverwacht	08:00–18:00
	Oshoek	07:00–22:00
	Waverley	08:00–16:00

Zimbabwe	Border Post	Opening hours
	Beit Bridge	24 hours

- **Visas:** For tourists with a South African passport, visas are only necessary for Mozambique and Zimbabwe. The Zimbabwean visa is available free at Zimbabwean airports or border posts.
- During holiday periods the hours of some border posts are sometimes extended.
- More information about the border posts can be obtained at: **www.home-affairs.gov.sa**.
- At Sendelingsdrift vehicles are ferried across the Orange River on a pontoon to prevent a detour of about 500km. If there is a very strong wind, the pontoon cannot be used.
- A new border post between South Africa and Zimbabwe is planned near Pafuri.
- The Mata-Mata border post can only be used after one has spent two nights in the Kgalagadi Transfrontier Park.

3. CONSERVATION AND ECOTOURISM

Table Mountain National Park

Marakele National Park

Kirstenbosch

Lion at Sabi-Sabi

Swellendam hiking trail

Tired from hiking

National parks

- Reservations for all the national parks can be made through South African National Parks on **012 428 9111**.
- The facilities in the camps of the national parks are constantly being enlarged and improved.
- Pensioners are entitled to a 40% discount on accommodation, on certain conditions.
- More information is available on the Sanparks website: **www.sanparks.org**.

Addo Elephant National Park

This park was established in 1931 in the Sundays River Valley, about 75km from Port Elizabeth. It was established to protect the last few remaining elephants in the Eastern Cape. Since then, the park has increased vastly in size and today covers 164 000ha. The park is still growing and will eventually cover 398 000ha, when it will be the third-largest national park in the country. A marine reserve of 120 000ha is also planned. The Alexandria State Forest and Tootabie Nature Reserve will become part of the new, enlarged park.

Addo landscape

The original 15 elephants have increased to more than 450. Buffalo, lion, leopard, eland, kudu and black rhino can also be seen. Guided game drives are offered and trail hikes can be undertaken. The park has a 4x4 route and a route for disabled people, which takes an hour to complete.

Self-catering accommodation is available in chalets, rondavels, wooden huts, furnished safari tents or campsites. There is also accommodation in private five-star lodges. There is also a shop, restaurant and swimming pool, and fuel is also available.

Elephant, Addo

Agulhas National Park

This park at the southernmost point of Africa was proclaimed in 1999. It covers 5 690ha. The area has about 2 000 indigenous plant species and the coast has a rich sea life. Because of the strong currents, high winds, rocks and stormy seas, many ships have been wrecked here. The Agulhas bank is one of the richest fishing grounds in the southern hemisphere. Archaeological finds in the area indicate early Khoisan habitation. Fish ponds used by the Khoisan can still be seen.

A memorial plaque has been erected at the southernmost point of the country. The lighthouse at L'Agulhas was built in 1848 and is the second oldest lighthouse in South Africa still in use. Seventy-one steps lead to the highest point of the lighthouse. It is a national monument and currently also serves as a museum and restaurant. Various hiking trails can be walked. A new, bigger restaurant is planned. In 2008 work was begun on accommodation in the park. Struisbaai and L'Agulhas also offer plenty of accommodation and facilities.

A tourist at the southernmost point of Africa

Agulhas Lighthouse

The Japanese cargo ship *Meisho Maru 38* sank on 22 July 1974 near Agulhas. The wreck remained visible from the land for a long time.

Meisho Maru

Many ships sank off the coast near L'Agulhas, Struisbaai and Waenhuiskrans (Arniston). The most famous of these is the *Arniston*, which sank on 30 May 1815. Only six of the 378 people on board were saved. In 1982 a large number of articles from the ship were salvaged **(see page 202)**.

Ai-Ais/Richtersveld Transfrontier Park

The park was established in 1991 and is a dry, mountainous desert area bordering on the Orange River and covering 162 445ha. An international agreement on the establishment of the Ai-Ais/Richtersveld Transfrontier Park was concluded in 2003.

Richtersveld landscape

The rainfall is less than 50mm a year. In the spring there are fields of flowers. This is an inhospitable wilderness where large animals are scarce, but it is the only place in the world where the Hartmann's mountain zebra is still found. Birds, reptiles and scorpions are abundant. An unusual succulent, the halfmens (*Pachypodium namaquanum*), is found everywhere in the park.

Richtersveld accommodation

There are different walking routes and swimming and angling is also permitted. At Sendelingsdrift there are fully-equipped luxury chalets with air-conditioning. At Potjiespram Rest Camp there are campsites and an environmental education centre where school groups can sleep in traditional Nama huts. The De Hoop, Richtersburg and Kokerboom rest camps all have camping facilities. Tatasberg and Ganakouriep have fully equipped self-catering units.

There are no shops or restaurants in the park, but cooldrinks and fuel can be purchased in Sendelingsdrift (weekdays only). This park is only accessible by 4x4. A pontoon takes vehicles across the Orange River at the Sendelingsdrift border post.

Halfmens Richtersveld
The halfmens is a stemmed succulent and reaches 2–3m in height. It is endemic to the Richtersveld and the south-west of Namibia. The halfmens often grows against cliffs and its leaves are always turned towards the sun.

Augrabies Falls National Park

Augrabies Falls

The park covers 51 430ha on the north and south banks of the Orange River and has been developed since 1966. The Augrabies Falls in the Orange River drop 56m over a vertical cliff – the Khoi-Khoi called the waterfall *Aukoerebis* ("the place of the great noise"). Baboon, klipspringer, springbok, eland, gemsbok, giraffe, jackal, leopard and black rhino can be seen here.

Guided 4x4 drives are on offer through the north of the park, where black rhinos can be seen. There are hiking routes as well as a route that allows hiking, canoeing and mountain biking. Two wooden pathways lead to viewing platforms, one of which is wheelchair friendly.

Accommodation consists of a rest camp with equipped chalets and rondavels, as well as a shady campsite and caravan park. Rondavels equipped for disabled people are available. There are communal kitchens and ablution blocks. All the sites have electrical outlets. In the kitchens two-plate stoves and sinks are provided. There are also three swimming pools, a restaurant, shop and a bar.

Kokerboom or quiver tree aloe

Mountain zebra

Mountain Zebra National Park

This park near Cradock in the Eastern Cape was established in 1937 to protect the endangered mountain zebra. It was one of the smallest parks in the country (6 536ha), but bordering farms were bought to eventually enlarge it to 28 412ha. As well as mountain zebra, the park has black wildebeest, red hartebeest, many types of antelope and birds. Black rhino and buffalo have also been released in the park. Guided night drives are on offer and short hiking trails have been laid out.

Accommodation consists of a restored Victorian farmhouse, smaller cottages and a campsite. A cultural history museum depicts the life of the early pioneers. The museum consists of an original homestead, dairy, wagon house and water mill. San rock art can be seen in a nearby cave. There is also a shop, restaurant, post office and swimming pool.

- At one time, there were only 100 surviving mountain zebras in the world. Six of them were on the farm Babylon's Toren, which was declared the Mountain Zebra National Park in 1937. In 1980 there were already more than 200 mountain zebras in the park, and there are currently around 300. The largest population of mountain zebras is now in the Mountain Zebra National Park and the second largest group is in the Karoo National Park.
- The mountain zebra has narrower stripes than a zebra, an orangey cast to its face and a white rump.

Mountain Zebra National Park

Bontebok National Park

The first Bontebok National Park was established near Bredasdorp in 1931 to save the bontebok from extinction. The park was later moved to its current location at the foot of the Langeberg near Swellendam. The park covers 2 786ha and is the smallest national park in South Africa. In 2000, the municipality of Swellendam donated an additional 700ha to the park. In 2007 a road that links the new area to the park was completed. There are also grysbok, mountain zebra, grey rhebok and small mammals to be seen.

The park borders on the Breede River, where swimming, angling and boating on the river (with own equipment) are permitted. There are two hiking trails along the river. A new rest camp, Lang Elsie's Kraal, was opened in 2007. There are chalets and a new reception centre. Other accommodation consists of a campsite on the river bank with facilities for caravans. There are no power points at the individual stands. There is a shop at the entrance to the park; fuel is only available in Swellendam.

Bontebok accommodation

Breede River

Golden Gate Highlands National Park

This park at the foot of the Maluti Mountains in the north-eastern Free State was proclaimed in 1963. It consists of 11 633ha, which includes magnificent rock formations and unspoilt grassveld. In 2008 the Qwa Qwa National Park was incorporated into the park, which enlarged it to 34 000 ha. The park is known for its many birds and unusual species, including the very rare ibis and bearded vulture (with a wingspan of up to 3m). Springbok, black wildebeest, zebra and blesbok are also abundant. Guided night drives, lectures and video shows are offered during peak periods and there are various hiking trails and facilities for tennis, bowls, table tennis and snooker (in the hotel). Horse rides can be booked.

The Glen Reenen Rest Camp has rondavels, cottages and a lovely caravan park and campsite next to a river. There is also accommodation available in a restored farmhouse, the North Brabant farmhouse. In the camp there is a natural swimming pool. In 2009 extensive improvements were embarked upon in the Golden Gate Brandwag Hotel in the Brandwag Resort. The restaurant will seat 300 people upon completion. The hotel is scheduled to reopen in April 2010. The Brandwag Resort looks out over the Sentinel, a large sandstone crag that is the best-known rock formation in the valley. The Highlands Mountain Retreat offers luxury accommodation

Golden Gate landscape

Golden Gate Glen accommodation

in wooden cabins. The Wilgenhof Centre in the park offers educational programmes and provides accommodation for up to 90 people in dormitories. There is also a Basotho cultural village with comfortable huts in the Basotho style. The park offers shops, a laundry, restaurant, gift shop, coffee bar and ladies' bar. Fuel is available.

Camdeboo National Park

This park is situated around the town of Graaff-Reinet in the Eastern Cape and was proclaimed in 2005. Currently it consists of around 19 405ha. There is a possibility that it could later become part of the Mountain Zebra National Park.

The Valley of Desolation is located in the park. Buffalo, mountain zebra, gemsbok, blesbok, springbok and kudu can be seen here. There are four picnic spots with facilities. The park also has walking routes for day trips and two overnight routes. An environmental education centre can accommodate 40 people and can also be used for conferences. Graaff-Reinet has a variety of accommodation.

Spandau Kop

Valley of Desolation

Karoo National Park

Karoo National Park

Karoo National Park swimming pool

This park of 77 094ha near Beaufort West was established in 1979 with the aim of preserving part of the Great Karoo as a nature reserve. Gemsbok, black wildebeest, springbok, impala, red hartebeest, eland, kudu, zebra and black rhino also occur here. There are also many birds – the black eagle is frequently seen.

Besides the routes for cars, there are 4x4 and walking trails and night drives are offered. The Springbok hiking trail of 36km is closed in summer. There is a fossil route that is accessible to blind and disabled people. Accommodation is available in lovely Cape Dutch cottages, caravan parks and campsites with electrical outlets. There are cottages equipped for disabled people. Accommodation in the cottages includes breakfast. The campsites have communal kitchens as well as a laundry with a tumble dryer. In the Nuweveld Mountains there is a camp with basic facilities. The park has conference facilities, a shop, restaurant and swimming pool.

- The Karoo is one of the richest areas for reptile fossils in the world.
- Six riverine rabbits, one of South Africa's most endangered species, were introduced to this park in 1994 **(see page 235)**.

Kgalagadi* Transfrontier Park
(formerly **Kalahari Gemsbok Park** and the **Gemsbok National Park** [Botswana])

The Kgalagadi Transfrontier Park is the first transfrontier park to be established in Africa. The Kalahari Gemsbok Park in South Africa, which was proclaimed in 1931 and covered 959 103ha, and the Gemsbok National Park in Botswana were combined to form the Kgalagadi Transfrontier Park, which covers 3,7 million hectares. Wildlife can move freely across the border. Apart from the herds of antelope and wildebeest, there are lion, leopard, cheetah, wild cat, brown hyena, hyena and

---

* The Kgalagadi were among the first people to inhabit this area.

Kgalagadi

jackal. The park is also known for its many bird species and birds of prey.

There are three traditional camps, namely Twee Rivieren, Mata-Mata and Nossob. Twee Rivieren in the south is the biggest. Accommodation is available in chalets.

At Twee Rivieren there is a shop, restaurant, swimming pool and public telephones. In the other traditional camps there are swimming pools and shops. Fuel is available in the traditional camps and these camps also have campsites.

Kgalagadi is the first national park offering accommodation in unfenced wilderness camps. There are six of these wilderness camps. The Kalahari Tent Camp has a swimming pool. In the park there are five picnic spots with braai facilities and ablution blocks. Drinking water is not available at these picnic spots. Some camps are accessible to the disabled. The !Zaus Inn is the first luxury accommodation with full catering in the Kgalagadi Transfrontier Park and belongs to the Khomani San and Mier communities. The chalets have thatched roofs and a view over a large salt pan. From the decks of the chalets animals at a watering hole can be observed.

Although the park has dirt roads, it is suitable for all vehicles. Various 4x4 routes are available. Passports are not necessary in Botswana if the same gate is used as entrance and exit.

Cheetah

The Mata-Mata border post in the park was opened in 2007. Anyone wanting to use the Mata-Mata border post must spend at least two nights in the Kgalagadi Transfrontier Park.

Kruger National Park

The Kruger National Park is named after President Paul Kruger of the former Zuid-Afrikaansche Republiek (ZAR). In 1898 the Sabie Game Reserve was proclaimed and in 1903, the Shingwedzi Game Reserve. In 1926 the two reserves were combined and renamed the Kruger National Park. Major James Stevenson-Hamilton was the first warden of the Sabie Game Reserve and later established the Kruger National Park as a large conservation area and tourist attraction. The Kruger National Park is South Africa's most important conservation area and one of the most famous game reserves in the world. It covered 1 963 268ha, but with the transfrontier park project the Kruger National Park becomes part of a conservation

Elephant River

Warthog

area of about 10 million ha. Seven great rivers flow through the area. Roads for viewing wildlife criss-cross the reserve. In the Kruger National Park there are 147 mammal species, of which the Big Five are the main attraction. There is also a rich bird life of more than 500 species.

Accommodation consists of the main rest camps, bush camps and private bush camps. There are 13 main rest camps where electricity, shops, restaurants or cafeterias, public telephones and fuel are available. All the camps, except Orpen, Punda Maria and Tsendze, are accessible to disabled people. Skukuza is the headquarters of the reserve and the biggest camp. (The name Skukuza is derived from the Shangaan word *uSikhukhuza*, which means "he who sweeps clean".) Satara is the next largest camp. There are campsites in many of the rest camps. Accommodation options are luxury guesthouses, rondavels (and luxury rondavels), family cottages, or tents. Tsendze has only campsites. Lodging is cleaned daily and linen, towels and soap are provided. Night drives, game drives and guided hikes on wilderness routes are undertaken from many of the camps. Holiday programmes are also offered in some of the camps.

Main Rest Camps

Name	Facilities
Berg-en-Dal	Shop, restaurant, cafeteria, laundry, swimming pool, fuel, internet café, conference facilities, DSTV (selected channels) only in guesthouses, cellphone reception
Crocodile Bridge	Shop, cafeteria, coffee shop, laundry, fuel, cellphone reception
Letaba	Shop, restaurant, cafeteria, laundry, swimming pool, fuel, DSTV (selected channels) only in guesthouses, cellphone reception
Mopani	Shop, restaurant, cafeteria, ladies' bar, laundry, swimming pool, fuel, conference facilities, DSTV (selected channels) only in ladies' bar and guesthouse, cellphone reception
Lower Sabie	Shop, restaurant, cafeteria, laundry, swimming pool, fuel, DSTV (selected channels) only in guesthouse, cellphone reception
Elephant Camp	Shop, restaurant, cafeteria, laundry, fuel, DSTV (selected channels) only in TV room and guesthouses, cellphone reception

Name	Facilities
Orpen	Shop, laundry, swimming pool, fuel, cellphone reception
Pretoriuskop	Shop, restaurant, cafeteria, laundry, swimming pool, fuel, DSTV (selected channels) only in guesthouses, cellphone reception
Punda Maria	Shop, restaurant, cafeteria, laundry, swimming pool, fuel, DSTV (selected channels) only in family rondavels, cellphone reception
Satara	Shop, restaurant, deli, laundry, fuel, eco-information centre, amphitheatre, DSTV (selected channels) only in guesthouses, cellphone reception
Shingwedzi	Shop, restaurant, cafeteria, laundry, swimming pool, fuel, DSTV (selected channels) only in guesthouse, cellphone reception
Skukuza	Shop, two restaurants, deli with internet café, laundry, post office, bank, museum, garage with workshop, nine-hole golf course, two swimming pools, library, fuel, auditorium and conference facilities, DSTV (selected channels) only in luxury units, cellphone reception, medical doctor
Tsendze	Two camp kitchens and two ablution blocks, hot water and two communal freezers. No electricity, shop, restaurant or fuel in the camp.

Malelane, Maroela, Tambotie and Balule are small camps with only basic facilities. Tsendze has no reception office and is managed from the Mopani camp. Guests must report at the Mopani camp at least one hour before the gate closes.

Kruger accommodation

Giraffe

Rhino

Leopard

Elephant

Bush Camps

The bush camps are smaller and more remote. Accommodation is luxurious and well equipped. Only overnight visitors who have booked are permitted. Besides a small shop that sells wood, ice, etc., there are no shops or restaurants. At most bush camps, game drives are offered. The bush camps are:

Name	Facilities
Bateleur	Electric lights, power points, air conditioning in main bedrooms and ceiling fans in other rooms, microwaves, TVs, braai facilities, a communal braai facility with TV, conference facilities
Biyamiti	Electric lights, power points, ceiling fans, braai facilities
Shimuwini	Solar power only for lights and ceiling fans, no power points, braai facilities, communal braai facilities
Sirheni	Solar power only for lights and ceiling fans, no power points, DSTV (selected channels) only in one unit, communal freezer, braai facilities, communal braai facilities, no cellphone reception
Talamati	Solar power only for lights and ceiling fans, power points, braai facilities, communal braai facilities

Bateleur is the most well-equipped bush camp.

The **private bush camps** (Boulders and Roodewal) each have a unique atmosphere. They must be booked as a whole. There are no shops or restaurants. Lights and ceiling fans are solar-powered. Only residents are allowed in these camps.

Impala

Lion

Luxury Lodges

Concessions were granted for very luxurious lodges that are privately managed. These places offer outstanding accommodation, facilities and service.

Lodge	Contact details
Imbali Safari Lodges	031 310 3333 www.imbali.com
Jock Safari Lodge	041 407 1000 www.jocksafarilodge.com
Lukimbi Safari Lodge	011 431 1120 www.lukimbi.com
Pafuri Camp	011 807 1800 www.pafuri.com
Rhino Walking Safaris	035 474 1473 www.rws.co.za
Shishangeni Private Lodge	011 463 3779 www.pinnaclecollection.com
Singita Lebombo Private Game Lodge	021 683 3424 www.singita.com
Tinga Private Game Lodge	013 735 8400 www.tinga.co.za

Krokodilbrug

Adventurous visitors can do guided wilderness trails under the guidance of experienced, armed game rangers. Hikers overnight in huts with flush toilets and showers behind reed screens. Meals are enjoyed in a lapa around a campfire. Simple, nutritious meals are provided. Only the relatively fit aged between 12 and 60 years old are permitted. The hike lasts three nights and two days and hikers leave from the rest camps in question on Wednesdays and Sundays.

Route	**Nearest gate**	**Nearest rest camp**
Bushman	Malelane	Berg-en-Dal
Metsi-Metsi	Kruger	Skukuza
Nyalaland	Punda-Maria	Punda-Maria
Olifants	Phalaborwa	Letaba
Napi	Numbi	Pretoriuskop
Sweni	Orpen	Satara
Wolhuter	Malelane	Berg-en-Dal

- Harry Wolhuter, a game ranger who worked with Stevenson-Hamilton, stabbed a lion to death in 1904 when the lion leapt on his horse and he dropped his rifle. After he killed the lion, he climbed into a tree to escape a second lion and tied himself to the branches so he would not fall out of the tree should he lose consciousness. His dog frightened off the second lion. Wolhuter was in a great deal of pain when he was found. His knife and the lion's skin can be seen in the Stevenson-Hamilton Memorial Museum in Skukuza.
- In 1926 the game ranger Mafuta, after shooting and wounding a lion, stabbed it to death with his knife. He himself died from loss of blood.

Lower Sabie

The game park has nine entrance gates – Malelane is the southernmost gate and Pafuri is the northernmost gate.

The gates are open at the following times:
November to February	05:30–18:30
March	05:30–18:00
April	06:00–18:00
May to July	06:00–17:30
August and September	06:00–18:00
October	05:30–18:00

Gate	Nearest Rest Camp
Crocodile Bridge*	Lower Sabie
Kruger*	Skukuza
Malelane*	Berg-en-Dal
Numbi*	Pretoriuskop
Orpen*	Satara
Pafuri	Punda Maria
Phabeni	Skukuza
Phalaborwa	Letaba
Punda Maria*	Punda Maria

* Visitors who have pre-booked can enter at these gates until 21.00 for an extra fee per vehicle. A game ranger will escort the vehicle to the camp.

- The term Big Five refers to the animals that are the most popular among tourists and visitors to national parks. These five animals are lion, elephant, leopard, buffalo and black rhino.
- In 2001 23 people burned to death in a runaway bush fire in the Kruger National Park. It was the biggest fire in the history of the park.
- South Africa, Mozambique and Zimbabwe came to an agreement in 2000 on the establishment of the largest transfrontier conservation area in the world: the Great Limpopo Transfrontier Park, formerly known as the Gaza-Kruger-Gonarezhou Transfrontier Park. The conservation area will be established in phases and could take up to 10 years to complete. It will eventually cover about 100 000km² and will be managed and maintained jointly by the three countries.

The Big Five built of sand on a Durban beach

Thulamela*

In the early 1990s, on a rocky hill in the northern reaches of the Kruger National Park, excavations began on the site of an unwalled settlement: Thulamela. This settlement, which dates from the late Iron Age (about 450–500 years BCE), forms part of the Zimbabwe culture that originated at Mapungubwe.

Tradition has it that this village was inhabited by the Nyai tribe of the Shona-speaking Lembethu. The Lembethu were apparently a Venda group who believed there is a mystical bond between the earth and their leader, who lived in isolation on the summit of the hill. The royal kraal housed about a thousand people. From the remnants of collapsed walls and signs of dwellings outside the walls, it can be deduced that up to 2 000 people lived here.

The site was apparently chosen for its fertile soil, in which different types of sorghum and manna were cultivated for porridge and beer. Clay spinning wheels indicate that cotton was probably also planted. The many potsherds are the remnants of clay pots of various sizes and shapes that were made by the Thulamela women and often were decorated. The men were accomplished goldsmiths and gold was their most important barter.

Thulamela was apparently an important centre of trade. Here gold and ivory were traded for corn and beads from traders who came from the present-day Mozambique to trade their goods north of the Limpopo River. There are also signs of contact with people from West Africa. Artefacts found at the site include beautiful bracelets of worked gold and beads, as well as harpoons for hunting hippos, royal gongs from West Africa, porcelain of the Chinese Ming dynasty and glass beads from India.

* *Thulamela* is a Karanga word meaning "place of birth". This name is appropriate because in the Shona-Karanga tradition the smithing of metal is seen as a process of birth.

Mapungubwe National Park (formerly **Vhembe-Dongola National Park**)

This park is located at the confluence of the Limpopo and Shashe rivers. It is a transfrontier park (Botswana, Zimbabwe and South Africa) that is still in the development phase. The park was declared a World Heritage Site in 2003. Lion, buffalo, elephant and other mammals are abundant. In the park is one of South Africa's most important archaeological sites, Mapungubwe, a city that was probably inhabited until about 1290 BCE **(see pages 88 & 128)**.

Baobab tree

Accommodation and outdoor shower   © SANParks.org

Accommodation in the main camp, Leokwe, is available in self-catering units with air conditioning and braai facilities. There is also a swimming pool. In the Tshugulu Lodge there is self-catering accommodation in luxury rooms with air conditioning. A swimming pool is also available. In the Limpopo bush tent camp there are tents with ceiling fans. There is a communal kitchen and braai facilities. In the Vhembe wilderness camp there are huts with communal kitchens and braai facilities and it is the only camp where meals can be ordered. In the Mazhou campsite there are sites for both tents and caravans. There are no restaurants or shops in the park and no fuel is available. Visitors must bring their own firewood.

Marakele* National Park

The park, which covers 50 726ha, was established in 1994 near Thabazimbi. It was originally known as the Kransberg National Park. The park protects the highest peaks of the Waterberg and has the country's largest breeding colony of Cape vultures. There are giraffes, elephants, white and black rhinos, leopards, hippos, zebras, elands and sable and roan antelopes, as well as many bird species.

The Tlopi tent camp is on the bank of the Matlabas River. Each tent has its own bathroom and a fully equipped kitchen. The Bontle campsite has 38 camping sites with power points. The Apies River bush camp can only be booked in its entirety (minimum six people). The area is very sandy and most of the roads are only suitable for 4x4 vehicles. There are no shops or restaurants in the park and no fuel is available. Own firewood must be brought.

* *Marakele* is a Tswana word meaning "sanctuary".

On top of the Waterberg

Tlopi tent camp

Mosu Lodge   Mosu Lodge

Mokala* National Park

The Mokala National Park is about 80km south-south-west of Kimberley and covers around 20 000ha. The park was opened in 2007. There are already plans to expand it. This park has a land claim against the then-Vaalbos Park near Barkly West to thank for its existence. Giraffe, rhino, buffalo, kudu, blue wildebeest, red hartebeest, Baster gemsbok and duiker can be seen here. Activities include mountain bike trails, day hikes, night drives and bush braais.

The Mosu Lodge offers luxury and semi-luxury accommodation. The Mofele Lodge, a semi-luxury lodge with a restaurant, can accommodate 30 people. The Lillydale Lodge has self-catering units with views over the Riet River. All the lodges have conference facilities. In the Haak-en-Steek camp there is only one self-catering cottage. There is a campsite without electricity or kitchen facilities and braai facilities are available in a lapa. A good telescope can be used for stargazing.

* *Mokala* is the Setswana name for the camel thorn tree.

Namaqua National Park

The park, which covers 60 000ha, was developed to protect the ecosystem of Namaqualand. The area is especially known for its floral beauty in the spring – there are around 3 500 flower species. The park has few mammals, but steenbok, duiker, baboon, porcupine and jackal are sometimes seen. There are short hiking trails, but the most important activity is going on tours in the spring to admire the wild flowers. There is a 50km 4x4 route with beautiful viewing spots. Mountain bikes are also available to hire. In the Skilpad Rest Camp there are four fully equipped self-catering cottages, each with a fireplace, a large veranda and an outdoor braai.

Klipspringers

Table Mountain National Park (formerly Cape Peninsula National Park)

The first part of this national park was proclaimed in 1998. The park covers 22 100ha and stretches from Vlaeberg above the Cape Town CBD over Table Mountain to Cape Point. In the park there are more than 2 285 plant species, many of which are found nowhere else in the world, including the well-known but rare red disa (*Disa uniflora*, also called the Pride of Table Mountain) and the king protea (*Protea cynaroides*). There are few mammals, but dassies (hyrax) and baboons are common. The scenery is breathtaking with beautiful beaches and Table Mountain, Cape Point, Boulders Beach at Simon's Town and Kirstenbosch are the most noteworthy sights.

Near Cape Point

   A cableway takes visitors to the top of Table Mountain. There is a restaurant on top of the mountain. A great variety of walking and climbing routes also leads to the top of the mountain. The first Table Mountain hiking trail with facilities for an overnight stay (exclusively for underprivileged youths) was opened in 2005. The trail – which can be completed in two days – starts at Constantia Nek and goes across Disa Gorge to Woodhead Dam, where the accommodation facilities are. Hikers can leave the park on the second day via Plattekrip Gorge or Kasteelpoort.

   The People's Trail is the first of four new hiking trails known collectively as the Hoerikwaggo* Trail. As well as the many hiking trails, there are beaches for water sports, picnic spots and mountain bike trails. The Olifantsbos self-catering unit is isolated and right on the beach. It is fully equipped. There is a master bedroom and two bedrooms with two beds each. There is also an annex that can accommodate six more people. The Eland and Duiker self-catering units have accommodation for six people each. The Wood Owl self-catering cottage is a restored forester's cottage in the Tokai forest. It can house six people. Many other types of accommodation are available in the Peninsula.

* *Hoerikwaggo* ("sea mountain") is how the Khoisan used to refer to Table Mountain.

Baboon

- Table Mountain is 1 086m high and South Africa's most famous landmark.
- The king protea grows up to 30cm in diameter and ranges from a creamy green to light pink and dark red.
- You should not hike on the mountain on your own and hikers should make sure they are home before dark.
- According to tradition, the ship *Flying Dutchman* disappeared off Cape Point in 1680. Apparently the captain, Hendrik van der Decken, said he would ask the devil for help if God did not come to his aid. As punishment he is doomed to an eternity of failed attempts to round the Cape. Richard Wagner's opera *Der fliegende Holländer* is based on this legend.
- The Indian tahrs on Table Mountain are the descendants of a breeding pair that escaped from the Groote Schuur Reserve in Cape Town in 1936. In 2000 authorities decided to exterminate these alien antelopes as they cause erosion and destroy indigenous plant species.
- In 1999 klipspringers were released on Table Mountain.

King protea

The World of Birds in Hout Bay

World of Birds is the largest bird park in Africa. There are more than 3 000 birds, monkeys, other small animals and alpacas. In the many walk-in cages small monkeys, for example, can be touched.

The Penguins of Boulders

There are only around 20 000 breeding pairs of African or jackass penguins in the world. Since 1958 Boulders in Simon's Town has offered protection to around 570 breeding pairs.

Tankwa Karoo National Park

The park was established in 1986 on the southern border of the Northern Cape near Calvinia. It is still expanding and today covers around 111 000ha. The succulent plant life has been damaged by overgrazing. After good rains the flowers in the area are beautiful. Smaller mammals like jackals, dassies (hyrax) and baboons are common and a variety of other mammals such as klipspringers and steenbok also occur.

The Paulshoek farmhouse and Varschfontein farmhouse offer self-catering accommodation. Both houses are fully equipped and have braai facilities. At Varschfontein there is a reservoir suitable for swimming. The Tanqua Guesthouse also offers self-catering accommodation and is sometimes used for team-building activities or as a wedding venue. There is a landing strip for light aircraft. In 2008, fully equipped self-

catering cottages were completed in the Elandsberg Wilderness Camp. Each cottage has a fireplace and undercover braai facilities. There are no electricity, shops or restaurants in the park. Fuel is also not available. During the winter months the road to Varschfontein is only suitable for 4x4 vehicles.

Garden Route National Park

The Garden Route National Park of about 121 000 ha was proclaimed in 2009. It consists of the former Knysna National Lake Area, the Wildernis National Park and Tsitsikamma National Park, all of which are now camps in the Garden Route National Park. It is the only national park in South Africa in which the unique combination of lagoons, indigenous forests, fynbos and mountain catchment areas have been included. No new gates or perimeter fencing has been erected. The establishment of this park forms part of the strategy to extend the preserved areas in South Africa to 8% of the total surface area of the country.

Knysna National Lake Area

Knysna Lagoon

The Knysna National Lake Area was proclaimed in 1985 to protect the area from development. The Knysna Lagoon is part of the conservation area. More than 230 bird species and 200 fish species occur here. There are few mammals but grysbok, duiker, bushbuck, bush pig, vervet monkey and baboon can sometimes be seen. The area is ideal for swimming, diving, canoeing and any other water sports. Boat trips are offered on the Knysna Lagoon. In 2007, Sanparks constructed wooden camping decks in the Diepwalle Forest Station. Each deck has a braai area and power point and can accommodate a three-man tent. Tents and mattresses can be hired. There is also a variety of accommodation in and around Knysna.

- The rare Knysna seahorse occurs in the Knysna Lagoon. These seahorses are about 7cm long and live off small crustaceans. Their eyes can move independently of each other. The female lays her eggs in the breeding sack of the male, where they can then be fertilised.
- South Africa's largest oyster farm is at Knysna.

Oyster Restaurant

Tsitsikamma* National Park

The park was established in 1964 in the Garden Route and in 2009 became a camp in the Garden Route National Park. It is the first marine reserve to be established in Africa, and dolphins, otters and whales are often seen. In the forested areas there are monkeys, blue duikers, bushbucks and many other small mammals.

* *Tsitsikamma* is a Khoi word meaning "running water".

The park offers several short hiking trails, while the famous five-day Otter Trail begins in the park. At the Storms River Mouth Rest Camp there are several types of self-catering accommodation, and many of the wooden chalets are right on the sea. The De Vasselot Rest Camp at Nature's Valley offers accommodation in huts, each of which comes with a canoe. Both camps also have campsites. The Storms River Rest Camp has a restaurant.

Wilderness Camp

This camp is near Wilderness. The lakes are suitable for canoeing, rowing, swimming and angling. Small boats and canoes can be hired. There are various hiking trails and two bird hides on the banks of two vleis. At the Ebb & Flow Rest Camp (south) there are chalets and wooden huts on stilts. At the northern camp there are rondavels with only basic facilities available. Both camps have campsites on the banks of the Touw River. There is no shop or restaurant in the camp, but both can be found in the nearby town of Wilderness.

West Coast National Park

This park was established in 1985 and covers 24 700ha. It surrounds the Langebaan Lagoon and protects four bird islands. On Jutten Island African penguins and oyster catchers breed and on Malgas Island oyster catchers and often about 60 000 Cape gannets breed. On Schaapen Island crowned cormorants breed while Marcus Island has the largest African penguin breeding colony in the country, as well as many breeding pairs of Cape cormorants.

At Postberg there are bontebok, red hartebeest, springbok and blue wildebeest. Postberg is also known for its beautiful spring flowers. At Churchhaven and Kraal Bay there are fish traps made by early fishermen. Salamander Point*, near Donkergat, was once the site the largest whaling station in the southern hemisphere. The area was also used a quarantine station for people suffering from smallpox.

* The *Salamander* was a Dutch ship that lay at her moorings in the bay because some of the crew members had smallpox.

Langebaan Lagoon

In the park there are various picnic spots, hiking trails and bird shelters. The Abrahamskraal self-catering unit, Duinepos chalets and Jo-Anne's Beach Cottage (near Churchhaven) are fully equipped. Flamingo Jo's Beach Camp provides accommodation in tents on decks. All meals are provided.

At Kraal Bay there is accommodation available in two houseboats, which can be booked with or without meals. Guided walking tours are offered. There is also a tea garden where light meals are offered.

National botanical gardens

Name	City/Town
Hantam National Botanical Garden	Nieuwoudtville
Harold Porter National Botanical Garden	Betty's Bay
Karoo Desert National Botanical Garden	Worcester
Kirstenbosch National Botanical Garden	Cape Town
KwaZulu-Natal National Botanical Garden	Pietermaritzburg
Lowveld National Botanical Garden	Nelspruit
Pretoria National Botanical Garden	Pretoria
Free State National Botanical Garden	Bloemfontein
Walter Sisulu National Botanical Garden	Roodepoort

Kirstenbosch

World Heritage Sites

World Heritage Sites are declared by the United Nations Educational, Scientific and Cultural Organisation (Unesco). In South Africa the following areas and places are World Heritage Sites:

Richtersveld

The top of Table Mountain

World Heritage Site	Date declared
Robben Island	1999
iSimangaliso (formerly Greater St Lucia) Wetland Park	1999
uKhahlamba/Drakensberg Park	1999
Cradle of Humankind, the Sterkfontein fossil hominid sites	1999
Mapungubwe Cultural Landscape	2003
Cape Floral Region Protected Areas (Boland mountain complex, Boosmansbos wilderness area, Cederberg wilderness area, De Hoop Nature Reserve, Groot Winterhoek wilderness area, Swartberg mountains, Table Mountain)	2004
Vredefort Dome	2005
Richtersveld Cultural and Botanical Landscape	2007

Well-known provincial and private reserves

Baviaanskloof

Baviaanskloof is located about 120km west of Port Elizabeth in the Eastern Cape. It stretches across about 200km² of unspoilt, rugged mountain landscape. Leopards, mountain zebras, buffalos, kudus, bushbucks and klipspringers, as well as other smaller mammals and birds, occur here. There are opportunities for mountain and rock climbing, hiking,

mountain biking, camping and bird watching. There is also a challenging 4x4 trail.

Baviaanskloof offers various campsites, but there is only one mountain hut with basic facilities. The mountain hut, the Bergplaas Hut, is deep in the wilderness and can accommodate 12 people. There is also accommodation available on private land near the reserve. One of these places is the very unusual Makkedaat Cave, which is on the border of the reserve (see photo above).

Blyde River Canyon

This nature reserve stretches about 57km along the Drakensberg escarpment, north of Graskop in Mpumalanga. It covers approximately 27 000ha and serves chiefly to protect the natural beauty of the area. Bushbuck, klipspringer, kudu, grey rhebok, duiker and bush pig, as well as baboon and three types of monkey, occur here. There are hiking trails and viewpoints. Accommodation is available in chalets and at a campsite, and there is a swimming pool, shop, restaurant, golf course, mini golf course, tennis court and facilities for horse riding.

Boesmanskloof

This exclusive reserve near Clanwilliam at the foot of the Cederberg in the Western Cape covers 7 200ha. Bontebok, black wildebeest, springbok, gemsbok, the rare Cape mountain zebra, wild dog and birds of prey can be encountered here. Accommodation is in luxurious cottages and there are restaurants. In 1998 the Manor House, which has four suites and all facilities, opened. Guided walking tours can be taken to the various San rock art sites. Other activities include mountain and river walks, swimming in rock pools and game drives. In spring the flowers are breathtaking.

De Hoop

This reserve near Waenhuiskrans on the Cape south coast stretches over 35 846ha and includes a coastline of 50km. As well as bontebok there are springbok, eland, grysbok, mountain zebra, steenbok and klipspringer. Approximately 260 bird species also occur here. Thousands of African coots, yellow-billed ducks, Cape shovellers and Egyptian geese

Accommodation

congregate at a 14km-long saltwater marsh. Smaller mammals such as the small grey mongoose (Cape grey mongoose), baboon, caracal and silver-backed jackal also occur here. De Hoop is also one of the best places in the Western Cape for whale watching.

Various types of accommodation, from basic to luxurious, are available. There are also ten campsites. At Potberg there is an environmental information centre, which has two dormitories with room for 60 people. Hiking

Restaurant

and mountain biking trails are marked out. In 2009 all the accommodation was upgraded and redecorated. There is also a new restaurant, bar, coffee shop and a curio shop. In 2009 the local population and Cape Nature Conservation agreed to further development in the reserve.

> Between January and April southern right whales migrate to the south-western Cape coast to mate and calf. The coast between Waenhuiskrans and Puntjie is one of the most important areas in the world as regards their calving. Up to fifty whales have been spotted in one day near the De Hoop Nature Reserve.

Hluhluwe-Umfolozi

This park of 96 453ha was, along with Lake St Lucia, proclaimed as a conservation area in 1895 and has the largest population of white and black rhinos in southern Africa. When the park was established there were only about 50 white rhinos left in the world, but thanks to the protection they enjoy in this park the population increased to 700 by 1960.

Since then white rhinos have been released in conservation areas around the world. The park also has lion, elephant, giraffe, buffalo, hippo, jackal, warthog and many types of antelope.

Various hiking trails are available and early morning and night drives are on offer. Accommodation is available in rest and bush camps with large and small cottages and huts. Extremely luxurious accommodation is also available. In some camps meals are offered, but there are also several picnic spots. The Mambeni craft market offers a large variety of traditional and handmade articles at very reasonable prices.

iSimangaliso* (formerly Great St Lucia Wetland Park)

Lake St Lucia is the focus of this reserve of 170 000ha. It supports crabs, fish and other marine life. Hippos and crocodiles are common. On the western shore of the lake there are approximately 385 bird species. The coastal dune forest is home to bushbucks, bush pigs, vervet monkeys and red squirrels. In the Mfabeni section there are rietbok, buffalo, impala and black rhino. Sodwana Bay is regarded as the best place for free diving on the South African coast. The marine life is breathtaking – coral grows on sandstone reefs and thousands of colourful fish are encountered. There are guided turtle tours in January and February when the leatherbacked and loggerhead turtles come to lay their eggs on the beach at night. In the Mkuzi reserve there is abundant wildlife and leopard and cheetah are sometimes seen.

Accommodation is in rest camps with chalets and huts, in bush camps and at campsites. In the different parts of the wetland park there are opportunities for a variety of activities: from swimming, snorkelling and diving to boat rides, game drives, bird watching, guided wilderness walks and night drives.

* iSimangaliso is a World Heritage Site.

- Leather-backed turtles can weigh up to 646kg and grow to up to 2,5m long. In January and February they lay their eggs on the beach at St Lucia. Out of every 1 000 baby turtles only about two will reach adulthood.
- The loggerhead turtle weighs up to 140kg and grows up to 1,2m long.

Itala

This park, in the north of KwaZulu-Natal, stretches over 30 000ha and borders on the Pongola River. The Big Five can be seen here. Giraffe, rhino, tsessebe and many other types of antelope occur. More than 320 bird species also occur here. Hikes, night drives and guided early morning and afternoon walks can be undertaken. Accommodation is available in rest and bush camps with chalets. In the main camp, Ntshondwe, there is a restaurant and shelter that looks out over a watering hole, which attracts many birds and animals. At Ntshondwe there is a swimming pool, shop and petrol pump.

The Itala Wildlife Reserve is the southernmost area where tsessebe occur. They are related to the bontebok and blesbok, have a shoulder height of about 1,3m and can reach a speed of 100km/h. Cows live in small herds with a territorial bull.

Kagga Kamma

This reserve is in the Cederberg north of Ceres and covers 15 000ha. It is known for its beautiful scenery and San rock paintings that are up to 6 000 years old. Bontebok, kudu, gemsbok, springbok, carakal and Cape vulture are often seen here. There are hiking trails and 4x4 game routes, as well as conference facilities for up to 45 people. Accommodation is available in luxury huts, caves or chalets. There is a restaurant, gift shop, open-air lapa and a landing strip for light aircraft.

San rock paintings

Royal Natal National Park

The focus of this park is the Amphitheatre, a rock wall 6km wide that towers 1 500m above the valleys. The second highest waterfall in the world, the Tugela Waterfall at 947m high, gushes over the edge of the Amphitheatre. Breathtaking views, beautiful hiking trails and mountain tracks that crisscross the park, and mountain streams for swimming make a visit to the park unforgettable. Horse riding can also be done. Accommodation is available in chalets and at a campsite.

> The Tweede Waterfall in Jonkershoek, Stellenbosch, is the highest uninterrupted waterfall in southern Africa.

Lapalala

Lapalala stretches over 35 000ha in the Waterberg in Limpopo. In 1990 it became the first private reserve to have black rhinos. There are also blue wildebeest, kudu, baster gemsbok and about 275 bird species. A wilderness school that teaches young people about nature conservation is available. There are no roads for viewing game, but there are short walking trails, while guided game drives are also offered. Accommodation is available in six camps overlooking the Lephalala River.

Phinda

This resource reserve borders on the Greater St Lucia Wetland Park in KwaZulu-Natal. Elephant, lion, cheetah, giraffe and white rhino are seen here. The reserve is also home to more than 300 bird species. Game drives, riverboat and canoe trips, bush walks and free diving at Sodwana Bay can be enjoyed. Accommodation is in the Forest Lodge and Phinda Nyala Lodge.

Pilanesberg National Park

The park of 55 000ha is situated on the eroded remains of a volcano. Although some of the camps are near the well-known Sun City, this has no effect on the peaceful atmosphere of the park. A wide variety of animals, including the Big Five, are often seen. Accommodation is in luxury lodges, chalets, tented camps and campsites. At the main entrance, Manyane, there are two walk-in aviaries with African birds. Game viewing in vehicles is undertaken and hot-air balloon rides over the park are also offered.

Sabie Sand Complex

Selati Camp, Sabi-Sabi

Little Bush Camp, Sabi-Sabi

Sabi-Sabi, Mala Mala and the Londolozi reserves combined form the Sabie Sand complex. It covers 70 000ha and is located in Mpumalanga north-west of Hazyview. The fence between this reserve and Kruger National Park has been removed and game can move freely between them. Reserves in the Sabie Sand complex differ in atmosphere, accommodation and tariffs, but all are luxurious. Mala Mala is the most luxurious and expensive bush camp in South Africa. Game is common and visitors can be virtually certain of seeing the Big Five.

Shamwari

This is the most important private reserve in the Eastern Cape and covers 8 000ha. Lion, elephant, giraffe, rhino, hippo, buffalo, eland, zebra and wildebeest can be seen here. Walks and game drives can be undertaken. Accommodation is in an Edwardian manor house or in farmhouses. There is also a cultural village that uses music, dance and stories to introduce visitors to traditional African culture. In 2003, Shamwari was named the best safari venture in the world at the World Travel Awards in New York.

Timbavati

This reserve lies north-east of Lydenburg in Mpumalanga. A wide variety of animals, including buffalo, lion, elephant, giraffe, zebra and many types of antelope, can be encountered here, as well as the rare white lion. There are more than 250 bird species. Accommodation is available in luxury rondavels or tents. Timbavati is popular with businesspeople and foreign tourists.

Twalu

This reserve covers 75 000ha at the foot of the Koranna Mountains in the Kalahari Desert and is the largest private reserve in South Africa. Lion, elephant, kudu and sable can be seen here. Accommodation is available in a luxury lodge. There is a landing strip for light aircraft.

uKhahlamba/Drakensberg Park*

This park is South Africa's third largest conservation area and covers 235 000ha. The highest mountain peaks in the country are here. The scenery and viewpoints are the park's biggest attractions. At Giant's Castle baboons and a wide variety of antelopes can be seen, of which the eland population of around 1 500 is the second largest in the country. There are easy and difficult hiking trails, guided tours to a vulture hide and many examples of San rock art. In the park there are facilities for trout fishing. At Hillside you can go horse riding, weather allowing, and overnight in caves or huts. There are several resorts and different types of accommodation, ranging from campsites to luxury hotels. More to the north, at Cathedral Peak and Monk's Cowl, there are mammals like baboons, bushbuck, blesbok and mountain reedbuck. It often snows in winter.

* The uKhahlamba/Drakensberg Park is a World Heritage Site.

> Fonteinedal, at the source of the Apies River in Pretoria, was Africa's first nature reserve. It was proclaimed in 1895 by President Paul Kruger.

Well-known hiking trails

1936

2009

Alexandria

This circular route begins at the forestry station south of Alexandria in the Eastern Cape. It winds through plantations and indigenous forests, where bushbuck, bush pig and blue duiker occur, and through duneveld with duiker, tree dassie, lynx, other mammals and a variety of birds.

A part of the route runs along the coast with beautiful views over the sea. At low tide one can walk further along the coast and later climb a rope ladder up the cliffs. The last section of the route runs across dunes and a grass plateau. The route is 36km long and can be completed in two days. There are two overnight huts. Making fires is forbidden and all rubbish must be removed.
 Reservations and enquiries: ☎ 046 653 0601

Amatola

The route begins at Maden Dam near King William's Town in the Eastern Cape, and ends at the Zingcuka forestry station. It is a one-way route that criss-crosses the Amatola Mountains. The route runs through pine plantations and indigenous forest and over grassveld, and offers breathtaking views. There are many waterfalls, streams and pools. A variety of birds, endangered amphibians and fish, bushbuck and bush pigs occur here. The Amatola is a demanding route of 100km that can be completed in six days. The overnight huts have braai facilities and firewood is supplied.
 Reservations and enquiries: ☎ 043 642 2571

Blyde River Canyon

This one-way route begins at God's Window in Mpumalanga and runs over the southern part of the Blyde River Canyon Nature Reserve. Mammals such as baboon, vervet monkey, kudu and duiker, as well as 227 bird species, are found here. It is a relatively easy route running through grassveld and bushveld. The view over the escarpment and Lowveld is beautiful. The route is 30,1km long and can be walked in three days. There are two overnight huts.
 Reservations and enquiries:
☎ 013 759 5432

Boland

The route starts at the Nuweberg forestry station near Grabouw in the Western Cape. Various one-way or circular routes can be followed. The routes run through fynbos in the mountains above Stellenbosch, Franschhoek and Somerset West. The lengths of the routes differ and the hikes can be completed within two or three days. Baboon, klipspringer, grysbok and leopard are sometimes encountered. At the overnight huts there are braai facilities. All the routes are closed in June and July and the Boegoekloof circular route is closed between April and September.
Reservations and enquiries: ☎ 021 659 3500

Fanie Botha

This is a one-way route through pine plantations, grassveld and indigenous forests between Sabie and Graskop in Mpumalanga. There are beautiful views. Bush pigs, antelope, dassies and baboons may be encountered. The longest route is 72,4km long and can be completed in five days. It ends at the Mac Mac Falls. Shorter circular routes can also be followed. Overnight huts have braai facilities and firewood is provided.
Reservations and enquiries: ☎ 013 754 2724

Giant's Castle

This circular route begins at the main camp of the Giant's Castle Nature Reserve in KwaZulu-Natal. There is beautiful scenery, many rivers and valleys, and San rock art. Blesbok, mountain reedbuck, eland and oribi are often encountered. The route is 58km long and can be completed in four days. Various shorter routes can also be followed. There are overnight huts.
Reservations and enquiries: ☎ 036 353 3718.

Giant's Cup

This route in KwaZulu-Natal runs through grassveld valleys in the foothills of the Drakensberg and ends at Boesmans Nek. Six rivers flow through the valleys where the path winds. Mountain reedbuck, duiker, oribi and various types of birds of prey are often seen. There are five overnight huts, all of which are located near water. The route is 59,3km long and can be completed in five days.
Reservations and enquiries: ☎ 033 845 1000

Harkerville

This hiking trail begins at Harkerville, near Plettenberg Bay. The route takes two days to complete and winds through beautiful indigenous forest. From the high cliffs there are breathtaking views of the rocky coastline. The steep path down has wooden steps in certain places. The coastal route is only around 4km long, but ladders and chains are used to climb cliffs. Twelve people can sleep in the Sinclair hut. There are beds and mattresses, and wood is available. The rest of the route is also demanding with more rocks that must be climbed with the help of chains and ladders. The route is not recommended for people with a fear of heights. The Outeniqua hiking trail ends here and the two routes can easily be combined to form a route of nine nights.

Reservations and enquiries: ☎ 044 302 5606

Oorlogs Kloof

The Oorlogs Kloof hiking trail is in the Oorlogs Kloof Nature Reserve and approximately 16km from Nieuwoudtville. There are two circular routes that take four to five days and four to seven days respectively.

There are also two routes for day hikes. The routes have views over the Knersvlakte, Moutonsberg, Tierberg, Van Ryns Pass and the Oorlogs Kloof River. Hikers must climb cliffs, sometimes with the help of a ladder and chain, and cross rivers. On the route there are rock art, kraals and stone cottages that speak of some of the history of the area. The name of the route refers to the clashes between the local farmers and the Khoisan.

Reservations and enquiries:
☎ 027 218 1010

Otter

The Otter Trail became South Africa's first official hiking trail in 1968. The route starts at the Storms River Nature Reserve, runs along the beautiful coastline and ends at Nature's Valley on the Garden Route. It is viewed as the country's most beautiful coastal hiking trail. The route is 41km long and the longest stretch that must be completed in one day is 14km. The hike is five days long. The Lottering and Bloukrans rivers must be crossed on the third and fourth day respectively. Hikers should consult a tide timetable so that they can cross the rivers at low tide. Waterproof bags for rucksacks are handy if one must swim the rivers.

Reservations must be made far in advance at: ☎ 012 426 5111

Outeniqua

The route begins at the Beervlei forestry station and ends at Harkerville in the forests west of Knysna. It runs through fynbos, pine plantations and indigenous forests where vervet monkey, bush buck, blou duiker, bush pig and a variety of birds can be seen. It often rains and the paths can be very slippery. The route is 180km long and the hike lasts seven days. Shorter routes can also be followed. Firewood is provided at

the overnight huts. New huts, showers, toilets, ablution facilities, wooden paths and wooden decks were completed in 2007 in the Diepwalle forest, where visitors can camp and braai.

Reservations and enquiries: ☎ 044 382 5863

Cederberg

The Cederberg is the Western Cape's biggest wilderness area. This is an unspoilt area with unusual rock formations that offers wonderful opportunities for hiking. There is a network of routes stretching over 250km and hikes of up to seven days can be undertaken. Baboon, klipspringer and grey rhebok are found here. Fires are not allowed in the wilderness area and there are no equipped overnight huts, only basic huts and campsites. There are also many campsites in the area.

Reservations and enquiries: ☎ 021 659 3500

Swellendam

This hiking trail is regarded as one of the most beautiful in the Western Cape. It follows a circular route through the Marloth Nature Reserve in the Langeberg mountains and winds through valleys and indigenous forest and over streams. It offers a view of the Breede River Valley and Little Karoo. The hiking trail is 76,8km long and six days are needed to complete it. Shorter routes can also be followed. Making fires is only permitted at the Wolfkloof hut.

Reservations and enquiries: ☎ 028 514 1410

Tsitsikamma

This hiking trail is an extension of the Otter Trail and begins at Nature's Valley. It runs through damp indigenous forest, fynbos, pine plantations and mountain landscapes and ends at the Paul Sauer Bridge over the Storms River near Humansdorp. The route is 60,8km long and the hike is five days long. The overnight huts have cooking facilities.

Reservations and enquiries: ☎ 042 281 1712

Tips for hikers

Clothing

- Preferably a pair of light trousers for hiking through forests and grass, to avoid scratches and cuts. A pair of trousers with removable legs works very well.

- A pair of light shorts or swimming trunks that dry quickly if the hike does not go through thick vegetation. A pair of cycling shorts under shorts prevents chafing.

- A long-sleeved shirt helps to prevent sunburn.

- Cotton underwear and wool socks are very effective.

- If the trail goes across rocky terrain, boots that support the ankles are best. Otherwise, ordinary walking shoes are fine. Shoes or boots must be worn in. New shoes can be worn in at home by wetting them on the wearer's feet and "walking them dry". Wear them as often as possible before the hike. Take extra shoelaces along.

- Take flip-flops that fit properly – it is never a good idea to walk through a river barefoot.

- A hat that protects the neck and ears is a necessity.

- A waterproof jacket with a lining is a good idea. The inner can then also be worn alone for warmth. Test the waterproof jacket as sometimes a poncho works better. A poncho is cheap and light and can be pulled over a rucksack when it begins to rain. Unfortunately it is very warm as it cannot "breathe".

- A woollen cap for the cold evenings.

- Good planning will prevent hikers from taking along too many clothes.

Equipment

- Your rucksack must be as light as possible. Side bags are not really important. Straps on the rucksack work just as well. The weight of a packed rucksack should preferably be no more than 20% of the hiker's body weight. Adjust the rucksack so that it rests on the hiker's hips, instead of the shoulders.

- A good-quality down sleeping bag is the best choice. Hikers who sleep badly because of the cold will not have the energy to walk very far the next day.

- A lightweight, waterproof tent that is easy to erect is a good choice.

- A cheap inflatable or foam mattress is a good idea. An inflatable pillow or clothes can be used as a pillow.

- A light aluminium walking stick is very useful on paths with loose rocks or inclines.

- Plan water rations well, in case the hike does not take place in an area with lots of water.

- Take the best sunscreen along.

- Use water purification tablets if the water purity is uncertain.

- Take enough toilet paper along.

- A pair of sunglasses and lip salve are important.

- A chamois cloth can be used instead of a towel.

- A few pieces of sponge are useful; they can be placed under the straps of the rucksack to avoid chafing and can also be used to wash dishes.

- Nylon rope and about 3m of thin wire are useful for repair work.

- A thick needle and thread for repair work is a good idea.

- A trowel is necessary on wilderness routes without toilet facilities.

- A headlamp is more useful than a torch, as you can use both hands for tasks like cooking.

- Pack a box of matches or a lighter.

- Black bags are multi-purpose and can, for example, be used to protect your sleeping bag and rucksack if it rains.

- A camping stove and gas bottle, a penknife with a can opener, as well as cutlery and washing-up liquid, are useful.

Useful food for hikes

- Instant oats
- ProNutro
- Muesli
- Rusks
- Coffee, tea and sugar
- Powdered milk
- Pro-Vita
- Instant soup
- Dehydrated mince
- Couscous
- Pasta
- Smash
- Vacuum-packed meat, frozen and wrapped in newspaper, can last up to four days
- Cans of tuna
- Tins of sardines
- Tins of mussels
- Biltong
- Salami (vacuum packed)
- Cheese wedges
- Energy bars, jelly sweets and chocolate
- Dried fruit and nuts
- Energy drinks
- Wine for a treat in the evening

- Pack every day's food in a separate Ziploc bag.
- Use empty plastic bottles and film or pill bottles for sugar, salt and jam. You can also keep body lotion or liquid soap in them.

Safety Guidelines

- Make sure you are fit enough for the hike.
- Do proper research and plan thoroughly.
- Keep someone informed of your whereabouts.
- Always take a good map with you, even if you have directions.
- A space blanket is light, can be folded up and could save someone's life. Make sure someone in the group takes one along.
- Make sure there are at least two fully charged cellphones in the group.
- A whistle is useful if there is a crisis and a search party needs to find you.
- Take a first aid kit with disinfectant, pain pills, antiseptic ointment, insect repellent, diarrhoea pills, rehydration salts, antihistamine, plasters, bandages and methylated spirits (for blistered feet or heels) along.

4. WELL-KNOWN MONUMENTS, CHURCHES AND ATTRACTIONS

The Statue of Energy at Rhodes Memorial

George's Dutch Reformed Church

Cango II, where visitors are not allowed

Table Mountain

Rickshaw

Canal Walk

Monuments

Afrikaans Language Monument, Paarl

The Afrikaans Language Monument (*Taalmonument*) is situated on Paarl Rock. The purpose of the monument is to commemorate the birth and growth of the Afrikaans language. It was designed by the architect Jan van Wijk. The monument was inaugurated in 1975. The three obelisks represent the contributions made by European languages to the development of Afrikaans, the three round hills represent Africa and its languages and a low wall represents the contribution of the Cape Malays. The tallest obelisk is 57m high.

Obelisk of the Language Monument

Blood River Monument, Dundee

Ox wagon laager at the Blood River Monument

Three monuments were erected on the site of the Battle of Blood River. The cornerstone of the first monument, an ox wagon of grey granite designed and made by Coert Steynberg, was laid in 1938. The second monument consists of a replica of an ox wagon laager cast in bronze. There are 64 life-size ox wagons, each weighing eight tons. There are also three replicas of cannons that were used in the battle. This monument was unveiled in 1971. In 1998 the Ncome Museum, the third monument, was erected on the opposite bank of Blood River, in remembrance of the Zulus who died in the Battle of Blood River.

Hector Pieterson Memorial

On 16 June 1976 masses of schoolchildren from Soweto took part in a demonstration after a meeting at the Orlando Stadium to protest against the use of Afrikaans as a language of instruction. The Transvaal Department of Education had decided that Afrikaans should be used as the medium of education in all black secondary schools, despite the fact that many black people could not speak or understand Afrikaans.

The demonstration became a riot when police used tear gas. The learners started throwing stones and the police began to shoot. Hundreds of learners were killed and wounded. Vehicles were destroyed and buildings set on fire. The

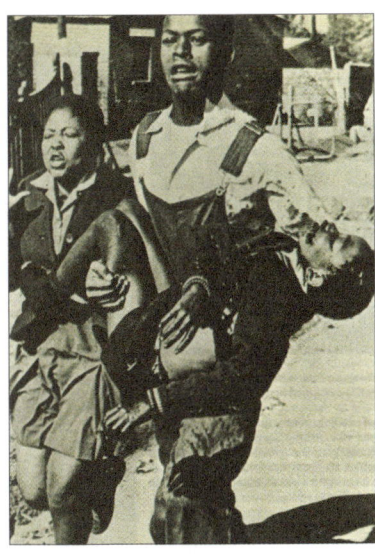

13-year-old Hector Pieterson was one of the learners who was wounded. The 18-year-old Mbuyisa Makhubo picked him up and he and Hector's sister took Hector to photographer Sam Mzima's car in which he was taken to a clinic. At the clinic, Hector was declared dead.

After the protests the Transvaal Department of Education rescinded its decision. The Hector Pieterson Museum was inaugurated in 2002 and has information about the events that led to the protests. The museum also has a register of all the children who died violent deaths between June 1976 and the end of 1977. Hector's sister is a guide in the museum. The museum is in Kumalo Street, Orlando West, Johannesburg.

Photograph in front of the Hector Pieterson Memorial

- The 15-year-old Hastings Ndlovu was shot before Hector, but it was not photographed and he did not become as famous.
- Hector and Hastings are both buried in the Avalon Cemetery in Soweto.

Huguenot Monument

The Huguenot Monument was erected to commemorate the arrival of the French Huguenots in South Africa in 1688. It was designed by J.C. Jongens, a Dutchman who worked for the city council in Cape Town. The monument is at the eastern entrance to Franschhoek.

The three arches symbolise the Trinity. Above the arches is a cross and the "sun of righteousness", a symbol of Christianity. The central figure, a woman standing on the globe with her feet in France, was made by the sculptor Coert Steynberg. The woman has a Bible in her right hand and a broken chain in her left hand, which symbolises religious freedom. In front of the monument is a pool and behind the monument is a colonnade in a semicircle. Near the monument is the Huguenot Memorial, which also houses the head office of the Huguenot Society of South Africa.

Castle of Good Hope, Cape Town

The Castle in Cape Town is the oldest built structure in South Africa and also the oldest building still in use. The cornerstones were laid in 1666 by Commander Zacharias Wagenaar and the construction work was completed in 1679. Stone was taken from Table Mountain, wood was cut at Hout Bay, shells (for chalk) were brought from Robben Island and bricks, tiles and special wood were imported from the Netherlands. Soldiers and slaves did the construction work.

The Castle's five bastions were named after the titles of the Prince of Orange: Leerdam, Katzenellenbogen, Nassau, Orange and Buuren. In the Castle there were living quarters, barracks for the local garrison, a gunpowder magazine, prison cells, workshops for gunsmiths, offices and kitchens. In a dark underground cell, the "black hole", offenders were locked up in solitary confinement. Some of their graffiti and scratch marks can still be seen there today.

The Kat is a beautiful balcony in front of a high wall built in the inner courtyard for extra protection. Louis Thibault (architect) and Anton Anreith (sculptor) designed and built it. Next to the balcony was the governor's residence and a large hall that was used for formal dances and other functions. Various alterations were made to the Castle in the 19th century. Currently, the Castle is the headquarters of the South African Army in the Western Cape. There is a maritime and military museum, as well as a collection of valuable Africana.

Entrance to the Castle

National Women's Monument, Bloemfontein

The National Women's Monument commemorates the approximately 27 000 Boer women and children who died during the Anglo-Boer War in British concentration camps and elsewhere. The monument was the brainchild of the last president of the Republic of the Free State, President M.T. Steyn, and his wife, Tibbie. Family and friends of the Steyns had died in the concentration camps. The design was done by the architect Frans Soff and the sculptor was the well-known Anton van Wouw. The monument is about 3km south

Statues in front of the Women's Monument

of the centre of Bloemfontein. The 35m-high memorial needle is encircled by a "whispering wall" that picks up any sound from the inside of the wall and broadcasts it around the wall. The group of sculptures in front of the monument consists of a standing woman who is gazing into the distance and a seated woman holding her emaciated child who has just died on her lap.

The Women's Monument was unveiled on 16 December 1913. Emily Hobhouse, who had dedicated herself to improving conditions in British concentration camps, could not attend the ceremony due to ill health, but her speech was read out. President M.T. Steyn, Tibbie Steyn, General Christiaan de Wet, Reverend J.D. Kestell and Emily Hobhouse are buried at the monument. There is also a War Museum on the grounds, which has relics from the Anglo-Boer War.

Rhodes Memorial, Cape Town

Rhodes Memorial, on the lower slopes of Devil's Peak, was erected in memory of the well-known politician Cecil John Rhodes. Rhodes was very attached to the place where the monument was erected. The design, by Sir Herbert Baker, is based on a Greek temple at Segesta. The monument consists of 49 massive steps (a step for every year of Rhodes's life) leading from a semicircular terrace to a U-shaped monument that consists of large granite pillars. The granite was quarried at Table Mountain. In front of the steps is a bronze statue of a horseman (Statue of Energy) sculpted by George Frederic Watts. It is symbolic of Rhodes's drive and determination. On each side of the steps are four bronze lions, made by John Swan. The monument also has a bust of Cecil John Rhodes, also designed by Swan. The monument was completed in 1912.

Rhodes owned large pieces of land on the slopes of Table Mountain, which he willed to the people of South Africa. Kirstenbosch Botanical Gardens and the University of Cape Town are also on land that used to belong to Rhodes. Behind the monument is a tea room and the area around it is popular with picnickers. There used to be a zoo in the grounds, but it closed in the 1970s. The area is closed from sunset to sunrise for safety reasons.

Voortrekker Monument, Pretoria

The Voortrekker Monument on Monument Hill just outside Pretoria was designed by the architect Gerard Moerdijk. It was built to honour the Voortrekkers who had left the Cape Colony and Natal between 1835 and 1854. The cornerstone was laid on 16 December 1938 and the monument was inaugurated on 16 December 1949 by Dr D.F. Malan, the then-prime minister.

The monument is 62m high. It is encircled by a symbolic laager of 64 ox wagons that have been carved out of stone on a circular wall. At the entrance there is a bronze sculpture of a Voortrekker woman and her two children – the last work of sculptor Anton van Wouw. At the four corners of the monument are statues of Andries Pretorius, Piet Retief, Hendrik Potgieter and an unknown leader who represents all the other Voortrekker leaders.

The Hall of Heroes is a large domed hall with a marble floor and frieze, the latter depicting scenes from the Great Trek. The frieze was designed by Frikkie Kruger, Hennie Potgieter, Peter Kirchoff and Laurika Postma and was carved in Italian marble by 46 Italians. The cenotaph is made of red granite and represents the symbolic graves of all the Voortrekkers who died during the Great Trek. In the Cenotaph Hall there is a flame that has been burning since the symbolic ox wagon trek in 1938. Every year on 16 December a beam of sunlight strikes the cenotaph, shining on the words "Ons vir jou South Africa" (Literally, "We for you, South Africa" although usually translated as "O, South Africa, dear land"). Just outside the monument is a museum depicting the lifestyle of the Voortrekkers.

A new Afrikaner Heritage Centre was erected in 2008 on the slopes of Monument Hill. It is a modern Art Deco-style three-storey building and was founded to be a comprehensive Afrikaner museum to protect the Afrikaner cultural heritage.

Freedom Park, Pretoria

Freedom Park was erected opposite the Voortrekker Monument on Salvokop. It was completed in 2009. The grounds cover 52ha. From Salvokop there is a view over the Union Buildings, Church Square and other well-known landmarks. Freedom Park symbolises democracy, humanity and the sacrifices made for freedom.

Amphitheatre and eternal flame

Isivivane

The park consists of a garden with an indoor chapel where people can pray or meditate, and an open-air theatre with an eternal flame in memory of the heroes who died for freedom and humanity. Sikhumbuto* houses a gallery of leaders where two African and two international leaders are honoured, a memorial wall with the names of South Africans who died for freedom or in concentration camps and an amphitheatre that can seat up to 2 000 people. Isivivane** consists of a symbolic cemetery and a venue where incense can be burned. Around the symbolic cemetery are nine stone blocks that represent the local and national government. An interactive museum and a reception and conference centre also form part of the park. From the top there is a view over a peaceful dam. The purpose of Freedom Park is to be a peaceful, spiritual place that can serve as a place of prayer and a place of healing, restitution and cleansing so a united nation can be built.

* *Sikhumbuto* is the Swazi word for "memorial".
** *Isivivane* is a Zulu word that, loosely translated, means "each must make a contribution to a communal goal".

Certain Historic Churches
(Original churches, rebuilt churches and churches built on the site of an earlier church)

The oldest places of worship in South Africa were in nature, where the Khoisan and South Africa's earlier black population groups practised their traditional religions centuries ago.

The Christian religion was the first of the monotheistic religions (Judaism, Christianity and Islam) brought by adventurers, officials, settlers and missionaries from Europe to South Africa. Shortly after Jan van Riebeeck's establishment of a victualling station at the Cape in 1652, devotees of Islam also came here. Most of them were slaves and political exiles from the Far East.

From 1652 to 1778, the only denomination acknowledged at the Cape by the Dutch administration was the Dutch Reformed Church. In 1778 the mostly German-speaking Lutherans received permission to start their own congregation and to erect a church building.

After the final British takeover of the Cape Colony in 1806, a variety of other church denominations such as the Anglicans, Methodists, Baptists and other Protestant denominations, as well as the Roman Catholic and Jewish communities, erected their own places of worship. In this regard Christian missionary groups played an important role.

The indigenous African churches developed from the 1800s.

In the early 1500s the explorer Joao da Nova built a stone structure in Mossel Bay for church services. This was the first "church" in South Africa. There is now only a stone cross where the building once stood **(see photo on page 277)**.

The foundations of the oldest true church building in South Africa were laid in 1686 in Stellenbosch. Before then church services were held in a room with animal skins and horns on the walls, in the old Good Hope Fort, or on board a ship in Table Bay.

The church in Stellenbosch was built of stone and clay. It had yellowwood beams, a simple gable and a thatched roof. The church was destroyed in a fire in 1710. Today the d'Ouwe Werf Hotel stands on the site. In the hotel one can see parts of the old walls of the church.

Moederkerk ("Mother Church"), Drostdy Street, Stellenbosch

The cornerstone of this church was laid in **1687** by the Reverend Johannes Overneij. The church was destroyed in a fire in 1710. A new church was built in 1722 and enlarged in 1814. It was rebuilt from 1862 to 1863 according to the design of the architect Otto Hager. Until 1952 it was the only Dutch Reformed church in the town.

Groote Kerk ("Great Church"), Adderley Street, Cape Town

The foundations of this church were laid in **1700** by governor Willem Adriaan van der Stel. The church was consecrated on 6 January 1704. When the roof nearly collapsed after heavy rains in 1835, it was decided that the foundations could not take the weight of a new roof. The whole building, except the church tower, was demolished and a larger church was erected. The new church was consecrated on 31 January 1841. The pulpit was made by the well-known sculptor Anton Anreith.

Moravian Church, Genadendal

Genadendal ("Valley of Grace"), the first Protestant mission in Africa, was established in **1738** by the Moravian missionary Georg Schmidt about 35km north-east of Caledon. The mission was first called Baviaanskloof but the name was changed in 1806 to Genadendal. The church was built in 1738, but when it became too small a new church was consecrated in 1800. A clock tower, which was used from 1796 to 1800 for services, is still there. One of Genadendal's most precious possessions is a copy of the New Testament printed in Amsterdam in 1694. The whole church square in Genadendal has been declared a national monument.

Oude Kerk, Tulbagh

This church was built between **1743** and **1748** by residents. The building material was imported from the Netherlands. A gable in the Baroque style was added in 1796. The church building was fully restored and turned into a museum, which opened in 1925. This is the oldest church in the country that retains its original cross shape. In 1940 it was declared a national monument.

Lutheran Church, Strand Street, Cape Town

Lutheran services were illegal and so this church was originally a warehouse, to deceive the Dutch East India Company. The church (warehouse) was completed in **1774**. It belonged to Martin Melck, who gave permission that it be used as a church. A few years later he agreed that it be converted into a proper church.

Dutch Reformed Church, Graaff-Reinet

In 1798 Reverend H.W. Ballot became the second minister of the Dutch Reformed congregation in Graaff-Reinet. One of his first tasks was to complete the half-built new church. (The first church building was already dilapidated and during this time was destroyed in a fire.) The new church was consecrated in **1800**, but in 1815 it was demolished. In 1822 the church was completely demolished and rebuilt. The third and current church was built in 1886 and consecrated in 1887. It was built from local sandstone and is one of the largest Dutch Reformed churches in the country. The design is loosely based on that of Salisbury Cathedral in England. The church has a valuable collection of silver that dates from 1809. The silver is used for christenings and communions, as well as for collections.

St Stephen's Church, Riebeeck Square, Cape Town

St Stephen's church is the only church building that was originally a theatre and also the only Dutch Reformed church named after a saint. The African Theatre was opened in the building in **1801**. In 1838 the theatre was closed because it had deteriorated into a brothel. In 1843 the Presbyterian and Lutheran churches bought the building and used it as a church for freed slaves. In 1857 the Dutch Reformed church bought the property and it has since become the only Dutch Reformed congregation

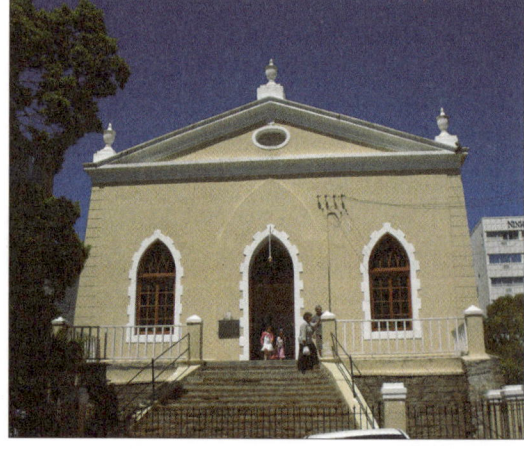

with a majority of coloured members, namely the St Stephen's congregation. The church was declared a national monument in 1965. In 2007 it was announced that the entire building would be restored and in January 2009 the restored church was consecrated. Another two restoration phases are being planned.

Dutch Reformed Church, Swellendam

The first church in Swellendam was built in **1802**. The old church was later demolished and the current building was built on the same site in 1910. The wall around the church dates from 1840. The church still has the first pulpit Bible printed in 1756. The original pulpit also forms part of the current pulpit.

Strooidak (Thatch Roof) Church, Main Street, Paarl

The Strooidak (Thatch Roof) Church, also known as the Huguenot Church, was consecrated in **1805** by the Reverend J.P. Serrurier. The church, shaped like a Greek cross, was designed by the architect Louis Thibault. Major G.C. Kuechler changed the design slightly by adding the characteristics of a traditional Cape-Dutch farmstead. Piet Retief was baptised in this church. In 1970 the walls had to be strengthened to prevent their collapse. The church building and family crypts were declared national monuments in 1966.

Het Gesticht (also known as the Zion Church), Main Street, Paarl

Missionary work began in Paarl in the early 19th century. This church was erected in **1813** by the Friends of the Missionary Society for the slaves and coloured people. They had earlier attended services in the Strooidak Church, but it was now too small to accommodate the whole community. The Paarl Missionary Society took over the building and teaching programmes in 1819 and later the church was bought by the DR Mission Institute. In 2001 the building was restored and turned into a museum. It can also be hired for weddings and functions.

Dutch Reformed Church, Caledon

The Dutch Reformed congregation was established in **1811**, but for a few years a converted wine cellar was used as a church. A church was consecrated in 1813. The current church was consecrated in 1876.

St George's Church, Simon's Town

The building that in **1814** became St George's Church was built in Simon's Town in 1806. The first Anglican church services in South Africa were held in this church. In 1819 it was seriously damaged by rain and in 1824 the greater part was destroyed by storm water. Thereafter services were temporarily held in another building until a new Anglican church, the St Francis Church, was completed in 1837.

Moravian Church, Mamre

The Moravian Missionary Society established the mission at Mamre, formerly known as Groenekloof, in **1808**. The church was built in 1816 and the gables were added later. The missionaries worked among the local Khoi people, but it was also a refuge for slaves. In 1967 it was declared a national monument.

Dutch Reformed Church, George

The first Dutch Reformed Church in George was built in **1817**. By 1821 the church was so dilapidated that a new one had to be built. The new church was consecrated in 1842. In 1905 the tower collapsed and was rebuilt in 1906. The walls of the church are about 1m thick and the ceiling is yellowwood. The pulpit is made of stinkwood.

Dutch Reformed Mission Church, Zoar

The town of Zoar was established in **1817** by the farmer and missionary P.J. Joubert, from the Zuid-Afrikaansche Zendelingsgenootschap (SA Missionary Society). The church was consecrated in 1819.

Settlers Church, Port Alfred

This church was built by the British settlers with stone from the area. It was consecrated in 1823. The church was destroyed twice during the border wars but rebuilt each time. Today the church is a national monument.

Baptist Chapel, Grahamstown

This is the oldest Baptist church in South Africa and was built in 1823.

Dutch Reformed Church, Cradock

The first church was built with stone from the area and was consecrated in **1823**. The church became too small for the number of congregation members and in 1868 a new church was completed. Architects Welchman and Read drew up the plans, based on the style of the well-known St Martin-in-the-Fields on Trafalgar Square in London.

Rhenish Missionary Church, The Braak, Stellenbosch

Het Stellenbosche Meedewerkende Zendelings Genoodschap (The Stellenbosch Co-operative Missionary Society) was established in 1801. The name was changed in 1838 to Het Stellenbosche Zendelings Genoodschap (The Stellenbosch Missionary Society). The church was consecrated in **1824**. A new wing and entrance were built in 1840. The pulpit in the Baroque style was made in 1853 by a Cape cabinetmaker, Londt, for the Dutch Reformed Church, and he donated it to the Rhenish Missionary Church in 1863. The society dedicated itself to the spiritual and educational needs of slaves. In 1948 the community joined the Dutch Reformed Mission Church, under the name "Rynse Nederduitse Gereformeerde Sendinggemeente" (Rhenish Dutch Reformed Missionary Congregation).

Congregational Church, Pacaltsdorp, George

This small mission was established a few kilometres south of George in **1812** by the Reverend Carl August of the London Missionary Society. The first minister was Charles Pacalt. The church was built in 1825 by the residents with stone from the Outeniqua mountains. In 1878 it was taken over by the Congregational Church. It is a popular church for weddings.

Dutch Reformed Church, Durbanville

The cornerstone of the first church was laid in **1825** and the church was consecrated in 1826. A circular wall, which still exists today, was built in 1833 to prevent wagons from pulling up too close to the church building. The church building was later enlarged.

St George's Church, Grahamstown

St George's Church was built in **1828** and was the second Anglican church in South Africa. After Grahamstown became a diocese in 1853, parts of this church were incorporated into the Cathedral of St Michael and St George.

Dutch Reformed Church, Clanwilliam   Dutch Reformed Church, Beaufort-Wes

Dutch Reformed Church, Clanwilliam

The first church in Clanwilliam was built in **1830**. In 1864 the current church was built on the site of the first church. The church was designed by Carl Otto Hager.

Dutch Reformed Church, Beaufort West

In **1830** a small thatch roof church was built. The church quickly became too small and in 1892 the current church was built.

Dutch Reformed Church, Worcester

This church opposite Church Square was built in **1832**. It originally had a short tower. In 1899 the tower was replaced with one made of tin. This tower could not withstand the windstorms and was replaced a second time. The current tower was built in 1927.

Wesleyan Chapel, Grahamstown

This chapel was built in **1832**.

Methodist Church, Bathurst

This church was built in **1832** by the British Settlers. During the border wars it was a fort and place of safety. It is a national monument.

St Mary's Church, Port Elizabeth

The cornerstone of St Mary's Church was laid in **1825**, but the church was first used only in 1832. It was built by Sir Francis Evatt. He was buried at the church, but was later reburied at Fort Frederick. The church burned down in 1895, but a new church was immediately built on the same site. The church was consecrated as a cathedral in 2003.

Dutch Reformed Church, Somerset East

The cornerstone was laid in **1830** and the church was consecrated in 1833. It was enlarged in the 1870s by the architect and builder Carl Otto Hagar. In 1950 it was modernised and it was restored in the 1970s. The church is a national monument.

Moravian Church, Wupperthal

Wupperthal was established in **1830** by the Rhenish Missionary Society. The thatched church was built in 1834. In 1965 the Moravian Church took over the mission.

Moravian Church, Elim

Elim was established in 1824. The church was built in **1834**. A large number of freed slaves established themselves here in 1836 and the missionaries taught them various trades, such as shoemaking, thatching and joinery. It is the largest Moravian church in the Western Cape. The church has the oldest working church clock in South Africa. It was made in 1757 in Germany and was given to the church in Elim in 1914. The whole town has been declared a national monument.

Church of St Francis, Simon's Town

This Anglican church was consecrated in **1837**. It is the oldest original Anglican church building in South Africa and is a national monument.

St John's Church, Bathurst

This Anglican church was consecrated in **1838**. In 1834, during the Sixth Border War, when the church was still incomplete, women and children loaded weapons for the men in the church until reinforcements arrived. Later, earthen barricades were erected around the church, making it a de facto fort, and it was used again in the Seventh and Eighth Border wars. The church is a national monument.

St Patrick's Catholic Church, Grahamstown

This church was built in **1839**.

- The Auwal Mosque is the oldest mosque in South Africa. It was built in 1798, during the first British settlement of the Cape.
- The oldest synagogue in South Africa was built in **1849** in Cape Town. It was called *Tikvath Israel* ("hope of Israel"). It currently houses a Jewish museum.
- The oldest Hindu temple in South Africa, the Shree Ambalavanaar Alayam Temple, was built in **1875** on the bank of the Umbilo River, about 2km south of Cato Manor in Durban. It was rebuilt after a flood washed it away and it is now a national monument.
- St Mark's Cathedral in George is the smallest cathedral in South Africa.
- The Dutch Reformed Church in Graaff-Reinet is the only Dutch Reformed church in the country with a fireplace in the vestry.
- Rev. Joan (Johannes) van Arckel, the first minister in South Africa, died in 1666 at the age of 26.
- The Groote Kerk in Cape Town is the oldest Dutch Reformed Church in South Africa still in use.
- The Oude Kerk in Tulbagh is the only church building that has retained its original cross shape.
- The St Stephen's Church is the only church building that was first a theatre and is also the only Dutch Reformed Church named after a saint.

Auwal Mosque

Interesting towns, places, attractions, events, phenomena and legends

Bourke's Luck Potholes

The Bourke's Luck Potholes are a natural wonder that consist of cylindrical potholes formed over thousands of years in rock formations through water erosion. These potholes are at the beginning of the Blyde River Canyon where the Treur River flows into the Blyde River, about 35km north of Graskop in Mpumalanga. The potholes are named after Thomas (Tom) Bourke, who was the owner of the farm and prospected for gold in the area. At the potholes there is a visitors centre with interesting exhibitions.

> The Blyde River Canyon is the largest vegetated canyon in the world and the third largest canyon in the world. The Grand Canyon in the USA is the largest and the Fish River Canyon in Namibia is the second largest.

Roaring Sands of the Kalahari

About 6km west of Olifantshoek in the Northern Cape there are white dunes covering roughly 3 200ha. Water can be found here by digging just a few centimetres. When one walks on the sand on a hot day, with the wind at the right speed and in the right direction, the dunes make a roaring sound that can be heard 400m away. It is thought that the roaring sound is produced by smooth grains of sand, of similar size, rubbing against each other.

Canal Walk and Ratanga Junction

The Canal Walk Shopping Centre and Ratanga Junction Theme Park near Cape Town are a shopping centre and fun park respectively. Canal Walk was opened in October 2000 and is the largest mall in Africa – there are more than 450 shops and places to eat.

Canal Walk

Ratanga Junction, South Africa's first full-scale theme park, was opened in December 1998. There are more than 30 different fun rides and snake and bird shows, among others, to entertain visitors.

Ratanga Junction

Durban's rickshaws

The rickshaw was designed in 1853 in Japan by a missionary, Jonathan Goble, for his invalid wife. It had a seat for just one person. A sugar magnate, Sir Marshall Campbell, imported them to Natal, had them rebuilt and trained Zulus to pull them. The Zulus were also taught to decorate themselves and the rickshaws. The rickshaws became a huge tourist attraction in Durban. In 1930 there were more than a thousand rickshaws; it was a boom time for the rickshaw business. Each year there was a competition for the best rickshaw and its "puller". The popularity of the rickshaws declined after World War Two. Traffic officials were not in favour of the rickshaws, there were accusations from the public that it was inhumane and many rickshaw pullers looked for other work. In 1960 there were only around 500 rickshaws left. By 1970 they had all but disappeared. Today there are just a few in holiday time on the beachfront.

Gamkaskloof ("The Hell")

Gamkaskloof lies in an isolated valley in the Swartberg. Little is known about how the first farmers came to settle in Gamkaskloof. According to one legend, a child, Danie Hartman, was kidnapped by the Khoi-Khoi and taken there. He escaped and told people about the wonderfully fertile valley. Another explanation is that farmers went to look for their cattle and came across the valley.

Farmers settled in the valley from 1830. Because of the high temperatures the valley was called "The Hell". The residents supported themselves by planting fruit and vegetables and keeping goats. In the past the valley could only be reached via a narrow footpath and the residents were cut off from civilisation. In 1962 a road was built that created access to the valley.

Road to Gamkaskloof

The farmers were very poor and began to leave the valley to look another means of livelihood. The last family left Gamkaskloof in 1991. In 1992 1 500ha was fenced to protect the area. In 1997 Gamkaskloof was declared a national monument. The restoration project under the leadership of Cape Nature was expanded and a number of Gamkaskloof cottages and a campsite were made available to visitors. The road is suitable for normal vehicles if one drives slowly and carefully.

Accommodation

"Hole in the Wall" on the Wild Coast

An interesting phenomenon in the sea on the Wild Coast is a rock with a hole in it as large as a double-decker bus. The waves roar through this hole. It is very difficult to climb the rock and many people have had to be rescued and brought to safety. Some have even died in an attempt to swim through the hole – they are dashed by the waves against the sharp rocks on the sides of the hole.

Gold Reef City

Gold Reef City, south of the Johannesburg CBD, was built around Shaft 14 of the old Crown Mines. There is a partially working museum and a replica of a mining town from the 1880s. There are shops and restaurants, a mining museum, a farmyard, casino and a theme park with entertainment for young and old. Visitors can enjoy underground tours, attend a demonstration of gold casting or visit historical exhibitions. Traditional dances, gumboot dances and a variety of other performances are also offered. A miniature train and a horse and carriage provide transport. The Gold Reef City Hotel offers accommodation in rooms with an old-world atmosphere.

Restaurant in Gold Reef City

Big Hole and Mining Museum, The

In 1871 the biggest diamond rush in history began when diamonds were discovered on Colesberg Hill in Kimberley. When the hill had been carted off, they began to dig deeper into the ground. This is how the second largest man-made hole in

Buildings in the mining town   Viewpoint

the world came into existence. The hole was dug 400m down, but it then became difficult to get the soil out. Cecil John Rhodes established larger companies to finance the project. The first shaft was sunk in 1889 and the hole was dug down another 700m. In 1914 the mine was closed at a depth of 1 100m. Diamonds of about 14,5 million karats were mined here. The diameter of the hole is about 470m and the circumference 1,5km.

The Mining Museum is next to the Big Hole. There is a replica of a mining town with small shops, pharmacies, bars, offices and other buildings, all of which are furnished and include exhibitions that depict early life at the diamond diggings. Some houses date from 1877. They were carefully disassembled at their original sites and re-erected here. There is also an exhibit of unusual vehicles, such as the homemade three-wheeler with which John Derbyshire travelled from Plettenberg Bay to Kimberley in 1880, Kimberley's first car, as well as a luxury train carriage that was specially imported for the directors of the De Beers Mining Company. In the De Beers Hall there are exhibits of uncut diamonds, jewellery and replicas of the 616, the largest uncut diamond in the world, and of the Eureka, the first diamond to be found in South Africa (at Hopetown in the Northern Cape).

Since 2006 there have been big developments at the Big Hole. A new viewpoint over the Hole, from where visitors have a good vertical view over the Big Hole, a new visitors centre with interesting exhibitions, a four-star guesthouse, bar, souvenir shop, a wine shop where wines from the Northern Cape can be bought and other shops were built. In 2007 a new four-star Protea Hotel opened near the edge of the Big Hole.

- In 2005 mine inspectors proved that the Jagersfontein Hole is the largest man-made hole in the world, not the Big Hole.
- With the closure of Bultfontein Road in 2008, after fears about the stability of the sides of the hole, rides on the old tram were stopped. The tram used to transport visitors from the Kimberley Town Hall to the museum.

Cango Caves

These world-famous limestone caves are in the foothills of the Swartberg Mountains and near Oudtshoorn in the Little Karoo. The cave complex stretches 3km into the earth and is the largest underground cave complex in the world. The Cango Caves were discovered in 1780 by a shepherd and Jacobus van Zyl, a farmer, was the first who dared to venture deeper into the caves.

The caves were created over millions of years when groundwater seeped in through cracks in the limestone layers and the acid in the groundwater eroded the limestone. This was how chambers and rooms came into existence. There are a number of rooms connected to each other with passageways and tunnels. A beautiful variety of stalagmites, stalactites and helictites make formations such as the Frozen Waterfall, Cleopatra's Needle and the Curtain. Visitors may only explore the caves on a guided tour. There is a more demanding route where one must crawl along low, narrow passageways and edge through the very narrow Chimney. This route is only recommended for those who are lean and fit.

In the 1970s chambers were discovered that reached a further 1 600m into the mountain. They are known as Cango II, III, IV and V and are not yet open to the public. It is known that the new chambers are far more beautiful than Cango I as they have not been damaged by pollution and vandals.

At the entrance to the Cango Caves are a curio shop, a crèche and a restaurant.

- Stalagmites are erect dripstones on the floor of a cave; stalactites are dripstones that hang from the roof of a cave and helictites are irregular dripstones with projections on the roof of a cave.
- Stalagmites in the Cango Caves grow 5–6mm every 100 years and stalactites grow 2-5mm every 100 years.
- In 2007 an overweight woman got stuck in the Tunnel of Love in the Cango Caves and 22 fellow tourists were trapped there for over 10 hours.

Kirstenbosch

Kirstenbosch, on the eastern slopes of Table Mountain, is the most important botanical garden in South Africa and is world-famous. The garden was proclaimed in 1913 to protect the indigenous flora of South Africa. It covers 560ha. The land belonged to Cecil John Rhodes and was left to the state at his death in 1902. There is a lane of wild almond trees that were planted in 1660 by Jan van Riebeeck to keep poachers away from the settlement.

Kirstenbosch has around 6 000 planted species of plants and 900 that grow naturally. The flowers are breathtaking, especially in spring and summer. There are big lawns, short and long footways, a cycad garden, a fragrance garden and a Braille trail. The Compton Herbarium is a research centre and contains 300 000 plant specimens. The Botanical Society conservatory houses a collection of thousands of plants that were collected around the country. The focus is a baobab, whose roots are artificially warmed to the right temperature. Sunset concerts are held in the garden on Sundays in the summer. There is a restaurant complex and at the entrance there are shops where seeds, snacks and souvenirs are sold. Kirstenbosch is managed by trustees who are appointed by the director.

Kruger Millions

The legend of the Kruger Millions came about at around 1900. During the Anglo-Boer War, gold to the value of about a million rand was transported from Pretoria to Maputo to prevent it falling into the hands of the British army. The gold was later shipped to Europe and sold there. The money was used for the war against the British. Rumours spread that there was also a large quantity of gold hidden somewhere on the Highveld. The authorities extended permits to people who wanted to look for the Kruger Millions; they had to undertake to give two-thirds of any find to the government. Many stories have been told about the Kruger Millions, but so far it has all been conjecture.

Laingsburg Flood

On Sunday 25 January 1981 the Buffalo River flooded the Karoo town of Laingsburg. The residents were caught unawares, as they didn't expect that the water level would rise so quickly – it rose at a rate of 1,5m per hour. Residents and rescue teams from the police and army rescued many people. Some people were washed to the Floriskraal Dam and were picked up there by helicopters. Helpless elderly people from the old-age home were helped to the roof of the building. The water later caused the roof to collapse and 18 people drowned. Rev. Malan Jacobs, the minister of the community who showed great courage in trying to help the elderly people, will always be remembered. He also drowned. Altogether 120 people died and many bodies were never recovered.

Mapungubwe

Mapungubwe Hill is just south of the Limpopo River, about 75km west of Musina. It is in the Mapungubwe National Park, previously known as the Vhembe-Dongola National Park. Although people had been living in the Limpopo valley since about 200 BCE, Mapungubwe only started to develop at about AD 1075. The king and his followers lived on the summit of the hill, his family members lower down and the ordinary people on the plain. Only a winding path gave access to the top of the hill. The total population was between 3 000 and 4 000 people.

Mapungubwe Hill

Gold was smelted in Mapungubwe, cotton was cultivated and ivory and clay articles were made. There was probably trade with seafarers from India and the Middle East. Mapungubwe was only a major settlement for about 60 to 80 years. Mainly a change in climate and a shortage of grazing for the ever-growing cattle herds led to a move to the north (over the Limpopo). In 1932, thanks to stories of gold treasure at Mapungubwe a farmer, E.S.J van Graan, his son and a few friends decided to find out exactly what the state of affairs was. They found pottery, potsherds, glass beads, golden articles and graves. The Van Graan son gave details of their find to Prof. Leo Fouché at the University of Pretoria, who in turn informed a colleague at the University of the Witwatersrand. The South African government bought the farm and the University of Pretoria was asked to investigate matters at Mapungubwe.

In 1984 the area was declared a national monument and everything dug up and found there was recorded by the University of Pretoria. Objects such as a golden sceptre, a small golden rhino and a golden bowl were found in the royal graves. The articles were made of wood and covered in gold. The golden objects were probably buried with royals or important people. From the characteristics of the skulls it would appear that black people had migrated from the east coast and intermarried with the Khoisan living in the vicinity of Mapungubwe. Mapungubwe is one of the most important archaeological sites in South Africa and was declared a world heritage site by Unesco (the cultural arm of the United Nations) in 2003.

Matjiesfontein

A Scot, Douglas Logan, developed this entire town in the Karoo, as well as a health resort where people with lung problems could recuperate in the Karoo air. In 1877, as a young man, he was on his way to Australia when he decided to stay in South Africa. He initially worked for the railways, and later bought large tracts of land at Matjiesfontein and began to farm. He also planted many trees and fruit trees.

Lord Milner Hotel

During the Anglo-Boer War Matjiesfontein was the headquarters of the British troops. Logan imported lamp posts from London and Matjiesfontein was the first town in South Africa to have electric light and a water sewerage system. The Lord Milner Hotel, which was built during the Anglo-Boer War, was used for a time as a military hospital. Logan died in 1920. After the war, Matjiesfontein's popularity began to decline, the hotel became delapidated and the town emptied.

In 1956 a hotelier from Stellenbosch, David Rawdon, bought the whole town and restored all the buildings to their original Victorian glory. The town has been declared a national monument.

Many ghost stories are told about Matjiesfontein. The most famous is that of a wounded British soldier who stands at the turn-off to the cemetery and suddenly disappears when he is approached.

Orania

A house in Orania

Orania's punt

Orania is located in the Northern Cape, on the southern bank of the Orange River, and is 164km from Kimberley and 200km from Bloemfontein. The town was established in 1967 as a construction camp for workers on the Vanderkloof canals. In 1991 the town, which was by then abandoned and neglected, was bought for R1,5 million. The buyers were members of the Afrikaner Freedom Foundation under the leadership of Prof. Carl Boshoff, the son-in-law of Dr Hendrik Verwoerd. The goal was to develop the town as a homeland for the Afrikaners.

The town is owned by a company, Vluytjeskraal Aandeleblok Ltd, and all residents are shareholders. Today it is a town of neat houses and gardens that has sports facilities, a post office, a school, church buildings, a library, a landing strip for light aircraft and helicopters, guesthouses, a caravan park, etc. There are more than 40 businesses in Orania. Irrigation from the Orange River means nuts, fodder, grain, fruit and vegetables can be cultivated. All work in the town is done by Afrikaners. In 2004 Orania got its own currency, the Ora, and in 2008 a request for a licence for a community radio station was granted.

In front of the swimming pool in Orania is this statue of a koeksister.

Pilgrim's Rest

Royal Hotel

This historic town in Mpumalanga came to exist after one Alec Patterson loaded all his possessions in a wheelbarrow in 1873 and discovered gold at Pilgrim's Creek. A gold rush ensued and a tin town sprang up in the spot. It quickly became a gold mining town with bars, shops, three bakeries and two banks. Small-scale gold prospecting ended in 1881 when a mining concession was granted to D.B. Benjamin.

In 1974 the Transvaal provincial administration bought the town. The buildings were carefully restored and many buildings were turned into museums. The hub of the town is the Royal Hotel with its historic bar. The white and red houses were turned into coffee shops, craft shops, restaurants and other businesses. The town was declared a national monument. Guided tours through the town are offered.

Robben Island*

This island in the Atlantic Ocean is 9km from Cape Town. It is 3,5km long and 2km wide and covers about 575ha. It is a rocky island with indigenous West Coast vegetation, exotic trees and shrubs, a large penguin population as well as wild antelope that graze on the grass. The sea around the island has an abundance of large crayfish and galjoen.

Over the years Robben Island became known as a prison. The first criminal was moved there in 1658. The prisoners had to work in quarries on the island. Stone quarried there was used to build the Castle and the Burger redoubt in Cape Town and shells were collected to be made into lime. In 1806 the British used the island as a quarantine station. The British built houses, laid out streets and built a post office and school, as well as a church

* Today Robben Island is a World Heritage Site.

in 1841. A whalery was built in 1940, which was quickly closed after some of the prisoners escaped in one of the factory boats. At one stage there were 600 lepers on the island, but they were moved to Pretoria in 1931. In 1939, at the outbreak of the Second World War, the island was used for the defence of Cape Town. After the war Robben Island became a training centre for the South African Navy. In 1961 the island was once again placed under the control of the then-Department of Corrective Services.

Some freedom fighters were held in the jail on the island for years. Former President Nelson Mandela spent 18 of his 27 years of imprisonment on Robben Island. Guided tours of the island are offered and interesting stories about the island and life in the prison are told. Ferries to the island leave from the V&A Waterfront in Cape Town.

> A male leper was found on the island in 1915 by missionaries after he had spent 45 years there.

Sardines of KwaZulu-Natal

Sardines are normally found in the cold water of the south and west coasts. Between June and August they gather in huge schools to spawn in the warm Mozambique current in the Indian Ocean. The schools are normally far from the coast, but between Port St Johns and just south of Durban sea currents drive them to the shore. Large predator fish follow them and millions of sardines are eaten. When the sardines "run", the water swarms with them. Everyone scoops them up with basins, cans, buckets, aprons or whatever containers are available. Every year this is a big event. It is not known how many fish survive this journey, but every female lays around 100 000 eggs and only one or two need to survive to keep their numbers stable.

Sun City and the Lost City complex

Sun City Hotel

This complex is world famous and is the largest hotel and casino complex in Southern Africa. It was the first of many luxury holiday resorts and casinos developed by hotel boss Sol Kerzner in South Africa. There are four luxury hotels, cinemas, a casino and facilities for every imaginable type of sport. In the beautiful gardens

there are walkways and a rich birdlife. The Superbowl, which has seating for 6 000 people, is a popular venue for international competitions and concerts. The newest hotel, The Palace of the Lost City, is surrounded by 25ha of man-made jungles and gardens and is a fantasy world with a fictitious ancient civilisation as its theme. The hotel has 338 rooms and is extremely luxurious. A big golf tournament takes place every December on the golf course, which was designed by Gary Player. Near Sun City is the well-known Pilanesberg National Park, a crocodile farm and a lion park.

Table Mountain (see also **Table Mountain National Park** page 82)

Table Mountain from Blouberg beach

Cable car

The 1 086m-high Table Mountain is one of the best known landmark in the whole of Africa. The mountain is visible up to 200km out to sea. Well-known peaks nearby are Devil's Peak, Lion's Head and Signal Hill (Vlaeberg). The view from Table Mountain is something special day and night. The easiest way to ascend the mountain is via cable car. This cableway was opened on 4 October 1929, but new cable cars have been in use since October 1997. Each cable car has room for 65 people and can reach a speed of 10m per second.

On the slopes of Signal Hill is a cannon that marks noon every day except Sunday. Table Mountain, which is part of a national park, has a rich plant and bird life. Large mammals are scarce, but baboons and dassies are common. On top of the mountain is a bistro, restaurant, gift shop, picnic facilities and many short walking routes to different lookout points. There are various climbing routes – which should not be attempted without experienced guides. The weather on the mountain is very changeable. Mountain biking is only allowed on the lower slopes (below Table Mountain Road).

- In the summer, especially when the South-Easter blows, a white cloud forms on Table Mountain. It is called "The Tablecloth of Table Mountain". Legend has it that on these days the devil and the pirate Van Hunks are locked in a smoking competition.
- Another legend has it that Antjie Somers used to live on top of Table Mountain. His name is used to frighten children and often appears in rhymes. There is also a South African musical comedy with the title *Antjie Somers*.

The cable car that was used between 1929 and 1997.

Owl House, Nieu-Bethesda, The (see also **Helen Martins** page 156)

The Owl House in Nieu-Bethesda was the home of the eccentric artist Helen Martins. It is an isolated village at the foot of the Sneeuberg Mountains, about 50km north of Graaff-Reinet. She decorated the walls, doors and ceilings of her house with ground coloured glass. The rooms are also filled with small sculptures, mainly of owls, mermaids and the sun. In the garden she, with the help of Koos Malgas, a resident of the town, made hundreds of cement sculptures of people, camels, owls, sphinxes and religious symbols – more than 500 sculptures in all. Today the Owl House is a national monument that attracts more than 10 000 people every year. Koos Malgas died on 20 November 2000 at the age of 63.

uShaka Marine World

This giant marine theme park on the Durban Waterfront covers 16ha and was opened in 2004. It is the largest marine theme park in Africa and among the five largest in the world. The shark tank is the largest in the southern hemisphere. The aquarium and a number of restaurants are in the life-sized replica of the wreck of a 1940s cargo steamer. The aquarium is regarded as the best in the country. Visitors can drift down a man-made river, snorkel among fish and sea animals, swim in a cage among sharks, scuba dive and take part in numerous water activities. Performances by dolphins, penguins and seals are also presented. Near the main entrance there is a wide variety of shops and restaurants.

Victoria & Alfred Waterfront

This development in the harbour area of Table Bay is one of Cape Town's most popular tourist attractions. There is a myriad shops, hotels, cinemas, bars, restaurants, art and craft markets and historic buildings. Historic navy craft can be seen and boat trips in the harbour and to Robben Island can be undertaken. There is also the Two Oceans Aquarium and an amphitheatre where artists and orchestras perform. Buskers and mime artists perform in the streets.

The Cradle of Humankind

The Cradle of Humankind is about 45km from Johannesburg, near Krugersdorp. The area covers 47 000ha and consists of the Sterkfontein caves, Swartkrans, Kromdraai and surrounding areas. It was declared a World Heritage Site in 1999. Some of the oldest humanoid fossils in the world were found here in dolomite rocks estimated at 2,5 million years old. Many fossils of animal

Entrance to the Maropeng visitors centre

and plant species have also been found here. This area is a source of important scientific information about the evolution of humankind over the past 3,5 million years.

In the Maropeng* Visitors Centre there are exhibitions that stretch over 2 500m^2. There is also an exhibition of original fossils from around the country that have been lent to Maropeng and are regularly changed. An underground boat ride depicts the creation of the earth up to the present. At Maropeng there is an open-air theatre, conference facilities, hotel and two restaurants. At Swartkrans proof has been found that controlled fires were made in this area more than 1 million years ago.

The Sterkfontein caves, in dolomite hills north of Krugersdorp in Gauteng, were discovered in 1896 by an Italian prospector. It is regarded as one of most important prehistoric finds in the world. There are six underground chambers with beautiful stalagmites and stalactites, as well as an underground lake. The largest chamber is 90m long and 23m high. The caves became world famous in 1947 when Dr Robert Broom found the first remains of an adult apeman, which was called Mrs Ples, in the caves. In 2002 French researchers used modern technology to prove, on the basis of the roots of the teeth, that Mrs Ples was most probably a young man. Over the years many other important humanoid fossils and the remains of extinct animals were discovered here. The caves belong to the University of the Witwatersrand. Guided tours to the caves are offered. There is a restaurant and the fossil digs of the university's researchers can be viewed.

* *Maropeng* is a Tswana word that means "to return to the place of origin".

Sterkfontein Caves

- Mrs Ples is kept in a fireproof display cabinet in the Transvaal Museum in Pretoria where visitors can view her.
- In 1994 Prof. Ron Clarke found the foot bones of a humanoid, named Little Foot, in a conservation room, and in 1997 almost the whole skeleton was found in a rock. Little Foot is still in the rock in the Sterkfontein Caves, and full analysis must still be carried out.
- About 2,5 million years ago the Cradle of Humankind was a shallow inland lake.

5. PEOPLE

Outa Lappies

Commanders and governors of the Cape Colony

Dutch commanders and governors

Term	Name
Commanders	
1652–1662	Johan (Jan) Anthonisz van Riebeeck
1662–1666	Zacharias Wagenaer
1666–1668	Cornelius van Qualbergen
1668–1670	Jacob Borghorst
1670–1671	Pieter Hackius
1671–1672	Coenraad van Breitenbach
1672 (Apr.–Oct.)	Albert van Breugel (acting)
1672–1676	Isbrand Goske
1676–1678	Johan Bax van Herenthals
1679 (June–Oct.)	Hendrik Crudop (acting)
1679–1691	Simon van der Stel
Governors	
1691–1699	Simon van der Stel
1699–1707	Willem Adriaan van der Stel
1707–1708	Johan Cornelis d'Ableing (acting)
1708–1711	Louis van Assenburg
1711–1714	Willem Helot (acting)
1714–1724	Lieutenant Colonel Maurits Pasques de Chavonnes
1724–1727	Jan de la Fontaine (acting)
1727–1729	Pieter Gysbert Noodt
1730–1736	Jan de la Fontaine (acting)
1737 (dies after three weeks in service)	Adriaan van Kervel
1737–1739	Daniël van den Henghel (acting)
1739–1751	Hendrik Swellengrebel
1751–1771	Ryk Tulbagh
1771–1785	Baron Joachim van Plettenberg (acting)

Term	Name
Commanders	
1785–1791	Cornelius Jacob van de Graaff
1791–1792	Johannes Izaak Rhenius (acting)
1792–1793	Sebastiaan Cornelius Nederburgh and Simon Hendrik Frijkenius (commissioners-general)
1793–1795	Abraham Josias Sluysken
1803–1804	Jacob Abraham Uitenhage de Mist
1803–1806	Lieutenant General Willem Janssens

In 1772 Baron Pieter van Rheede of Oudtshoorn was appointed governor of the Cape, but he died while on his way to Cape Town. Oudtshoorn is named after him.

British governors

Term	Name
1797–1798	Lord George Macartney
1798–1799	Lieutenant General Francis Dundas (acting)
1799–1801	Sir George Young
1801–1803	Lieutenant General Francis Dundas (acting)
1806–1807	Sir David Baird (acting)
1807 (Jan.–May)	Lieutenant General Henry George Grey (acting)
1807–1811	Du Pré Alexander, Earl of Caledon
1811 (July–Sept.)	Lieutenant General Henry George Grey (acting)
1811–1814	Sir John Francis Cradock
1813–1814	Robert Meade (acting)
1814–1826	Lord Charles Somerset
1820–1821	Sir Rufane Donkin (acting)
1826–1828	Sir Richard Bourke (acting)
1828–1833	Sir Galbraith Lowry Cole
1833–1834	Thomas Francois Wade (acting)

Term	Name
1834–1838	Sir Benjamin D'Urban
1838–1844	Sir George Thomas Napier
1844–1847	Sir Peregrine Maitland
1847 (Jan.–Dec.)	Sir Henry Pottinger
1847–1852	Sir Henry ("Harry") Smith
1852–1854	Sir George Cathcart
1854 (May–Dec.)	Sir Charles Henry Darling (acting)
1854–1861	Sir George Grey
1859–1862	Sir Robert Henry Wynyard (acting)
1862–1870	Sir Philip Wodehouse
1870 (May–Dec.)	Lieutenant General Charles Craufurd Hay (acting)
1870–1877	Sir Henry Barkly
1877–1880	Sir Henry Frere
1880 (15–27 Sept.)	Sir Henry Hugh Clifford (acting)
1880–1881	Sir George Cumine Strahan (acting)
1881–1889	Sir Hercules George Robert Robinson
1881 (April–Aug.) and 1883–1884	Sir Leicester Smyth (acting)
1886 (Apr.–Jul.)	Sir Henry D'Oyley Torrens (acting)
1889 (May–Dec.)	Sir Henry Augustus Smyth (acting)
1889–1895	Lord Henry Brougham Loch
1891–1892 and 1894 (May–Jul.)	Sir William Gordon Cameron (acting)
1895–1897	Sir Hercules George Robert Robinson
1897 (Apr.–May)	Sir William Howley Goodenough (acting)
1897–1901	Lord Alfred Milner
1898–1899	Sir William Francis Butler (acting)
1901-1910	Sir Walter F. Hely-Hutchinson
1909 (Jun.–Sept.)	Sir Henry Jenner Scobell (acting)

Prime ministers of the Union and Republic of South Africa (1910–1984)

Name	Political party	Term
General Louis Botha	South African Party	1910–1919
General Jan Christiaan Smuts	South African Party	1919–1924
General James Barry Munnik Hertzog	National Party (until 1934) and United Party (from 1934)	1924–1939
General Jan Christiaan Smuts	United Party	1939–1948
Dr Daniël Francois Malan	National Party	1948–1954
Advocate Johannes Gerhardus Strijdom	National Party	1954–1958
Dr Hendrik Frensch Verwoerd	National Party	1958–1966
Balthazar Johannes Vorster	National Party	1966–1978
Pieter Willem Botha	National Party	1978–1984

(State) presidents* of the Republic of South Africa (1961–present)

Name	Political party	Term
Charles Robberts Swart	National Party	1961–1968
Jacobus Johannes Fouché	National Party	1968–1975
Dr Nicolaas Diederichs	National Party	1975–1978
Balthazar Johannes Vorster	National Party	1978–1979
Marais Viljoen	National Party	1979–1984
Pieter Willem Botha	National Party	1984–1989
Frederik Willem de Klerk	National Party	1989–1994
Nelson Rolihlala Mandela	African National Congress	1994–1999
Thabo Mvuyelwa Mbeki	African National Congress	1999–2007
Kgalema Petrus Motlanthe (interim)	African National Congress	2007–2009
Jacob Gedleyihlekisa Zuma	African National Congress	2009-

*The title "state president" was changed in 1994 to "president".

- In 1994 Nelson Mandela became South Africa's first black president.
- The two official residences of the president are Genadendal, on the Groote Schuur estate in Cape Town, and Mahlambandlovu in Pretoria.

Presidents and secretaries general of the African National Congress (ANC)

Presidents

Name	Term
Dr John L. Dube	1912–1917
Sefako M. Makgatho	1917–1924
Rev. Zaccheus R. Mahabane	1924–1927
Josiah T. Gumede	1927–1930
Dr Pixley ka Isaka Seme	1930–1936
Revd Zacheus R. Mahabane	1937–1940
Dr Alfred B. Xuma	1940–1949
Dr James S. Moroka	1949–1952
Chief Albert J. Luthuli	1952–1967
Oliver R. Tambo	1967–1991
Nelson R. Mandela	1991–1997
Thabo M. Mbeki	1997–2008
Jacob G. Zuma	2008–

Secretaries General

Name	Term
Sol T. Plaatje	1912–1917
H.L. Bud Mbelle	1917–1919
Saul Msane	1919–1923
T.D. Mweli Skota	1923–1927
Eddie J. Khaile	1927–1930

Name	Term
Revd Elijah Mdolomba	1930–1936
Revd James A. Calata	1936–1949
Walter Sisulu	1949–1955
Oliver R. Tambo	1955–1958
Duma Nokwe	1958–1969
Alfred Nzo	1969–1991
Cyril Ramaphosa	1991–1997
Kgalema Motlanthe	1997–2007
Gwede Mantashe	2007–

Speakers of Parliament (1910–present)

Name	Term
Sir James Molteno	1910–1915
C.J. Krige	1915–1924
Dr E.G. Jansen	1924–1929
J.H.H. de Waal	1929–1933
Dr E.G. Jansen	1933–1944
C.M. van Coller	1944–1948
J.F. Naudé	1948–1950
J.H. Conradie	1951–1960
H.J. Klopper	1961–1974
A.J. Schlebusch	1974–1976
J.J. Loots	1967–1981
J.P. du Toit	1981–1983
J.W. Greeff	1983–1987
L. le Grange	1987–1991
E. van der Merwe Louw	1991–1994
Dr Frene Ginwala	1994–2004
Baleka Mbete	2004–2008
Gwen Mahlangu-Nkabinde	2008–2009
Max Sisulu	2009–

Economists of the year

An annual competition to appoint South Africa's economist of the year was instituted in 1988 by the Absa bank group. Media24's business supplements and newspapers are also involved. The following list names the year in which the prize is won (although the prize is only awarded the following year); the prize winner, as well as the firm with which the person was affiliated when the prize was awarded.

Year	Winner	Company/Institution
1988	Johan Louw	Sanlam
1989	Prof. Johan du Pisanie	Senbank
1990	Ulrich Joubert	Transnet
1991	Louis Geldenhuys	Senekal, Mouton & Kitshoff
1992	Dave Mohr	Old Mutual
1993	Ulrich Joubert	Transnet
1994	Louis Fourie	Citadel
1995	Nico Czypionka	Standard Bank
1996	Edward Osborn	Edey Rogers
1997	Dr Riaan Lombard	AHI
1998	Herman van Papendorp	BoE
1999	Dave Mohr	Citadel
2000	Anne-Marie Wiehahn	Sasol
2001	Ulrich Joubert	Transnet
2002	Jac Laubscher	Sanlam Investment Management
2003	Dr Johan Willemse	Indepedent agricultural economist
2004	Dr Roelof Botha	PriceWaterhouseCoopers
2005	Mike Schüssler	T-sec
2006	André Mellet	North-West University
2007	Mike Schüssler	T-sec
2008	Christo Luüs	Ecoquant

Business leaders of the year

This award was initiated in 1990 by the Cape daily *Die Burger* and the Cape Town Chamber of Commerce. The list below indicates the firm with which the person was affiliated when the prize was awarded.

Year	Winner	Company/Institution
1990	Johann Rupert	Remgro and Venfin
1991	Dr Christo Wiese	Pepkor Group
1992	Ton Vosloo	Naspers
1993	Pierre Steyn	Sanlam
1994	Raymond Ackerman	Pick n Pay
1995	Mike Levett	Old Mutual plc
1996	David Jack	V&A Waterfront
1997	Whitey Basson	Shoprite Group
1998	Bill McAdam	BoE
1999	Dr Anton Rupert	His overall contribution to the business world.
2000	Peter Swartz	SunWest and Grand Parade Investments
2001	Pam Golding	Pam Golding Properties
2002	Dr Leon Vermaak	Sanlam
2003	Johan Ferreira	Intercape bus service
2004	Dr Edwin Hertzog	Medi-Clinic
2005	Graham Power	Power Construction
2006	Jannie Mouton	PSG
2007	Dr Iqbal Survé	Sekunjalo Investments
2008	Andrew Boraine	Cape Town Partnership (CEO)
2009	Philip Krawitz	Cape Union Mart

Nobel Prize Winners

The following South Africans have won the Nobel Prize.

Year	Name	Category
1951	Dr Max Theiler (later emigrated to the USA)	Medicine
1960	Chief Albert Luthuli	Peace
1979	Allan Cormack (later emigrated to the USA)	Medicine
1982	Sir Aaron Klug (born in Lithuania – moved to SA as a toddler)	Chemistry
1984	Archbishop Desmond Tutu	Peace
1991	Nadine Gordimer	Literature
1993	Nelson Mandela and F.W. de Klerk	Peace
2002	Sydney Brenner	Medicine
2003	J.M. (John Maxwell) Coetzee (later emigrated to Australia)	Literature

Some famous South Africans

Barnard, Prof. Christiaan Neethling

Christiaan Neethling Barnard was born on 8 November 1922 in Beaufort West. He was one of four sons of a missionary minister. He studied medicine at the University of Cape Town and thereafter worked as a GP in Ceres. In 1951 he returned to Cape Town and in 1953 received his Masters degree from the University of Cape Town. The same year he also received his doctorate in medicine. In 1956 he was awarded a postgraduate bursary to study at the University of Minnesota in the USA. Here his interest in heart surgery developed. He obtained a Masters degree and doctorate from this university in 1958. Upon his return to South Africa in 1958, he was appointed as a cardiothoracic surgeon at Groote Schuur Hospital in Cape Town. He designed a new artificial heart valve, started doing open heart surgery and experimented with heart transplants on dogs.

Prof. Christiaan Neethling Barnard

In 1967 he performed the first heart transplant in the world at Groote Schuur Hospital in Cape Town. Louis Washkansky (53) received the heart of Denise Darvall (25). A team of 30 people were involved in the transplant and the operation lasted nine hours. As a result of this, Prof. Barnard became world-famous. Although the heart transplant was a success, Louis Washkansky died 18 days later of pneumonia.

He gained recognition as a brilliant surgeon and in 1972 became a professor at the University of Cape Town. In 1974 he performed the world's first heterotopic heart transplant. The patient who survived the longest after a heart transplant by Prof. Barnard was Dorothy Fisher. She lived for 24 years after her heart transplant.

He was married three times. In 1983, at the age of 61, he resigned from the University of Cape Town because arthritis made it difficult for him to perform surgery. He dedicated himself to writing and lecturing worldwide and helped to establish a new heart transplant programme in Oklahoma, USA. He received various awards from countries and organisations around the world. He died during a visit to Cyprus in 2001 following an asthma attack.

The Beaufort West Museum houses a permanent exhibition about Prof. Barnard. In 2002 the City Park Hospital in Cape Town was renamed the Christiaan Barnard Memorial Hospital and in 2003 improved heart wards at Groote Schuur were named after him. In 2007 an improved and expanded new museum, the Heart of Cape Town Museum, was opened at Groote Schuur Hospital.

De Klerk, Frederik Willem (F.W.)

Frederik Willem de Klerk was born on 18 March 1936 in Johannesburg. His father was Jan de Klerk, a former senator and minister in the South African government. He completed his schooling in Krugersdorp and in 1958 earned B.A. and LL.B.

Frederik Willem de Klerk

degrees at the University of Potchefstroom. He then worked for a law firm in Vereeniging, which he also helped establish, and became active in politics. In 1969 he became the Member of Parliament for Vereeniging. That year he also married Marike Willemse. They had two sons and a daughter.

In 1978 he became a cabinet minister and under John Vorster and P.W. Botha he held six different portfolios. In 1982 he became the leader of the National Party in Transvaal. In 1989 he became the head of the National Party and declared himself in favour of a non-racial South Africa and negotiations to change the political future of the country. In the same year he also became the acting state president and, after Botha's resignation, became state president. In this manner the way was paved for negotiations that led to the end of apartheid and minority government, when the ANC and other organisations were unbanned in 1990.

On 10 February 1990 De Klerk announced that Nelson Mandela would be released. In 1993 he and Nelson Mandela jointly received the Nobel Peace Prize for their role in the peaceful end to apartheid. In 1994 Mandela became president and De Klerk served for two years as joint executive deputy president in the official government. In 1996 he withdrew from the Government of National Unity. He retired from active politics in 1997 and distanced himself from both state policy and the National Party.

In 1998 he divorced Marike after a marriage of 38 years. He married Elita Georgiades, the former wife of a Greek shipping magnate. In December 2001 the whole of South Africa was shocked when Marike de Klerk was murdered in her luxury apartment. In 2002 he established the F.W. de Klerk Foundation, which campaigns for equality, democracy, property rights, cultural rights and language rights. In 2002 the Order of Mapungubwe (gold) was awarded to De Klerk and Mandela for their contribution to the peace process, national reconciliation and nation-building in South Africa. In 2004 he resigned from the New National Party after this party announced its merger with the ANC.

De Klerk has won numerous international prizes and awards. He takes an active role in international conferences and is involved in many organisations. Since March 2008 he and his wife have been living in the upmarket neighbourhood of Upper Fresnaye in Cape Town.

Kruger, Stephanus Johannes Paulus

Paul Kruger was born on 10 October 1825 on the farm Bulhoek near Cradock. He had only three months of formal education. When the Great Trek began in 1836, his father joined Hendrik Potgieter's trek. They settled in the Rustenburg area, where Kruger started farming at the foot of the Magaliesberg. In 1842 he married Maria du Plessis. She and their baby son died, probably due to malaria. He later married Gezina du Plessis, who was his devoted partner until her death in 1901.

They had seven daughters and nine sons.

Kruger was an important leader of the resistance against the British. He played a leading role in negotiations with the British and often travelled to England and Europe. In December 1880 he became president of the Zuid-Afrikaansche Republiek. He was elected president four times, the last time in 1898. He also played a leading role in the proclamation of the Sabie Game Reserve, which, along with the Shingwedzi Game Reserve, became the Kruger National Park. After the outbreak of the Anglo-Boer War in 1899, he left South Africa on the warship *De Gelderland* sent by the Netherlands' Queen Wilhelmina. His wife could not accompany him due to ill health. He departed from Lourenço Marques (now Maputo) for France. In 1904, when his health deteriorated drastically, he was moved to Switzerland, where he died on 14 July 1904. An interim funeral was held on 26 July 1904 in The Hague in the Netherlands. His remains were embalmed and brought to South Africa. He was buried on 16 December 1904 in the Heroes' Acre in Pretoria. His former residence in Pretoria is now the Kruger House Museum. The room in the house in Clarens (Switzerland) where he spent his last days and eventually died, has been declared a monument and can be visited.

- The Kruger National Park is named after him.
- There are statues of Paul Kruger on Church Square in Pretoria and at the Kruger Gate of the Kruger National Park.
- The golden Krugerrand is also named after him.

Langenhoven, Cornelis Jacob

Cornelis Jacob Langenhoven was born in 1873 at Hoeko, near Ladismith in the Cape. He later moved to Oudtshoorn and became the town's most famous resident. He studied at the Victoria College (later the University of Stellenbosch) and earned B.A. and LL.B. degrees. In 1897 he married Lenie van Velden, who was ten years his senior. They had one daughter, Engela, who was born in 1901.

In 1912 he became editor of the newspaper *Het Zuid-Westen*. Later he became a member of parliament and senator. He wrote serious and humorous newspaper articles and editorials as well as a variety of books that was very popular. It made him thé Afrikaans writer of the period between 1920 and 1940. He was also a founding member of *Die Burger*. At his suggestion Afrikaans became the second

language of instruction in schools up to standard four (grade six) in 1914. In 1931 he received an honorary doctorate in literature from the University of Stellenbosch. As a writer, Langenhoven tackled virtually every genre, from ghost stories, children's stories and poetry to sayings and much more. He was especially famous as the person who wrote the words of the former South African national anthem, "Die Stem" ("The Call of South Africa") **(see page 7)**, in 1918. He died in 1932. His house in Oudtshoorn, *Arbeidsgenot*, has been restored and turned into a living museum. In 2003, "Sagmoedige Neelsie" and "Vroutjie", as Langehoven sometimes referred to himself and his wife in his novels, were reburied in the garden of *Arbeidsgenot*. The University of Stellenbosch's student centre is called The Neelsie in his honour.

Langenhoven had an imaginary elephant, Herrie, who appeared in many of his stories. He carved Herrie's name in a rock alongside the N12 highway near Meiringspoort. The rock is known as "Herrie's Rock" and is a national monument.

Mandela, Nelson Rolihlahla

Rolihlahla Mandela was born on 18 July 1918 in Mvezo, a village in the district of Umtata. The family moved shortly afterwards to the nearby Qunu. His father died when he was just nine years old, and he was placed in the care of a guardian. He was only later given the name Nelson, when he started going to school. From 1934 to 1938 he studied at Methodist colleges and in 1939 and 1940 he studied at the University of Fort Hare. In 1940 he was expelled from the university because of his involvement in a student boycott. In 1941 he moved to Johannesburg and finished his studies by correspondence.

He initially worked on the mines and was later appointed as an article clerk. From 1943 to 1949 he studied law at the University of the Witwatersrand. In 1943 he became a member of the ANC and, along with Walter Sisulu and Oliver Tambo, founded the ANC Youth League. After his first marriage, to Evelyn Mase, ended in divorce, he married Nonzamo Winnifred Madikizela (born 1936) in 1958.

After the Sharpeville Massacre in 1960, the ANC was banned and Mandela formed an underground military wing of the ANC. The ANC's military wing Umkhonto we Sizwe ("Spear of the Nation") was established under

under his leadership in 1961. In 1962 he underwent military training in Algeria. On his return he was taken into custody because of his political activities and in the Rivonia Trial in 1964 he was sentenced to life in jail for high treason. He spent a large part of his prison years on Robben Island. In 1968 and 1969 his mother and son died and he was not allowed to attend their funerals. He refused repeated offers from the government to free him with the proviso that he desisted from further political activities.

In 1990 President F.W. de Klerk unbanned the ANC and after protracted negotiations, Mandela was unconditionally released on 27 February 1990. In 1993 Mandela and De Klerk were jointly awarded the Nobel Peace Prize for their efforts to change conditions in South Africa.

In 1994 he was elected president of a democratic South Africa. He held this post for five years. After his second marriage ended in divorce, he married Graça Machel on his eightieth birthday in 1998. In 1999 he retired and retreated from public life. Mandela spent 27 years of his life in South African prisons. He is one of the world's most beloved and revered statesmen and is an important unofficial ambassador for South Africa. He has honorary degrees from more than 50 international universities.

Naudé, Dr Christiaan Frederik Beyers

Beyers Naudé was born in Roodepoort on op 10 May 1915. He was one of eight children and his father was a minister and a founding member of the Afrikaner-Broederbond (Afrikaner Brotherhood). He matriculated in Graaff-Reinet and achieved a Masters degree in languages and a degree in theology at the University of Stellenbosch. As a minister of the Dutch Reformed Church he served several congregations. In 1940 he became the youngest member yet of the Afrikaner Broederbond.

He began to express his opposition to apartheid and after the Sharpeville Massacre in 1960 he finally rebelled against the apartheid government. As a result of his denouncements and rejection of apartheid, he had to resign as a Dutch Reformed minister and also resigned as a member of the Broederbond in 1963. He became an underground supporter of the anti-apartheid movement and helped ANC activists flee the country. He also dedicated himself to the freeing of political prisoners and the lifting of the ban on the ANC and other organisations. He was banned from 1977 to 1984. In spite of his long association with the ANC he never joined the party. He and his family were harassed for years by the security police and high-ranking members of government. After the end of apartheid in 1994, he was invited to preach in the Dutch Reformed community of Aasvoëlkop in Johannesburg, where he had been the minister from 1959 to 1963.

Although he was initially branded as a traitor, he was later honoured for his struggle against apartheid and hailed worldwide for his role against apartheid and in the dissolution of the old South Africa. He was awarded nine honorary doctorates and eight international prizes. He died in 2004 at the age of 89 and was given an official state funeral, which was attended by President Thabo Mbeki and other dignitaries. His ashes were scattered in Alexandria just outside Johannesburg. A street and a square in Johannesburg are named after him and he was granted the Freedom of Johannesburg.

Oppenheimer, Sir Ernest

Ernest Oppenheimer was born in 1880 in Friedberg, Germany. His father and family encouraged him and his brothers to seek their fortune elsewhere. At 16, he became a messenger at the London diamond broker Anton Dunkelsbulher, who also had business interests in South Africa. He later began to grade diamonds and his talents were noticed.

In 1902 he became Dunkelsbuhler's representative in Kimberley. Within a short period he became one of the most respected diamond dealers in the business. He started various companies that were primarily involved in the diamond and gold mining industries. From 1912 to 1915 he was mayor of Kimberley. In 1915 he established himself in Johannesburg where he befriended the American engineer W.L. Honnold. As a result of anti-German riots during the First World War he emigrated to England in 1915 and accepted British citizenship. In 1916 he again settled in South Africa and in 1917 he and Honnold started the Anglo-American Corporation, of which Oppenheimer was chairman. This company became one of the most important mining companies in the world. In 1921 he was knighted by the British king. Oppenheimer also acquired shares in De Beers Consolidated Mines and in 1929 he became the chairman of that company. He later started the Diamond Producers' Association, which handles 95% of the world's diamond yield. He died in 1957 from a heart attack and was succeeded by his son, Harry.

- In 1915 Oppenheimer changed his name from Ernst to Ernest.
- Today Anglo-American is a business conglomerate with worldwide subsidiaries and is one of the largest single companies listed on the JSE.

Player, Gary

Gary Player was born in 1935 in Johannesburg. His mother died of cancer when he was eight years old. At the age of 14 he began to play golf and at 17 he became a professional golfer. In 1957 he married Vivienne Verwey and in 1959 he won his first British Open title.

Player won nine major championships. He won the British Open three times (1959, 1968 and 1974), the American Open once (1965), the American Masters three times (in 1961, 1974 and 1978) and the American PGA twice (in 1962 and 1972). He also won various other major titles.

In 2003 he received the Laureus Lifetime Achievement Award in Monaco. He has received numerous awards, as well as three honorary doctorates from international universities. On the golf course he always wears black, earning him the nickname "The Black Knight".

Today he is a sought-after designer of golf courses, and has been involved in more than 250 projects worldwide. He has interests in various organisations, including a racehorse stud farm

and the Player Foundation, which establishes and supports educational institutions. Player is regarded as one of the greatest sportsmen South Africa has ever produced. He was named South Africa's Sportsman of the Century in 2000. In 2008 at the age of 72 he played in his 52nd masters tournament.

Rupert, Dr Anthony Edward (Anton)

Anton Rupert was born in 1916 in Graaff-Reinet. He studied medicine at the University of Pretoria, but had to drop out due to a lack of funds. He later earned a degree in chemistry. He was a lecturer for a short time and then started a dry-cleaning business. Then, along with two investors, he started making cigarettes in his garage. From this small beginning came the Rembrandt Group. In 1941 he married Huberte Goote.

Today this group owns hundreds of companies in more than 35 countries. Not only was he a brilliant business pioneer and a visionary entrepreneur, he also made an important contribution to the advancement of nature conservation and the arts (especially fine arts and music). He established the international industrial giant Rembrandt and was one of the founding members of the World Wildlife Fund (WWF) and the Peace Parks Foundation. On the cultural front he made a contribu-

tion of inestimable value with the conservation of historic buildings, including at his birthplace of Graaff-Reinet as well as in Stellenbosch. The Rupert family is also involved in the wine industry and own the wine estates L'Ormarins and La Motte. They have a partnership with the Rothschild family and founded Rupert & Rothschild Vignerons, which has become well known for good wines. The Rembrandt Group also owns the Medi-Clinic private hospitals and has a large share in Distell.

Anton Rupert died in 2006 at the age of 89 (about a year after his wife) in his house in Stellenbosch. He will be remembered around the world as a great entrepreneur, businessman and conservationist.

Shuttleworth, Mark

Mark Richard Shuttleworth was born in 1973 in Welkom in the Free State. He completed his schooling at the Diocesan College (Bishops) in Rondebosch, Cape Town, and earned a business science degree in finance and information systems at the University of Cape Town.

In 1995 he started Thawte, a company specialising in digital certificates and internet security. In 1999 he sold the company to VeriSign for R3,5 billion. In 2000 he started HBD Venture Capital, in 2001 he established the non-profit Shuttleworth Foundation and in 2004 he established Canonical Ltd. In 2005 he also started the Ubuntu Foundation and made an initial investment of US$10 million. The funds of the Ubuntu Foundation are used to pay Ubuntu co-workers. In 2005 he bought a 65% stake in ImpiLinux.

Shuttleworth's flight in the Soyuz spacecraft took two days and he was on the International Space Station for eight days. Here he participated in experiments related to Aids and genome research. He returned to Earth on 2 May 2002. He was the first African in space. He currently lives in London and has both South African and British citizenship.

Sisulu, Walter

Walter Sisulu was born in 1912 at Engcobo in the Transkei. His mother was a housekeeper and his father was a civil servant. He was brought up by his mother's family. At the age of 15 he finished standard four (grade six) at a local missionary school and went to Johannesburg to work on the mines. However, he was too young to be employed and had various jobs until he started an estate agency. This estate agency later became a place of refuge for black people looking for help and many black people were also recruited here for resistance organisations. Here Sisulu met Nelson Mandela and a lifelong association began.

In 1940 he, along with Nelson Mandela and Oliver Tambo, founded the ANC Youth League. He also played a major role in the establishment of the military wing of the ANC, Umkhonto we Sizwe ("Spear of the Nation"). He became secretary general of the ANC and the political commissioner of Umkhonto we Sizwe. In 1944 he married Albertina Mnyila. They had five children and adopted four more. His wife and children also played an active part in the struggle against apartheid. He was taken into custody numerous times or placed under house arrest. After the Rivonia trial in 1964 he, along with Nelson Mandela and others, was taken to Robben Island and imprisoned there for 25 years. He was eventually freed in 1989.

Sisulu died at the age of 90 in 2003 and was buried in the Croesus Cemetery outside Soweto. He is regarded as one of the giants in the struggle against apartheid.

Smuts, Jan Christiaan

Jan Smuts was born in 1870 on a farm near Riebeek West. He first went to school at the age of 12. He was a brilliant student at Victoria College in Stellenbosch and in 1891 left for Cambridge to read law. In 1894 he was awarded an LL.B degree. In 1897 he married Isabella Krige. They had six children.

He returned to South Africa and in 1898 was appointed state attorney by President Kruger. In this post he regarded as his most important task the rooting out of corruption and inefficiency in the government. With the British occupation of Pretoria, Smuts joined the commando of General de la Rey. Under his and other leaders' guidance, guerrilla commandoes carried out successful attacks on isolated enemy divisions, bridges and railway lines. In 1901 he left with a Boer army for the Cape Colony to continue the guerrilla war there. This attempt failed and there was great loss of life.

In 1902 Smuts played an important role in the conclusion of the Peace of Vereeniging and again in 1908 in the National Convention. He later played a leading role in the Botha cabinet, the campaign in German West Africa (1915), the Imperial Conference, as a member of the British War Cabinet, and as a representative at the Paris Peace Conference. In 1910 he helped to write a constitution for the Union of South Africa and in 1919 he succeeded Botha as prime minister.

In 1924 his party lost the general election and he became leader of the opposition. He later formed a coalition with General Hertzog and became the minister of justice. 1n 1936 Smuts became chancellor of the University of Cape Town. In 1939 the coalition cabinet split and he once again became prime minister until 1948, when he again became leader of the opposition. When the United Party was defeated in 1948, Smuts became chancellor of the University of Cambridge.

He died in 1950 on his farm at Irene near Pretoria. Some of Smuts's decisions caused great divisions among South Africans, but internationally he enjoyed great admiration.

Theron, Charlize

Charlize Theron was born in 1975 on a farm near Benoni. At the age of 13 she went to Johannesburg for her high school education. When she was 15, her mother shot her father in self-defence, killing him. After she had won a local beauty contest, she travelled to Milan (Italy) at the age of 16 with a modelling contract.

After the contract had ended, she went to New York where she received ballet training and also did modelling work. Because of a knee injury she had to give up ballet at the age of 18.

She then moved to Los Angeles where, in 1995, she earned her first role as an actress in the movie *Children of the Corn III*. From 1996 to 2007 she had lead roles in 25 movies. For her powerful performance in 2004 in the movie *Monster*, in which she played the role of lesbian serial killer Aileen Wuornos, she won an Oscar. She also won a Golden Globe for her role in *Monster* and, along with Sandino Moreno, was named best actress at the Berlin Film Festival in 2004. She has also won several other prizes and awards. According to *The Hollywood Reporter* she was, in 2006, seventh on the list of the most highly paid actresses in Hollywood. She lives with her long-term boyfriend Stuart Townsend in Los Angeles.

Tutu, Archbishop Desmond Mpilo

Desmond Tutu was born in 1931 in Klerksdorp. In 1953 he was awarded a diploma in education and in 1954 he earned a BA degree from the University of Cape Town. He studied theology and completed his Masters degree at King's College in London. In 1955 he married Leah Shenxane; they had four children. After his return to South Africa in 1967 he trained black theologists. From 1972 to 1975 he held an important position with the World Council of Churches as co-director of the Theological Education Fund. In 1976 he was appointed as bishop in Lesotho. In 1977 he returned to South Africa and in 1978 he became secretary general of the World Council of Churches, which opposed the South African government politically.

Tutu campaigned across the world for the institution of economic sanctions against South Africa. While he was viewed by the oppressed as a symbol of freedom, supporters of the government regarded him as a dangerous agitator. In 1979 his passport was revoked. The publicity that surrounded him when he received an honorary degree from Columbia University in 1982 and when he was awarded the Nobel Peace Prize in 1984, helped him with his sanction campaign. He received a variety of awards and honorary degrees from various institutions and international universities.

In 1994 he dedicated himself to building the Rainbow Nation and in 1995 he became the chairman of the Truth and Reconciliation Commission. He still plays a prominent role in South Africa and in the world.

Interesting South Africans

Monkey boy of KwaZulu-Natal

In 1988 a mentally disabled five-year-old boy was found among the monkeys on the north coast of KwaZulu-Natal. It was suspected that his mother, after finding out that he was disabled, left the baby in the forests outside Stanger. He was then raised by the monkeys for five years. He ate the same food as the monkeys and walked on all fours through the bushes and trees. Local residents took him to the hospital in Stanger. He was called Saturday and transferred to the Ikhwezi Home for the disabled in Mandini. He was very frightened and ran away, climbed on the roof and in the trees and spent hours sitting in the veld, staring. At first he would only eat raw food, even raw meat, and refused ordinary food. He also bit the other children. Although he still cannot speak (he makes only unintelligible noises), he eventually improved with the help of psychologists. He now eats ordinary food (with his hands) and walks upright. It is suspected that he is deaf. His feet are deformed, possibly because he walked on all fours for so many years. He will probably have to remain in the home for his entire life.

Eliza Meiring

Eliza Meiring was a beautiful girl who lived on the farm Clovelly in the Hex River Valley in the middle of the 18th century. To get rid of all her unwanted suitors, she said she would only consider marrying the man who brought her a rare disa from the inhospitable parts of the Matroosberg Mountains.

A friend, whom she loved dearly, intended to surprise her with the disa but fell to his death in the mountains. Eliza lost her sanity and had to be locked up in the house's loft. She scratched her initials on the windowsill in 1768. One night she managed to open the door, fell down the stairs and died. It is a true story and the farm Clovelly, with the homestead and loft in which Eliza Meiring was locked up, still exists.

A different version of the story says that she jumped out of the window and died. The legend of a heartbroken woman who sometimes wanders in the Matroosberg on dark nights is probably related to her.

Helen Martins (see also Owl House page 134)

Helen Martins, the youngest of six children, was born in 1897. After she earned a teaching diploma in Graaff-Reinet and for a short time was married to a farmer, Johannes Pienaar, she left Nieu-Bethesda for a few years. In the 1930s she returned to take care of her elderly parents. After their deaths she began making artworks.

Helen Martins's memorial

She decorated the walls, doors and ceilings of her home with finely ground, coloured glass. In 1978, at the age of 77, Miss Helen, as she was known, committed suicide by drinking caustic soda. She was convinced that she was going blind. It is suspected that her eyes had been damaged by the fine fragments of glass with which she worked. The well-known playwright Athol Fugard depicted Martins's life in his *The Road to Mecca*. A film was also made, with Yvonne Bryceland in the leading role.

Modjadji, the Rain Queen

The story goes that a princess in Zimbabwe had a son by her brother. She was banned from the royal kraal but before her departure her mother gave her the rain medicine and beads and taught her how to use them to make rain.

She and a few followers established themselves in a grove of cycads near Duiwelskloof in Limpopo. She called herself Modjaji and founded the Lobedu tribe. Her reputation as a rain-maker spread around South Africa. When a rain queen became too old to rule, she was expected to commit suicide by drinking poison. This forest of modjaji palms (*Encephalartos transvenosus*) is one of the highest in the world. Modjadji III adopted Christianity and refused to commit suicide. Her successors, Modjadji IV and V, were also Christians.

Even today the Modjadji queens must live in isolation and may only be seen by specially authorised people. They are not allowed to marry but may still have children. The secret of making rain is still handed down from mother to daughter. In July 2001 Modjaji IV died at the age of 20. Modjaji V died three days later in a hospital in Pietersburg (now Polokwane). In April 2003 the new rain queen, Modjadji VI, was crowned. During the ceremony it began to rain, even though there had been no sign of rain earlier. Modjadji VI died in 2005 at the age of 27.

After the death of a rain queen there is an official morning period of a year. A rain queen chooses her successor herself. The rain queen is the only female traditional leader in South Africa. In 2009 no successor for Modjaji VI had been appointed yet.

- Some people claim that Modjadji II was white, with long brown hair and blue eyes.
- The book *She* by H. Rider Haggard is based on this story.

Nongqawuse

In April 1856 Nongqawuse, a 14-year-old Xhosa girl of the Gcaleka tribe in the current Eastern Cape, claimed that the ancestors has spoken to her. She said the ancestors would return and drive off the white people, but the Xhosas had to demonstrate their faith by making certain sacrifices. They had to kill all their cattle and destroy their crops. The people who refused to do this would turn into frogs, mice and ants and be blown into the sea. For ten months the Gcalekas, encouraged by their leader Sarhili, destroyed everything they possessed. 18 February 1857 would be the day of their "salvation". Nongqawuse foretold that the sun would rise blood red, come to a halt and set again in the east. Nothing happened and about 30 000 people later died of hunger. Nongqawuse fled to King William's Town. For her own safety she was kept for a short time on Robben Island. Later she went to live on a farm in the Eastern Cape. She died in 1898.

Outa Lappies

Outa Lappies has roamed across the whole country, but currently lives next to a tarred road on the farm Botterkraal near Prince Albert. His real name is Jan Schoeman and he estimates that he is between 75 and 80 years old. He makes artworks from all kinds of rubbish such as rope, tins, pieces of glass, pine cones and bits of fabric. He also embroiders sayings and events from his life in fine cross stitch on cloth. He only attended school until grade four. From a young age he picked up all kinds of objects and made them into something else. A teacher apparently told him about Vincent van Gogh and showed him one of the artist's works. Since then Outa Lappies has had a great admiration for Van Gogh.

His artworks are exhibited in galleries in Cape Town and Johannesburg, and galleries in the Netherlands and Belgium have invited him to exhibit there. Busloads of tourists often stop at his home. In 2000 he was named Western Cape tourism personality of the year. Outa Lappies is not only an artist, but also a philosopher, poet and storyteller.

Sarah Baartman

The Khoi woman Sarah Baartman was born in 1789 in the Gamtoos River Valley. Her buttocks and sexual organs apparently were especially large. She was a slave in Cape Town when she was spotted by a British ship's surgeon, William Dunlop. He promised her a lot of money and convinced her to go with him to London. In 1810 she left with him for London. There she was exhibited almost naked in circuses, museums, bars and on the street. She was called the "Hottentot Venus" and had to obey all her handler's commands like an animal. In 1815 she was taken to Paris where she experienced the same inhumane treatment. The French became tired of her performance and she became a prostitute. She died in 1815 at the age of 25.

An imprint was made of her body and her skeleton, brain and sexual parts were exhibited in the Musée de l'Homme (the Museum of Man) in Paris. About 160 years later it was still being exhibited, but in 1974 it was removed from public view. In 1994 President Nelson Mandela suggested that her remains be returned to

Sarah Baartman's grave

South Africa. Her remains arrived back in South Africa in 2002 and, amid great public interest, were buried near Hankey in the Gamtoos Valley. At her funeral President Mandela said that she should never have been exhibited, but that she had been a lonely African woman who was handled with barbaric brutality. Diana Ferrus wrote a poem for her, many books have been written about her and the Department of Environmental Affairs named a patrol boat after her in 2005.

Well-known South African heroes and heroines

South Africa has many heroes and heroines. The following is just a small selection from some of the best known from history.

Dick King

Richard (Dick) King was a British settler in present-day KwaZulu-Natal. In 1842 he rode his horse from Durban to Grahamstown in the Eastern Cape in ten days, a distance of more than 900km, to call for reinforcements for the English troops. His 16-year-old Zulu outrider Ndongeni went with him, but could not complete the ride as he did not have a saddle or stirrups. Each was rewarded with a piece of land: Ngondeni was given land on the bank of the Mzimzulu

Statue of Dick King

River and King was given land at Isipingo, where he operated a sugar mill until his death in 1871. In Durban there is a statue of Dick King designed by Wallace Pato and made by the sculptor H.H. Grellier.

Dirkie Uys

Dirkie Uys is one of South Africa's most famous child heroes. He was 12 years old when he, during the Battle of Italeni, bravely fought alongside his father Piet Uys against the Zulus. There are different versions of the event, but the one that is commonly accepted is that he was ahead of his father, but turned around when his father was wounded and fell from his horse. They were both stabbed to death.

Japie Greyling

Japie Greyling was born in 1890 on a farm in the Hoopstad district. When the Anglo-Boer War broke out in 1899, he was too young to go on commando with his father and older brothers and had to stay behind on the farm. In March 1901 the English began to burn down farms in the Hoopstad area. A group of Boers came to warn the Greylings. Shortly after the Boers left, the English came to the farm. They wanted Japie to tell them where the Boers had gone and where the Boer commandos were. Although he knew, Japie refused to tell them. Captain Jack Seely made him stand against a wall and ordered six soldiers to stand in a half-moon around Japie with their rifles trained on him. He quietly told the soldiers not to shoot. Japie said they might as well shoot him because he wasn't going to talk. Seely then ordered the soldiers to lower their weapons and congratulated Japie on his bravery. Japie Greyling was very modest and years later hadn't even told his children about this.

Klara Majola

Klara Majola lived with her parents on a farm called *Die Eike* in the district of Ceres. She was the oldest child of April and Maria Jansen. Her father was a shearer on the farm and also worked in the fruit orchards. He became blind, but often still took his walking stick and went to look for wood. On 25 July 1950 it was a cold, misty day and April again went to look for wood. Because he was blind he didn't mind going in the dark. His family became worried and the eight-year-old Klara offered to go and look for him. She did not return. It began to rain and snow and even though everyone was looking for her, they could not find her. The next morning her body was found near a stream. She had gotten lost and eventually froze to death. A poem by D.J. Opperman, "Klara Majola", is based on this event.

Racheltjie de Beer

Racheltjie de Beer and her family for a time lived on a farm in the south-east Highveld near the Drakensberg in the middle of the 1840s. One winter afternoon Racheltjie and her little brother went to look for a lost calf, but were overtaken by the dark and got lost themselves. It was icy cold and began to snow. She put her brother in a hollow ant heap and covered him in all her clothes to keep him warm. To try and stop the cold, she lay against the opening of the ant heap. The next morning the two children were found there. Her little brother was still alive, but Racheltjie was dead. The poem "Sneeuwitjie" by A.G. Visser is based on this event.

Wolraad Woltemade

In May 1773 *De Jonge Thomas*, a ship of the Dutch East India Company, was smashed to pieces by waves on the beach at Woodstock in Cape Town. The crew clung to the wreck and called for help, but no one on the beach could come to their aid. Great trouble was taken to salvage the wreck's cargo, but nothing was done to save the crew. Wolraad Woltemade, a dairy farmer of over 60 years, rode into the stormy sea on his faithful horse. Each time he rescued two people. In this way he rescued 14 people. The eighth time he reached the ship, a group of people grabbed hold of him and his horse in a panic and he and his horse disappeared under the waves. Altogether 138 people drowned and 53 made it to the beach. The Company later named the ship *Held Woltemade* after him, but he received little other acknowledgement. Today there is a statue of Wolraad Woltemade at the entrance to Mutual Park in Pinelands, Cape Town. Capetonians also thought it fitting to name the large city cemetery after him.

Statue of Wolraad Woltemade

- A heroic deed similar to that of Wolraad Woltemade, but not as well known, is that of the brave Francis Rose. On 4 January 1821 three ships, the *Indian Packet*, the *Emma* and the *Dorah*, ran aground on the rocks in Table Bay. The 17-year-old Francis and his father went to the beach to see if they could help. Francis went to fetch his horse from home, rode into the waves and one by one saved the crew members of one of the ships. On his last ride he was too exhausted and drowned.
- According to legend, a farmer shot and killed his son when he could not get him out of a crevice into which he had fallen. The son begged his father to shoot him. It is not known whether this really happened or where it may have happened. The poem "Waar ruwe rotse" by C.M. van den Heever is based on this event.

6. LITERATURE

The Dewey System (shortened version)

This indexing system was developed in 1876 by an American, Melville Dewey. Before this system was used, books in libraries were arranged alphabetically or according to size or colour.

000		**Computer Science, Knowledge and General Works**
004		Computer Science
010		Bibliography
020		Library and Information Sciences
030		Encyclopaedias and books of facts
050		Magazines, journals and serials
060		Associations, organisations and museums
070		News media, journalism and publishing
080		General collections
090		Manuscripts and rare books
100		**Philosophy and Psychology**
130		Paranormal phenomena
150		Psychology
200		**Religion**
220		The Bible
230–280		Christian theology
290		Other & comparative religions
300		**Socials Sciences**
301		Sociology and Anthropology
305		Social groups
310		General statistics
320		Political science
330		Economics
340		Law
350		Public administration
355		Military science
360		Social services, associations
364		Criminology
370		Education
380		Commerce, communications, transport
390		Customs, etiquette, folklore
400		**Language**
410		Linguistics
420		English and Old English
430		Germanic languages; German
439.36		Afrikaans
440		Romance languages; French
450		Italian; Romanian; Rhaeto-Romanic
460		Spanish and Portuguese languages

470	Italic; Latin
480	Hellenic languages; Classical Greek
490	Other languages
500	**Natural Sciences and Mathematics**
510	Mathematics
520	Astronomy
530	Physics
540	Chemistry
550	Earth sciences (geology, etc)
560	Palaeontology (sciences concerning fossils)
570	Life sciences
574–575	Biology
580	Plants
590	Zoological sciences
600	**Technology**
610	Medical sciences
620	Engineering
630	Agriculture
640	Home economics
650	Management
657	Accounting
660	Chemical engineering
670–680	Manufacturing products and processes
690	Buildings
700	**Arts**
710	Civic and landscape art
720	Architecture
730–770	Fine arts, sculpture, drawing, painting, etc.
780	Music
790	Recreational and performing arts
796–799	Sport
800	**Literature and Rhetoric**
810	American
820	English
830	Germanic
840	Romance languages
850	Italian
860	Spanish and Portuguese
870	Latin
880	Greek
890	Other languages
900	**History, Geography and Biography**
910	Geography and travel
920	Biography

929	Genealogy, names, insignia
930	History of ancient world
930.1	Archaeology
940–990	Modern history

South African literary awards
(in alphabetical order and not a complete list)

Alan Paton Award
This award for English non-fiction is sponsored by *The Sunday Times* and has been awarded annually since 1989. The prize is named after Alan Paton, who is best known as the author of *Cry, the Beloved Country*. The date indicates the year in which the prize was awarded.

Breyten Breytenbach (1994)

Winners

Year	Winner	Work
1989	Marq de Villiers	*White Tribe Dreaming*
1990	Jeff Peires	*The Dead Will Arise*
1991	Albie Sachs	*Soft Vengeance of a Freedom Fighter*
1992	Thomas Pakenham	*Scramble for Africa*
1993	Tim Couzens	*Tramp Royal*
1994	Breyten Breytenbach	*Return to Paradise*
1995	Nelson Mandela	*Long Walk to Freedom*
1996	Margaret McCord	*The Calling of Katie Makanya*
1997	Charles van Onselen	*The Seed is Mine*
1998	John Reader	*Africa: A Biography of a Continent*
1999	Antjie Krog Stephen Clingman	*Country of My Skull* *Bram Fischer: Afrikaner Revolutionary*
2000	Anthony Sampson	*Mandela: The Authorised Biography*
2001	Henk van Woerden	*A Mouthful of Glass*
2002	Jonathan Kaplan	*The Dressing Station*
2003	Jonny Steynberg	*Midlands*
2004	Pumla Gobodo-Madikizela	*A Human Being Died That Night*
2005	Jonny Steinberg	*The Number*

Year	Winner	Work
2006	Edwin Cameron Adam Levin	*Witness to AIDS* *Aidsafari*
2007	Ivan Vladislavic	*Portrait with Keys*
2008	Mark Gevisser	*Thabo Mbeki – The Dream Deferred*
2009	Peter Harris	*In a Different Time*

Alba Bouwer Prize

This prize, which was instituted in 1989, is awarded every three years by the South African Academy for Science and Arts to any children's book for readers between the ages of seven and 12. Original Afrikaans books are in contention for the prize. The prize is awarded for the three years prior to the award year.

Winners

Year	Winner	Work
1989	Freda Linde	*Strepie en Kurfie*
1992	Barrie Hough Marietjie de Jongh	*Droomwa* *Braam en die engel*
1995	Corlia Fourie	*Die towersak en ander stories* and *Die wit vlinder*
1998	Philip de Vos	*Moenie 'n mielie kielie nie*
2001	Martie Preller	*Die Balkie-boek*
2004	Leon de Villiers	*Droomoog Diepgrawer*
2007	Jaco Jacobs	*Wurms met tamatiesous en ander lawwe rympies*

Philip de Vos (1998)

Eugène Marais Prize

The Eugène Marais Prize has been awarded since 1961 by the Academy for Science and Arts. It is awarded to a first or early belletristic publication in Afrikaans. The date indicates the year in which the prize was awarded.

Winners

Year	Winner	Work
1961	Audrey Blignault	*In klein maat*, *Die vrolike lied* and her contribution to *Die dammetjie*
1963	André P. Brink	*Caesar*
1964	Dolf van Niekerk	*Skepsels*
1965	George Louw	*Koggelstok*
1966	Henriëtte Grové	All her dramatic work
1967	Abraham de Vries	All his prose work
1968	M.M. Walters	*Cabala*
1970	P.G. Hendriks	*Die weg van 'n man*
1971	Sheila Cussons	*Plektrum*
1972	Lina Spies	*Digby Vergenoeg*
1973	Antjie Krog	*Januarie-suite*
1974	Leon Strydom	*Geleentheidsverse*
1975	P.J. Haasbroek	*Heupvuur*
1976	J.C. Steyn	*Die grammatika van liefhê*
1978	Marlene van Niekerk	*Sprokkelster*
1979	Eveleen Castelyn	*Tussen hemel en aarde*
1980	Petra Müller	*Patria*
1981	Annesu de Vos	*Gebed van 'n groen perske en ander verse*
1982	Louis Krüger	*Die skerpskutter*
1983	E. Kotzé	*Halfkrone vir die nagmaal*
1984	Etienne van Heerden	*My Kubaan*
1985	Alexander Strachan	*'n Wêreld sonder grense*
1986	Freek Swart	*Spinola se rooi angelier*
1987	Deon Opperman Joan Hambidge	*Môre is 'n lang dag/Die teken* *Bitterlemoene*
1988	P.C. Haarhoff	*Uit 'n ander wêreld*

Year	Winner	Work
1989	Philip de Vos	*Daar's bitterals in die heuningwals*
1990	H.J. Pieterse	*Alruin*
1991	Pieter Stoffberg	*Die hart van 'n hond*
1992	Riana Scheepers	*Dulle Griet*
1993	Marita van der Vyver	*Griet skryf 'n sprokie*
1994	Mark Behr Ronel de Goede	*Die reuk van appels* *Skoop*
1995	Johan Myburg	*Kontrafak*
1996	A.H.M. Scholtz	*Vatmaar*
1997	Jaco Fouché	*Die ryk van die rawe*
1999	Christoffel Coetzee	*Op soek na generaal Mannetjies Mentz* (awarded posthumously)
2000	S.P. Benjamin	*Die lewe is 'n halwe roman*
2001	Tom Dreyer	*Stinkafrikaners*
2002	Dine van Zyl	*Slagoffers*
2003	Barbara Fölscher	*Reisgenoot*
2004	Ilse van Staden	*Watervlerk*
2005	Prize withdrawn*	
2006	Marlize Hobbs	*Flarde*
2007	Danie Marais	*In die buitenste ruimte*
2008	Helena Gunter	*Op 'n plaas in Afrika*
2009	Ronelda Kamfer Loftus Marais	*Noudat slapende honde* *Staan in die algemeen nader aan vensters*

* The Eugène Marais Prize was withdrawn in 2005 and an embargo was placed on the distribution of the poetry collection *Waterbreker* by Melanie Grobler. This occurred after a literary storm broke over the marked similarities between her poem "Stad" and a poem by the Canadian poet Anne Michaels.

Helena Gunter (2008)

Herman Charles Bosman Prize

This prize was initiated in 1997 and is awarded to writers who have published English books with one of Media24's imprints during the previous calendar year.

Winners

Year	Winner	Work
1997	Rayda Jacobs	*Eyes of the Sky*
1998	Achmat Dangor	*Kafka's Curse*
1999	No award	
2000	Peter Horn	*My Voice is Under Control Now*
2001	Willemien le Roux	*Shadow Bird*
2002	K. Sello Duiker	*The Quiet Violence of Dreams*
2003	Ingrid de Kok	*Terrestrial Things*
2004	Rayda Jacobs	*Confessions of a Gambler*
2005	Keorapetse Kgositsile	*This Way I Salute You*
2006	Simao Kikamba	*Going Home*
2007	Maxine Case Kgebeti Moele	*All We Have Left Unsaid* *Room 207*
2008	No award	
2009	Michiel Heyns	*Bodies Politic*

Rayda Jacobs (1997, 2004)

Hertzog Prize

The Hertzog Prize was instituted in 1914 by the South African Academy for Science and Arts. General J.B.M. Hertzog donated £1 200 towards the prize, which is the most sought-after in Afrikaans literature. The prize is awarded annually in the categories of prose, poetry and drama (in turns). The date indicates the year in which the prize was awarded.

Winners

Year	Winner	Work (genre in brackets)
1915	Totius	*Trekkerswee* (poetry)
1917	Jochem van Bruggen	*Teleurgestel* (prose)
1920	Leon Maré	*Ou Malkop* (prose)
1925	Jochem van Bruggen	*Ampie: die natuurkind* (prose)
1926	A.G. Visser J.F.W. Grosskopf D.F. Malherbe	*Gedigte* (poetry) *As die tuig skawe* and *Drie eenbedrywe* (drama) *Die meulenaar* (prose)
1927	Jochem van Bruggen C.J. Langenhoven	*Ampie: die meisiekind* (prose) *Skaduwees van Nasaret* (prose)
1928	A.G. Visser C.M. van den Heever	*Rose van herinnering* (poetry) *Die nuwe boord* (poetry)
1930	D.F. Malherbe G.C. en S.B. Hobson	*Hans die skipper* (prose) *Kees van die Kalahari* (prose)
1933	Jochem van Bruggen	*Die sprinkaanbeampte van Sluis* (prose)
1934	Totius C. Louis Leipoldt W.E.G. Louw	*Passieblomme* (poetry) *Skoonheidstroos* (poetry) *Die ryke dwaas* (poetry)
1935	H.A. Fagan	*Die ouderling en ander toneelstukke* (drama)
1936	Mikro	*Toiings* and *Pelgrims* (prose)
1937	I.D. du Plessis	*Vreemde liefde* en *Ballades* (poetry)
1940	N.P. van Wyk Louw	*Die halwe kring* (poetry)
1942	C.M. van den Heever	*Laat vrugte* (poetry)
1943	Elisabeth Eybers	*Die stil avontuur* and *Belydenis in die skemering* (poetry)
1944	C. Louis Leipoldt	*Die heks* and *Die laaste aand* (drama)
1945	Sangiro	All his prose works
1947	D.J. Opperman	*Heilige beeste* (poetry)

Year	Winner	Work (genre in brackets)
1951	Toon van den Heever	Gedigte (1919) in 1931 rewritten as Eugene en ander gedigte (poetry)
1952	Gerhard Beukes	Langs die steiltes, Salome dans, As ons twee eers getroud is and eight one-act plays (drama)
	W.A. de Klerk	Die jaar van die vuur-os, Drie vroue, Drie dramas and Vlamme oor La Roche (drama)
1953	M.E.R.	All her prose work
1956	D.J. Opperman	Periandros van Korinthe (drama)
1957	Elise Muller	Die vrou op die skuit (prose)
1958	N.P. van Wyk Louw	Die mens agter die boek, Maskers van die erns, Lojale verset and Berigte te velde (prose)
1960	N.P. van Wyk Louw	Germanicus (drama)
1961	F.A. Venter	Swart pelgrim and Geknelde land (prose)
1962	Ernst van Heerden	Die klop (poetry)
1964	Etienne Leroux	Sewe dae by die Silbersteins (prose)
1965	N.P. van Wyk Louw	Tristia (poetry)
1968	Boerneef	Posthumous; all his poetry collections
1969	D.J. Opperman	Voëlvry (drama)
1970	Karel Schoeman	By fakkellig, 'n Lug vol helder wolke and Spiraal (prose)
1971	Elisabeth Eybers	Onderdak (poetry)
1972	P.G. du Plessis	Siener in die suburbs and Die nag van legio (drama)
1973	Chris Barnard	Mahala and Duiwel in die bos (prose)
1974	Uys Krige	Uys Krige: 'n Keur uit sy gedigte (poetry)
1976	Anna M. Louw	Kroniek van Perdepoort (prose)
1977	Wilma Stockenström	Van vergetelheid en van glans (poetry)
1978	Bartho Smit	Putsonderwater, Moeder Hanna, Christine and Die verminktes (drama)
1979	Etienne Leroux	Magersfontein, o Magersfontein (prose)
1980	D.J. Opperman	Komas uit 'n bamboesstok (poetry)
1981	Henriette Grové	Ontmoeting by Dwaaldrif and all her other dramas
1982	Hennie Aucamp	All his prose work

Year	Winner	Work (genre in brackets)
1983	Sheila Cussons	All her poetry collections
1984	Breyten Breytenbach Henriette Grové	*Yk* (poetry)* *Die kêrel van die Pêrel* (prose)
1985	Uys Krige	All his dramas
1986	Karel Schoeman	*'n Ander land* (prose)
1987	T.T. Cloete	*Idiolek* and *Allotroop* (poetry)
1989	Etienne van Heerden	*Toorberg* (prose)
1990	Antjie Krog	*Lady Anne* (poetry)
1991	Chris Barnard	All his dramas
1992	Wilma Stockenström	*Abjater wat so lag* (prose)
1993	T.T. Cloete	*Met die aarde praat* (poetry)
1994	Reza de Wet	*Vrystaat* trilogy and *Trits: Mis, Mirakel, Drif* (drama)
1995	Karel Schoeman	*Hierdie lewe* (prose)
1996	Ina Rousseau	*'n Onbekende jaartal* (poetry)
1997	Reza de Wet	*Drie susters twee* (drama)
1998	Elsa Joubert	*Die reise van Isobelle* (prose)
1999	Breyten Breytenbach	*Oorblyfsels: 'n roudig* and *Papierblom* (poetry)

* In 1984 Breyten Breytenbach refused the Hertzog Prize for his poetry collection *Yk* for political reasons.

Etienne van Heerden (1989)

Marlene van Niekerk (2007)

Year	Winner	Work (genre in brackets)
2000	André P. Brink	*Die jogger* (drama)
2001	André P. Brink	*Donkermaan* (prose)
2002	Henning Pieterse	*Die burg van hertog Bloubaard* (poetry)
2003	Pieter Fourie	All his dramas (drama)
2004	Ingrid Winterbach	*Niggie* (prose)
2005	Petra Müller	*Die aandag van jou oë* (poetry)
2006	Deon Opperman	His drama oeuvre, *Vyfmylpaal* (drama)
2007	Marlene van Niekerk	*Agaat* (prose)
2008	Breyten Breytenbach	*Die Windvanger* (poetry)
2009	Deon Opperman	*Kaburu* (drama)

Ingrid Jonker Prize

The Ingrid Jonker Prize was instituted in 1965. It is awarded in turn to debut poetry collections in Afrikaans or English. The prize consists of a medal by the sculptor Bill Davis and a cash prize. The judges must be published poets. The date indicates the year in which the prize was awarded. Incomplete list.

Winners

Year	Winner	Collection
1965	Ruth Miller	*Floating Island*
1966	D.P.M. Botes	*Wat is 'n gewone man?*
1968	M.M. Walters	*Cabala*
1969	Sinclair Beiles	*Ashes of Experience*
1970	Sheila Cussons	*Plektrum*
1972	Lina Spies	*Digby Vergenoeg*
1973	Wally Serote	*Yakhal'Inkomo*
1974	Leon Strydom	*Geleentheidsverse*
1976	J.C. Steyn	*Die grammatika van liefhê*
1977	Colin Style	*Baobab Street*
1978	Marlene van Niekerk	*Sprokkelster*
1979	Mike Nicol	*Among the Souvenirs*

Year	Winner	Collection
1981	T.T. Cloete	*Angelliera*
1982	Johann de Lange	*Akwarelle van die dors*
1983	Jeremy Cronin	*Inside*
1984	Johann Lodewyk Marais	*Die somer is 'n dag oud*
1987	Donald Riekert	*Heuning uit die swarthaak*
1988	Graham Walker	*The Complete Libby Destrudo Songbook*
1989	Rosa Smit	*Krone van die narsing*
1990	John Eppel	*Spoils of War*
1991	Henning Pieterse	*Alruin*
1992	Heather Robertson	*Under the Sun*
1993	Paul Bosman	*Ryp geel kring*
1995	Gert Vlok Nel	*Om te lewe is onnatuurlik*
1996	Steve Shapiro	*In a Borrowed Tent*
1997	Charl-Pierre Naudé	*Die nomadiese oomblik*
1998	Dan Wylie	*The Road Out*
1999	Trienke Laurie	*Skietspoel*
2000	Brian Walter	*Tracks*
2001	Zandra Bezuidenhout	*Dansmusieke*
2002	Kobus Moolman	*Time like Stone*
2003	Martjie Bosman	*Landelik*

Lina Spies (1972)

Year	Winner	Collection
2004	Finuala Dowling	*I, Flying*
2005	Ilse van Staden	*Watervlerk*
2006	Rustum Kozain	*This Carting Life*
2007	Danie Marais	*In die buitenste ruimte*
2008	Megan Hall	*Fourth Child*

MER Prize

The MER Prize was instituted in 1983 and is awarded to the best children's or young adult book published the preceding year by one of Media24 imprints. The prize is named after M.E. Rothman. The prize is awarded to Afrikaans or English books for young readers, written and illustrated by local writers and artists. Since 2004 the prize has been awarded separately to young adult and children's literature.

Winners

Year	Winner	Work
1984	Alba Bouwer	*Vlieg, swaeltjie, vlieg ver*
1985	Rona Rupert	*Al Everest se voëls*
1986	Dolf van Niekerk	*Die haasvanger*
1987	No award was made	
1988	Jenny Seed	*Place Among the Stones*
1989	Linda Rhode (compiler) Alida Bothma (illustrator)	*Goue fluit, my storie is uit*
1990	Lawrence Bransby	*Down Street*
1991	Corlia Fourie	*Die meisie wat soos 'n bottervoël sing*
1992	Nel Swart	*Elk vir mekander*
1993	Allan Jermieson	*The Delmonico*
1994	Elizabeth van der Merwe	*Kaljander van die Karoo*
1995	Corlia Fourie	*Die towersak en ander stories*
1996	Philip de Vos	*Moenie 'n mielie kielie nie*
1997	Jenny Robson	*One Magic Moment*

Year	Winner	Work
1998	Leon de Villiers	*Die pro*
1999	Barrie Hough	*Skilpoppe*
2000	Freda Linde	*Eenders en anders*
2001	Jan Vermeulen	*Geraamtes dra nie klere nie*
2002	Dianne Hofmeyr	*The Waterbearer*
2003	Jackie Nagtegaal	*Daar's vis in die punch*
2004	Willem van der Walt Martie Preller	*Ragtime en rocks* *Ek is Simon*
2005	Anoeschka von Meck Wynand Louw	*Vaselinetjie* (young adult book) *Mr Humperdinck's Wonderful Whatsit* (children's book)
2006	Fanie Viljoen Marita van der Vyver (writer) Piet Grobler (illustrator)	*Breinbliksem* (young adult book) *Mia se ma* (children's book)
2007	Jenny Robson Fanie Viljoen (writer) Karl Stephan (illustrator)	*Praise Song* (young adult book) *Geraamte in die klas* (children's book)
2008	S.A. Partridge Wendy Hartman (writer) Marjorie van Heerden (illustrator)	*The Goblet Club* (young adult book) *Nina and Little Duck* (children's book)
2009	Derick van der Walt Mari Grobler (writer) Elizabeth Pulles	*Lien se lankstaanskoene* (young adult book), *Siyolo se trui/Siyolo's Jersey* (children's book)

Dolf van Niekerk (1986)

Olive Schreiner Prize

The Olive Schreiner Prize was instituted by the English Academy of South Africa to encourage and give recognition to first-time authors and poets. This prize is awarded annually in the categories of prose, drama and poetry in turn. The date indicates the year for which the prize is awarded, although it is only announced the following year.

Winners

Year	Winner	Work (genre in brackets)
1990	Norman Coombe	*A Snake in the Garden* (drama)
1991	Ivan Vladislavic	*Missing Persons* (prose)
1992	Tatamkhulu Afrika	*Nine Lives* (poetry)
1993	No award	
1994	Deena Padayachee	*What's Love Got to Do with It?* (prose)
1995	Allan James	*Morning near Genadendal* (poetry)
1996	Zakes Mda	*The Nun's Romantic Story* (drama)
1997	Zakes Mda	*Ways of Dying* (prose)
1998	Dan Wylie	*The Road Out* (poetry)
1999	Moira Lovell	*Bedtime Stories* (drama)
2000	Antjie Krog	*Country of My Skull* (prose)
2001	Mzi Mahola	*When Rains Come* (poetry)
2002	Xoli Norman	*Halleluja* (drama)
2003	Hugh Lewin	*Bandiet out of Jail* (prose)

Zakes Mda (1996, 1997)

Antjie Krog (2000)

Year	Winner	Work (genre in brackets)
2004	Isobel Dixon	*Weather Eye* (poetry)
2005	John Kani	*Nothing but the Truth* (drama)
2006	Russel Brownlee Jane Taylor	*Garden of the Plagues* (prose) *Of Wild Dogs* (prose)
2007	Rustum Kozain	*This Carting Life* (poetry)

Recht Malan Prize

This prize is awarded by Media24 for the best non-fiction work in Afrikaans or English published the previous year by an imprint in the Media24 group.

Winners (since 2000)

Year	Winner	Work
2000	J.C. Kannemeyer	*Leipoldt: 'n Lewensverhaal*
2001	Gregg Mills	*The Wired Model*
2002	Karel Schoeman	*Dogter van Sion*
2003	Karel Schoeman	*Die laaste Afrikaanse boek*
2004	Hermann Giliomee	*The Afrikaners: Biography of a People*
2005	Uma Dhupelia-Mesthrie	*Gandhi's Prisoner: The Life of Gandhi's Son Manilal*

Hermann Giliomee (2004)

Year	Winner	Work
2006	Antony Altbeker	*The Dirty Work of Democracy*
2007	Leon Rousseau	*Die groot avontuur – Wondere van die lewe op aarde*
2008	Mark Gevisser	*Thabo Mbeki: The Dream Deferred*
2009	Tony Leon Jonny Steinberg	*On the Contrary* *Three-Letter Plague*

Sunday Times Fiction Award

This prize has been awarded since 2001. The date indicates the year in which the prize was awarded.

Winners

Year	Winner	Work
2001	Zakes Mda	*The Heart of Redness*
2002	Ivan Vladislavic	*The Restless Supermarket*
2003	André Brink	*The Other Side of Silence*
2004	Rayda Jacobs	*Confessions of a Gambler*
2005	Justin Cartwright	*The Promise of Happiness*
2006	Andrew Brown	*Coldsleep Lullaby*
2007	Marlene van Niekerk Michiel Heyns (translator)	*Agaat*
2008	Ceridwen Dovey	*Blood Kin*
2009	Anne Landsman	*The Rowing Lesson*

André Brink (2003)

Tienie Holloway Medal

This prize was instituted in 1969 by the South African Academy for Science and Arts. The prize is named after Mrs Tienie Holloway, a well-known author of literature for young children. Since 1976 it has been awarded every three years. The date indicates the year in which the prize was awarded.

Corlia Fourie (1991)

Winners

Year	Winner	Work
1970	M.E.R.	*Karlien en Kandas*
1971	Pieter W. Grobbelaar	All his books for young children
1973	Freda Linde	*Jos en die bok*
1976	Hester Heese	All her books for young children
1979	Tienie Holloway (posthumously)	*Rympies van Tienie Holloway* and *Versies van Tienie Holloway*
1982	Hester Heese	*Sy wat die soen op haar voorkop dra*
1985	Freda Linde	*Die Keiserkroon*
1988	Rona Rupert	*Nou wil almal sien*
1991	Corlia Fourie	*Die meisie wat soos 'n bottervoël sing*
1994	Elizabeth van der Merwe	*Kaljander van die Karoo*
1997	Marita van der Vyver and Piet Grobler	*Olinosters op die dak*
2003	Martie Preller	*Babalela* and *Lisa het 'n plan*
2006	Martie Preller, Erica and Andries Maritz	*Diep, diep in 'n donker bos*
2009	Alana Bailey Emily Bornoff	*Prinses van die Afrikavlaktes*

W.A. Hofmeyr Prize

This prize has been awarded since the fifties by Naspers to works released the previous year by an imprint in the Media24 group.

T.T. Cloete (1981, 1986, 1990)

Winners (since 1980)

Year	Winner	Work
1980	D.J. Opperman	Komas uit 'n bamboesstok
1981	T.T. Cloete	Angelliera
1982	Sheila Cussons	Die woedende brood
1983	Elisabeth Eybers	Bestand
1984	Henriette Grové	Die kêrel van die Pêrel
1985	Karel Schoeman	'n Ander land
1986	T.T. Cloete	Allotroop
1987	Etienne van Heerden	Toorberg
1988	Ernst van Heerden	Amulet teen die vuur
1989	Elsa Joubert	Missionaris
1990	T.T. Cloete	Driepas
1991	Sheila Cussons	Die knetterende woord
1992	Wilma Stockenström	Abjater wat so lag
1993	Chris Barnard	Moerland
1994	Eben Venter	Foxtrot van die vleiseters
1995	Alexander Strachan	Die werfbobbejaan
1996	Elsa Joubert	Die reise van Isobelle
1997	Eben Venter	Ek stamel, ek sterwe
1998	George Weideman	Die onderskepper
1999	André P. Brink	Duiwelskloof
2000	Ingrid Winterbach	Buller se plan
2001	Etienne van Heerden	Die swye van Mario Salviati
2002	Dine van Zyl	Slagoffers
2003	Dan Sleigh	Eilande
2004	Eben Venter	Begeerte
2005	Marlene van Niekerk	Agaat
2006	Etienne van Heerden	In stede van die liefde
2007	Ingrid Winterbach	Die boek van toeval en toeverlaat
2008	Breyten Breytenbach	Die windvanger
2009	Etienne van Heerden	30 Nagte in Amsterdam

7. TRANSPORT

South Africa's national roads

Route descriptions usually begin in the north or west.

Name	From	To	Route
N1	Zimbabwe	Cape Town	Zimbabwe (Beit Bridge border post), Polokwane, Mokopane, Pretoria, Johannesburg, Winburg, Bloemfontein, Colesberg, Hanover, Three Susters, Beaufort West, Worcester, Cape Town
N2	Cape Town	Ermelo	Cape Town, Swellendam, Mossel Bay, George, Port Elizabeth, Ncanara, Grahamstad, King William's Town, East London, Umtata, Durban, Piet Retief, Ermelo
N3	Johannesburg	Durban	Johannesburg, Harrismith, Ladysmith, Pietermaritzburg, Durban
N4	Botswana	Mozambique	Botswana (Skilpad Gate border post), Pretoria, Witbank, Middelburg, Mozambique (Lebombo border post)
N5	Winburg	Harrismith	Winburg, Bethlehem, Harrismith
N6	Bloemfontein	East Londen	Bloemfontein, Queenstown, East London
N7	Namibia	Cape Town	Namibia (Vioolsdrift border post), Springbok, Cape Town
N8	Bloemfontein	Lesotho	Upington, Kimberley, Bloemfontein, Ladybrand, Lesotho (Maseru Bridge border post)
N9	Colesberg	George	Colesberg, Middelburg, Graaff-Reinett, George

Name	From	To	Route
N10	Namibia	Ncanara	Namibië (Nakop border post), Upington, Britstown, De Aar, Hanover, Middelburg, Cradock, Ncanara
N11	Botswana	Ladysmith	Botswana (Groblers Bridge border post), Mokopane, Middelburg, Ermelo, Ladysmith
N12	George	Witbank	George, Beaufort West, Three Susters, Britstown, Kimberley, Warrenton, Klerksdorp, Potchefstroom, Johannesburg, Witbank
N14	Springbok	Pretoria	Springbok, Upington, Vryburg, Krugersdorp, Centurion, Pretoria
N15	Worcester	Swellendam	Worcester, Robertson, Swellendam
N17	Johannesburg	Swaziland	Johannesburg, Leandra, Bethal, Ermelo, Swaziland (Oshoek border post)
N18	Botswana	Warrenton	Botswana (Ramatlabama border post), Mafikeng, Vryburg, Warrenton

South Africa's road network is 534 131km long. It is the longest road network in Africa.

South African cars of the year

This competition is held by the South African Guild of Motoring Journalists in association with the main sponsor, WesBank. Finalists are chosen from all the cars released the preceding year. Each car is subject to a strict judging process and is evaluated according to a range of criteria, including quality, dynamics, performance, appearance and value for money. The winner is announced the year after the release of the car.

Mazda2 1.5 Individual (2007)

Year	Car	Year	Car
1986	Toyota Corolla Twin Cam	1998	Ford Fiesta Fun
1987	Mercedes-Benz 260	1999	Alfa Romeo, 156 T-Spark
1988	BMW 735.	2000	Renault Clio 1,4 RT
1989	Toyota Corolla Gli Exec	2001	BMW 320d
1990	BMW 53	2002	Audi A4 1.9 Tdi
1991	Opel Monza 160 Gsi	2003	VW Polo 1.4 Tdi
1992	Nissan Maxima 300 SE	2004	Renault Megane 1.9 dCi
1993	BMW 316i	2005	Volvo S40, 2.4
1994	Opel Kadett 140	2006	Audi A3 Sportback 2.0T FSI
1995	Opel Astra 160 iS	2007	Honda Civic 1.8 Vxi
1996	Audi A4 1.8	2008	Mazda2 1.5 Individual
1997	BMW 528i	2009	Honda Accord 2.4i Executive

The first car in South Africa was a single cylinder Benz Voiturette, which was imported from Germany in 1897 by two Pretorians. It had an engine with $1\frac{1}{2}$ horsepower and could reach speeds of up to 22,5km per hour.

Tips for purchasing a second-hand car

- Don't just rush out and buy a car – investigate a few options before you decide.

- Find out what are the market-related prices of cars of the same model and year.

- Take note of the safety and fuel efficiency of the car.

- Try to buy a second-hand car from a reputable dealer. They usually offer reliable after-sales service and guarantees.

- If you buy a car at a dealership, ask for the previous owner's contact details and phone the person.

- If you buy the car from a private person, meet the person at a safe place, such as the parking lot of a shopping centre, and preferably during the day. Do not provide your home address.

- If you buy from a private person, obtain a certificate from the police confirming that the car has not been stolen.

- Insist on a roadworthy certificate.

- To calculate the total price of the car, you must also take into account any repair work that needs to be done.

- Inspect the car in broad daylight and not in a garage.

- Make sure that the car has a full service history. It gives you an indication of the mechanical condition of the car.

- Insist on a second set of keys.

- Do not buy a car that has an average mileage of above 30 000km a year. Most cars in South Africa travel between 25 000 and 30 000km a year.

- If there are colour differences between panels, the car was probably in an accident. Also check to see if there are rust patches.

- Wide gaps or doors that don't close properly are also signs that the vehicle was in an accident.

- The headlights must be correctly adjusted.

- If the upholstery or the rubber on the pedals looks worn while the kilometre reading is low, it is possible that the kilometre reading may be false.

- Make sure that the boot lid works properly and can lock.

- Turn the engine on and look at the exhaust fumes. If the car smokes a great deal or if the smoke is blue or grey, the rings could be in a bad condition.

- The engine oil must be clean.

- Look under the vehicle to see if there are fluid leaks. Only water from the air conditioning may leak.

- The car must have a valid licence and the car's chassis number on the licence must correspond with the number on the chassis. You should also check the registration certificate.

- The tyres, as well as the spare tyre, must be in a good condition. If the tyres have worn unevenly there could be a problem with the wheel balance, wheel alignment or shock absorbers.

- Take a test drive and feel if the gears change smoothly and the brakes work well; test the windows and doors, air conditioning, radio, locks and central locking.

- Test the handbrake on a slope.

- It is a good idea to have the car tested by the Automobile Association (AA) (083 843 22) before you buy it. They can determine if the car has been stolen or written off and rebuilt, and can also determine if the car is fully paid off.

> - If you sell a car privately, make sure that the money is in your bank account before you give the car to the buyer.

Tips for a safe journey

- Ensure that your car is regularly serviced.
- The car's seatbelts must be in working condition and all passengers must use them. Children under two should be in a car seat facing backwards. Children under 10 should sit in a booster seat, which prevents them from being injured by the seat belt.
- If the front air bag is not deactivated, no one shorter than 1,4m may sit in the front seat. The air bag could hit the person in the face and cause serious injuries. Children's car seats may also not be used in the front if the air bag is not deactivated.
- Ensure that the tyres are not flat or worn.
- There must always be enough fuel in the vehicle.
- Have the oil and water checked regularly.
- Keep an eye on the temperature gauge so the car does not overheat.
- Make sure that all lights work properly.
- The windscreen wipers must be in a good condition.
- Lock all doors when you are driving.
- Do not exceed speed limits.
- Maintain a safe distance between your car and the car in front of you.
- Do not drive for long hours without taking breaks.
- Drive slowly in rain or mist.
- Do not speak on a cellphone, change CDs or do anything else while you are driving.
- Avoid alcohol if you are planning to drive.

- Avoid dangerous roads.

- Do not pick up hitchhikers.

- Phone the police (10111) or your cellphone's emergency number (112) if your car breaks down by the side of the road.

The correct conduct at a vehicle accident

An accident without injured persons

- Stop immediately and put on your hazard lights.

- Inspect the damage, but be very careful of oncoming traffic.

- Do not take any alcohol or tranquillizers.

- If no one is injured, move the cars out of the road.

- Do not accept any responsibility, offer compensation for damages or discuss the accident with anyone other than the police or traffic police.

- Take down the names, addresses and vehicle registration numbers of the other drivers and witnesses.

- Give your name, address and vehicle registration number to the involved parties or the police.

- Make a sketch or take a photo of the accident scene, if possible.

- Report the accident within 24 hours at the nearest police station, showing your driver's licence, and get a case number for insurance purposes.

An accident with injured persons or fatal injuries

Do not stop at the scene of an accident if emergency personnel are already there. If no help has arrived yet, call an emergency number immediately – 112 (from cellphones) or 10111 (police) and 10177 (ambulance) from any telephone.

- If you come across a car accident, park your car out of the way and be careful of oncoming traffic.

- Turn on your car's emergency lights and place warning triangles, if available, in the road.

- Notify the police, a doctor and an ambulance.

- If you are involved in the accident, ask a passing motorist for help if necessary.

- Do not move the vehicles without the permission of the police.

- Do not try to turn an overturned car back onto its wheels unless the car has caught fire and it is the only way to free the injured.

- If a car must be moved due to dangerous circumstances, the vehicle's position on the road must be marked.

- Do not walk around the scene. Evidence may be lost.

- Keep children away from the accident scene. They may be injured and it could harm them psychologically.

- Give first aid where possible and help the people who are most seriously hurt first.

- Do not give injured people anything to drink or move them unless there is danger of fire.

- Where possible, keep the injured warm with blankets.

- Try to keep the injured calm and keep talking to them so they do not panic.

- Follow the further steps as set out above for an accident without injured people.

> **Useful items to keep in a car**
> A torch
> A first aid kit
> Contact numbers of emergency services
> Contact numbers of towing services
> Warning triangles
> A blanket
> A fire extinguisher
> Chalk
> Surgical gloves

Tips for saving fuel

- Take fuel consumption into account when buying a new car.

- Drive as little as possible and join lift clubs where the members take turns to use their cars.

- Ensure that your type pressure is correct. If the tyre pressure is too low, the fuel consumption increases.

- Do not overfill your fuel tank.

- Do not overload your car.

- Do not start your car before you are ready to depart.

- Do not use the clutch unnecessarily at stop streets – use your hand brake.

- Switch off your car when you are stuck in traffic for long periods.

- Keep the windows closed while you are driving. Open windows reduce speed and cause higher petrol consumption.

- Drive smoothly and not too fast. The faster you drive, the more fuel is used.

- Plan shopping trips so everything can be bought in one trip.

- Plan ahead when you drive so there is more than one reason to drive. If you pick up the children from school, for example, do your shopping and pay accounts at the same time.

- Try to drive as little as possible at peak times.

- Do not look for a parking place for a long time – take the first available.

- Remove roof racks when they are not in use.

- Use the car's air conditioning as little as possible.

Vehicle repair
- Write down the odometer reading so you can check that car has not been driven unnecessarily.
- Be specific about what you want done and what problems you have with the car.
- Ask for a written quotation or that you are phoned before any repair work is done. Make sure that no work is done on the vehicle without your permission.
- When you go to collect the car, check that the job sheet specifies what has been done.
- If work has been done without your permission, you can refuse to pay for it and it must be removed from your invoice.
- Ask to see parts that have been replaced.
- Keep all statements and invoices and get written guarantees.

The development of trains and railway lines in South Africa

1845	The Cape of Good Hope Western Railway is established, but due to a lack of interest no development takes place.
1853	The Cape Town Railways and Dock Company is established.
1858	The Cape Town Railways and Dock Company begins to build a railway from Cape Town to Wellington – it is the first railway line in the then Cape Province.
1859	The first locomotive is delivered to South Africa. It is now on exhibition at Cape Town Station. The Natal Railway Company is established and a railway line of 3,5km is built between Durban and the Point.
1860	The first train in South Africa begins to run from Durban to the Point.
1862	The railway line between Cape Town and Wellington is completed.
1864	The railway line between Cape Town and Wynberg is opened.
1870	The first railway line in the Eastern Cape, between Port Elizabeth and Uitenhage, is built.
1873	The government takes over the two Cape railway companies and Cape Government Railways is born.
1877	Natal Government Railways is established.
1880	The railway line from Durban reaches Pietermaritzburg.
1885	The railway line from Cape Town reaches Kimberley.
1890	The railway line from Cape Town reaches Bloemfontein. The first railway line in the former Transvaal, between Johannesburg and Boksburg, is completed.
1892	Cape Town, Johannesburg, East London and Port Elizabeth are linked by rail.
1896	The first electric trams, imported from America, begin to run in Cape Town.
1898	Durban and Johannesburg are linked by rail.
1910	South African Railways and Harbours is established.
1923	South Africa begins to electrify trains.
1927	The first electric railway line in South Africa, between Ladysmith and Estcourt in what is now KwaZulu-Natal, is opened.
1939	The Blue Train, one of the most luxurious trains in the world, is unveiled.
1949	Steel carriages for main-line trains are used for the first time in South Africa.
1958–1959	The first diesel locomotives are adopted into use.

1972	The withdrawal of steam trains is announced.
1976	A bogie designed by Dr Herbert Scheffel is unveiled and used in all South African railway carriages.
1977	The railway line from Dingleton (Sishen) to Saldanha is completed.
1981	SAR&H becomes the South African Transport Services.
1990	South African Transport Services becomes Transnet.
1991	The last steam train in South Africa is taken out of service in Kimberley.
2006	Work begins on the Gautrain project. The route will link Johannesburg, O.R. Tambo Airport and Pretoria. This speed train will also serve seven other stations on the approximately 80km route.
2007–2009	Luxury speed trains (Business Express trains), meant primarily for daily commuters, are announced in the Western Cape and Gauteng **(see page 195)**.

- The longest train tunnel in South Africa is the Hex River Tunnel – 13,4 km.
- The Dingleton-Saldanha railway line is 861km long and has only three turns. In 1989 the world's longest train took a cargo of iron ore (71 209t) from Dingleton (formerly Sishen) in the Northern Cape to Saldanha on the West Coast. Nine electric locomotives and seven diesel locomotives pulled the 660 trucks of ore. The train was 7,3km long. In 2001 this record was broken by a train in western Australia, which transported 82 000t of iron bars in 682 trucks. The train was 7,35km long.
- In 1996 15 people were trampled to death in a stampede when security guards at Tembisa Station near Johannesburg tried to control a crowd.

South Africa's trains

Apple Express
This historic narrow-gauge railway line, the longest in the world, was completed in 1906. The total length of the railway line is 285km. It was built to transport fruit from the Langkloof area to Port Elizabeth. There was later also a suburban train service on this line that was closed in 1928. These days only a tourist train offers regular rides between Humewood (Port Elizabeth) and Assegaaibos Station just outside Kareedouw. Before 2008 the Apple Express ran irregularly, and then only to Loerie. The train runs over the Van Stadens Bridge (77m high), which is the highest narrow-gauge railway bridge in the world. The old train carriages date from the time of the Cape Government Railways and the Natal Government Railways (before 1910). All the personnel on the train are volunteers. Along the route there is a great variety of accommodation and open-air activities that can be booked.

The Great Train Race, in which athletes in relay teams race against the Apple Express, takes place annually. The first race was in 1980. In 1999 nearly 5 000 athletes took part and the winning team beat the train by just two seconds. The distance is 72km and the race ends in Loerie. In 2005 the race did not take place because of objections from Athletics South Africa, but after a court case it resumed in 2006.

Blue Train
The Blue Train officially acquired its name in 1946. In 1972 a new Blue Train was announced. In 1997 and 1998 two new Blue Trains were adopted into use. The two Blue Trains have space for 74 and 58 passengers respectively. The trains are 336m long and have 16 and 17 carriages respectively. Their top speed is 110km/h. Each compartment has its own bathroom, air conditioning, television and telephone. Each train also has two luxury carriages with three suites, which are much larger than the standard units. The main routes of the Blue Train are Cape Town–Pretoria–Cape Town, Cape Town–Port Elizabeth–Cape Town and Pretoria–Victoria Falls–Pretoria. The Blue Train is also used for special tours. The Blue Train was chosen in 1998 by more than 250 000 travel agents from more than 180 countries as the most luxurious train in the world. In 2009 the standard tariff for a one-way trip from Cape Town to Pretoria was between R9 955 and R17 045 a person.

Choo Tjoe
The Choo Tjoe is a steam train that used to run regularly between Knysna and George. After major floods and mud slides in 2006 the route was changed and now runs from the Dias Museum complex in Mossel Bay to George (or from George to Mossel Bay). There are two journeys a day,

except Sundays. If it is very dry and there is a danger of fire, a diesel locomotive is used.

Luxury speed trains (Business Express trains)

In 2007 luxury speed trains aimed primarily at commuters in Gauteng and the Western Cape were unveiled. In 2009 the fourth train was adopted into service. The four trains run between Cape Town and Khayelitsha, Johannesburg and Soweto, Johannesburg and Pretoria, and Cape Town and the Strand respectively. The trains have comfortable, luxurious seats. There are LCD screens and built-in wifi access. The cabin staff serve complimentary beverages and free newspapers are also available. These are safe trains with security guards on duty. Only monthly tickets are sold for them. More similar trains are being planned.

Metro trains

These are suburban trains that are used in and near the big cities.

Premier Classes

The first Premier Class train was launched in 2001 and could accommodate only 24 passengers. In 2007 a new train was unveiled that can transport 126 people. It is a luxury train and passengers are welcomed in a special lounge at the station before the train departs. The train offers a choice of different sleeping compartments and linen, bathrobes and toiletries are provided. The bathrobes and linen may not be removed. Each compartment has a telephone so food and beverages can be ordered and meals are served in a dining car. All meals are included in the tariff. In 2009 the tariff for a one-way trip from Cape Town to Johannesburg was between R1 380 and R2 250.

Rovos Rail

This private luxury train service was established in 1989. The carriages were collected around the country and rebuilt and restored. Steam, electric and diesel locomotives are used. There are two trains with 20 carriages each that are always in use and a third train with 13 carriages that can be hired. The Edwardian carriages with wooden panelling offer five-star accommodation. The suites have air conditioning, a

personal safe and a fridge full of beverages of the passenger's choice. There is a range of suites of which the most luxurious is about 16m^2 and the less luxurious are around 7m^2. Each train has two dining cars that can accommodate 42 passengers each. The dining cars have a Victorian atmosphere with beautiful woodwork and lamps. Fine porcelain crockery and silver cutlery are used and the food is superb. Rovos Rail claims that these are the most luxurious trains in the world. Excursions are offered at the places where the train stops. A one-way trip from Cape Town to Pretoria takes three days with excursions at Matjiesfontein and Kimberley. In 2009 the cheapest ticket for this trip was R11 000 and the most expensive was R22 000.

Shongololo Express

Since 1995 this luxury train has undertaken tours from Johannesburg and Cape Town to Namibia, Swaziland, Mozambique, Zimbabwe, Botswana and Zambia. Each train also transports a number of air conditioned minibuses with which tourist attractions can be visited. The train has different classes of accommodation, from units with a sit-sleep section and a bathroom to a sleeping compartment without a bathroom. Compartments have enough space for luggage, and linen and towels are provided. Breakfast and dinner is served on the train. In 2009 a tour (one-way) from Cape Town to Windhoek cost between R37 100 and R46 500 a person.

Shosholoza Meyl

This is a very affordable long-distance Spoornet train. Trips to different cities are available. There are six-sleeper units and three-sleeper units. On long trips only four people are booked into a six-sleeper unit. There is a dining car that serves meals one pays for. Each carriage has two toilets and a hot shower. There are also carriages that only have seats and are much cheaper. In 2009 a one-way ticket from Cape Town to Johannesburg in a sleeping car cost R560.

> Since 1 January Spoornet no longer hires out trains to tour companies, and as a result many train tours have had to be stopped. JB Train Tours uses Spoornet's Shosholoza Meyl tourist trains, the luxury Premier Class trains and the Shongololo speed train. Breakfasts and dinners are served on the trains. The dining cars in the tourist trains are air conditioned and there is security on the trains. Tour busses are used with the trains on many of the tours. In 2009 a nine-day tour by train and bus from Cape Town to Johannesburg, the Kruger National Park, Blyde River Canyon, God's Window, Bourke's Potholes, Pilgrims Rest and Sabie and back to Cape Town cost around R6 620 a person.

South African airlines

SAL

1 Time

Comair (South Africa is the concession holder) (www.comair.co.za)
kulula.com (www.kulula.com)
Mango (www.flymango.com)
1Time (www.1time.co.za)
SAA (www.flysaa.com)
South African Airlink (www.saairlink.co.za)
Sunair (website not available – book through travel agents)

kulula.com

New names of South African airports

Old name	New name
Ben Schoeman	East London Airport
B.J. Vorster	Kimberley Airport
D.F. Malan	Cape Town International Airport
H.F. Verwoerd	Port Elizabeth Airport

Cape Town International Airport

Durban International Airport

J.B.M. Hertzog
Johannesburg International Airport (formerly Jan Smuts)
Louis Botha
Pierre van Ryneveldt
P.W. Botha

Bloemfontein Airport
O.R. Tambo Airport

Durban International Airport
Upington Airport
George Airport

Inkwazi, the South African presidential jet

The *Inkwazi* (meaning "fish eagle") is a repurposed Boeing 737-800 with a top speed of 870km/h. The plane can fly about 11 500km without needing to refuel, has a gigantic bed for the president, a lounge and conference room and is equipped for 20 passengers. The *Inkwazi* was rebuilt in Switzerland at a cost of more than R700 million and was adopted into use in 2002. It is managed by the South African Air Force.

- It is said that a South African, Goodman Household, made a controlled flight in 1871, long before the Wright brothers or Lilienthal. It took place at Karkloof near Howick in the current KwaZulu-Natal. After he studied a vulture he'd shot he made a glider of bamboo, oiled paper and steel pipes. With the help of his brother and a few Zulus he "flew" off the rocks near the Howick Falls. He glided about 250m over a cliff and collided with a tree. He broke his leg and, for his mother' sake, stopped his experiments.
- M.J. Weston built the first aeroplane in Africa from 1907 to 1909. In 1911 he flew it for the first time in Kimberley; it was in the air for $8^{1}/_{2}$ minutes. The last version of his aeroplane engine can be seen in the National Museum in Bloemfontein.
- In 1920 two South Africans, Major C.J. Brand and Lieutenant Colonel H.A. van Ryneveld, became the first people to fly from Europe to South Africa.
- In 2001 a South African, Bill Green, became at the age of 89 the oldest person to walk on an aeroplane's wing while in the air.

Luggage allowances on flights

- The allowances sometimes differ between airlines. Therefore, find out what the luggage allowance for your airline is before you leave.

- One personal item such as a laptop or a handbag.

- One suitcase, no heavier than 8kg and no larger than 115cm in total in length, width and height.

Hand luggage

Maximum weight of checked luggage on most international flights

Economy class   20 kg/50 lb
Business class   30 kg/66 lb
First class   40 kg/88 lb
If luggage exceeds the maximum weight, additional fees are charged.

Checked luggage

International security regulations regarding hand luggage

Everyone who travels overseas must adhere to these regulations. They have been in effect since 1 June 2007 at all international airports.

With respect to the following items: liquids, creams, perfume, lip gloss, mascara, oils, aerosols, shaving cream, pastes like toothpaste, gel and any other liquid mixture and any items with a similar composition, the following regulations are applicable:

- Items may not be in a container of more than 100 ml if they are carried in hand luggage.

- The containers must be packed in a transparent, resealable plastic bag of 20 x 20cm. The total capacity must not exceed 1 litre.

- Only one bag per passenger is permitted and the bag must be shown to airport security officers.

- Baby food and milk may be brought along but must be shown to security officers.

- Medicines are permitted but must be shown to security officers. Officers can insist on being provided with a medical prescription.

- Duty-free items may be brought along. These items must be sealed and may not be opened before you have reached your final destination.

- To save time and to make the checking-in process easier, it's better to pack these items in your checked luggage.

Dangerous items that may not be packed in any luggage

- Compressed gasses like butane, oxygen, lighter fluid and scuba equipment.

- Corrosive liquids like acids, alkalis, items containing mercury or batteries.

- Explosives, firearms, ammunition, fireworks and flare pistols.
- Inflammable liquids or solids like matches, cigarette lighters, paint, paint thinners and refills for cigarette lighters.
- Radioactive substances.
- Briefcases with alarm systems installed.
- Oxidising agents like bleach and peroxide.
- Poisons, contaminants and dangerous substances like insect spray, pesticides and live viruses.
- Dangerous articles like magnetic, repellent or irritating material.

Animals on aeroplanes

- Animals can travel in a transport or luggage area with air conditioning and air pressure.
- Only pets are permitted.
- The cage must adhere to the requirements.

Requirements for animal cages

- The cage must be waterproof and safe so that the animal cannot escape.
- There must be sufficient ventilation, but no part of the animal may protrude from the cage.
- The animal must be able to stand and turn around in the cage.
- The cage must be made of metal, wood, hard plastic or another hard substance.
- There must be absorbent material in the cage.
- The handles must be of such a nature that no direct contact need be made with the animal and that the cage can be carried upright.
- The cage must be securely closed but must not be locked.
- The cage must have the words "Living animal" in letters no smaller than 3cm on top and on at least one side.

South Africa's submarines

SAS *Assegaai* (formerly SAS *Johanna van der Merwe*)
SAS *Umkhonto* (formerly SAS *Emily Hobhouse*)
SAS *Spear* (formerly SAS *Maria van Riebeeck*)
SAS *Manthatisi* (new in 2006)
SAS *Charlotte Maxeke* (new in 2007)
SAS *Queen Modjadji* (new in 2008)

The South African tugboat *Smit Amandla* (formerly known as the *John Ross*) is the largest tugboat in the world.

Notable shipping disasters

Achille Lauro

The Italian cruise liner *Achille Lauro* sank on 2 December 1994 off the coast of Somalia after a fire broke out in the engine room on 30 November. There were 1 390 crew and passengers on board. Among the passengers were 257 South Africans. Many of the passengers were still on the ship after the captain and crew had already abandoned it. Some of the crew members had even been wearing life jackets the day before the disaster. The entertainment artist and hero of the *Oceanos*, Moss Hills, was also on the *Achille Lauro* and once again heroically rescued many people from the sea **(see page 204)**. Only two people died and eight were injured.

Figurehead of the Marie Elise (1877)

Apollo Sea

The Chinese ore carrier *Apollo Sea* sank on 20 June 1994 south-west of Dassen Island. The ship had 2 400t of fuel oil on board, which led to the worst-ever oil spill. All 36 crew members were saved. Despite concerted efforts to save as many endangered African penguins as possible, about 10 000 penguins died. The clean-up process cost more than R7 million.

Arniston

The *Arniston*, a British troop ship of 1 498t, ran aground on the rocks near Waenhuiskrans on 30 May 1815. The ship was returning to England from Ceylon with wounded soldiers and sailors on board. It was built in 1794 and was 53,8m long, 13,2m wide and had three decks. The crew saw land and thought it was Table Bay. All efforts to turn the ship back into deeper waters were in vain. The ship quickly broke up once it hit the rocks and of the 350 people on board, only six reached the beach by drifting on planks. Two weeks after the disaster more than 300 bodies were discovered on the beach. Local residents buried the bodies in groups of ten in the dunes. The six survivors walked in the direction of Mossel Bay, but returned to the wreck when they realised they were walking in the wrong direction. There they were found by a farmer's son, stayed for a week on the farm and then left for Cape Town. On 26 June 1815 the survivors arrived in Cape Town.

Wreckage and salvage from the ship were sold in August 1815 at a public auction. In May 1816 a monument was erected on the dunes. It was one of the first monuments in South Africa. With the passage of time, the monument collapsed but the stone memorial was later re-erected on the bluff in Waenhuiskrans. The wreckage that washed up on the beach was gradually covered with sand. The wreck of the *Arniston* was discovered in January 1982 and declared a national monument. Divers recovered porcelain, copper, cannons, glassware, pottery, jewellery and coins from the wreck.

The *Birkenhead*

The HMS *Birkenhead* was a British troop carrier of 1 900t that departed from Simon's Town on 25 February 1852. On board were many British soldiers, seven women, 13 children and a number of horses. Near Danger Point the ship ran aground on rocks. On the lowest deck hundreds of soldiers drowned in their bunks. Of the eight lifeboats, only three could be used. The women, children and as many men as possible were loaded into the boats. The horses were thrown into the sea so they could try to reach the shore by themselves. Although Captain Robert Salmond gave the com-

Birkenhead (painting)

mand that each man should save himself, the soldiers, on the order of their commanding officer Lt. Col. Alexander Seton, stood still on the deck of the ship until it sank 20 minutes later. One lifeboat reached the coast at Hawston. The survivors in the other two boats were picked up by a ship. Altogether 68 people and eight horses reached the shore. Of the 638 people on board, only 193 were eventually saved, which included all the women and children on board. The captain also drowned. Over the years many attempts have been made to recover the stash of gold that was apparently on the *Birkenhead*, but nothing of value has ever been found.

- The *Birkenhead* disaster is world famous because it established the tradition of "women and children first".
- The Birkenhead Brewery is at Stanford, near Hermanus.

The *Grosvenor*

The *Grosvenor* had 150 people and, according to legend, billions of rand in treasure on board. The ship sank on 4 August 1782 off the Wild Coast near Port Elizabeth. The crew succeeded in getting a cable to the beach and some people reached the shore by hanging on to the cable. All the women and children reached

Grosvenor

the shore safely. The castaways decided, under the leadership of Captain John Coxon, to walk to the Cape. On the way they were attacked and their provisions were stolen. The sailors decided to go on ahead and reached the Cape. Although the Dutch were at war with the British, they sent a party to look for the other survivors. However, most of the survivors were never seen again.

Various people and companies have tried unsuccessfully to find the treasure of the *Grosvenor*. An attempt was even made to dig a tunnel to the wreck. All that has been found thus far is a number of silver and gold coins and a few cannons. Some of the cannons can be seen at the Old Fort in Durban, in a park in Port St Johns, at the Royal Hotel in Lusikisiki and in the museum in Umtata in the Eastern Cape.

The *Oceanos*

The luxury Greek cruise liner the *Oceanos* departed from East London for Durban on 31 August 1991 with 581 passengers and crew. Just a few hours later a distress signal was received from the ship. It had begun to sink in stormy seas off the Transkei coast. The captain and crew abandoned ship first and left the passengers to their fate. The ship's entertainers, Moss and Tracy Hills, put a rescue plan in action. The SA Navy and SA Air Force also helped with rescue operations. Many passengers could not find a place in the lifeboats and had to stay on board. Some were saved by SA Air Force helicopters only minutes before the ship sank. It was the biggest sea rescue operation ever on the coast of Africa and it is considered a miracle that there was no loss of life.

Treasure

The Chinese ore carrier MV *Treasure* sank on 23 June 2000 near Melkbosstrand. The ship was on its way from Brazil to the Far East and had 140 000t iron ore and 1 300t bunker fuel on board. The ship was first allowed to moor in Table Bay, but after divers discovered a hole of about 10m by 19m in a cargo hold, the tugboat *John Ross* (*Smit Amandla*) tried to tow the carrier to deeper waters. The tow rope broke and the *Treasure* sank. All the crew members were rescued in time. Coast-guard vessels immediately began to clean up the oil spill and conservationists and volunteers began to catch the penguins covered in oil and clean them. On Dassen Island and Robben Island there are large breeding colonies of the endangered African penguins. It took months to clean the penguins and release them, and many were released in Port Elizabeth to temporarily avoid the pollution. It was the largest sea rescue in the world and only 10% of the 20 000 penguins that were cleaned and released, died **(see page 233)**.

The *Waratah*

The *Waratah*, an Australian steam ship, was built in 1908 in Scotland. On 26 July 1909 the *Waratah* left Durban for Cape Town. There were 211 people on board. The following day the vessel was spotted by the cargo ship *Clan Macintyre* and it seemed as though the ship was steaming ahead normally. The weather then deteriorated drastically – the captain of the *Clan Macintyre* stated that it was the worst storm he had ever experienced. The *Waratah* was scheduled to arrive in Cape Town on 29 July but failed to do so. The ship had vanished without a trace – no wreckage washed up on shore and search attempts by British and Australian ships were fruitless. The search was abandoned on 23 August. There have been several claims that the wreck of the *Waratah* had been found, but the claims could never be substantiated.

- In 1722 ten sailing ships came unmoored in Table Bay. The ships were wrecked on the beach at Woodstock and six hundred people drowned. Poor people gathered some of the wreckage on the beach, only to be arrested by Kompanjie officials and hanged from nine gallows right on the beach.
- In 1766 the captain of the *Meermin* let slaves move around freely instead of keeping them chained below deck. The slaves eventually took over the ship. The captain regained control of the ship on the condition that they sail to Madagascar. At Agulhas the captain convinced them they were near Madagascar and that 50 slaves should go ashore and light bonfires as a sign to the other slaves to come ashore as well. The captain had in the meantime written a note about what had happened, sealed it in a bottle and thrown it overboard. The bottle washed up on the beach. Farmers did what the captain asked and lit bonfires on the beach. This was the sign the other slaves were waiting for. Instead of using the rowboats, they cut the anchor so the ship could drift to the shore. The captain and crew watched helplessly as the ship broke up on the rocks. No significant loss of life occurred and 112 slaves were taken to the Cape.

- During the night of 17 May 1865, 30 ships ran aground on the beach at Woodstock. Fires were made on the beach to help survivors reach the shore. More than 50 people drowned. One steam ship, the *Athens*, managed to sail out again, but was dashed to pieces on the rocks at Mouille Point. Everyone on board drowned.
- The *Oriental Pioneer* (35 746t) ran aground on the rocks near Struisbaai in July 1974. There was no loss of life. Neither the owners nor the insurers would cooperate with the police and no attempts were made to salvage the vessel.
- In May 2009 the MSC *Melody*, a luxury cruise liner that often sails in South African waters, was attacked by a motorboat of armed pirates near the Seychelles. The cruise liner was heading for Italy. There were 114 South Africans on board. The ship's security personnel fired shots in the air and used high pressure fire hoses. The ship also executed zigzag manoeuvres to create high bow waves. This presented difficulties to the pirates' smaller boat and the pirates had to give up the chase. Nobody was injured.

8. ECONOMY AND FINANCES

The South African currency

Coins

Value	Metal	Picture (front)	Year issued
1c	Red copper	Sparrow	1990
2c	Red copper	Fish eagle	1991
5c	Red copper	Blue crane	1990
10c	Brass	Arum lily	1990
20c	Brass	Protea	1992
50c	Brass	Strelitzia	1991
R1	Nickel	Springbok	1991
R2	Nickel	Kudu	1989
R5	Nickel	Black wildebeest	1994
R5	Bronze and silver	Black wildebeest	2004

- The coins are made of steel and plated with copper, nickel or bronze.
- A.L. Sutherland designed the front of the coins.
- Coins are minted by a private company, the South African Mint Company (Mint), in Gateway near Pretoria.
- A new R5 coin was released in 2004 to make counterfeiting harder.

Banknotes

Value	Colour	Design (front)	Year issued
R10	Green	Rhinoceros	1993
R20	Brown	Elephant	1993
R50	Red	Lion	1992
R100	Blue	Buffalo	1994
R200	Orange	Leopard	1994

- The rand is named after the Witwatersrand, which is known as the "Rand".
- The rand replaced the pound on 14 February 1961 when it became South Africa's official currency.

New South African banknotes in 2005

The new notes of 2005 look much like the previous ones, with the same paper, sizes, motifs and colours.

Changes to the new banknotes

- The coat of arms appears on all the notes.
- The wording on the front of the notes is in English, and on the back in two other official languages.
- The watermark is smaller.
- The "R" that could be seen whenever the note was held up to the light, has been changed to the denomination of the note.
- The unique number of the note has been moved to two places on the back of the note.
- The "South African Reserve Bank" in micro letters appears in English next to the animal's ear.
- Geometric symbols for those with impaired sight have been changed and made clearer.

Languages on the back of the bank notes

Note	Languages
R10	Afrikaans and Swazi
R20	Tswana and Ndebele
R50	Xhosa and Venda
R100	Northern Sotho and Tsonga
R200	Zulu and Southern Sotho

Geometric shapes on the front for those with impaired sight

Note	Shape
R10	Diamond
R20	Square
R50	Circle
R100	Elongated hexagon
R200	Standard hexagon

Previous currencies

1. ZAR coins from 1892
2. British pound from 1923
3. Decimal rand and cent from 1961
4. Updated electroplated coins from 1990
5. Updated bank notes from 1992
6. Current bank notes from 2005

Before money came into use, a barter system was used. After 1652, for example, cattle from the Khoi were exchanged for iron, copper, tobacco and alcohol.

Personal budget

- Make a list of all major expenses such as a house mortgage and car payments.
- Estimate what amount is spent monthly and annually on expenses such as tax, water, electricity, telephone, car maintenance, petrol and food.
- Budget for relaxation, entertainment and eating out.
- Every month, set aside an amount for holidays or unexpected expenses.
- If your expenses are greater than your income, you are living beyond your means.
- Always give an amount to charity – buy food for a hungry person or animal.
- Where two people are involved, money should be jointly managed.
- If you differ about money matters, try to find a compromise.
- Each person must have some personal freedom. Budget so that each person has an allowance to spend as they wish.
- Keep to your budget.

Financial tips

- Live simply and be content with what you have. Don't buy luxury items just because your neighbours and friends have them. Don't covet things all the time.
- Be positive about saving and save as much as possible. Try to save at least 10% of your income every month.
- Plan short term goals like a great holiday – it will motivate you to save a bit extra.
- Leave your credit card at home when you go shopping.
- Make a list before you go grocery shopping and do not buy unnecessary items. It is a good idea to draw up a menu for the week and then only buy what you need.
- Keep an eye on newspapers for bargains.
- Buy vegetables and fruit loose – pre-packed produce is usually more expensive.
- Do not go grocery shopping when you are hungry.
- Look at the price per kilogram and compare the products.
- No-name products are usually cheaper than those with well-known brand names.
- Buy in bulk, but make sure it's cheaper – sometimes it isn't.
- Do not use your credit card to pay off other debt.

- Do not open unnecessary accounts, for example clothing accounts.
- Do not create debt. Save until you can buy things with cash.
- Do not invest in a pyramid scheme. It is illegal and usually collapses.
- Do not lend money to friends. It is difficult to say no, but there is always a good chance that it can seriously damage the friendship.
- Do not accept increased credit limits.
- Avoid places where gambling takes place.
- It is dangerous to take money out of your house mortgage. If the interest rate increases, you could struggle to keep up with the bond repayments.
- Do not use pension money for other things.
- Do not leave all the decisions to a financial advisor. Make sure you have all the information about the products and make final decisions about your money yourself.
- Do not borrow money to invest in the stock market.
- Do not sell shares when the stock market falls.
- Do not purchase a financial product until you are sure of the costs associated with it. Negotiate for lower costs.
- Do not invest in a product you do not understand.
- Do not invest in unfamiliar institutions that make unrealistic promises. If it looks too good to be true, it probably is.
- Making extra payments on a house mortgage is an excellent way to save.
- Financial decisions must be made objectively and soberly.
- Make provision for your children's studies and start planning for your retirement from an early age.
- When you get older, your investments must be more conservative.

Children and finances

- Children see how their parents work with money, and therefore parents should always set a good example. Children should realise that money must be earned and they should get pocket money as soon as they can count. Teenagers should have a budget instead of pocket money, and it should be set by the child and parents together.
- Give your children a fixed amount of pocket money until the age of ten. Emphasise that a portion of the pocket money should be saved for something the child really wants and must buy for himself.
- Children must have their own bank account as early as possible so they can learn to manage their money themselves.

- Set up a quarterly budget with a teenager. Decide together what the money should cover. The amount should be determined by your lifestyle.

- Be realistic and find out what things cost that the child must buy. Too little money will dishearten the child and too much pocket money encourages recklessness.

- Do not make too many money rules. Give the child the freedom to spend his money on things that are important to him.

- Older teens must be encouraged to save and invest.
- Encourage children to do weekend and vacation work.
- Children can do chores for extra money, but it must be kept apart from their set allowance.
- If you lend money to your child, let him sign a "contract" that determines how and when he must pay it back.
- If pocket money is managed irresponsibly, for example on alcohol or drugs, it can be temporarily stopped.

Bank costs

- Compare the costs of different banks.
- Banks are often prepared to negotiate about bank costs.
- Study your bank statements and make sure you are not paying too much in bank costs.
- Make sure that you know what you will pay for a specific account.
- Make sure that every mistake on your bank statement is corrected, even if it is a small amount.
- Plan your transactions so that you need to do as few of them as possible.
- Electronic bank transactions are much cheaper.
- Withdraw large amounts of cash rather than small amounts.
- Ensure that you have enough money in your account so you don't have to pay unnecessary fines or interest.
- Keep a record of all correspondence with the bank.
- If you are not happy with the bank's service, change your bank.

9. PLANTS AND ANIMALS

Common weeds and alien plants

Jakaranda tree

Port Jackson

Name	Scientific name	Area of origin
American blackberry	*Rubus cuneifolius*	North America
Australian blackwood	*Acacia longifolia*	Australia
Babylon willow	*Sesbania punicea*	Brazil
Black wattle	*Cascuta campestris*	North America
Blackjacks	*Tribulus terrestris*	China
Brazilian rattlebox	*Centaurea cyanus*	Europe
Castor oil tree	*Oxalis corniculata*	Asia, Europe
Cluster pine	*Acacia pycnantha*	Australia
Common thorn apple	*Hakea gibbosa*	Australia
Cornflower	*Hakea suaveolens*	Australia
Cosmos	*Hakea sericea*	Australia
Creeping woodsorrel	*Jacaranda mimosifolia*	Argentina
Dodder	*Hypericum perforatum*	Europe
Dubbeltjie, Devil's thorn	*Tagetes minuta*	South America
Golden wattle	*Salvinia molesta*	Zimbabwe/Zambia
Honey mesquite	*Ricinus communis*	Central Africa
Jacaranda	*Bidens pilosa*	North America
Jointed cactus	*Galinsoga parviflora*	Central America
Kakiebos, khaki weed	*Bidens formosa*	South America
Kariba weed	*Lantana camara*	South America
Knoppieskruid, gallant soldier	*Opuntia aurantiaca*	South America

Name	Scientific name	Area of origin
Lantana	*Melia azedarach*	Asia
Long-leaved wattle	*Argemone mexicana*	Mexico
Mesquite	*Araujia sericifera*	Peru
Mexican poppy	*Prosopis glandulosa*	Americas
Moth catcher	*Nerium oleander*	Europe
Oleander	*Datura stramonium*	North America
Oleander	*Chromolaena odorata*	South America
Paraffin bush	*Campuloclinium macrocephalum*	Brazil
Pompom weed	*Acacia saligna*	Australia
Port Jackson	*Eucalyptus camaldulensis*	Australia
Portulaca	*Striga lutea*	Namibia
River red gum	*Acacia cyclops*	Australia
Rock Hakea	*Nerium oleander*	Europe
Rooiblom, witch weed	*Acacia dealbata*	Australia
Rooikrans	*Portulaca quadrifida*	India
Silky hakea	*Pinus pinaster*	Europe
Silver wattle	*Albizia lophantha*	Australia
St John's wort	*Prosopis glandulosa*	North and Central America
Stinkboom, silk acacia	*Acacia melanoxylon*	Australia
Sweet hakea	*Acacia mearnsii*	Australia
Syringa	*Salix babylonica*	China
Turkish fig	*Opuntia ficus-indica*	Mexico
Water hyacinth	*Eichornia crassipes*	South and Central America
Wild tobacco	*Solanum mauritianum*	South America

Lantana

Oleander

In 1978 poison from the castor oil tree, known as ricin, was used to murder Georgi Markov, a Bulgarian journalist who criticised the Bulgarian government. He was stabbed with the tip of an umbrella at Waterloo Station in London. A pellet was found in his leg that allegedly contained poison extracted from castor beans.

Popular indigenous trees, shrubs, flowers and climbers

Common name	Botanical name	Details
Trees		
Karee	*Searsia lancea*	A lovely dense shade tree with a soft, round canopy and olive-green leaves. It has a textured dark-brown trunk. A hardy and drought-resistant tree. Needs full sun and moderate water. Flowers: July–September.
Coral tree	*Erythrina lysistemon*	A fast grower and very drought resistant. The trunk is smooth and the canopy is sparse. The branches and leaves have thorns. In the spring the tree is covered in beautiful bright red flowers. It has an aggressive root system and should not be planted near buildings. Needs full sun and little water. Flowers: July–August.
Olive	*Olea Europeea* subsp. *africana*	A good shade tree or screen plant with a dense, wide canopy. The leaves are dark green on top and greyish underneath. The tree has rows of white-green flowers. The blackish fruit is eaten by birds and animals. A hardy plant that grows well in dry areas. Needs full sun and little water. Flowers: October–February

Maidenhair fern

Barberton daisy

Common name	Botanical name	Details
Trees		
Outeniqua yellowwood	*Podocarpus falcatus*	The tallest South African forest tree, it can grow up to 60m high. The tree has small, dark-green leaves with a greyish cast. The wood is sought after for furniture, ceilings, floors and window frames. The tree grows about a metre a year. Needs full sun and moderate water.
Natal mahogany	*Trichilia emetica*	A lovely tree with a dark green, dense canopy. The creamy green flowers and fruit attract many kinds of birds. It is a fast grower and an outstanding shade and screen tree. Needs full sun and moderate water. Flowers: August–October.
Silver tree	*Leucadendron argenteum*	A fast grower and lovely decorative tree with silky, silver-grey leaves. The male flowers are an apricot colour with a silver sheen and the female flowers are silvery cones. Needs full sun and moderate water. Flowers: August–September.
Sweet thorn	*Acacia karroo*	A fast grower and a good shade tree. White thorns and golden yellow flowers. Monkey, birds, livestock and wild animals eat the flowers and pods. Needs full sun and moderate water. Flowers: October–February.
Sycamore fig	*Ficus sycomorus*	A slow grower with a very large, dark-green, wide-branching canopy. A good shade tree for very large gardens and farms. The figs are eaten by many birds and animals. The figs make a mess when they fall and the roots can damage buildings. Needs full sun and plenty of water. Fruits: July–December.
White milkwood	*Sideroxylon inerme*	A slow grower with a large, dense, wide-branching canopy. The small golden yellow flowers have an unpleasant smell. A good shade or screen tree. An ideal tree for a coastal garden and the thick canopy offers protection for birds. Needs full sun and plenty of water. Flowers: January–July.

Common name	Botanical name	Details
Trees		
White stinkwood	*Celtis africana*	A common and widespread tree on the Highveld. Very resistant to drought and fast growing. The tree has small, light yellow flowers. It offers shade for livestock. Birds and animals eat the fruit. A good shade tree in the garden. Needs full sun and moderate water. Flowers: August–October.
Shrubs, flowers and climbers		
African daisy	*Dimorphotheca jucunda*	Climbing shrub and groundcover. Lovely pink or purplish daisy flowers that only open in sunshine. The plant spreads quickly. Needs full sun or partial shade and moderate water. Perennial. Flowers: March–September
African daisy	*Arctotis fastuosa*	Herbaceous shrub. A bushy shrub with grey-green leaves and lovely orange daisy flowers on long stems. The innermost petals have a dark-brown fleck at the base. Needs full sun and moderate water. Annual. Flowers: September–October.
African iris	*Dietes bicolor*	Small shrub. Light-green, tape-like leaves and masses of yellow flowers with black spots on long stems. A very popular shrub. Needs full sun and moderate water. Flowers: October–January.

Bietou

Aloe

Afican daisy

Livingstone daisy

Common name	Botanical name	Details
Shrubs, flowers and climbers		
African lily	*Agapanthus africanus*	Flowering plant. A fast grower with ribbon-shaped leaves and round heads with white and blue tubular flowers on long stems. Needs full sun or partial shade and moderate water. Perennial. Flowers: December–March.
Agapanthus	*Agapanthus praecox*	Flowering plant. A fast-growing and hardy plant with long narrow leaves and round flower heads with blue or white tubular flowers on long stems. Needs full sun or partial shade and moderate water. Perennial. Flowers: December–January.
Aloe	*Aloe ferox*	Shrub. A slow grower with a single stem, thick, thorny, fleshy leaves and tubular, orange-red flowers. The sap of the leaves is used in medicine and beauty products. An outstanding shrub for a rock garden. Needs full sun and moderate water. Flowers: May–September.
Barberton daisy	*Gerbera jamesonii*	Flowering plant. A plant with lovely daisy flowers on long stems. Various colours are available. Grows fairly quickly. Needs full sun and moderate water. Perennial. Flowers: September–November

Common name	Botanical name	Details
Shrubs, flowers and climbers		
Bietou, Tickberry	*Chrysanthemoides monilifera*	Climbing plant. A fast and easy grower. grey-green foliage and yellow daisy flowers. In the past, the berries were an important source of food for the Khoi people. Excellent for a hedge or windbreak at the coast. Needs full sun and moderate water. Perennial. Flowers in spring.
Black-eyed susan	*Thunbergia alata*	Climbing plant. A fast and easy grower. Between the small, heart-shaped leaves are a mass of trumpet-shaped orange or yellow flowers with a black spot in the middle. Needs full sun and moderate water. Perennial. Flowers in summer.
Blue daisy	*Felicia amelloides*	Small flowering shrub. A hardy, fast-growing plant with small leaves and lovely blue daisy flowers with yellow crowns. Spreads easily and must be cut back regularly. Needs full sun or partial shade and moderate water. Perennial. Flowers: September–March.
Cancer bush, balloon pea	*Sutherlandia frutescens*	Small shrub. A fast grower with silver-grey foliage, orange sweet pea-like flowers and pinkish-red petals. This shrub has many medicinal uses. Needs full sun and little water. Flowers: July–December.

Agapanthus

Black-eyed susan

Strelitzia

Tanager gazania

Common name	Botanical name	Details
Shrubs, flowers and climbers		
Cape dandelion, Cape marigold	*Arctotheca calendula*	Groundcover. A hardy plant with green leaves that are grey on the underside. Lovely yellow daisy flowers are constantly produced. Spreads very quickly and is resistant to drought. Needs full sun and little water. Perennial. Flowers at any time.
Cape honeysuckle	*Tecoma capensis*	Shrub. A fast grower that is drought resistant. A large dark-green shrub with lovely orange, yellow, salmon or red trumpet-shaped flowers. The shrub is a climber that spreads, and must be pruned to keep it neat. Needs full sun and moderate water. Flowers in spring and autumn.
Coral creeper	*Barleria repens*	Small shrub. A fast grower with shiny, light green leaves and purple or pink-red tubular flowers. The plant spreads easily. Needs partial shade and moderate water. Flowers: February–April.
Ericas	*Erica* species	Small shrub. Small, needle-like leaves. Flowers can be bell- or lantern-shaped or tubular. Various colours are available. Deadhead regularly. Needs full sun and moderate water. Flowering times vary.

Common name	Botanical name	Details
Shrubs, flowers and climbers		
Gladiolus	*Gladiolus* species	Bulb. A fast grower with flowers in various colours. Bulbs must be kept dry until they are replanted. Various species are available. Needs full sun and moderate water. Perennial. Flowers at various times.
Hen-and-chickens, spider plant	*Chlorophytum comosum*	Groundcover. A fast grower that spreads quickly. Soft, ligulate green leaves with white in the middle. Leaves root where they touch the ground and form new plants. Needs shade or partial shade and moderate water. Perennial.
Honey euryops	*Euryops virgineus*	Small shrub. A dense, bushy shrub with fine, dark-green foliage and masses of small yellow flowers. Needs full sun and moderate water. Flowers: July–September.
King protea	*Protea cynaroides*	Shrub. A compact, hardy shrub that grows to about 1m. It has the largest flower head of all the proteas and is South Africa's national flower. Adult plants can survive veld fires. Needs full sun and moderate water. Flowers: May–December.
Livingstone daisy	*Dorotheanthus bellidiformis*	Small flowering plant. The plant has small, multicoloured flowers in different colour combinations. Needs full sun and very little water. Annual. Flowers in spring.
Maidenhair fern	*Adiantum capillus-veneris*	Fern. A delicate fern with flat, heart-shaped foliage on thin, black stems. Needs shade or partial shade and lots of water. Perennial.

Cape honeysuckle

Blue daisy

Cape honeysuckle

Common name	Botanical name	Details
Shrubs, flowers and climbers		
Namaqualand daisy	*Dimorphotheca sinuata*	Flowering plant. South Africa's most popular spring flower. Its large orange or yellow flowers open only in sunlight and always turn to the sun. Needs full sun and moderate water. Annual. Flowers: July–mid September.
Nemesia	*Nemesia strumosa*	Small flowering plant. Bilabiate flowers in a variety of colours grow on erect stalks. Lovely in gardens, rock gardens or pots. Various species are available. Needs full sun and moderate water. Annual. Flowers in spring.
Pincushion flower	*Scabiosa africana*	Flowering plant. A fast grower with grey-green foliage and lovely light purple flowers on long stems. It can also be used as a groundcover. Needs full sun and moderate water. Perennial. Flowers: September–February.
Pincushion protea	*Leucospermum cordifolium*	Small shrub. A neat bush with salmon pink to apricot-coloured flowers. Needs full sun and moderate water. Flowers: July–December.
Pink sage	*Orthosiphon labiatus*	Small shrub. A fast grower with heart-shaped leaves and light pinkish-purple flowers. Prefers morning sun and then shade. Needs moderate water. Flowers: November–April.

Common name	Botanical name	Details
Shrubs, flowers and climbers		
Plectranthus	*Plectranthus fruticosus*	Small shrub. A fast grower with big heart-shaped leaves and masses of pink or blueish purple flowers on spikes. Needs partial shade and plenty of water. Flowers: December–February.
Queen sugarbush	*Protea magnifica*	Shrub. A round shrub with grey-green leaves and pink flowers with soft white hair. The middle hairs are often black or brown at the tips. A hardy shrub, but must be planted in well-drained soil. Needs full sun and moderate water. Flowers: June–January.
Red flush, red vygie	*Lampranthus coccineus*	Flowering plant. A fast growing climbing plant with small fleshy leaves and shiny, bright red flowers that only open on sunny days. Many other related species are available. Needs full sun and little water. Flowers in spring.
Red hot poker	*Kniphofia praecox*	Flowering plant. The plant has ribbon-like leaves with orange flowers on long stems that become yellow when they open. Grows relatively fast. Needs full sun and plenty of water. Flowers in winter.
Star jasmine	*Jasminum multipartitum*	Climber. Dark green foliage with white jasmine flowers that are dark pink underneath. The flowers attract many birds. Used for herbal tea and pot pourri. The plant must be staked. Needs full sun to partial shade and moderate water. Perennial. Flowers: August–January.
Strelitzia	Strelitzia reginae	A slow grower with leaves that look like those of the banana tree and orange and blue flowers that resemble birds. It is one of South Africa's most successful export products. It is wind-resistant and suitable for coastal gardens. Full to partial shade and moderate water are necessary. Flowers: March–October.
Sun marigold	*Dimorphotheca pluvialis*	Flowering plant. The plant has narrow, blunt, toothed leaves and large, white daisy flowers that only open in sunshine and always turn to the sun. Needs full sun and moderate water. Annual. Flowers: July–mid September.

Common name	Botanical name	Details
Shrubs, flowers and climbers		
Tanager gazania	*Gazania krebsiana*	Flowering plant. A fast grower. It has daisy flowers on long stems that only open in sunshine. Available in many colours. Perennial. Flowers in spring and summer.
Tree aloe	*Aloe arborescens*	Shrub. A round, fast-growing shrub with fleshy, blue-grey leaves and bright red tubular flowers on spikes. Needs full sun and little water. Flowers: May–July.
Yellow bush daisy	*Euryops pectinatus*	Small shrub. A fast grower with silver-grey leaves and bright yellow flowers. Needs full sun and moderate water. Perennial. Flowers: June–October.

South Africa's trees of the year (2001–2015)

To make the public more aware of South Africa's indigenous trees, special attention is given to two or three trees every year during National Arbor Week.

Year	Scientific name	Common name
2001	*Loxostylis alata* *Ptaeroxylon obliquum*	Tarwood Sneezewood
2002	*Pittosporum viridiflorum* *Alberta magna*	Cheesewood Natal flame bush
2003	*Searsia chirindensis* *Pterocarpus angolensis*	Red currant Wild teak
2004	*Kirkia acuminata* *Kirkia wilmsii* *Combretum bracteosum*	White seringa Mountain seringa Hiccup nut
2005	*Schefflera umbellifera* *Adansonia digitata*	False cabbage tree Baobab
2006	*Burchellia bubalina* *Raphia australis*	Wild pomegranate Kosi palm
2007	*Searsia pyroides* *Pavetta schumanniana*	Common wild currant Poison bride's bush
2008	*Harpephyllum caffrum* *Diospyros whyteana* *Markhamia zanzibarica*	Wild plum Bladdernut Bell bean tree

Year	Scientific name	Common name
2009	*Acacia galpinii* *Halleria lucida* *Pterocarpus rotundifolius*	Monkey thorn Tree fuchsia Round-leaved teak
2010	*Acacia xanthophloea* *Rothmannia capensis* *Rothmannia globosa* *Cladostemon kirkii*	Fever tree Cape gardenia Bell garden Tonga kerrie
2011	*Pappea capensis* *Genus Pavetta* *Nuxia congesta*	Jacket plum Bride's bushes Common wild elder
2012	*Syzygium cordatum* *Protorhus longifolia* *Bruguiera gymnorrhiza*	Water berry Red beech Black mangrove
2013	*Virgilia oroboides* *Grewia occidentalis* *Barringtonia racemosa*	Blossom tree / Keurboom Cross berry Powder puff tree
2014	*Genus Heteropyxis* *Vepris lanceolata*	Lavender trees White ironwood
2015	*Combretum kransii* *Heteromorpha trifoliata*	Forest bushwillow Parsley tree

The first Arbor Day was held in 1983. Since 1999 Arbor Week has been celebrated every year between 1 and 7 September.

Baobab (2005)

The gestation of animals

Animal	Gestation	Number of offspring
Aardvark (*Orycteropus afer*)	7 months	1
Aardwolf (*Proteles cristatus*)	95–110 days	2–4
Baboon (*Papio ursinus*)	187 days	1
Bat, common slit-faced (*Nycteris thebaica*)	5 months	1
Blesbok (*Damaliscus dorcas phillipsi*)	246 days	1
Blue wildebeest (*Connochaetes taurinus*)	8–8½ months	1
Bontebok (*Damaliscus dorcas dorcas*)	8 months	1
Buffalo (*Syncerus caffer*)	11–11½ months	1
Bushbaby (*Galago senegalensis*)	4 months	2
Bushbuck (*Tragelaphus scriptus*)	6–6½ months	1
Bush pig (*Patamochoerus porcus*)	4 months	3–4
Caracal (*Felis caracal*)	70–78 days	2–4
Cat, domestic (*Felis domesticus*)	63 days	2–5
Cheetah (*Acinonyx jubatus*)	90–95 days	1–5
Cow	9–9½ months	1–2
Dassie (*Procavia capensis*)	7–8 months	1–3
Dog (*Canis familiaris*)	53–71 days	4–8
Dolphin (*Delphinus delphis*)	10–11 months	1
Donkey (*Equus asinus*)	12 months	1
Duiker (*Sylvicapra grimmia*)	3 months	1

Squirrel, 40–44 days

Elephant, 22 months

Animal	Gestation	Number of offspring
Eland (*Taurotragus oryx*)	8–9 months	1
Elephant (*Loxodonta africana*)	22 months	1
Gemsbok (*Oryx gazella*)	9 months	1
Genet cat (*Genetta genetta*)	10–11 weeks	2–4
Giraffe (*Giraffa camelopardalis*)	15 months	1
Goat (*Capra hircus*)	145–155 days	1–2
Ground pangolin (*Manis temminckii*)	5 months	1
Grysbok (*Raphicerus melanotis*)	6 months	1
Hare, Cape/Brown (*Lepus capensis*)	1½ months	1–2
Hedgehog (*Erinaceus frontalis*)	1½ months	2–4
Hippopotamus (*Hippopotamus amphibius*)	8 months	1
Honey badger (*Mellivora capensis*)	6–7 months	1–4
Horse	329–345 days	1
Hyena, brown (*Hyaena brunnea*)	3 months	1–4
Impala (*Aepyceros melampus*)	194–200 days	1
Impala (*Aepyceros melampus*)	6½–7 months	1
Jackal, Bat-eared (*Otocyon megalotis*)	51–63 days	4–6
Jackal, red (*Canis mesomelas*)	51–63 days	4
Jackal, silver (*Vulpes chama*)	51–63 days	1–4
Klipspringer (*Oreotragus oreotragus*)	6–7 months	1
Kudu (*Tragelaphus strepsiceros*)	7 months	1
Leopard (*Panthera pardus*)	90–100 days	2–3
Lion (*Phanthera leo*)	14–15 weeks	1–4
Meerkat (*Suricata suricata*)	77 days	2–4
Mole rat, Cape dune (*Bathyergus suillus*)	2–2½ months	1–4
Mongoose, Cape grey (*Galerella pulverulenta*)	50 days	2–4
Monkey (*Cersopithecus pygerythrus*)	7 months	1
Mouse	19–31 days	2–8
Njala (*Tragelaphus angasii*)	7 months	1
Oribi (*Ourebia ourebi*)	7 months	1
Otter, Cape (*Aonyx capensis*)	60–70 days	1–2
Pig (*Sus domesticus*)	112–115 days	8–15
Polecat, African (*Ictonyx striatus*)	1½ months	1–3

Animal	Gestation	Number of offspring
Porcupine (Hystrix cristata)	2 months	1–4
Rabbit (Oryctolagus cuniculus)	29–35 days	4–6
Rat	3 weeks	6–12
Rhinoceros, black (Diceros bicornisen)	15–16 months	1
Rhinoceros, white (Ceratotherium simum)	16 months	1
Riverine rabbit (Bunolagus monticularis)	35–36 days	1
Sable antelope (Hippotragus niger)	8–9 months	1
Seal, Cape fur (Arctocephalus pusillus)	8–10 months	1
Seal, elephant (Mirounga leonina)	8–10 months	1
Serval (Felis serval)	3½ months	1–3
Sheep	5 months	1–2
Springhare (Pedetes capensis)	2–3 months	1–3
Springbok (Antidorcas marsupialis)	6 months	1
Squirrel (Sciurus carolinensis)	40–44 days	1–3
Steenbok (Raphicerus campestris)	5½ months	1
Warthog (Phacochoerus aethipicus)	5½ months	1–5
Whale, blue (Balaenoptera musculus)	11 months	1
Wild dog (Lycaon pictus)	2–2½ months	7–10
Wildcat (Felis lybica)	2 months	2–5
Zebra, Cape mountain (Equus zebra zebra)	12 months	1

The feeding of small kittens and puppies

Pet shops and vets usually have excellent substitute products for cat and dog milk. If none is available, use the following formulae:

Formula for kittens

120ml Ideal milk
120ml water
1 egg yolk
1 teaspoon honey
1–2 drops Vi-Daylin
Mix well

Formula for puppies

1 tin Ideal milk
2 cups water
1 cup yoghurt (full cream)
1 dessert spoon honey
1 dessert spoon mayonnaise
1–2 egg yolks
Mix well

- Newborn kittens and puppies must be fed every two hours.
- Use a dropper or small bottle with a teat.
- Make sure the opening in the teat is big enough. Do not cut a hole in the teat; rather cut a slit with scissors.
- The mixture must be lukewarm.
- Be wary of over-feeding.
- Rub the excretory organs lightly with a warm, damp cloth after each feed to stimulate urination and excretion. From about three weeks old, they should be able to urinate and excrete on their own.
- The mixture can later be given less often, but more at a time.
- After about four or five weeks you can start them slowly on solid food.

The largest mammals in the world (All except the Blue Whale can be found in South Africa)

Animal	Weight
Blue whale (*Balaenoptera musculus*)	150t (up to)
Elephant (*Loxodonta africana*)	4–9t
White rhinoceros (*Ceratotherium simum*)	2–3t
Hippopotamus (*Hippopotamus amphibius*)	2t
Black rhinoceros (*Diceros bicornis*)	1,8t
Buffalo (*Syncerus caffer*)	750kg
Eland (*Taurotragus oryx*)	730kg

- The mammal that causes the most deaths in South Africa is the hippo.

Remarkable animals of South Africa

Diamant (Kaapsche Hoop wild horse)

Diamant, the leader of the wild horses, and six others were trapped in a fire in 2008. A journalist, Mark Stansfield, was also overcome by flames. Diamant had given birth to a foal just minutes before the fire started, but despite this she led the six horses and Stansfield to safety. After the fire, a local farmer, Gordon Mullin, looked after Diamant and her foal on his farm. Because of shock she did not pass the afterbirth and this caused a serious infection. In spite of treatment by a vet, the infection spread and she had to be put down.

Huberta (hippo)

In 1926 the hippo Huberta began a journey of 1 600km, walking in a southern direction from Zululand. Everywhere she went, she was followed by curious onlookers and photographers. Many people gave her food. The Johannesburg Zoo was looking for a hippo and there were attempts to catch her. This caused chaos and it was decided to leave her in peace. One night, when she had fallen asleep in the middle of a bridge, a motorist hit her with his bumper; Huberta left in a huff. Huberta wandered around Durban and Pinetown, where everyone loved her and spoiled her with treats. She even walked right through the middle of Durban's central business district with a crowd in tow. In Anerley, Indians made an offering of a buck to her. In 1931 Huberta reached East London, where she fell asleep on a main railway line. Eventually an engineer had to nudge her gently off the tracks with the locomotive. Huberta's life ended when three hunters shot her while she was bathing in the Keiskamma River. They were each given a negligible fine. Huberta's remains were taken from the river and are kept in a museum in Pietermaritzburg.

Jack (Cape baboon)

He was the pet of James Wide, a signalman who had lost both his legs. Jack pushed Wide to work in his wheelchair every day for nine years and also learnt how to work the signals. Later he could pump and carry water and fetch firewood. The railway administration paid for his food. For nine years he was Wide's helper and friend, until he died of TB in 1890. His skull is kept in the Albany Museum in Grahamstown.

Jock (Staffordshire terrier)

Jock belonged to the writer Percy Fitzpatrick. Jock was born in 1885 in the Kruger National Park and although he was the runt of the litter, he was clever, brave, agile and involved in many fights with wild animals. Jock was accidentally shot dead when he was mistaken for a dog that stole chickens at night. The guilty dog, which had already been killed by Jock, was found dead. Fitzpatrick's book, *Jock of the Bushveld*, became a classic work of literature in South Africa.

Statue of Jock in front of the Barberton Town Hall.

Just Nuisance (Great Dane)

Just Nuisance was a Great Dane born in 1937 in the Cape. He became a great friend of the British sailors in Simon's Town. He got his name because he often lay on the gangplank of the HMS Neptune, getting in the sailors' way. He also began to ride on the train with them. When the conductor chased him off the train, he simply climbed back in through a window or waited for the next train. In 1939 Ordinary Seaman Just Nuisance was officially inducted into the British Navy and began to serve on the HMS Afrikaner in Simon's Town. His name, rank and number were on his collar and he was given a seaman's hat with a band under his muzzle, as well as a permanent free train pass. He accompanied drunken sailors from the train back to their base and sometimes also helped other drunkards get there as well. He also separated sailors who were fighting. Just Nuisance was quickly promoted to Able Seaman. He had his own bed but sometimes committed the offence of sleeping in the officers' quarters. Just Nuisance was very fond of people, but bit two dogs from other ships to death. He also caused trouble at closing time in pubs. In 1943 he died at the age of seven. He was buried with full military honours on Red Hill; a granite stone marks his grave. On Jubilee Square in Simon's Town there is a bronze statue of him, and Leslie Steyn wrote a book about him called *Just Nuisance: Able Seaman Who Leads a Dog's Life*.

Max (gorilla)

In 1997 Max the Gorilla got hold of a fleeing robber who had jumped into his enclosure in the Johannesburg Zoo. He hit the robber a few times on the chest. The trespasser shot Max three times before police took him into custody. Max was taken to an animal hospital and recovered quickly. He died in his sleep in 2004 at the age of 33.

Nancy (springbok)

In 1915 David McLarren from the farm Vierfontein in the former Orange Free State gave Nancy as a mascot to the South African Scottish regiment. They were involved in the Battle of Delville Wood. She only injured a horn in the war and in 1918 she attended the first memorial service at Delville Wood. Nancy died in 1918 and was buried in Belgium with full military honours. She was later exhumed and stuffed and is now in a glass case in the Johannesburg Military Museum.

Percy, Pamela and Peter (penguins)

Percy, Pamela and Peter are three penguins that were covered in oil when the Chinese cargo ship MW *Treasure* sank on 23 June 2000 near Melkbosstrand on the Cape West Coast, causing a large oil spill. They were among thousands of penguins that were cleaned and released on 30 June 2000 at Port Elizabeth. Percy, Pamela and Peter were fitted with satellite tracking devices and the public followed their progress with great interest on the Internet. Pamela began to look around for food, but Percy immediately began to swim home. On 27 July, in spite of a shark-infested sea, he arrived safely on Dassen Island after an 800km journey. Pamela also arrived safely a few days later. Peter was missing for a short time, but apparently arrived on Robben Island on 17 July. He was recognised thanks to a unique number on a metal band around one of his fins.

Sauer (dobermann pinscher)

Detective sergeant Herbert Kruger trained the police dog Sauer. In 1925 Sauer followed a rustler's tracks for 160km in the Great Karoo and caught him. This earned him a place in the Guinness World Records.

Wild horses of South Africa, The

There are three groups of wild horses in South Africa: near Kleinmond, in the Kouga and at Kaapsche Hoop near Barberton. It is thought that the wild horses of Kouga are the descendants of Arabian horses that came with the British settlers on the ship *Albany* and landed at Algoa Bay (Port Elizabeth). Kouga's wild horses are very seldom seen, while the wild horses of Kaapsche Hoop were probably taken there by sheep farmers from the Highveld. Kleinmond's wild horses are possibly a subgroup of the Boland carthorses of the 18th and 19th centuries.

Wild horses at Kaapsche Hoop

Extinct and endangered South Africa mammals

The red data list is a list of all the endangered animals in the world. The list is revised every year by the International Union for the Conservation of Nature (IUCN). The full list is available on the Internet: **www.redlist.org**.

Extinct animals

Name	Scientific name
Blue buck	*Hippotragus leucophaeus*
Cape lion	*Leo leo capensis*
Quagga	*Equus quagga*

- The last quagga died in 1883 in the Amsterdam Zoo. In 1986 a quagga project was started to bring back the extinct quagga through breeding. The project's first foal was born in 1988, but it was a laborious process and the stripes and colour of the new quaggas are still not right.
- In 1989 a few mounted blue buck horns were found in Cape Town. These are the only remains of the blue buck in South Africa.

- The Lichtenstein's hartebeest is extinct in South Africa, but in the 1980s a few were imported and released in the north of the Kruger National Park, re-establishing them in the country.
- The Cape lion lived in the old Cape Province and the Free State. They were larger than other lions and had very long, dark manes. The last Cape lion was shot in 1865.
- In 2001 a lion closely resembling a Cape lion was found in a zoo in Siberia. Two of its cubs were donated to the Tygerberg zoo where they will be used in a breeding programme to try and breed a Cape lion. In 2009 they were still in the zoo.

Critically endangered and endangered animals

The most endangered animal in South Africa is the riverine rabbit (*Bunolagus monticularis*). Other critically endangered species are the black rhino (*Diceros bicornis*), four types of mole and two bat species. Endangered animals include the African elephant (*Loxodonta africana*), the wild dog (*Lycaon pictus*) and the mountain zebra (*Equus zebra*).

- The riverine rabbit is one of the 12 most endangered species of hare in the world. There are only about 250 adult riverine rabbits left in South Africa and they only occur in a small area in the central Karoo between Calvinia, Sutherland, Beaufort West, Victoria West, Carnarvon and Williston. Riverine rabbits only live for three years and only have one or two offspring per litter. The riverine rabbit's natural enemies are wild cats, caracals, jackals and owls. Their habitat is under threat because of overgrazing on farms and agricultural development. They are also being decimated by hunters and feral dogs and are sometimes caught in traps.
- The most endangered animal in the world is the Yangtze River dolphin (*Lipotes vexillifer*), of which there are possibly less than 20 remaining.

Illnesses transmitted by pets

Pets must be dewormed regularly. Families that keep pets must also take deworming medication to prevent illness.

Hookworm

Hookworm usually occurs in areas with poor health conditions. The larvae bore through the skin and spread to the blood-

stream and intestines. An itchy patch forms where the parasite entered the skin. The parasite has four hooked teeth with which it attaches itself and lays a large number of eggs. One or more of the following symptoms can occur: stomach pain, peptic sores, diarrhoea, bloody stools and anaemia.

Hydatid disease

This parasitic worm disease is caused by a very small tapeworm. The disease is common in the north-west Cape and not at all in urban areas. Dogs are carriers of the adult tapeworm. In people, the eggs can breed in the intestines and spread to the bloodstream. It spreads to the intestines where it can cause cysts in the liver, lungs, brain and other organs. Hydatid disease, or echinococcosis as it is also known, is a dangerous illness and parts of organs must sometimes be removed. The diagnosis is made with computer tomography.

Rabies

Rabies is a very dangerous, lethal disease that attacks the nervous system. The virus occurs in the saliva of infected animals and is transmitted to people by a bite or an open wound. A rabid animal salivates excessively, has uncontrolled movements, chews on everything and behaves strangely and with aggression. The average time from the bite to the onset of symptoms is four to eight weeks. Sometimes it can be shorter, but it can also be longer than a year before symptoms appear. The patient's symptoms are fever, restlessness, delirium, convulsions and thirst, but due to paralysis of the throat, he is not be able to drink water. Treatment involves repeated immunisation injections, intravenous feeding, painkillers, tranquillisers and supportive treatment of the heart and respiratory system.

Cat-scratch disease

People are infected with this disease by a cat's scratch or bite. The symptoms are fever and swollen lymph nodes appearing seven to 21 days after the disease is contracted. Diagnosis is through a skin test. There is no specific treatment and the patient recovers after a few weeks. The cat is asymptomatic.

> Some people are allergic to the saliva on cat hair and can suffer asthma attacks as a result.

Tapeworm

Tapeworm eggs occur in the excrement of vertebrates. Infection with dog tapeworm is common. Swallowed tapeworm eggs develop into embryos and the larvae end up in the bloodstream, from where they spread to the brain and other organs. It is a dangerous disease that can cause epilepsy and blindness.

Ornithosis

This is an infectious disease of birds, especially parrots, doves and parakeets, that can be transmitted to humans. Pigeon breeders often fall victim. Flu symptoms are experienced, and later the symptoms of pneumonia also appear with blood in the sputum. Treatment is supportive.

Psittacosis (parrot fever)

Parrots, doves, canaries and parakeets are infected with a micro-organism. Humans are infected when particles of the infected excrement of the birds are inhaled, especially when cleaning the cages.

Ringworm

This highly infectious fungal infection is transmitted by dogs and cats. In animals, it causes bald, round spots in the fur. In humans, it causes scabby red patches on the skin. Ointment and antibiotics are available for humans and animals.

Roundworm

This is common in children, especially in areas with poor health conditions. The eggs appear in the excrement of infected animals, which then infect the soil. They are often swallowed with food or are ingested when children play in infected soil and put their hands in their mouths. The eggs develop in the intestines.

Salmonella

This is caused by the salmonella bacterium that is also carried by animals, especially dogs. The symptoms are stomach pain, vomiting and diarrhoea. Treatment includes medication to prevent vomiting and diarrhoea and the prevention of dehydration. Intravenous feeding is sometimes necessary.

Scabies

This highly infectious skin disease is sometimes caught from dogs and spreads quickly from person to person through skin contact. It is caused by the scabies mite under the skin and usually appears on the hands and feet, and is extremely itchy. Medical treatment is necessary.

Toxocara

This disease is most common in puppies. It is caused by a small roundworm. The eggs are in the excrement and infect the soil. In humans, the eggs hatch in the intestines and spread to other organs like the lungs, brain, liver and eyes. It then causes allergic reactions like asthma and can also cause convulsions and blindness (if an egg lands behind the eye). Diagnosis is done by sputum analysis or a liver biopsy. In the event of serious infection, hospitalisation is necessary.

Toxoplasmosis

This disease is caused by ingesting unpasteurised milk and eating meat (especially pork) that is not properly cooked. It multiplies in the intestines of cats and the eggs are excreted. Humans are infected by touching an infected cat or its excrement and not washing their hands. It causes miscarriages, still births and deformity in babies. Toxoplasmosis is diagnosed by a blood test. Most people have a natural resistance to the disease. Treatment includes the administration of anti-malarials and sulphanilamide.

Fish tank disease

This disease is caused by bacteria that grow in fish tanks. Humans are infected by contact with an open wound when cleaning the fish tank.

Flea allergy

Some people have a severe allergic reaction to flea bites.

Bird lovers' disease

This is an allergic reaction to a protein in the blood of birds. The protein is in the bird's excrement and is inhaled when the cage is cleaned. After a few hours, flu-like symptoms develop.

South Africa's most poisonous snakes

Berg adder (*Bitis atropos*)

Appearance: The colour varies from grey-olive to dark brown or black with small, triangular patterns on the body and a dark arrow-shaped pattern on the triangular head.
Length: 30–60 cm
Distribution: Cape Peninsula, Cederberg, southern coastal mountain ranges, Drakensberg and Limpopo.
Venom: Neurotoxins with a specific effect on the optical and facial nerves that temporarily cause a loss of smell and taste, dizziness and drooping eyelids. Is not fatal, but medical treatment is necessary. Unlike other adders, the poison is not cytotoxic (does not destroy tissue).
Antivenom: Not necessary as it does not neutralise the venom.

Boomslang (*Dispholidus typus*)

Appearance: Young snakes are light brown with large green eyes. The colours vary widely. The females are often olive coloured while the males are bright green with black and gold flecks or dark brown to black with a yellow belly.
Length: 1,2–2 m
Distribution: The whole of South Africa, except in dry areas where there are no trees.
Venom: The venom is a haemotoxin (inhibits the clotting of blood) and slow working, but bleeding can lead to death.
Antivenom: Available.

- Boomslangs can open their jaws up to 17cm wide.
- Contrary to popular belief, they do not fall out of trees onto their prey.
- Boomslangs are often confused with the black or green mamba.

Forest cobra (*Naja melanoleuca*)

Appearance: A yellow-brown snake with darker spots on the back and body, and a black tail. The belly is cream or yellow. The scales are shiny. The snake makes a narrow hood when threatened.
Length: 1,5–5 m
Distribution: Forested areas of KwaZulu-Natal.
Venom: Neurotoxic. Immediate treatment is necessary to prevent the patient's death from paralysis and suffocation.
Antivenom: Available.

- This snake is often confused with the black mamba.
- Forest cobras are excellent swimmers.

Egyptian cobra (*Naja haje annulifera*)

Appearance: The snake is yellow-brown and darkens to blue-black as it ages. The belly is a dull yellow with dark flecks. Adult snakes have approximately 10 cross-bands. Young snakes have dark bands around their throats. It makes a wide hood when threatened.
Length: 1,2–3 m
Distribution: KwaZulu-Natal to Angola.
Venom: Neurotoxic. Immediate treatment is necessary to prevent the patient's death from paralysis and suffocation.
Antivenom: Available.

Gaboon viper (*Bitis gabonica*)

Appearance: A brown, pink or purplish snake with geometric patterns on its body that are richer in colour than those of a puff adder. The head is triangular.
Length: 90 cm–1,8 m
Distribution: North-eastern coastal area of KwaZulu-Natal.
Venom: Cytotoxic. The snake injects more venom than the puff adder. Immediate medical attention is necessary to prevent death.
Antivenom: Available.

Cape cobra (*Naja nivea*)

Appearance: The colour varies from yellow to yellow-brown flecked with darker spots and a dark reddish brown. Young snakes have a dark band around the throat that becomes lighter as they reach adulthood. The Cape cobra makes a hood when threatened.
Length: 1,2–2 m
Distribution: Western, Northern and Eastern Cape and Free State.
Venom: Neurotoxic. Immediate treatment is necessary to prevent the patient's death from paralysis and suffocation.
Antivenom: Available.

Green mamba (*Dendroaspis angusticeps*)

Appearance: Young snakes are blue-green and adult snakes are bright green with a lighter belly.
Length: 1,8–2,5 m
Distribution: Coastal areas of KwaZulu-Natal.
Venom: Neurotoxic. Immediate treatment is necessary to prevent the patient's death from paralysis and suffocation.
Antivenom: Available.

- The green mamba lives in trees and is often mistaken for a boomslang.

Mozambique spitting cobra (*Naja mossambica*)

Appearance: The snake is light brown or light grey in colour. Each scale has a dark ring. The belly is pink or yellow with dark crossbands and there are spots on the throat.
Length: 1–1,5 m
Distribution: Mpumalanga, Limpopo and KwaZulu-Natal.
Venom: Cytotoxic. It is not lethal, but immediate treatment is necessary to prevent tissue damage, which may necessitate skin grafts. Venom must immediately be washed out of the eyes.
Antivenom: Available.

Puff adder (*Bitis arientans*)

Appearance: The colour varies from grey to brown, orange-brown and light yellow. The snake has clear patterns with chevrons and dark bands on the tail. The head is triangular.
Length: 90 cm–1,7 m
Distribution: Everywhere in South Africa.
Venom: Cytotoxic. The patient experiences great pain and develops swelling and blistering around the bite. The venom works slowly, but immediate medical attention is necessary.
Antivenom: Available.

Rinkhals / Spitting Cobra (*Hemachatus haemachatus*)

Appearance: The colours vary from olive to dark brown with two or three crossbands over the throat.
Length: 1–1,5 m
Distribution: Western Cape, Eastern Cape, Gauteng, Mpumalanga, Free State and KwaZulu-Natal.
Venom: Neurotoxic. Venom is spat from distances of up to 2,4m. The snake makes a hissing sound when it spits.
Antivenom: Available.

Black mamba (*Dendroaspis polylepis*)

Appearance: Olive-green or grey, with a light green belly with dark spots. Young snakes are lighter in colour than adult snakes. The snake makes a hood when threatened.
Length: 2,5–4,5 m.
Distribution: Coastal areas of KwaZulu-Natal.

Venom: Neurotoxic. The snake bites a few times in quick succession and the venom works quickly. Immediate treatment is necessary to prevent the patient's death from paralysis and suffocation.
Antivenom: Available.

- The black mamba is one of the deadliest snakes in the world and the longest venomous snake in Africa.
- If one is encountered, walk backwards slowly and carefully. Sudden movements will make the snake bite suddenly and in rapid succession, often with fatal consequences.
- The black mamba is often confused with the mole snake.

Black-necked spitting cobra (*Naja nigricollis woodi*)

Appearance: The young snake is grey with a black head. The adult snake is completely black. The snake makes its head into a hood when threatened.
Length: 1,2–2 m
Distribution: Cape West Coast and the Karoo.
Venom: Cytotoxic. Serious tissue damage can occur.
Antivenom: Available.

The black button spider is the most poisonous spider in South Africa. A bite can be deadly.

Symptoms of a black button spider's bite
The symptoms develop over hours.
1. Nausea and vomiting
2. Muscle pain and spasms
3. Sweat
4. Abnormal salivation
5. Respiratory problems
6. Quickened pulse
7. Rise or fall in blood pressure

An antivenom is available and medical treatment is necessary.

10. SPORT

South African Olympic winners

Year	Athlete (gold)	Event
1908	Reginald Walker	Athletics (100m sprint)
1912	Kenneth McArthur Charles Winslow Charles Winslow and Howard Kitson Rudolph Lewis	Athletics (marathon) Tennis (men's singles) Tennis (men's doubles) Cycling (320km road race)
1920	Bevil Rudd Louis Raymond Clarence Walker	Athletics (400m sprint) Tennis (men's singles) Boxing (bantamweight)
1924	Willie Smith	Boxing (bantamweight)
1928	Sydney Atkinson	Athletics (110m hurdles)
1932	Laurie Stevens David Carstens	Boxing (lightweight) Boxing (light heavyweight)
1948	Gerald Dreyer George Hunter	Boxing (lightweight) Boxing (light heavyweight)
1952	Esther Brand Joan Harrison	Athletics (high jump) Swimming (100m backstroke)

Due to political pressure, South Africa could not participate in the Olympics from 1964 to 1988. In 1992 the country was readmitted to the Games.

Year	Athlete	Event
1992	Elana Meyer (silver) Wayne Ferreira and Piet(ie) Norval (silver)	Athletics (10 000m) Tennis (men's doubles)
1996	Penny Heyns (gold) Penny Heyns (gold) Josiah Thugwane (gold) Hezekiel Sepeng (silver) Marianne Kriel (bronze)	Swimming (100m breaststroke) Swimming (200m breaststroke) Athletics (marathon) Athletics (800m) Swimming (100m backstroke)
2000	Hestrie Cloete (silver) Terence Parkin (silver) Llewellyn Herbert (bronze) Frantz Kruger (bronze) Penny Heyns (bronze)	Athletics (high jump) Swimming (200m breaststroke) Athletics (400m hurdles) Athletics (discus) Swimming (100m breaststroke)

Year	Athlete	Event
2004	Roland Schoeman (gold) Ryk Neethling (gold) Darian Townsend (gold) Lyndon Ferns (gold)	Swimming (4 x 100m freestyle relay)
	Roland Schoeman (silver)	Swimming (100m freestyle)
	Mbulaeni Mulaudzi (silver)	Athletics (800m)
	Hestrie Cloete (silver)	Athletics (high jump)
	Roland Schoeman (bronze)	Swimming (50m freestyle)
	Donovan Cech and Ramon di Clemente (bronze)	Rowing (coxless pair)
2008	Khotso Mokoena (silver)	Athletics (long jump)

- At the 2004 Olympics in Athens, the South African 4 x 100m freestyle relay swimming team beat the world record by half a second.
- At the 2005 Deaf Olympics in Melbourne, Australia, Terence Parkin won 12 gold medals and one silver medal. He also broke five world records in swimming.
- At the 2004 Paralympics in Athens, Oscar Pistorius won a gold medal in the 200m sprint. He is the first athlete without legs to complete this distance in under 22 seconds. In 2008 he won three gold medals at the Paralympic Games.
- Natalie du Toit broke six world records at the 2004 Paralympic Games in Athens and won five gold medals for swimming. In 2008 she won five gold medals at the Paralympic Games.

Comrades Marathon

The Comrades Marathon is run in KwaZulu-Natal. The route of 89,006km leads athletes annually either from Durban to Pietermaritzburg (up) or from Pietermaritzburg to Durban (down). The first Comrades took place in 1921. In those days, only parts of the road were tarred and dust and sharp rocks made the race very unpleasant. Women and black athletes were only allowed to officially participate from 1976. Since 1986, the song "Chariots of Fire" is played at the beginning of the race. The Comrades Marathon traditionally took place on or near 31 May. In 2006 the race took place on 16 June, Youth Day. Since 2007, it has taken place on the Sunday closest to 16 June.

Winners

Men				
Year	Winner	Country	Time	Direction
1921	Bill Rowan	South Africa	08:59:00*	Down
1922	Arthur Newton	South Africa	08:40:00*	Up
1923	Arthur Newton	South Africa	06:56:07*	Down
1924	Arthur Newton	South Africa	06:58:22*	Up
1925	Arthur Newton	South Africa	06:24:45*	Down
1926	Harry Phillips	South Africa	06:57:46*	Up
1927	Arthur Newton	South Africa	06:40:56	Down
1928	Frank Sutton	South Africa	07:49:07	Up
1929	Darrel Dale	South Africa	07:52:01	Down
1930	Wally Hayward	South Africa	07:27:26	Up
1931	Phil Masterson-Smith	South Africa	07:16:30	Down
1932	Bill Savage	South Africa	07:41:58	Up
1933	Hardy Ballington	South Africa	06:50:37	Down
1934	Hardy Ballington	South Africa	07:09:03	Up
1935	Bill Cochrane	South Africa	06:30:05	Down
1936	Hardy Ballington	South Africa	06:46:14*	Up
1937	Johnny Coleman	South Africa	06:23:11*	Down
1938	Hardy Ballington	South Africa	06:32:26*	Up
1939	Johnny Coleman	South Africa	06:22:05*	Down
1940	Allen Boyce	South Africa	06:39:23	Up
1941–1945 No Comrades (due to the Second World War)				
1946	Bill Cochrane	South Africa	07:02:40	Up
1947	Harry Ballington	South Africa	06:41:05	Down
1948	Bill Savage	South Africa	07:13:52	Up
1949	Reg Allison	South Africa	06:23:21	Down
1950	Wally Hayward	South Africa	06:46:25	Up
1951	Wally Hayward	South Africa	06:14:08:*	Down
1952	Trevor Allen	South Africa	07:00:02	Up
1953	Wally Hayward	South Africa	05:52:30*	Down
1954	Wally Hayward	South Africa	06:12:55*	Up
1955	Gerald Walsh	South Africa	06:06:32	Down

Men				
Year	Winner	Country	Time	Direction
1956	Gerald Walsh	South Africa	06:33:35	Up
1957	Mercer Davies	South Africa	06:13:55	Down
1958	Jackie Mekler	South Africa	06:26:26	Up
1959	Trevor Allen	South Africa	06:28:11	Down
1960	Jackie Mekler	South Africa	05:56:32*	Up
1961	George Claassen	South Africa	06:07:07	Down
1962	John Smith	Great Britain	05:57:05	Up
1963	Jackie Mekler	South Africa	05:51:20*	Down
1964	Jackie Mekler	South Africa	06:09:54	Up
1965	Bernard Gomersall	Great Britain	05:51:09*	Down
1966	Tommy Malone	South Africa	06:14:07	Up
1967	Manie Kuhn	South Africa	05:54:10	Down
1968	Jackie Mekler	South Africa	06:01:11	Up
1969	Dave Bagshaw	South Africa	05:45:35*	Down
1970	Dave Bagshaw	South Africa	05:51:27*	Up
1971	Dave Bagshaw	South Africa	05:47:06	Down
1972	Mick Orton	Great Britain	05:48:57*	Up
1973	Dave Levick	South Africa	05:39:09*	Down
1974	Derek Preiss	South Africa	06:02:49	Up
1975	Derek Preiss	South Africa	05:53:00	Up
1976	Alan Robb	South Africa	05:40:43	Down
1977	Alan Robb	South Africa	05:47:00*	Up
1978	Alan Robb	South Africa	05:29:14*	Down
1979	Piet Vorster	South Africa	05:45:02*	Up
1980	Alan Robb	South Africa	05:38:25	Down
1981	Bruce Fordyce	South Africa	05:37:28*	Up
1982	Bruce Fordyce	South Africa	05:34:22	Down
1983	Bruce Fordyce	South Africa	05:30:12*	Up
1984	Bruce Fordyce	South Africa	05:27:18*	Down
1985	Bruce Fordyce	South Africa	05:37:01	Up
1986	Bruce Fordyce	South Africa	05:24:07*	Down
1987	Bruce Fordyce	South Africa	05:37:01	Up

Men

Year	Winner	Country	Time	Direction
1988	Bruce Fordyce	South Africa	05:27:42*	Up
1989	Sam Tshabalala	South Africa	05:35:51	Down
1990	Bruce Fordyce	South Africa	05:40:25	Up
1991	Nick Bester	South Africa	05:40:53	Down
1992	Jetman Msutu	South Africa	05:46:11	Up
1993	Charly Doll	Germany	05:39:41	Down
1994	Alberto Salazar	USA	05:38:39	Up
1995	Shaun Meiklejohn	South Africa	05:34:02	Down
1996	Dmitri Grishine	Ukraine	05:29:33	Up
1997	Charl Mattheus	South Africa	05:28:37	Down
1998	Dmitri Grishine	Ukraine	05:26:25*	Up
1999	Jaroslaw Janicki	Poland	05:30:11	Down
2000	Vladimir Kotov	Russia	05:25:33*	Up
2001	Andrew Kelehe	South Africa	05:25:52	Down
2002	Vladimir Kotov	Russia	05:30:59	Up
2003	Fusi Nhlapo	South Africa	05:28:52	Down
2004	Vladimir Kotov	Russia (now lives in Cape Town)	05:31:22	Up
2005	Sipho Ngomane	South Africa	05:27:11	Down
2006	Oleg Kharitonov	Russia	05:35:19	Up
2007	Leonid Shvetsov	Russia	05:20:41*	Down
2008	Leonid Shvetsov	Russia	05:24:49*	Up
2009	Stephen Muzhingi	Zimbabwe	05:23:26	Down

* Record (There is a record for the up race and a record for the down race.)

In 2005 Robert Mtshali, the first black athlete to complete the Comrades Marathon, at last won a medal. In 1935, the year he completed the race, there was no medal for him because black people could not officially enter the marathon.

Women				
Year	Winner	Country	Time	Direction
1975	Elizabeth Cavanagh	South Africa	10:08:00*	Up
1976	Lettie van Zyl	South Africa	09:05:00*	Down
1977	Lettie van Zyl	South Africa	08:58:00*	Up
1978	Lettie van Zyl	South Africa	08:25:00*	Down
1979	Jan Mallen	South Africa	08:22:41*	Up
1980	Isavel Roche-Kelly	South Africa	07:18:00*	Down
1981	Isavel Roche-Kelly	South Africa	06:44:35*	Up
1982	Cheryl Winn	South Africa	07:04:59	Down
1983	Lindsay Weight	South Africa	07:12:56	Up
1984	Lindsay Weight	South Africa	06:46:35*	Down
1985	Helen Lucre	South Africa	06:53:24	Up
1986	Helen Lucre	South Africa	06:55:01	Down
1987	Helen Lucre	South Africa	06:48:42	Up
1988	Frith van der Merwe	South Africa	06:32:56*	Up
1989	Frith van der Merwe	South Africa	05:54:43*	Down
1990	Naidene Harrison	South Africa	07:02:00	Up
1991	Frith van der Merwe	South Africa	06:08:19	Down
1992	Frances van Blerk	South Africa	06:51:05	Up
1993	Tilda Tearle	South Africa	06:55:07	Down
1994	Valentina Liakova	Russia	06:41:23	Up
1995	Maria Bak	Germany	06:22:45	Down
1996	Ann Trason	USA	06:13:23*	Up
1997	Ann Trason	USA	05:58:25	Down
1998	Rae Bisschoff	South Africa	06:38:57	Up
1999	Brigitte Lennartz	Germany	06:31:03	Down
2000	Maria Bak	Germany	06:15:35	Up
2001	Elwira Kolpakova	Russia	06:13:53	Down
2002	Maria Bak	Germany	06:14:21	Up
2003	Elena Nurgalieva	Russia	06:07:46	Down
2004	Elena Nurgalieva	Russia	06:11:15	Up
2005	Tatiana Zirkova	Russia	05:58:51	Down
2006	Elena Nurgalieva	Russia	06:09:24*	Up

Women				
Year	Winner	Country	Time	Direction
2007	Olesya Nurgalieva	Russia	06:10:11	Down
2008	Elena Nurgalieva	Russia	06:14:38	Up
2009	Olesya Nurgalieva	Russia	06:12:08	Down

* Record (There is a record for the up race and a record for the down race)

- In 1948 the marathon was started by the "cock crow" of Max Trimborn, just before the official start to the race. He has since passed away, but a recording of his crow is still played at the beginning of the race.
- Wally Hayward won the Comrades for the first time in 1930 at the age of 21. After 1954 he could not participate for many years as he had been declared a professional sportsman because of his training in London. In the 1970s he regained amateur status. He won the Comrades five times and earned seven medals. In 1988 at the age of 80 he completed his last Comrades. He died in 2006 at the age of 97.
- In 1983 Colin Goosen crawled 30m to the finish line to earn the last gold medal.
- In 1989 Sam Tshabalala was the first black athlete to win the Comrades.
- Bruce Fordyce won the marathon nine times; his record of 5:24:07 stood for 21 years. It was broken in 2007 by Leonid Shevetsov with a time of 5:20:49.
- In 1999 Sergio Motsoeneng lost his gold medal after he admitted that his brother had run parts of the race in his name.
- Since 2008 athletes are no longer allowed to be helped over the finish line.

Rugby

Important rugby stadiums in South Africa

City/Town	Stadium
Bloemfontein	Vodacom Park (formerly Free State Stadium)
Durban	Absa Stadium (formerly Kings Park)
George	Outeniqua Park
Johannesburg	Coca Cola Park (formerly Ellis Park)
Cape Town	Newlands (formerly Norwich Park)

City/Town	Stadium
Kimberley	Absa Park (formerly Hoffe Park)
East London	Absa Stadium (formerly Basil Kenyon Stadium)
Port Elizabeth	Telkom Park (formerly Boet Erasmus Stadium)
Potchefstroom	Olën Park
Pretoria	Loftus Versfeld (for a short time Securicor Loftus)
Springs	Pam Brink Stadium
Welkom	North West Stadium
Wellington	Boland Stadium
Witbank	Puma Stadium

The Springboks

The general consensus about the name "Springboks" is that it originated in 1906 with Paul Roos, who was captain of the South African rugby team on their tour to England. The story goes that he visited a zoo in England, saw a springbok there and decided to call his team the Springboks.

Absa Stadium, Durban

Springbok jersey

In March 1903 Gerald Orpen, a Transvaal representative on the South African Rugby Council, suggested green and gold jerseys with an embroidered springbok on the left breast. The jerseys were worn for the first time on 27 September 1906 when Paul Roos led his team onto the field in Northampton, England.

Springbok emblem

The designer of the Springbok emblem was a German, Heinrich L. Egersdörfer of Woodstock, Cape Town. He returned to Germany and later settled in London. In 1996, after much debate, the National Sports Council decided to retain the combined springbok-protea emblem in rugby. Since 2009 the springbok emblem has been on the right breast and the protea on the left breast of the Springbok jersey.

The first rugby match in South Africa took place in 1862 in Green Point, Cape Town.

Springbok captains (according to the *Sasol SA Rugby Annual 2009*)

Year*	Captain	Number of Tests as captain
1891	Herbert H. Carstens	1
1891	Robert C. (Bob) Snedden	1
1891	Alfred R. (Alf) Richards	1
1896	Ferdinand T.D. (Ferdy) Aston	3
1896	Barry (Fairy) Heatlie	2
1903	Alexander (Alex) Frew	1
1903	John M. (Jackie) Powell	1
1906	Harold W. (Paddy) Carolin	1
1906	Paul J. Roos	3
1910	Douglas F.T. (Dougie) Morkel	2
1910	William Alexander (Billy) Millar	5
1912	Frederick J. (Uncle) Dobbin	1
1921	Theodorus B. (Theo) Pienaar	0
1921	William H. (Boy) Morkel	3
1924	Pieter K. (Pierre) Albertyn	4
1928	Phillipus J. (Phil) Mostert	4
1931	Benjamin L. (Bennie) Osler	5
1933	Philip J. (Flip) Nel	8
1937	Daniel H. (Danie) Craven	4
1949	Felix du Plesis	3
1949	Basil J. Kenyon	1
1951	Hendrik S.V. (Hennie) Muller	9
1955	Stephen P. Fry	4
1956	Stefanus S. (Basie) Viviers	5
1956	Jacobus A. (Salty) du Rand	1
1958	Johannes T. (Johan) Claassen	9
1960	Desmond C. (Des) van Jaarsveldt	1
1960	Royden G. (Roy) Dryburgh	2

Year*	Captain	Number of Tests as captain
1960	Avril S. Malan	10
1963	Gabriël F. (Abie) Malan	4
1964	Cornelius M. (Nelie) Smith	4
1965	Dawid J. (Dawie) de Villiers	22
1969	Thomas P. (Tommy) Bedford	3
1971	Johannes F.K. (Hannes) Marais	11
1972	Pieter J.F. (Piet) Greyling	1
1975	Morné du Plessis	15
1980	Marthinus T.S. (Theuns) Stofberg	4
1981	Wynand Claassen	7
1984	David J. (Divan) Serfontein	2
1986	Hendrik E. (Naas) Botha	9
1989	Johannes C. (Jannie) Breedt	2
1993	Jacobus F. (Francois) Pienaar	29
1994	Christiaan P. (Tiaan) Strauss	1
1995	Adrianus J. (Adriaan) Richter	1
1996	Gary H. Teichmann	36
1999	Cornelius P. J. (Corné) Krige	18
1999	Johan (Rassie) Erasmus	1
1999	Joost H. van der Westhuizen	10
1999	André N. Vos	16
2001	Robert B. (Bob) Skinstad	12
2003	John W. Smit	55
2007	Victor Matfield	10
2007	Gysbert J. (Johann) Muller	1

* Year first chosen as captain.

Springbok records (according to the *Sasol SA Rugby Annual 2009*)

Captain in the most Tests:
John Smit (55).

Most Tests played:
Percy Montgomery (102).

Most points scored in Test matches:
Percy Montgomery (893) in 102 Tests (1997–2008).

Most points in a Test match:
Percy Montgomery (35) in 2007 against Namibia in Cape Town.

Most tries in a Test match:
Tonderai Chavhanga (6) in 2005 against Uruguay in East London.

Most conversions in a Test match:
Percy Montgomery (12) in 2007 against Namibia in Cape Town.

Most penalties in a Test match:
Percy Montgomery (7) in 2006 against Scotland in Port Elizabeth.

Percy Montgomery

Most points in all Springbok matches:
Percy Montgomery (906) in 104 matches (1997–2008)

Most tries in Test matches:
Joost van der Westhuizen (38) in 89 Tests (1993–2003).

Most tries in all Springbok matches:
Joost van der Westhuizen (56) in 111 matches (1993–2003).

Most conversions in Test matches:
Percy Montgomery (153) in 102 Tests (1997–2008).

Most conversions in all Springbok matches:
Percy Montgomery (157) in 104 matches (1997–2008).

Most penalties in Test matches:
Percy Montgomery (148) in 102 Tests (1997–2008).

Most penalties in all Springbok matches:
Percy Montgomery (148) in 104 matches (1997–2008).

Most drop goals in Test matches:
Naas Botha (18) in 28 Tests (1980–1992).

Most drop goals in all Springbok matches:
Naas Botha (27) in 40 matches (1980–1992).

Currie Cup winners (since 1980)

The Currie Cup competition was held for the first time in 1889.

Year	Winner	Place
1980	Northern Transvaal	Pretoria
1981	Northern Transvaal	Pretoria
1982	Western Province	Cape Town
1983	Western Province	Pretoria
1984	Western Province	Cape Town
1985	Western Province	Cape Town
1986	Western Province	Cape Town
1987	Northern Transvaal	Johannesburg
1988	Northern Transvaal	Pretoria
1989	Northern Transvaal and Western Province	Cape Town
1990	Natal	Pretoria
1991	Northern Transvaal	Pretoria
1992	Natal	Johannesburg
1993	Transvaal	Durban
1994	Transvaal	Bloemfontein
1995	Natal	Durban
1996	Natal	Johannesburg
1997	Western Province	Cape Town
1998	Blue Bulls	Pretoria
1999	Lions	Durban
2000	Western Province	Durban
2001	Western Province	Cape Town
2002	Blue Bulls	Johannesburg
2003	Blue Bulls	Pretoria
2004	Blue Bulls	Pretoria
2005	Cheetahs	Pretoria
2006	Cheetahs and Blue Bulls	Bloemfontein
2007	Cheetahs	Bloemfontein
2008	Sharks	Durban

Tri Nations Rugby winners (since 1996)

South Africa, Australia and New Zealand participate in the Tri Nations Tournament. It took place for the first time in 1996.

Year	Winner
1996	New Zealand
1997	New Zealand
1998	South Africa
1999	New Zealand
2000	Australia
2001	Australia
2002	New Zealand

Year	Winner
2003	New Zealand
2004	South Africa
2005	New Zealand
2006	New Zealand
2007	New Zealand
2008	New Zealand
2009	South Africa

The Super 14

The Super 10 competition was expanded in 1996 to the Super 12. In 2006 the Super 12 series was expanded to include 14 teams from South Africa, Australia and New Zealand.

Super 14 teams

Blues (New Zealand)
Brumbies (Australia)
Bulls (South Africa)
Cats (South Africa)
Central Cheetahs (South Africa)
Chiefs (New Zealand)
Crusaders (New Zealand)

Highlanders (New Zealand)
Hurricanes (New Zealand)
Reds (Australia)
Sharks (South Africa)
Stormers (South Africa)
Waratahs (Australia)
Western Force (Australia)

Super 12 winners

Year	Team	Country
1996	Blues	New Zealand
1997	Blues	New Zealand
1998	Crusaders	New Zealand
1999	Crusaders	New Zealand
2000	Crusaders	New Zealand

Year	Team	Country
2001	Brumbies	Australia
2002	Crusaders	New Zealand
2003	Blues	New Zealand
2004	Brumbies	Australia
2005	Crusaders	New Zealand

Super 14 winners

Year	Span	Country
2006	Crusaders	New Zealand
2007	Bulls	South Africa
2008	Crusaders	New Zealand
2009	Bulls	South Africa

World Cup winners and host countries

Year	Winner	Host country / countries
1987	New Zealand	Australia and New Zealand
1991	Australia	Great Britain and France
1995	South Africa	South Africa
1999	Australia	Wales
2003	England	Australia and New Zealand
2007	South Africa	France
2011		New Zealand

- The international governing body for rugby is the International Rugby Board (IRB).
- In South Africa rugby is controlled by the South African Rugby Football Union (Sarfu).
- In 2004 Schalk Burger was named rugby player of the year by the IRB.
- In 2007 Bryan Habana was named rugby player of the year by the IRB.
- In 2008 Bryan Habana and Percy Montgomery were both awarded with national honours, the Order of Ikhamanga (silver), for their role in the advancement of rugby in the country.

Cricket

Important cricket stadiums in South Africa

City / Town	Stadium
Centurion	SuperSport Park
Durban	Kingsmead/Absa Stadium
Johannesburg	Wanderers
Cape Town	Newlands
East London	Buffalo Park
Paarl	Boland Park
Port Elizabeth	St George's Park

Currie Cup, Castle Cup and SuperSport Series

The Currie Cup series was held for the first time in 1889. In 1991 the name was changed to the Castle Cup. Since 1997 it has been known as the SuperSport Series.

Currie Cup winners (since 1990)

Year	Winner
1990/1991	Western Province
Castle Cup winners (since 1991)	
1991/1992	Eastern Province
1992/1993	Orange Free State
1993/1994	Orange Free State
1994/1995	Natal
1995/1996	Western Province

SuperSport Series winners (since 1996/1997)

The SuperSport Series is a four-day series. Since the 2004/2005 season the provincial teams have been changed to six regional teams.

Year	Winner
1996/1997	KwaZulu-Natal
1997/1998	Free State
1998/1999	Western Province
2000/2001	Western Province
2001/2002	KwaZulu-Natal
2002/2003	Easterns
2003/2004	Western Province
2004/2005	Undecided (Eagles and Dolphins share trophy)
2005/2006	Undecided (Titans and Dolphins share trophy)
2006/2007	Titans
2007/2008	Eagles
2008/2009	Titans

Standard Bank Series/Standard Bank Pro 20 Series

The Standard Bank Series is a one-day series that took place for the first time in the 1996/1997 season. Only 20 innings are played. The six regional teams also take part in this series.

Year	Winner
1996/1997	Natal
1997/1998	Gauteng
1998/1999	Griquas
1999/2000	Boland
2000/2001	KwaZulu Dolphins
2001/2002	KwaZulu Dolphins
2002/2003	Western Province
2003/2004	Lions
2004/2005	Eagles
2005/2006	Eagles
2006/2007	Lions
2007/2008	Titans
2008/2009	Cape Cobras

Cricket World Cup

The World Cup takes place every four or five years and is a one-day tournament.

Year	Winner	Host country/countries
1975	West Indies	England
1979	West Indies	England
1983	India	England
1987	Australia	India and Pakistan
1992	Pakistan	Australia and New Zealand
1996	Sri Lanka	Pakistan, India and Sri Lanka
1999	Australia	England
2003	Australia	South Africa
2007	Australia	West Indies
2011		Bangladesh, India, Pakistan and Sri Lanka

- The governing body of international cricket is the International Cricket Council (ICC).
- In South Africa cricket is controlled by Cricket South Africa.
- In 1808 the first recorded cricket match in South Africa took place between two army teams.
- South Africa was banned from the ICC in 1970 because of its political policies, and was readmitted in 1991.
- The first international cricket match in South Africa was played at Matjiesfontein.
- South Africa participated in the World Cup for the first time in 1992.
- In 1999 Jonty Rhodes made the fastest century in South African Test cricket. He made 103 runs off 95 balls at Centurion Park against the West Indies.
- The famous cricket captain Hansie Cronje was banned from cricket for life in 2001 after he was found guilty of match fixing. In 2002 he died at the age of 32 when an aircraft in which he was travelling with two crew members to George crashed in the Outeniqua Mountains.
- In 2004 Jacques Kallis became the first South African to score centuries in four consecutive Tests.
- Irreplaceable items were destroyed in 2004 when a fire gutted the Wanderers Cricket Club in Johannesburg.
- In 2005 Jacques Kallis scored his 22nd test century and thus beat Gary Kirsten's record (21).

- In 2003 Graeme Smith became the South African to achieve the highest score in the history of Test cricket when he made 277 runs in the first Test against England. He also achieved the second-highest score (259 at Lord's) a few days later – the 333 of England's Graham Gooch is the highest ever score. Smith's thousand Test runs are the fastest recorded by a South African batsman (17 innings).
- In 2007 Shaun Pollock achieved a world record with his score of 312 wickets in One Day Internationals. He is also the only bowler to bowl more than 300 maiden overs in ODI.
- In 2008 Shaun Pollock and Makhaya Ntini were both awarded the Order of Ikhamanga (silver) for their role in the advancement of cricket in the country.

Soccer

Important soccer stadiums in South Africa

City/Town	Stadium
Bloemfontein	Vodacom Park
Durban	Kings Park
Johannesburg	Ellis Park ENB Stadium FNB Soccer City
Cape Town	Athlone Stadium Green Point Stadium Hartleyvale Newlands
Kimberley	Kimberley Stadium
Nelspruit	Mbombela Stadium
East London	Absa Stadium
Orkney	Oppenheimer Stadium
Polokwane	Peter Mokaba Stadium
Port Elizabeth	Port Elizabeth Stadium
Pretoria	Loftus Versfeld Rainbow Junction
Rustenburg	Royal Bafokeng Stadium
Thohoyandou	Thohoyandou Stadium

African Cup Tournament

Year	Winner	Host country
1990	Algeria	Algeria
1992	Ivory Coast	Senegal
1994	Nigeria	Tunisia
1996	South Africa	South Africa
1998	Egypt	Burkina Faso
2000	Cameroon	Nigeria
2002	Cameroon	Mali
2004	Tunisia	Tunisia
2006	Egypt	Egypt
2008	Egypt	Ghana
2010		Angola
2012		Gabon and Equatorial Guinea
2014		Libya

Soccer World Cup winners

Year	Winner	Host country
1930	Uruguay	Uruguay
1934	Italy	Italy
1938	Italy	France
1950	Uruguay	Brazil
1954	Germany	Switzerland
1958	Brazil	Sweden
1962	Brazil	Chile
1966	England	England
1970	Brazil	Mexico
1974	Germany	Germany
1978	Argentina	Argentina
1982	Italy	Spain
1986	Argentina	Mexico
1990	Germany	Italy
1994	Brazil	USA

Year	Winner	Host country
1998	France	France
2002	Brazil	Korea and Japan
2006	Italy	Germany
2010		South Africa
2014		Brazil

World Cup stadiums for 2010

Town/City	Stadium
Bloemfontein	Vodacom Park/ Free State Stadium
Durban	King Senzangakhona
Johannesburg	Ellis Park
Johannesburg, Soweto	Soccer City
Cape Town	Green Point
Nelspruit	Mbombela
Rustenburg	Royal Bafokeng
Port Elizabeth	Nelson Mandela
Polokwane	Peter Mokaba
Pretoria	Loftus Versfeld

- The international governing body for soccer in the International Federation of Association Football (Fifa).
- In South Africa soccer is under the control of the South African Football Association (Safa).
- Bafana Bafana is the nickname of South Africa's national soccer team.
- Amaglug-glug is South Africa's under-23 team.
- South Africa's under-20 team is called Amajita.
- Banyana Banyana is the nickname of South Africa's women's soccer team.
- South Africa was banned from Fifa in 1964 and only readmitted in 1992.
- On 11 April 2001 the biggest disaster in South African sport occurred when 43 spectators died at Ellis Park. Some people were trampled to death while others suffocated in a stampede.
- In 2008 the Order of Ikhamanga (silver) was awarded posthumously to the soccer star Patrick "Ace" Ntsoelengoe.

Tennis

South African Wimbledon winners

Men's doubles

Year	Players
1967	Bob Hewitt and Frew McMillan
1972	Bob Hewitt and Frew McMillan
1978	Bob Hewitt and Frew McMillan
2005	Wesley Moodie (with Stephen Huss of Australia)

Women's doubles

Year	Players
2005	Liezel Huber (with Cara Black of Zimbabwe)
2007	Liezel Huber (with Cara Black of Zimbabwe)

Mixed doubles

Year	Players
1949	Sheila Summers and Eric Sturgess
1950	Eric Sturgess (with Louise Brough of the USA)
1977	Greer Stevens and Bob Hewitt
1978	Frew McMillan (with Betty Stove of the Netherlands)
1979	Greer Stevens and Bob Hewitt
1981	Frew McMillan (with Betty Stove of the Netherlands)
1982	Kevin Curren (with Anne Smith of the USA)

- South Africa's first Wimbledon champions were Sheila Summers and Eric Sturgess. They won the mixed doubles in 1949.
- In 2005 Johan Kriek and Kevin Curren of South Africa won the men's doubles for players older than 45 for the third consecutive year.

Golf

Famous golf courses in South Africa

Not all the golf courses in the city/town/place are named.

City/town/place	Course (designed by)
Ballito	Zimbali Golf Club (Tom Weiskopf, 1998)
Durban	Durban Country Club (L. Waters, G. Waterman, 1922; S.V. Hotchkin, 1930; B. Grimsdell, 1959) Beachwood Golf Course (Sid and Jock Brews, 1930; Gary Player Design Co., 1996)
Edenvale	Glendower Golf Club (A.F. Tomsett and C.H. Alison, 1937)
George	George Golf Club (C.M. Murray, 1931; P. Basson, 1993) Fancourt Montagu (Gary Player Design Co., 1991–1992) Fancourt Outeniqua (Gary Player Design Co. 1992 and 1997) Fancourt The Links (Gary Player Design Co., 2000)
Hartbeespoort Dam	Pecanwood Golf Course (Jack Nicklaus, 1998)
Johannesburg	Houghton Golf Course (Copland 1923, S. Brews 1930s; Gary Player, 1974; P. Matkovich, 1994) Royal Johannesburg and Kensington Golf Club (Bob Grimsdell, 1935; Golf Data, 1998)
Cape Town	Royal Cape Golf Course (C.M. Murray, 1928; Golfscape, 2000) Steenberg Golf Course (Peter Matkovich, 1996)
Kathu	Sishen Golf Club (Bob Grimsdell, 1979)
Kleinmond	Arabella Golf Estate (Peter Matkovich, 1999)

Arabella Golf Estate, Kleinmond

City/town/place	Course (designed by)
Knysna	Sparrebosch Golf Course (Ronald Fream and David Dale, 2000)
Malelane	Leopard Creek Golf Course (Gary Player Design Co., 1996)
East London	East London Golf Course (G. Peck, 1923; S.V. Hotchkin, 1929)
Phalaborwa	Hans Merensky Golf Course (Bob Grimsdell, 1967)
Port Edward (nearby)	Wild Coast Country Club (Robert Trent Jones, 1983)
Port Elizabeth	Humewood Golf Course (Col. S.V. Hotchkin, 1931)
Randburg	Randpark Golf Course (S. Brews and K. de Beer 1971; Golf Data, 1993)
Somerset-West	Erinvale Golf Club (Gary Player Design Co., 1995)
Sandton	The River Club Golf Course (Bob Grimsdell, 1968; Rob O'Friel, 1998)
Stanger	Prince's Grant Golf Course (Peter Matkovich, 1994)
Sun City	Gary Player Country Club (Gary Player and Ron Kirby, 1979) Lost City Golf Course (Gary Player Design Co., 1993)

Winners of the South African Nedbank Golf Challenge (since 1990) (formerly the Sun City Million Dollar Golf Challenge)

In 2008 the tournament's prize money was $1 200 000.

Year	Winner	Country
1990	David Frost	South Africa
1991	Bernhard Langer	Germany
1992	David Frost	South Africa
1993	Nick Price	Zimbabwe
1994	Nick Faldo	Great Britain
1995	Corey Pavin	USA
1996	Colin Montgomerie	Scotland
1997	Nick Price	Zimbabwe
1998	Nick Price	Zimbabwe
1999	Ernie Els	South Africa
2000	Ernie Els	South Africa
2001	Sergio Garcia	Spain
2002	Ernie Els	South Africa

Sun City Golf Course

Year	Winner	Country
2003	Sergio Garcia	Spain
2004	Retief Goosen	South Africa
2005	Jim Furyk	USA
2006	Jim Furyk	USA
2007	Trevor Immelman	South Africa
2008	Henrik Stenson	Sweden

- The governing body of amateur golf in South Africa is the South African Golf Association.
- Since 1927, professional golf in South Africa has been under the aegis of the Professional Golfers' Association of South Africa.
- The first ladies' golf tournament took place in 1811 in Scotland.
- The first golf club in South Africa, the Cape Golf Club (later Royal Cape Golf Club), was established in 1885.
- Golf was played officially for the first time in South Africa in 1885 on Waterloo Green in Wynberg, Cape Town.
- Bobby (Arthur D'Arcy) Locke was the first South African to make a name for himself in international golf. He was just 17 when he won the South African Open for the first time in 1935, a feat he managed a total of nine times. He also won the British Open four times and is in the World Golf Hall of Fame. Locke was always dressed like a gentleman in a long-sleeved shirt, jacket and cap whenever he participated in a tournament. He died in 1987. There is an annual Bobby Locke Golf Tournament in Robertson.
- South African Gary Player won nine major championships. He won the British Open three times (in 1959, 1968 and 1974), the American Open once (1965), the American Masters three times (in 1961, 1974 and 1978) and the American PGA twice (in 1962 and 1972). He also won many other important titles. In 2003 he received the Laureus Prize in Monaco for lifelong achievement. On the course he always wore black, which earned him the nickname "The Black Knight". Player is regarded as one of the best sportsmen South Africa has ever produced. He was named South Africa's sportsman of the 20th century. In 2008 Gary Player played in his 51st Masters Tournament.
- In 2008 Trevor Immelman became the second South African to win the American Masters.

Horse races

Winners of the Durban July (since 1990)	
Year	Winner
1990	Jungle Warrior
1991	Olympic Duel
1992	Divine Master
1993	Empress Club
1994	Pas de Quoi
1995	Surfing Home
1996	La Fabulous
1997	London News
1998	Imperious Sue
1999	Horse Chestnut
2000	Badger's Coast

Winners of the Metropolitan Handicap (since 1990)	
Year	Winner
1990	Illustrador
1991	Flaming Rock
1992	Spanish Galliard
1993	Dancing Duel
1994	Space Walk
1995	Teal
1996	London News
1997	Super Quality
1998	Classic Flag
1999	El Picha
2000	El Picha

Winners of the Durban July (since 1990)	
Year	Winner
2001	Bunter Barlow
2002	Polo Classic
2003	Angus
2004	Yard-Arm
2005	Alastor
2006	Zebra Crossing
2007	Pocket Power
2008	Pocket Power
2009	Pocket Power

Winners of the Metropolitan Handicap (since 1990)	
Year	Winner
2001	Trademark
2002	Ipi Tombe
2003	Dynasty
2004	Greys Inn
2005	Dunford
2006	Eyeofthetiger
2007	Hunting Tower
2008	Pocket Power and Dancer's Daughter
2009	Big City Life

Athletics

Important athletic stadiums in South Africa

City/Town	Stadium
Bellville	Bellville Velodrome
Germiston	Herman Immelman Stadium
Johannesburg	RAU Stadium
Port Elizabeth	UPE Stadium
Potchefstroom	Kenneth McArthur Stadium
Pretoria	Pilditch Stadium
Roodepoort	Ruinsig Stadium
Stellenbosch	Coetzenburg Stadium

South Africans who broke world records in athletics

+ Unofficial
* Equalled world record
° South African athlete competing for another country

Name	Year: Record
Budd-Pieterse, Zola	**1984:** 5 000m+; 2 000m° (Great Britain) **1985:** 5 000m° (Great Britain)
Burke, Barbara	**1935:** 100 yards; 220 yards **1937:** 80m hurdles*
Clark, Marjorie	**1928:** High jump **1930:** 80m hurdles **1931:** 80m hurdles
Duncker, Vincent	**1909:** 120 yard hurdles
Fiasconaro, Marcello	**1973:** 800m° (Italy)
Joubert, Danie	**1931:** 100 yards*
Lavery, Tom	**1938:** 120 yard hurdles+
Malan, Danie	**1973:** 1 000m
Maree, Sydney	**1983:** 1 500m° (USA)
Meyer, Elana	**1991:** 15km road run **1999:** Half marathon
Nash, Paul	**1968:** 100m*
Potgieter, Gert	**1957:** 440 yard hurdles **1958:** 440 yard hurdles **1960:** 440 yard hurdles
Robb, Daphne	**1949:** 100 yards+ **1950:** 4 x 110 yards. South African team **1951:** 4 x 110 yards. (Florence Wills, Sally Black, Edna Maskell, Daphne Robb)
Van Heerden, Esther (later Brand)	**1941:** High jump
Van Reenen, John	**1975:** Discus
Walker, Reggie	**1909:** 120 yards+
Weightman-Smith, George	**1928:** 110m hurdles

- International athletics is controlled by the International Association of Athletics Federations (IAAF).
- In South Africa athletics is regulated by Athletics South Africa (ASA).
- Vincent Duncker was the first South African athlete to set a world record.
- In 1964 De Villiers Lamprecht became the first South African to run the mile in under four minutes – 10 years after Roger Bannister became the first person in the world to do so.
- South Africa was expelled from the IAAF in 1976. The ban was only lifted 16 years later, in 1992.
- In 2001 Hestrie Cloete became the high jump world champion with a jump of 2m in Edmonton. Her best jump was 2,06m, which she achieved in 2003 in Paris. In 2003 the IAAF named her the best female athlete of the year.
- In 2004 the wheelchair athlete Ernst van Dyk set four world records (400m, 800m, 10km and 25km). In 2006 he achieved his sixth consecutive victory in the wheelchair section of the Boston Marathon and was awarded the prestigious Laureus Prize as disabled sportsman of the year. At the 2008 Paralympic Games he won a gold medal in the road race for hand cycling.
- Since 2004 the IAAF has also acknowledged road records.
- In 2008 Paralympic athlete Oscar Pistorius was the holder of three Paralympic world records – the 100m, 200m and 400m. In 2008 the IAAF ruled that, because of his prosthetic limbs, he had an advantage over able-bodied athletes and could therefore not participate in the 2008 Olympic Games in Beijing for able-bodied athletes. He appealed and the Court of Arbitration of Sport in Switzerland decided that he may compete. Unfortunately, he failed to qualify. He won three gold medals at the Paralympic Games in 2008.

Swimming

South African swimmers who broke world records

° South African swimmer who competed for another country

Name	Year: Record
Fairly, Ann	**1966:** 110m backstroke
Heyns, Penny	**1999:** 50m breaststroke; 100m breaststroke; 200m breaststroke
Muir, Karen	**1965:** 110m backstroke **1966:** 220m backstroke
Neethling, Ryk	**2005:** 200m freestyle
Schoeman, Roland	**2005:** 50m butterfly (twice in two days) **2006:** 50m freestyle
°Skinner, Jonty	**1976:** 100m freestyle (USA)
Van den Burg, Cameron	**2009:** 50m breaststroke

- South Africa's Karen Muir was 12 when she set her first world record.
- Between July and September 1999 Penny Heyns broke the world records in the 50m, 100m and 200m 11 times. She is the first woman to hold world records in all her events.
- The South African Gordon Pugh became the world record holder for the longest cold water swim in 2005 when he swam 1 000m in the Arctic Ocean in water colder than 2° C.
- Since 2000 the Paralympic swimmer Natalie du Toit has set several world records for disabled swimmers. In 2008 she set another two records, in the 200m freestyle and 50m butterfly. She qualified for the able-bodied Olympic Games in Beijing, but did not win a medal. She did, however, win gold medals in all five of the swimming events she entered at the Paralympics. In Beijing she won the Whang Youn Dai Award and was also named Swimming South Africa's (SSA) personality of the year.
  In 2009 she broke the 22-year-old record for swimming between Robben Island and Bloubergstrand, a distance of 7,5km. The previous record was set by a Belgian, Annemie Landmeters, in a time of 1:40. Du Toit's time was 1:35.45.

Highlights of South Africa's sports calendar

Absa Cape Epic

The first Cape Epic mountain bike race took place in 2004. This highly demanding cycle race for mountain bikers covers over 900km from Knysna to Somerset West. Bikers must participate in teams of two, and they are responsible for the maintenance of their own bicycles. In 2008, 60 teams (of two riders each) from 40 countries entered the race. The route, which sometimes varies, is completed over nine days.

Argus/Pick 'n Pay Cycle Tour

This cycle race took place for the first time in 1978. Every year participants come from all over the world to take part in this cycle tour of 109km around the Cape Peninsula. The highest point on the route is Chapmans Peak, which is 169m above sea level. With more than 35 000 cyclists it is the biggest cycle race of its kind in the world, and also the biggest sport gathering in South Africa. The oldest person to enter to date was 89 years old (in 2008).

Argus Cycle Tour

Berg River Canoe Marathon (Isuzu)

The first Berg River Marathon was held in 1962. The canoe race from Paarl to Velddrif takes four days and takes place in July. More than 200km of the route is on the Berg River. It is regarded as the most demanding canoe race in the world.

Die Burger Sanlam Cycle Tour

This cycle tour was held for the first time in 1988. Since then it has become one of the Western Cape's top sporting activities. There is a route of just over 100km and a shorter route of approximately 50km for less serious cyclists.

Comrades Marathon

The Comrades Marathon takes place every year in KwaZulu-Natal. The route of about 89km goes either from Durban to Pietermaritzburg or from Pietermaritzburg to Durban in alternate years. The first Comrades was run in 1921, and in 2009 the 84th race took place.

Durban July Handicap

This horse race, the biggest in South Africa, takes place on a track of 2 200m at Greyville, Durban. It was run for the first time in 1897. The prize money is R1,25 million and more than R100 million is usually bet. The cigarette company Rothmans sponsored the race for 38 years, but because of a ban on cigarette advertising a new sponsor (Vodacom) has been involved since 2002.

Duzi Canoe Marathon

The Duzi Marathon begins on the Umsinduzi River at Pietermaritzburg, joins the Umgeni River in the Valley of a Thousand Hills and ends three days later at Blue Lagoon in Durban. The route is about 120km long. The first Duzi Marathon was held in 1951.

Metropolitan Handicap Horse Race

This horse race is held every January over a distance of 2 000m on the Kenilworth racecourse in Cape Town.

Midmar Mile

This demanding swimming event takes place annually on the Midmar Dam near Pietermaritzburg. It also attracts international swimmers. There are eight batches of swimmers who swim over four days. In 2008 approximately 17 000 swimmers participated.

Nedbank Golf Challenge (formerly the Sun City Million Dollar Golf Challenge)

This challenge is held every December at Sun City and attracts many international participants. The course was designed by Gary Player.

Two Oceans Marathon

The Two Oceans Marathon is run over a distance of 56km around the Cape Peninsula. Participants can also run a half marathon of 21,1km.

Foot of Africa Marathon

This 42,2km marathon is held every year in Bredasdorp. It took place for the first time in 1978. There is also a half marathon, a 10km road race and a 4km fun run/walk. The route winds through beautiful fynbos vegetation.

11. HISTORY

Replica of a Khoi hut

Cross on the site of Joao da Nova's church

Groot Constantia

Chris Barnard's gravestone

Ship's trunk (Huguenot)

Langenhoven's house, Arbeidsgenot

Highlights of South African history and interesting events in South Africa

Statue of Jan van Riebeeck

Statue of Maria van Riebeeck

- **Approximately 25 000 years ago**
  People belonging to an early Stone Age hunter-gatherer culture leave behind a legacy of rock art in Southern Africa.
- **Approximately 500 BCE**
  Cattle farmers who also keep sheep and make earthen pots live in small groups in the south Cape.
- **Approximately 300 AD**
  Oldest traces of an Iron Age culture are left in the interior of South Africa by people who live in the lowveld of what is now Mpumalanga and KwaZulu-Natal.
- **Approximately 1050 to 1290 AD**
  The settlement at Mapungubwe Hill in the current Limpopo Province is built by people who keep cattle.

1488
The Portuguese explorer Bartolomeu Dias (ca. 1450–1500) sails around the southern tip of Africa and in February goes ashore at what is today Mossel Bay. He erects the first stone cross on the South African coast.

1497
Vasco da Gama (1460–1524), another Portuguese explorer, sails round the southern tip of Africa and opens up the sea route to India in 1498.

1500
Pedro de Alaide leaves a letter in a shoe or iron pot under a milkwood tree in Mossel Bay. This was the first "post office" in South Africa, the Post Office Tree.

Statue of Dias in Mossel Bay

1501
The Portuguese explorer Joao da Nova builds a small stone structure in Mossel Bay to serve as a place of worship.

1503
Antonio de Saldanha lands in Table Bay, which was called the Bay of Saldanha. He becomes the first European to climb Table Mountain.

Approximately 1580
Sir Francis Drake (1545–1596), an English admiral, reached the Cape of Good Hope during his journey around the world and describes it as "the fairest cape in the whole circumference of the earth".

1591
An English seaman, James Lancaster, explores the coast of Southern Africa and in Table Bay barters for sheep with the Khoi-Khoi.

1601
A Dutch navy under the command of Joris van Spilbergen drops anchor in the Bay of Saldanha and names it Table Bay. The original name, Bay of Saldanha, is given to today's Saldanha Bay.

1602
The Dutch East India Company (VOC), with its head office in Amsterdam, is established to increase Dutch trade with the spice lands of the Far East.

1620
Two English ships' captains, Shillinge and Fitzherbert, raise the British flag

Discussions with the "strandlopers"

at Vlaeberg (Signal Hill) in Table Bay, but England refuses to recognise the annexation.

1632
Autshumao (also known as Herry, ca. 1600–1663), the chief of the Goringhaikona (the so-called "strandlopers" or beach walkers) at the Cape, accompanies an English ship's captain on a voyage to the Far East and learns some English. After the arrival of the Dutch in 1652 he acts as translator for Jan van Riebeeck and as spokesman for the local inhabitants.

1647
The VOC cargo ship *De Nieuwe Haerlem* runs aground in Table Bay.

1652
Johan (Jan) Anthonisz van Riebeeck (1619–1677) arrives in Table Bay on 6 April with three ships (the *Drommedaris*, *Reijger* and *Goede Hoope*).

Replica of the Drommedaris

His task is to build a victualling station for the VOC's fleet. He builds a small clay fort (known as the Fort de Goede Hoop) and digs a garden to grow fresh produce.

1655
The first vineyards and mealies are planted in the Company gardens.

1657
Van Riebeeck gives permission to nine VOC officials to farm near the Liesbeek River for their own gain. They must sell all their produce to the Company. It is an attempt to meet the demand for fresh produce from passing ships.

1658
Two hundred slaves from Benin and Angola arrive in Table Bay on the VOC ship Amersfoort.

1659
The first wine is made at the Cape, about 14 litres.

1660
The first horses are imported by the VOC to the Cape from Batavia. Batavia is known today as Jakarta, the capital of Indonesia.

Jan van Riebeeck

Groot Constantia

Today's Franschhoek Valley

1662
It is generally accepted that the person in this well-known picture is Jan van Riebeeck, but in reality it is Bartholomeus Vermuyden. Jan van Riebeeck leaves the Cape for a new post in Batavia. His successor as commander is Zacharias Wagenaer (1614–1668).

1665
The first Reformed minister at the Cape, Joan (Johannes) van Arckel (1640–1666), arrives in Table Bay.

1666
Building work on the stone castle De Goede Hoop begins. It replaces the already dilapidated fort that Van Riebeeck built.

1667
The first group of Malay slaves arrive at the Cape.

1674
– Sugar cane is planted and the first brandy is distilled. Brandy is used in trade with the Khoi-Khoi.
– Krotoa, the first Khoi woman to be baptised (with the name Eva), dies.

1679
– Simon van der Stel is appointed as commander of the Cape.
– The Castle of Good Hope is completed after 13 years **(see page 108)**.

1680
Simon van der Stel establishes a new settlement on the banks of the Eerste River and calls it Stellenbosch.

1688
The first group of French Huguenots arrive at the Cape on board the Voorschoten. They brought their French minister, Pierre Simond, with them and are given land at Stellenbosch, Drakenstein and Franschhoek.

1699
Simon van der Stel is succeeded as governor by his son, Willem Adriaan. He develops the farm Vergelegen at Somerset West.

1700
Colonists establish themselves in the Land of Waveren, the district around the current town of Tulbagh.

1704
The first church building at the top of Adderley Street in Cape Town is taken into use **(see page 113)**.

1706
W.A. van der Stel is relieved of his duties by the VOC and ordered to return to the Netherlands.

1713
A deadly smallpox epidemic breaks out at the Cape. Entire Khoi tribes, who had no immunity to European diseases, die. About a quarter of the small white population also dies.

1738
The first Protestant mission in Africa is established by the Moravian Mission Society among the Khoi-Khoi at Genadendal, about 35km north-east of Caledon. The first missionary is Georg Schmidt (1709–1785) **(see page 113)**.

1739
Hendrik Swellengrebel becomes the first governor of the Cape to be born in South Africa.

1751
Ryk Tulbagh (1699–1771) becomes governor of the Cape. During Tulbagh's time in office the so-called "Prag- en Praalwette" (sumptuary laws) are enacted to curb the extravagant lifestyles of certain officials and their wives at the Cape.

1755
A second smallpox epidemic breaks out at the Cape, again with devastating consequences, especially for the Khoi inhabitants.

1765
– The first church service is held at the first Groote Kerk in Cape Town.
– The *Meermin* sails from the Cape to buy slaves in Madagascar. After a fight on board near Cape Agulhas, the ship is wrecked. Only 122 of the 140 slaves reach the Cape.

1767
A third smallpox epidemic breaks out at the Cape.

1773
– The first Dutch Reformed church (Roodezand Church) is built in Tulbagh **(see page 113)**.
– The ship *De Jonge Thomas* is wrecked at Woodstock and Wolraad Woltemade rescues 14 people **(see page 160)**.

De Jonge Thomas

Gable of the wine cellar at Groot Constantia.

1778
- The Fish River is set as the eastern border of the Cape Colony by Governor Joachim van Plettenberg (1739–1793).
- After a long struggle the Lords XVIII give permission that a Lutheran church be built in Cape Town **(see page 114)**.
- Captain Robert Jacob Gordon, a Dutch explorer, botanist and soldier, names the great river that forms the northern border of the Cape Colony the Orange River in honour of the Prince of Orange. The river was called the Gariep by the Khoi-Khoi.

1779
The First Border War at the Cape's eastern border breaks out between white cattle farmers and Xhosa groups who cross the Fish River to rustle cattle from the farms.

1782
The first paper money (*riksdaalders*) is used at the Cape. The Grosvenor is wrecked on 4 August on the Wild Coast **(see page 203)**.

1786
The first magistracy is established at Graaff-Reinet.

1789
- The Second Border War breaks out. Xhosa groups that carry out raids on the farms of white colonists in the Suurveld are driven back by the commandos.
- The "Hottentot Venus", Sarah (Saartjie) Baartman, is born.

1791
The German-born sculptor Anton Anreith (1754–1822) designs the ornamental gable of the wine cellar at Groot Constantia. Anreith, working in the German Baroque style, also made the pulpits of the Groote Kerk and the Lutheran Church in Cape Town and the two lions along Government Avenue in the Company Gardens.

1794
The Portuguese ship *São José* is stranded in Camps Bay and about 200 of the 500 slaves on board drown.

The Battle of Muizenberg

1795
- The first British occupation of the Cape. The British troops easily overwhelm the small Dutch force in the Battle of Muizenberg.
- Farmers in the districts of Graaff-Reinet and Swellendam rebel against the VOC because they are not protected against the Xhosa raids. They establish the republics of Swellendam and Graaff-Reinet, but the British forcibly take back control.

1797
Lady Anne Barnard (1750–1825) (pictured left) travels from England to the Cape as the wife of a British official, Andrew Barnard (1762–1807). She is a vivacious and gifted woman. In her letters and diaries about her journeys in the interior, she gives an accurate, lively and humorous picture of the events and social life at the Cape. She is also a talented artist.

1798
- The VOC, which has been experiencing financial problems for years, has its assets and debts taken over by the Dutch government.
- The first post office in the Cape is built in Woodstock.
- The first mosque (Auwal Mosque) in South Africa is built in Cape Town **(see page 121)**.

1799
- The Third Border War, which lasts until 1801, breaks out.
- Two Dutch missionaries from the London Missionary Society arrive at the Cape. Rev. Johannes Jacobus Kicherer (1775–1825) first tries to convert the San between the Sak River and the Orange River, but later becomes the minister of the Dutch Reformed congregation at Graaff-Reinet. Dr Johannes Theodorus van der Kemp (1747–1811) establishes the mission Bethelsdorp near Port Elizabeth.

1800
The first printing press in South Africa is operated by the business firm Walker & Robertson.

Approximately 1800
Unrest that is to last several years breaks out among black tribes in the whole of Southern Africa. It is called the *Mfecane*, from the Nguni word meaning "crush in war".

1803
The Cape is returned to the Netherlands according to the terms of the Peace of Amiens. Lieutenant General Jan Willem Janssens (1762–1838) becomes governor of the Cape.

1805
The second oldest Dutch Reformed church in South Africa still in use, the Strooidak (Thatch Roof) Church in Paarl, is consecrated **(see page 115)**.

Lieutenant General Jan Willem Janssens

1806
– The British occupy the Cape for the second time. In the Battle of Bloubergstrand the British defeat the small force of Governor Janssens. Sir David Baird becomes governor of the Cape.
– A regular postal service between Cape Town and Algoa Bay (the current Port Elizabeth) is established.

1807–1808
The British outlaw slavery and no more slaves are brought to the Cape.

1811
The British governor, the Earl of Caledon (1777–1839), issues a proclamation that forces the Khoi-Khoi to have a permanent abode. They may also not migrate to other districts without written permission.

1811–1812
– Sir John Francis Cradock becomes governor of the Cape.
– In the Fourth Border War the British forces under command of Lieutenant Colonel John Graham (1778–1821) and Boer commandos succeed in pushing the Xhosas who have established themselves in the Suurveld, back over the Fish River.

1814
Lord Charles Somerset (1767–1831) is appointed governor of the Cape.

1815
– The Slagtersnek Rebellion: a group of border farmers in the Bosberg openly rebel against the British authorities. The leaders are arrested and six of them are sentenced to death by hanging. One is later pardoned, but the other five are executed in March 1816. The ropes of four of the men break, but despite pleas from onlookers, the men are hanged one after the other with the same rope.
– The British troop ship the *Arniston* is wrecked at Waenhuiskrans on the Cape south coast. Of the 350 people on board, only six survive the disaster.
– Sara Baartman, the "Hottentot Venus", dies in Paris **(see page 158)**.

1816
Shaka (born ca. 1787) becomes king of the Zulus. His kingdom will become the most powerful in south-east Africa. He does not hesitate to spill blood, even that of his own people.

1819
- The Fifth Border war begins. Xhosa warriors of the chief Ndhlambe are driven out of the area around Grahamstown by the British garrison and Boer commandos.
- The British authorities declare the area between the Fish and Keiskamma River neutral ground and try to resettle all the people living there.

1820
- About 4 000 British settlers land in Algoa Bay (today's Port Elizabeth) and are established in the Albany district around the town of Grahamstown.
- The British ship *Waterloo* sinks with a group of bandits on board during a storm in Table Bay. Only 98 of the nearly 300 people on board are rescued.

Shaka

1822
Lord Charles Somerset announces that English will replace Dutch over a period of a few years as the only official language of the Cape Colony. This causes great dissatisfaction among the Afrikaners.

1824
- The British administration declares the Orange River the northern border of the Cape Colony.
- The British settlers John Fairbairn (1794–1864) and Thomas Pringle (1789–1834) establish South Africa's first private newspaper in Cape Town, *The South African Commercial Advertiser*.
- The Moravian mission Elim is established near Bredasdorp **(see page 113)**.

1826
A teenager, John Ross, walks 1 000km from Durban to Delagoa Bay to seek medical assistance for his colleagues.

The wrecking of the *Waterloo*

1828
– Shaka is murdered by his half-brother Dingaan, who succeeds him as king of the Zulus.
– The British authorities proclaim that no person may have their freedom of movement limited or be forced into labour on the grounds of their race.

1829
– The Zuid-Afrikaansche Athenaeum is established in Cape Town. It later develops into the South African College and University of Cape Town (1918).
– The first four missionaries of the Rhenish Missionary Society arrive in the Cape from Germany. In 1830 one of them, Johann Gottlieb Leipoldt, establishes the mission Wuppertal in the Cederberg. He is the grandfather of the Afrikaans poet C. Louis Leipoldt.

Houses at Elim

1830
The first Dutch weekly in the Cape, *De Zuid-Afrikaan*, appears for the first time in Cape Town.

1834
– Slavery is outlawed by an act of the British parliament in all its colonies, and therefore also at the Cape. This leads to dissatisfaction among the many slave owners in the Cape. The compensation offered to the slave owners by the government, as well as the way in which the money has to be claimed, leads to great bitterness.
– The Sixth Border War breaks out. The British colonel (later Sir) Harry Smith (1787–1860) suppresses the Xhosa resistance particularly brutally. He has the Xhosa chief Hintsa shot dead in cold blood when he tries to escape in 1835.
– The Xhosas are driven to the far side of the Kei River, but the destruction of farms becomes one of the major causes of the Great Trek.
– The Berlin Missionary Society establishes its first mission, Bethanie, in the Orange Free State.
– The original St George's Cathedral of the Anglican Church is built at the top of the current St George's Street in Cape Town.

Mission at Bethanie (sketch)

1835
The Great Trek begins. The first group to leave is that of Louis Trichardt (1783–1838).

1836
Two groups of trekkers, under the leadership of Andries Potgieter (1792–1852) and Gert Maritz (1797–1838) respectively, reach the current northern Free State. The Voortrekkers defeat the warriors of Mzikilazi (ca. 1800–1868) in the Battle of Vegkop.

The Great Trek

1838
- The formal emancipation of slaves takes place.
- More Voortrekkers, under the leadership of Piet Uys (1797–1838) and Piet Retief (1780–1838), join the Maritz and Potgieter treks. Disagreements among the leaders result in Potgieter and his followers going north of the Vaal. The other groups choose Natal and make the difficult journey over the Drakensberg.
- Retief visits the Zulu king Dingaan at his royal kraal, Umgungundhlovo, with a small Voortrekker commando. Dingaan gives his permission that the Voortrekkers settle south of the Tugela. On a second visit to Dingaan, Retief, along with 71 of his comrades and 30 servants, is murdered on Dingaan's orders.
- After the death of Retief and his comrades, Dingaan sends his troops to attack the Voortrekker laagers at the current Weenen. Altogether 281 white trekkers and about 200 black workers are killed.
- A punitive expedition against Dingaan by the Voortrekkers fails when the Zulu forces lead them into an ambush at Italeni. Piet Uys and his 15-year-old son, Dirk Cornelis, are killed.
- Andries Pretorius (1798–1853) joins the Natal Voortrekkers, and is appointed their commandant general. The Voortrekkers defeat a large Zulu army on 16 December in the Battle of Blood River. Dingaan is forced to flee and shortly afterwards is killed by a Swazi.

Ox wagon

Piet Retief

1839
The Voortrekkers establish the Natalia Republic with Pietermaritzburg as its capital.

1840
Cape Town's municipality is established.

1841
In Cape Town the current Groote Kerk is consecrated on the site of the previous church **(see page 113)**.

1843
A British force occupies Port Natal and Natal is proclaimed a British colony. Many of the Voortrekkers leave Natal and settle in the Free State and Transvaal.

1845
The Berlin Missionary Society establishes a mission at Pniel in the Drakenstein Valley.

1846
– The Seventh Border War ("War of the Axe") breaks out on the Cape's eastern border. More of the Xhosa territory comes under British control.
– Sugar cane plantations are planted in Natal.

1848
Sir Harry Smith (now governor of the Cape Colony) defeats a Voortrekker commando under the leadership of Andries Pretorius in the Battle of Boomplaats.

1849
– The Diocesan College School of the Anglican Church is established in Rondebosch by Bishop Robert Gray. This school is still commonly known as Bishops.
– The first Jewish congregation is established in Cape Town **(see page 121)**.
– The Heerengracht in Cape Town is renamed Adderley Street.

1850
During the Eighth Border War, which lasts until 1852 and causes great losses on both sides, more Xhosa territory comes under British control.

1852
– The independence of the Zuid-Afrikaansche Republiek (South African Republic, Transvaal), is acknowledged by Great Britain at the Sand River Conference.
– The British troop carrier *Birkenhead* sinks on 26 February near Danger Point **(see page 203)**.

Bishops

1854
– The Orange Free State becomes a republic with the signing of the Bloemfontein Convention.
– The first Cape parliament is elected.

1855
Pretoria is established and from 1860 it is the official seat of the government.

1857
– The so-called "National Suicide" of the Xhosas takes place **(see page 157)**.
– M.W. Pretorius is elected president of the Zuid-Afrikaansche Republiek (South African Republic, Transvaal).

1859
M.W. Pretorius is elected president of the Orange Free State.

1860
– The first Indians arrive in Natal to work on the sugar plantations.
– The first train in South Africa to be pulled by a locomotive begins to run over a distance of 3,2km in Durban between the Point and Mark Square.

1862
The first rugby match in South Africa, between the Military and the Civilians, takes place on the Green Point common in Cape Town.

1863
– M.W. Pretorius steps down as president of the Free State Republic and returns to the Transvaal. He is succeeded by Jan Hendrik Brand (1823–1888). Jan Brand's motto is: "Everything will work out, as long as everyone does their duty."
– The *Alabama*, a privateer from the southern states of America, arrives in Table Bay. This warship sank various merchant ships during the American Civil War and in Table Bay, in front of a crowd of curious onlookers, forces the sailing ship *Sea Bride* to surrender. The *Alabama* is later sunk off the coast of France.
– The first regular train service in South Africa is established between Cape Town and Wellington.

The *Alabama* (painting by Samuel Walters)

1866
The long-running clashes between the Orange Free State and the Basotho people under the leadership of Mosheshwe are ended with the Treaty of Thaba Bosiu.

1867
Erasmus Jacobs discovers the first diamond (21 carats) in South Africa at Hopetown.

1870
– A rich source of diamonds is discovered at Kimberley. It leads to a rush of prospectors, adventurers and financiers. The best known among them by far is the young Englishman Cecil John Rhodes.
– General Jan C. Smuts is born in Riebeek West.

Dorsland Trek

1871
– Alluvial gold is found at Pilgrims Rest and shortly afterwards at Lydenburg in the ZAR.
– A postal service is established between Cape Town and Kimberley.

1872
Great Britain grants the Cape Colony autonomy.

1874
– The Dorsland ("Thirstland") Trek to Damaraland and Angola begins. One of the chief reasons for the trek is dissatisfaction with the rule of President Thomas François Burgers. Many of the trekkers eventually settle in southern Angola. Others later return to the Transvaal. Most of the descendents of the trekkers who stay in Angola are resettled in 1928 in the north of what is today Namibia.
– The Burgerspond, South Africa's first coin, is released.

1875
The *Genootskap van Regte Afrikaners* (GRA) (Society of Real Afrikaners) is established in Paarl by Reverend S.J. du Toit (1847–1911). It is the beginning of the First Afrikaans Language Movement.

1876
– The GRA publishes the first Afrikaans magazine, *Die Afrikaanse Patriot* (The Afrikaans Patriot), with C.P. Hoogenhout (1843–1922) as the editor.
– Walvis Bay is annexed by the Cape Colony.

1877
– Great Britain annexes the ZAR. It will henceforth be a British colony with the name Transvaal. Paul Kruger leads a small delegation to London to try to convince the British government to nullify the annexation of the ZAR. The attempt is unsuccessful **(see page 147)**.

Paul Kruger

– The Ninth Border War breaks out on the Cape's eastern border.

1879
– The Anglo-Zulu War breaks out in Natal. On 22 January the Zulu forces defeat the British army in the Battle of Isandlwana. On 12 March 2 000 Zulus attack a British camp at Ntombi River and only 15 of the 60 men escape. On 4 July the Zulus are defeated at Ulundi, ending the war.

Battle of Isandlwana

1880
– Reverend S.J. du Toit forms the Afrikanerbond in Paarl.
– The First Anglo-Boer War begins. At a national meeting at Paardekraal, near Krugersdorp, about 5 000 Transvaal citizens under the leadership of Paul Kruger decide to take up arms against Great Britain to regain the independence of the ZAR.

1881
– The war between the Boers and Brits ends with the signing of the Pretoria Convention.
– Gold is discovered at Barberton.

1882
Dutch may be used alongside English as a language of instruction in schools.

1883
Paul Kruger becomes president of the Transvaal.

1884
The London Convention restores the independence of the Transvaal and the state can once again call itself the Zuid-Afrikaansche Republiek.

1885
The railway link between Cape Town and Kimberley is opened.

1886
Gold is discovered on the Witwatersrand.

1887
The name of the Stellenbosch Gymnasium is changed to Victoria College, which later becomes the University of Stellenbosch.

1888
De Beers Consolidated Mines is established by Cecil John Rhodes in Kimberley.

1889
The Chamber of Mines is established in Johannesburg.

1890
Cecil John Rhodes becomes premier of the Cape Colony.

1892
The railway line between Cape Town and Johannesburg via Bloemfontein is completed.

1893
Great Britain allows the white inhabitants of Natal autonomy.

1894
The ZAR's own railway line from Lourenço Marques (now Maputo) to Pretoria is opened. It creates a link to the sea for the ZAR that does not run through British territory.

Cecil John Rhodes

1896
- In the Jameson Raid, British troops under the leadership of Dr Leander Starr Jameson (1853–1917) try to topple the government of the ZAR. The British troops surrender at Doornkop.
- Rinderpest, a viral disease affecting mostly cattle, breaks out north of the Limpopo and spreads to South Africa. This worsens the poverty of black people and becomes one of the factors leading to the emergence of "poor whites".
- The first electric tram service is installed in Cape Town, between Adderley Street and Mowbray.
- Cecil John Rhodes is forced to resign as prime minister because of his involvement in the Jameson Raid.
- The first teachers' college in South Africa is opened in Wellington.
- The first magazine in Afrikaans, *Ons Klyntji*, appears.

1898
The first game reserve in the world, the Sabie Game Reserve (predecessor of the Kruger National Park), is proclaimed on the recommendation of Paul Kruger **(see page 72)**.

1899
- Negotiations between the Kruger government and the British colonial authorities fail and the Second Anglo-Boer War breaks out on 12 October.
- Boer forces besiege Mafeking and Kimberley. Other commandos besiege Ladysmith in Natal.
- In the Battle of Magersfontein on 11 December, the Boer forces under the command of generals Koos de la Rey (1847–1914) and Piet Cronjé (1836–1911) achieve a significant victory over the British army.
- In the same week as the Battle of Magersfontein the Boer forces also achieve victories at Stormberg and Colenso. Winston Churchill (1874–1965), a war correspondent accompanying the British army in Natal, is captured by the Boers and held as a prisoner of war in Pretoria, from where he escapes.

After the Battle of Magersfontein

- The Mount Nelson Hotel is opened in Cape Town. It is still a world-renowned hotel.

1900
- The British war hero Field Marshal Lord Frederick Sleigh Roberts (1832–1914), arrives in Cape Town as the new commander-in-chief of all British forces in South Africa. His chief of staff is Lord Horatio Kitchener (1850–1916).
- The Boer forces of Louis Botha achieve another victory in January over a strong British force at Spioenkop in Natal. The British losses are around 1 000 men.

Mount Nelson Hotel

- In February, Kimberley is attacked by a large British army force under General John French, while General Sir Redvers Buller ends the Boers' siege of Ladysmith.
- At Paardeberg, near the Modder River, General Piet Cronjé, with 4 000 men, has to surrender to the British. An attempt by the brilliant Free State general Christiaan de Wet (1854–1922) to save Cronjé's commando fails.
- British forces under Roberts take Bloemfontein on 13 March and shortly afterwards annex the whole Free State under the name Orange River Colony.
- Johannesburg and Pretoria fall into British hands on 31 May and 5 June respectively. The ZAR is annexed as the Transvaal colony.
- Commandant General Joubert of the ZAR dies and is succeeded by Louis Botha.
- The British administration begins to send Boer prisoners of war to camps in St Helena, Ceylon, Bermuda and India. According to British figures, during the course of the war around 25 000 men are sent to these camps.
- Guerrilla forces under De Wet continue attacks on British forces.
- The ageing Kruger leaves for Europe on board the *Gelderland* **(see page 147)**.
- Roberts returns to England in December under the impression that the war is as good as over. He hands control of the British forces to Kitchener.

Boer guerrillas

The Gelderland

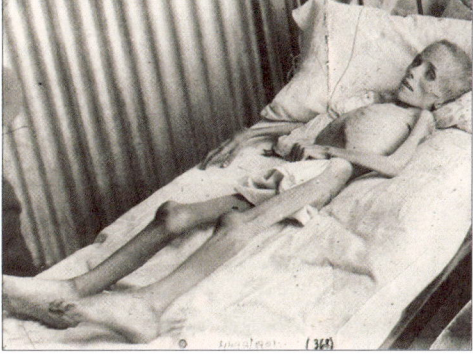
Lizzie van Zyl, a camp victim

- Increasing numbers of Boer women and children, as well as elderly Boer men, are sent by the British to concentration camps where they are housed in terrible conditions. Around 26 000 of them eventually die in these concentration camps.
- About 20 000 black people die in the separate concentration camps the British built for them. The conditions here are even worse than in the camps for the white people.
- The British relief worker Emily Hobhouse is one of the founders of a relief fund in England for women and children in the concentration camps. She visits the concentration camp at Bloemfontein and dedicates herself to the improvement of conditions in the camp. When she attempts to return to South Africa after a trip to England, she is denied entrance to the country by the British government.

1901
- Kitchener gives his forces the order to use a "scorched earth" tactic to force the Boers to surrender. Thousands of farmhouses are burnt down and the harvests and cattle destroyed. Kitchener also puts up block houses.
- The famous folk song "Sarie Marais" is written near Vryheid when soldiers under Louis Botha rewrite "Ellie Rhee", a slave ballad.
- Bubonic plague breaks out in Cape Town.

Block house, Leeu-Gamka

Melrose House

1902
- The Boer leaders realise that continued resistance will result in the annihilation of their people. The Peace of Vereeniging is signed on 31 May in Melrose House in Pretoria; formally bringing an end to the Second Anglo-Boer War.
- The Premier Diamond Mine at Cullinan, near Pretoria, is opened. Gold mining activities on the Witwatersrand are resumed.
- Rhodes dies in his humble beach cottage at Muizenberg on the Cape Peninsula.
- Major James Stevenson-Hamilton becomes the first warden of the Kruger National Park.

1903
Emily Hobhouse returns to South Africa.

1904
- The 78-year-old Paul Kruger dies in exile in Clarens, Switzerland. His remains are laid to rest on 16 December in Pretoria.
- Solomon (Sol) Tshekisho Plaatje publishes the first Tswana-English weekly, *Koranta ea Bechuana*.
- The first Chinese labourers (62 000) arrive in South Africa to satisfy the demand for unskilled mineworkers on the Witwatersrand.
- The Afrikaanse Christelike Vrouevereniging (ACVV) (Afrikaans Christian Women's Society) is established by Elizabeth Roos in Cape Town to undertake and coordinate welfare services.

1905
- Emily Hobhouse establishes the first weaving school at Philippolis in the Free State. There are eventually more than 25 such schools. She dies in England in 1926 and is buried at the National Women's Monument in Bloemfontein.
- The Second Afrikaans Language Movement begins with the publication of Eugène N. Marais's (1871–1936) poem "Winternag".
- The world's largest diamond, the 3 106 carat Cullinan, is found by Fred Wells in the Premier Mine at Cullinan near Pretoria.

1906
- The Transvaal is granted autonomy.
- The *Sunday Times*, the first Sunday newspaper in South Africa, appears. George Herbert Kingswell is the first editor.
- Pierre Basson, South Africa's first documented mass murderer, commits suicide while the police search for the bodies of at least nine people in the backyard of a house in Claremont, Cape Town.

1907
- The Orange River Colony (later the Orange Free State) is granted autonomy.
- Louis Botha's Het Volk party wins the general election and he becomes premier of the Transvaal.

Eugène N. Marais

Louis Botha

The Union Buildings

1908
The first meeting of the National Convention takes place in Durban. It is a meeting of the most important white political leaders of all four British colonies in South Africa (the Cape, Natal, Transvaal and the Free State).

1909
– A draft constitution for the Union of South Africa is approved by the four colonies and the British government accepts it as the South Africa Act.
– According to the terms of the South Africa Act, Pretoria will be the administrative capital, Bloemfontein the judicial capital and Cape Town the legislative capital. Coloured and black people in the Cape can vote if they meet certain qualifications, but in the other three provinces they have no franchise. Only white people can be members of parliament.
– South Africa becomes the first member of Fifa (the International Football Association) outside Europe.
– The South African Academy for Science and Art is established to promote the Afrikaans language, literature and culture.
– The *Waratah*, an Australian steamship, disappears on 26 July between Durban and Cape Town **(see page 205)**.

1910
– The Union of South Africa comes into being with Louis Botha as prime minister.
– The cornerstone of the Union Buildings is laid on Meintjeskop in Pretoria. The Union Buildings are completed in 1913.

1911
General Jan Smuts and General Louis Botha start the South African Party (SAP).

1912
The South African National Congress is established to promote the political and other interests of black people in South Africa. Dr John L. Dube

John Dube

(1871–1946) is elected as the first president. The name of the organisation is changed to the African National Congress (ANC) in 1923.

1913
- The Union Parliament accepts the Natives Land Act, which states that black people may own only about 10,5 million morgen of land in South Africa (about 7,3% of the total surface area). Most of this land is in the existing reserves for black people and not particularly suitable for agriculture. It hastens the impoverishment of rural black people and their migration to the cities.
- A deputation of black leaders under the leadership of Sol T. Plaatje goes to London to protest against the Natives Land Act to the British government, but does not achieve anything with this protest.
- Hertzog resigns as a member of Botha's cabinet.
- The Kirstenbosch National Botanical Gardens are proclaimed **(see page 127)**.
- South Africa's first flight school opens in Kimberley.
- The National Women's Monument in Bloemfontein is unveiled **(see page 108)**.
- The South African Police comes into existence.
- White mine workers strike in Johannesburg in support of five dismissed colleagues. Riots break out and more than 100 strikers and bystanders are killed in the violence.

1914
- General J.B.M. Hertzog starts the National Party in Bloemfontein.
- After the Forster Gang (William Forster, John Maxim and Carl Mezar) shoot eight people during a bank robbery gone wrong, the two surviving members of the gang (Mezar was shot dead earlier) and Forster's wife commit suicide in a cave where they are hiding.
- The Boer general Koos de la Rey and two other men are killed by a ricocheting bullet. This happens when they, due to a misunderstanding, drive through a roadblock set up by the police to find the infamous Forster Gang. Because of the political implications of this incident, there are persistent rumours for a long time that it was not an accident.
- The 1914 Rebellion breaks out when more than 11 000 citizens take up arms against the government. The rebellion is against the government's decision to declare war on Germany and invade German South-West Africa. They also hope to restore the independence of the republics. The poorly equipped and disorganised rebels are eventually forced to surrender. Beyers drowns in the Vaal River while fleeing his pursuers. De Wet and one of the other leaders are arrested and sentenced to prison and Jopie Fourie dies in front of a firing squad.
- Afrikaans, along with Dutch and English, is acknowledged as a language of instruction in schools up to standard four (grade six). From 1925 Afrikaans may be used as a language of instruction in all classes.

J.B.M. Hertzog

- The Hertzog Prize for literature is established by the SA Academy for Science and Art and is awarded for the first time in 1915. The poet Totius (J.D. du Toit, 1877–1953) is the first winner with his collection *Trekkerswee*.
- Mining at the Big Hole in Kimberley is halted **(see page 124)**.

A deserted trench after the Battle of Delville Wood

1915
- South African troops under the command of generals Botha, Smuts and Jaap van Deventer defeat a small German force in German South-West Africa.
- Botha's SAP wins the second general election in the Union.
- The Cape Town daily *Die Burger* appears for the first time.

1916
- Union troops are sent to Europe to take part in the trench war on the Western Front. Later in the war South African troops are also involved in military operations in North Africa and the Middle East. More than 12 000 South Africans die in this four-year war.
- In the Battle of Delville Wood in France, the Union troops earn great acclaim for their courageous stand against the enemy, but the death toll is terrible: of the 3 153 officers and privates who take part in the battle, only 750 survive.
- The first edition of the magazine *Die Huisgenoot* (now *Huisgenoot*) appears in Cape Town.
- The South African Native College is opened in the Eastern Cape. It later becomes the University of Fort Hare.

1917
- Smuts is appointed to the British war cabinet in London by the British prime minister, David Lloyd George. Smuts becomes an important advisor to the Allied forces. One of his proposals leads to the establishment of the Royal Air Force.
- Ernest Oppenheimer **(see page 151)** and the American engineer W.L. Honnold establish the Anglo American Corporation.
- The Industrial and Commercial Workers Union of Africa (ICU) is founded in Cape Town by Clements Kadalie as the first trade union that tries to further the interests of black workers.

1918
- Botha and Smuts represent the Union of South Africa at the peace negotiations after the First World War at Versailles, France.
- South Africa, like the rest of the world, is plagued by a deadly flu epidemic, the so-called Spanish Influenza. About 140 000 people in South Africa die. Most deaths are in the age group 25–34 years.
- The Koöperatiewe Wijnbouwers Vereniging van Zuid-Afrika (KWV) (Cooperative Wine Farmers' Association of South Africa) is established in Paarl.

- The Afrikanerbroederbond (AB) is formed in Pretoria. The goals are to protect and promote the interests of the Afrikaner community. Until the organisation amends its constitution in the 1990s, only white Protestant Afrikaner men are accepted as members.
- The University of South Africa (Unisa) is established.
- Victoria College in Stellenbosch becomes the University of Stellenbosch, and the South African College in Cape Town becomes the University of Cape Town.
- Sanlam and Santam are established in Cape Town.
- C.J. Langenhoven **(see page 148)** writes "Die Stem van Suid-Afrika" **(see page 7)**.
- Nelson Mandela is born on 18 July in Mvezo, a village in the Umtata district **(see page 149)**.

Jan Smuts

1919
- Premier Louis Botha dies and is succeeded by Jan Smuts **(see page 154)**.
- Dr Abdullah Abdurahman becomes the first coloured member of the Cape Provincial Council.
- The Potchefstroom College of Education is opened.

1920
- Hertzog's NP wins the general election.
- The Union of South Africa is given an international mandate to govern South-West Africa.
- Two South African pilots complete the first flight from Great Britain to South Africa in four days, 13 hours and 30 minutes.

1921
- After the Unionist Party and the SAP coalesce, a new election is called. The reconstituted SAP wins the most seats.
- The South African Reserve Bank comes into existence.
- The Comrades Marathon takes place for the first time **(see page 245)**.

1922
- A general mineworker strike begins on the Witwatersrand, when mine owners decide to lower the wages of white workers and hire more low-paid black workers. The first violent clashes between white workers and the police break out in February. The strike quickly becomes a full-scale revolt. People are attacked, cars vandalised, telephone lines are cut and a railway line is blown up. Smuts declares a state of emergency and government troops are called in. On 17 March the strike is called off by the trade unions. About 153 people die and more than 650 are injured. A total of 853 people are arrested and four strike leaders are sentenced to death and hanged.
- The University of the Witwatersrand is opened in Johannesburg.
- The South African Reserve Bank issues its first banknotes.

1923
– Platinum deposits are discovered in the Waterberg area in the Transvaal.
– The first radio broadcast in South Africa takes place.

1924
– The Labour Party and Hertzog's NP merge and form the Pact Government, which wins the election. Hertzog becomes prime minister.
– A professor from Wits, Raymond Dart, identifies a fossil skull found at Taung as that of an anthropoid that lived more than a million years ago.

1925
– Afrikaans replaces Dutch as the second official language of South Africa.
– The geologist Dr Hans Merensky discovers rich diamond deposits at Alexander Bay in Namaqualand.

Taung skull

1926
– The Shingwedzi and the Sabie game reserves are given the name Kruger National Park. It is the first national park in South Africa **(see page 72)**.
– One of the biggest diamond rushes in the world takes place on the farm Elandsputte near Lichtenburg. At one stage, more than 30 000 people take part in an organised race for the pegging off of claims.

1927
– The first OK Bazaar opens in Johannesburg.
– Huibrecht Jacob de Leeuw dies on the gallows. He caused the deaths of all three members of a committee investigating allegations of fraud against him when he blew up the Dewetsdorp town hall with dynamite.

1928
– The new Union flag is raised on 31 May in Cape Town **(see page 11)**. This flag was already used two months earlier, on 30 March, at an international conference in Havana, Cuba, in which representatives from South Africa participated.
– At the first official raising of the Union flag, "Die Stem van Suid-Afrika" is sung for the first time **(see page 7)**.
– Iscor (the South African Iron and Steel Industrial Corporation) is established by the state.
– The Carnegie Commission is constituted to investigate the "poor white question" in South Africa.

The Union flag

1929
– The Pact Government, under the leadership of Hertzog, increases its majority in the general election.
– The Table Mountain cableway is used for the first time **(see page 133)**.
– The Federasie van Afrikaanse Kultuurverenigings (FAK) (Federation of Afrikaans Cultural Societies) is established in Bloemfontein to promote and coordinate Afrikaners' cultural activities.
– South Africa's first airline, Union Airways, flies with a small aeroplane from Johannesburg to Port Elizabeth. This airline is later taken over by the government and renamed South African Airways.

The Table Mountain cableway

1930
– White women over the age of 30 are given the right to vote.
– The University of Pretoria formally comes into existence out of the former Transvaal University College, which was established in 1908.
– The worldwide Great Depression, which began in 1929 with the collapse of the American stock market (the Wall Street Crash), reaches South Africa. Mines, businesses, factories and shops close and unemployment rises. White and black South Africans live in utter poverty.
– The Afrikaanse Taal- en Kultuurvereniging (ATKV) (Afrikaans Language and Cultural Society) is established in Cape Town.
– The first Afrikaans movie with sound, *Moedertjie*, with Stephanie Faure, Pierre de Wet and André Huguenot in some of the leading roles, is released.

1932
– The cornerstone of Groote Schuur Hospital in Cape Town is laid. The hospital is opened in 1938.
– The famous opera singer Mimi Coertse is born in Durban. She earns international fame at a young age when she begins to sing as a coloratura soprano in Vienna, Austria. She plays many opera roles in the famed Vienna State Opera House. After 17 years, she returns to South Africa in 1973. She institutes the Mimi Coertse Bursary to lend financial support to talented young opera singers.

Mimi Coertse

– Miriam Makeba (nicknamed Mama Afrika) is born in Johannesburg. She becomes world famous as a singer. She also makes a name for herself as a political activist and acts as a UN delegate for the African state of Guinea, speaking out against South Africa's apartheid policies in the General Assembly. In 1960 she is forced into exile by the South African government. In 1965 she becomes the first black woman to win a Grammy. She fights for the emancipation of South Africa from racial discrimination and in 1986 is awarded the Dag Hammerskjöld Peace Prize. She returns to South Africa in 1990. In 2008 she dies of a heart attack.
– Daisy de Melker is executed on the gallows. Between 1923 and 1932 she poisoned her three husbands and her son.

Miriam Makeba

1933
– Hertzog's National Party and Smuts's South African Party form a coalition government with Hertzog as the leader.
– The first translation of the Bible into Afrikaans is completed and 10 000 copies arrive in Cape Town from London.

1934
– The NP and SAP coalesce to form the United Party (UP), with Hertzog as leader and Smuts as the deputy leader. A group that does not agree with this step starts a "purified" National Party under the leadership of D.F. Malan.
– The first South African Grand Prix takes places in East London.

1935
The South African First Aid League is established.

1936
– The South African Broadcasting Corporation (SABC) is established.
– The first Afrikaans daily in Johannesburg, *Ons Vaderland* (later *Die Vaderland*), appears.
– The laying of the cornerstone of the Voortrekker Monument in Pretoria **(see page 110)** and the Symbolic Ox Wagon Trek takes place.
– The Battle of Blood River is commemorated **(see page 106)**.
– The UP wins the general election.

Voortrekker Monument

- A living coelacanth is discovered by Dr Marjory Courtney-Latimer and Prof. J.L.B. Smith near East London. It was previously accepted that these primeval fish had died out about 70 million years ago. Since 1938 more living coelacanths have been discovered.

1939
- The Ossewabrandwag (OB) (Ox Wagon Sentinel) is established in Bloemfontein. Colonel J. Laas is the leader. The goal of the organisation is to unite Afrikaners and protect their interests. All members take an oath that they will not rest until the freedom of Afrikaners is regained. In 1942 Dr Malan rules that no member of the National Party may join the Ossewabrandwag. Many members resign and in 1952 the organisation is finally dissolved.
- After a bitter struggle between Prime Minister Hertzog and his deputy, Smuts, Smuts's motion that South Africa should enter the Second World War on the side of the Allies is passed. Hertzog resigns and Smuts takes over as prime minister.
- Malan's "purified" NP and some of Hertzog's supporters form the Herenigde Nasionale Party (HNP) (Reunited National Party). Hertzog dies in 1942 and Malan succeeds him as leader of the HNP.

1940
- The Industrial Development Corporation (IDC) is established by the government.
- Dr Alfred Bitini Xuma is elected president of the ANC.

1941
Smuts is awarded the rank of field marshal in the British army. He is the only South African ever to receive this honour.

1942
- The Second SA Division, along with other Allied troops, is forced to surrender at Tobruk by Field Marshal Rommel. It is regarded as one of Rommel's greatest victories.
- Black urbanisation picks up quickly because of the many industrial job opportunities, but also because of the impoverishment of people living in the reserves for black people.

1943
- South African forces participate in the Allied victory over Rommel in North Africa.
- About 80 000 Italian prisoners of war are brought to South Africa over the course of the war. They work on farms and road-building projects.

1944
- The Youth League of the ANC is established. They propose a more militant form of resistance against racial discrimination in South Africa. Among the early members are Nelson Mandela (1918–), Walter Sisulu (1912–2003) and Oliver Tambo (1917–1993).

1945
- South Africa becomes a founding member of the United Nations.
- Gideon Brand van Zyl (1873–1956) becomes the first person born in South Africa to hold the post of governor-general of the Union.

- The serious food and fuel shortages experienced during the war years continue.

1946
About 70 000 black mine workers strike on the Witwatersrand. The strike is organised by the African Mineworkers' Union (AMU).

1947
- The British royal family (King George VI, Queen Elizabeth and the princesses Elizabeth and Margaret) visit South Africa.
- Dr Robert Broom discovers a million-year-old skull in the Sterkfontein Caves **(see page 136)**.

The British royal family in South Africa

1948
- The NP under the leadership of Malan narrowly wins the general election against Smuts's UP. Malan becomes prime minister.
- The Huguenot Monument is unveiled in Franschhoek **(see page 107)**.
- Eighty-three German children orphaned in the Second World War arrive in South Africa.

1949
- About a quarter of a million people attend the inauguration of the Voortrekker Monument in Pretoria on 16 December.
- Riots break out between black people and Indians in Natal; 106 people die.
- The socialite Bubbles Schroeder is murdered in Johannesburg. Hyman Leibman and David Polliack are arrested, but are later released due to insufficient evidence.

1950
- The Suppression of Communism Act, the Population Registration Act, the Group Areas Act and the Immorality Amendment Act are all approved.
- General Jan Smuts dies on his farm Doornkloof near Pretoria.
- A South African air force squadron distinguishes itself in the Korean War.
- Sasol (the South African Coal, Oil and Gas Corporation) is established by the state.
- The University of the Orange Free State in Bloemfontein is given full university status.
- Vic Toweel becomes South Africa's first world boxing champion.
- The first Afrikaans full-length film, Jamie Uys's *Daar Doer in die Bosveld*, is released.
- The first Duzi Canoe Marathon takes place.

1951
- South Africa's first quadruplets of the same sex (four boys), the Lombard quadruplets of Loeriesfontein, are born on 13 February in the Voortrekker Hospital in Calvinia.

1952
– The Van Riebeeck festival is celebrated in Cape Town by mainly white South Africans to commemorate the 300th anniversary of Jan van Riebeeck's arrival.
– The ANC mounts a campaign by black people to protest apartheid. Protest leaders are prosecuted and about 6 000 people are arrested.

1953
– The NP under Malan wins the general election with a much bigger majority.

1954
– The statue of Paul Kruger in Pretoria is moved to its current position on Church Square.
– Malan steps down as prime minister. He is succeeded by J.G. (Johannes Gerhardus) Strijdom.

Paul Kruger statue

1955
– About 60 000 black inhabitants of the neighbourhood Sophiatown in Johannesburg are forcibly moved to Meadowlands by police. Sophiatown is declared a white area and renamed Triomf. In February 2006 the neighbourhood's original name is reinstated at a celebration.
– Great Britain returns the Simon's Town Naval Base to South Africa. The formal handover to the SA Navy takes place in 1957.
– The Oppenheimer jewels, valued at £250 000, are stolen from the family's residence in Parktown, Johannesburg. Most of the jewellery is found and returned.

1956
– Coloured voters are taken off the voters' roll.
– Thousands of black women take part in a protest march to the Union Buildings in Pretoria to protest against the expansion of the hated pass laws.

1957
The Union flag becomes South Africa's only flag and "Die Stem van Suid-Afrika" the only national anthem **(see pages 7 & 11)**.

1958
– The NP under Strijdom wins the general election. Strijdom dies a few months later and is succeeded as premier by Dr H.F. (Hendrik Frensch) Verwoerd. He supports the idea of independent homelands for black people.
– The Pan-Africanist Congress (PAC) is established by Robert Sobukwe in Soweto.

1959
– The limited representation black people have had in the Union Parliament is scrapped.

- Members of the UP, under the leadership of Helen Suzman, break away and start the Progressive Party (PP).

1960
- The blue crane is accepted as South Africa's national bird.
- The police shoot 69 people who are part of a demonstration against the pass laws in Sharpeville. A state of emergency is declared. About 30 000 black people march to the Parliament Buildings in Cape Town. The government bans the ANC and PAC.
- David Pratt wounds Dr Verwoerd when he shoots him twice in the head during his opening address at the annual Rand Easter Show. Pratt is later declared mentally disturbed and sent to a psychiatric institution, where he commits suicide in 1961.
- The biggest mining disaster yet in South Africa occurs at Clydesdale (in today's KwaZulu-Natal). Altogether 435 mine workers die, despite weeks of attempts to save them.
- In a referendum in which only white people can take part, voters vote in favour of the declaration of a republic.
- Chief Albert Luthuli (1898–1967), president of the ANC, receives the Nobel Peace Prize.
- South Africa takes part in the Olympics Games for the last time; South Africa is only readmitted in 1992.

Blue crane

1961
- A decimal currency is taken into use in South Africa.
- The South African government's request that the country remain a member of the Commonwealth after becoming a republic, is denied.
- The Republic of South Africa is formally declared on 31 May. The first state president is C.R. (Charles Robberts) Swart (1894–1982).
- The ANC decides to take up armed struggle against the government. The organisation starts a military wing called Umkhonto we Sizwe (MK – "Spear of the Nation").

1962
- Nelson Mandela is sentenced to five years in prison for his involvement in the banned ANC **(see page 149)**.
- The United Nations (UN) institutes sanctions against South Africa.
- The government announces the construction of the Orange River Scheme.

1963
- Walter Sisulu and other leaders of the ANC are arrested in Johannesburg after a police raid on their secret headquarters in Rivonia, near Johannesburg **(see page 153)**.

1964
- In the Rivonia Trial Nelson Mandela's five-year prison sentence is lengthened to a life sentence.

District Six

– Wilbur Smith's first book, *When the Lion Feeds*, appears; it is banned in South Africa.

1965
– The Afrikaans poet Ingrid Jonker commits suicide by walking into the sea at Three Anchor Bay in Cape Town.

1966
– Verwoerd is stabbed to death in his seat in the House of Assembly in Cape Town by Dimitri Tsafendas (1918–1999). Tsafendas is declared insane and in 1999 dies at the age of 81 in the Sterkfontein Psychiatric Hospital. Verwoerd is succeeded by Balthazar Johannes (John) Vorster. District Six, near the CBD of Cape Town, is declared a white area. The houses are demolished and residents are moved to the Cape Flats.

1967
– Prof. Christiaan Neethling Barnard performs the first heart transplant in the world at Groote Schuur Hospital, Cape Town **(see page 146)**.
– A Vickers Viscount SAA aeroplane, the Rietbok, falls into the sea near London with 25 people on board.
– Martin Thembisile (Chris) Hani succeeds Joe Slovo as chief of staff of Umkhonto we Sizwe.

1968
– The Rand Afrikaans University (RAU) begins lectures in temporary lecture halls in Braamfontein, Johannesburg, and remains there until its ultra-modern new campus in Auckland Park is completed in 1974.
– Steve Biko and his colleagues establish the South African Students' Organisation (SASO).

1969
– The Herstigte Nasionale Party (HNP) (Refounded National Party) is established.
– Steve Biko starts the Black Students' Organisation.
– An earthquake damages many buildings in Tulbagh.
– The first Coloured People's Representative Council is elected.

1970
– The NP wins the white general election with a slightly smaller majority than in 1966.

1971
The first yacht race from the Cape to Rio begins on 16 January.

1973
- The South African National Observatory is opened in Sutherland. In the following decades this Karoo town becomes the centre of astronomical research in Southern Africa.
- Steve Biko is banned by the government.

1974
- The NP increases its majority in the white general election.
- The 1820 Settlers' Monument in Grahamstown is inaugurated.
- The Rosenkowitz Six, the first South African sextuplets to survive, are born in Groote Schuur Hospital in Cape Town.
- The 16-year-old Marlene Lehnberg pays the disabled Marthinus Choegoe to murder the wife of her lover, Christiaan van der Linde, in their home in Bellville. Both receive the death penalty, but this is later commuted to a prison sentence. They are both freed in 1986.

Afrikaans Language Monument

1975
- The jurist and political activist Bram Fischer dies shortly after being released from prison.
- South Africa military forces enter Angola to stop cross-border attacks from this country on what is now Namibia and to help Jonas Savimbi's Unita rebel forces in their efforts against the Angolan government and their Cuban military supporters.
- The government declares that all black children will receive free and compulsory education.
- The first TV broadcast in South Africa takes place.
- The Afrikaans Language Monument on Paarl Rock is unveiled **(see page 106)**.

1976
- Riots on 16 June by school children in Soweto and the actions of the police lead to widespread unrest across the country in which about 600 people die **(see page 106)**.
- The government declares the Transkei a completely independent black state. Neither the rest of the world nor the majority of black people in South Africa accept this step.
- The harbour at Richards Bay is put into use.

1977
- Steve Biko dies in police custody of brain injuries.

- The *Windsor Castle*, the last passenger ship of the Union-Castle Line, leaves Cape Town on her final voyage.
- The Information Scandal comes to light. It appears that the Vorster government has been illegally misusing large amounts of state funds.
- The UP is formally dissolved.
- The United Nations forbids weapon sales to South Africa.
- The Progressive Federal Party is created by the merger of the Progressive Reform Party with a breakaway group from the United Party.

Windsor Castle

1978
- Coloured students are permitted to attend the University of Stellenbosch for the first time.
- Vorster is forced to resign as prime minister. He then becomes state president and dies in 1983. He is succeeded by P.W. Botha.
- Dr Robert Smit, NP MP for Springs, and his wife are murdered in their home. The crime is never solved.

1979
Dr Frederik van Zyl Slabbert becomes the leader of the PFP.

1980
A lift falls in the Vaal Reef gold mine and the 24 mine workers who are in the lift die.

1981
The Buffalo River at Laingsburg in the Karoo bursts its banks. Altogether 120 people drown and serious damage is caused **(see page 128)**.

1982
- Dr A.P. (Andries Petrus) Treurnicht (1921–1993) establishes the Conservative Party (CP).
- The South African navy ship SAS *President Kruger* sinks after a collision with the SAS *Tafelberg* and 16 members of the SA Navy die.
- Ruth First, the anti-apartheid activist and wife of Joe Slovo, dies in a letter bomb attack in Maputo.

1983
- The Botha government pushes through constitutional amendments. It creates a Tricameral Parliament consisting of a House of Assembly for white voters, a House of Representatives for coloured people and a House of Delegates for Indians.
- The United Democratic Front (UDF) is established in Cape Town.
- A powerful bomb planted by ANC members explodes in Church Street, Pretoria; 18 people die and many more are injured.
- The Stander Gang (André Stander, Patrick McCall and Allan Heyl) rob more than 15 banks in the Johannesburg area. Stander and McCall are later shot dead.

Heyl is extradited from Great Britain to South Africa and in 2005 is released from a South African prison.

1984
- Violent resistance to apartheid breaks out in neighbourhoods like Sebokeng on the East Rand and quickly spreads to other parts of the country.
- The Anglican clergyman Dr Desmond Tutu receives the Nobel Peace Prize **(see page 155)**.

1985
- In the worst bus accident ever in South Africa 42 learners die when a school bus crashes into the Westdene Dam in Johannesburg.

1986
- Frederik van Zyl Slabbert resigns as leader of the PFP and as member of parliament.
- Passbooks are scrapped.
- The president of Mozambique, Samora Machel (born 1933), dies in a plane crash in South African airspace. The cause of the accident is never determined.

1987
- Sixty Afrikaners start talks with the ANC leadership in exile in Dakar, Senegal. These are followed by a series of meetings between white and black South Africans.
- In the KwaMakhutha massacre 13 people, mainly women and children, die and many are injured when the house of UDF activist Bheki Ntuli is attacked with AK-47s.
- A 48-year-old grandmother, Pat Anthony of Tzaneen, becomes the first surrogate mother in the world to give birth to her own grandchildren (triplets).
- The *Helderberg*, an SAA Boeing 747, crashes into the sea near Mauritius. All 160 people on board die. Based on new information in 2001 it is suspected that there were highly flammable substances on board.

1988
- P.W. Botha has a mini stroke and resigns as state president. He is succeeded by F.W. (Frederik Willem) de Klerk **(see page 146)**.
- South African forces withdraw from Angola.
- Barend Strydom (the "White Wolf") shoots seven black people and an Indian in cold blood in Pretoria.

1989
- Beaches and many other public places are opened to all races.
- The student activists Thabo Mohale, Portia Shabangu and Derrick Mashobane are shot dead in Swaziland by members of the South African police's Vlakplaas unit.
- The Democratic Party (DP) is formed. It consists mainly of members of the former PFP, white voters who formerly belonged to the NP and various smaller political groups.
- Walter Sisulu **(see page 153)** and six other ANC leaders are released from prison.

1990
- On 2 February F.W. de Klerk announces the unconditional release of Nelson Mandela and the unbanning of the ANC, PAC and SA Communist Party (SACP).
- On 11 February Nelson Mandela walks out of the Victor Verster Prison near Paarl to freedom. It is seen by millions of people around the world. Later that afternoon he addresses a huge crowd on the Grand Parade in Cape Town.

House in Orania

- The Groote Schuur Minute is signed in May by the ANC and the government and paves the way for negotiations. The ANC announces the halt of its armed struggle.
- The leader of the South African Communist Party, Joe Slovo, returns after 27 years in exile. Many other political exiles also return to South Africa in this period.
- On the East Rand 143 people die in clashes between supporters of the Inkatha Party (of which Mangosuthu Buthlezi is the leader) and residents of Tokoza, Vosloorus and Katlehong who support the ANC.

1991
- Codesa (the Convention for a Democratic South Africa) begins on 20 December in the World Trade Centre in Kempton Park, Johannesburg.
- Orania, which is developed as a homeland for white Afrikaners, is bought by the Afrikaner Vryheidstigting (Afrikaner Freedom Foundation) under the leadership of Prof. Carel Boshoff, the son-in-law of Dr Verwoerd **(see page 130)**.
- The Group Areas Act is repealed and the adoption of children across the colour bar becomes legal.
- Ismail Mahomed becomes South Africa's first black judge.
- South Africa again becomes a member of the International Olympic Committee and is readmitted to the International Cricket Board.
- South African author Nadine Gordimer receives the Nobel Prize for Literature.
- Winnie Mandela, the wife of Nelson Mandela, is sentenced to six years in prison for her role in the death of Stompie Sepei. The sentence is later commuted to a fine of R15 000.
- The passenger ship *Oceanos* sinks on 4 August off the Wild Coast. There is no loss of life. The captain and many of the crew members leave the ship before the passengers **(see page 204)**.

1992
- In a referendum white voters vote in favour of De Klerk's reform policy by an overwhelming majority.
- De Klerk and Mandela jointly receive the Felix Houphouet-Boigny Peace Prize in Paris.

- A massacre occurs at Boipatong when an ANC-aligned community is attacked by mainly Zulu residents of a hostel for migrant workers; 46 people die.
- South Africa is readmitted to the International Football Association (FIFA), from which it was expelled in 1976.

1993
- Chris Hani, secretary-general of the SACP and a prominent leader in the ANC, is shot dead in cold blood at his home in Boksburg by Janusz Waluz.
- Amy Biehl, an American student volunteering at an aid project for black people in Cape Town, is murdered in Guguletu by political agitators.
- In the St James Church in Kenilworth, Cape Town, 11 people die and 49 are injured when a group of men with machine guns open fire on the congregation.
- At negotiations in Kempton Park an Interim Constitution for South Africa is accepted.
- De Klerk and Mandela jointly receive the Nobel Peace Prize.

1994
- Walvis Bay is handed over to Namibia.
- The ANC wins the first democratic elections in South Africa and Nelson Mandela becomes the first black president of South Africa.
- The new South African flag is raised for the first time on 10 May **(see page 11)**.
- A multi-party government for South Africa is formed in which the NP and Inkatha Freedom Party also participate. De Klerk (NP) and Thabo Mbeki (ANC) are appointed deputy presidents.
- The respected Dutch Reformed theologian Prof. Johan Heyns is shot dead in his house in Pretoria. The crime is never solved.
- Three members of the Afrikanerweerstandsbeweging (AWB) (Afrikaner Resistance Movement) are shot dead by the Bophuthatswana army.
- In the massacre at Shell House (the headquarters of the ANC), eight Inkatha Freedom Party members are shot dead when security officers begin to shoot at protestors. In violence resulting from this massacre, 50 more people die in and around Johannesburg.

1995
- South Africa is the host country of the World Cup Rugby Tournament and beats New Zealand in the final 15 – 12.

1996
- The first sitting of the Truth and Reconciliation Commission (TRC), under the chairmanship of Desmond Tutu, is held in East London.
- After a marriage of 38 years, Nelson Mandela divorces Winnie **(see page 149)**.
- Mandela signs the new South African Constitution as president after it is approved by parliament.
- The National Party withdraws from the multi-party government.
- Josiah Thugwane becomes the first black South African to win an Olympic gold medal when he wins the men's marathon at the Olympic Games in Atlanta, USA. The South African swimmer Penny Heyns also wins a gold medal.

1997
- Eugène Terre'Blanche, leader of the Afrikanerweerstandsbeweging (AWB), is sentenced to six years in prison for the assault and attempted murder of two black men.
- The first oil is pumped from the Oribi oil field at Mossel Bay.

1998
- President Nelson Mandela marries Graça Machel, widow of the former president of Mozambique, at the age of 80 **(see page 149)**.
- President Bill Clinton and his wife, Hillary, are the first American presidential couple to visit South Africa.
- A bomb explodes at the Planet Hollywood restaurant in the Waterfront, Cape Town. Two people die and 27 are injured.
- The four murderers of American student Amy Biehl are granted amnesty by the TRC.

Nelson Mandela and Graça Machel

1999
- The ANC wins the second democratic election.
- Nelson Mandela steps down as president and is succeeded by deputy president Thabo Mbeki.
- Tito Mboweni becomes the first black president of the South African Reserve Bank.
- The African People's Liberation Army (Apla), the armed wing of the PAC, is disbanded.
- The well-known South African tenor Gé Korsten commits suicide at the age of 71.
- A total of 26 British tourists and a tour guide die in a bus accident in the Long Tom Pass, Mpumalanga.

2000
- Dr Allan Boesak, a respected theologian, is found guilty of embezzling about R1,3 million and sentenced to three years in prison.
- The Chinese ore carrier *Treasure* sinks on 23 June near Melkbosstrand, causing oil pollution.

2001
- The biggest disaster in South African sport occurs on 11 April at a soccer match at Ellis Park, Johannesburg, when 43 spectators die in a stampede.
- Prof. Christiaan Barnard dies on 2 September in Cyprus following a serious asthma attack.

- Mrs Marike de Klerk, ex-wife of former president F.W. de Klerk, is murdered in her flat in Table View, Cape Town **(see page 147)**.
- The Ukkasie Festival, the first Afrikaans arts festival held abroad, takes place in London.

2002
- Dr Wouter Basson, head of the former government's secret chemical warfare programme, is acquitted on charges of murder, conspiracy, possession of drugs and fraud.
- The Khoi woman Sarah Baartman's remains arrive in South Africa **(see page 158)**.
- Mark Shuttleworth becomes the first South African to travel into space, as a paying member of the crew of a Russian Soyuz space craft **(see page XX153)**.
- The former Protea cricket captain Hansie Cronjé dies in a plane crash in the mountains near George.

2003
- Walter Sisulu dies at the age of 91.
- The Conservative Party, the Afrikaner-Eenheidsbeweging (EAB) (Afrikaner Unity Movement) and the Freedom Front unite to establish a new party, the Freedom Front Plus (FF+).
- J.M. Coetzee receives the Nobel Prize for Literature.
- Eskom erects three wind turbines on an experimental wind farm at Klipheuwel, near Durbanville.
- The first 46664 concert, organised by the Nelson Mandela Foundation to create awareness of HIV/Aids, takes place.

2004
- President Thabo Mbeki is inaugurated for a second term after the ANC wins the country's general election with an overwhelming majority.
- The South African-born Charlize Theron wins a Golden Globe and an Oscar as best actress for her role as the American serial killer Aileen Wuornos in the movie *Monster* **(see page 154)**.
- On 15 May, South Africa is named host country of the 2010 Fifa Football World Cup.
- After poor election results the New National Party (NNP) dissolves. Many of its former members join the ANC.
- Dr Beyers Naudé, internationally famous theologian and anti-apartheid activist, dies at the age of 89 **(see page 150)**.
- Six people die and more than 100 are injured in a gas explosion at the Sasol plant in Secunda, Mpumalanga.

Wind turbine

- The singer Brenda Fassie dies after taking an overdose of drugs.
- The South African-born Michael Melvill becomes the first person to make a space flight with a craft developed by a non-governmental organisation. On 21 June he reaches a height of 100km with the SpaceShipOne spaceplane built by the American aerospace company Scaled Composites.
- The four South African swimmers Roland Schoeman, Lyndon Ferns, Ryk Neethling and Darian Townsend win the gold medal at the Olympic Games in Athens. At the same time they smash the world record in the 4 x 100m freestyle relay.

Brenda Fassie

2005
- After 12 years in jail Allan George Heyl, the last surviving member of the Stander Gang, is released.
- Deputy President Jacob Zuma is relieved of his post by President Thabo Mbeki after allegations of corruption.
- The South African a capella group Ladysmith Black Mambazo win their second Grammy.

2006
- The business leader Anton Rupert dies at the age of 89 in Stellenbosch **(see page 152)**.
- Jacob Zuma is found not guilty of rape by Judge Willem van der Merwe.
- South African director Gavin Hood's movie *Tsotsi*, based on the novel by Athol Fugard, wins an Oscar for best film in a foreign language.
- The music icon and TV personality Taliep Petersen, who is especially known for musicals such as *Fairyland*, *Kat and the Kings* and *Ghoema*, is murdered in his home in Athlone, Cape Town. His wife, Najwa, and three suspects are later arrested.

2007
- Dr Piet Koornhof, a former cabinet member and ambassador, dies at the age of 82 in Stellenbosch.
- Marais Viljoen, South Africa's last ceremonial president, dies.
- Prof. Russel Botman becomes the first coloured rector of the University of Stellenbosch.
- The reggae singer Lucky Dube is shot dead in Rosettenville, Johannesburg.
- South Africa's Soweto Gospel Choir wins a Grammy for the best world music album for their CD *Blessed*.
- Ten soldiers from the Air Defence Regiment in Lohatla, Kimberley die and 14 are seriously injured when an anti-aircraft gun goes out of control during a training exercise.

Taliep Petersen

- The South African boxer Cassius Baloyi becomes the first South African to win five world title boxing matches.

2008
- A serious electricity crisis develops in South Africa. Eskom and the government appeal to the public and manufacturing sector to save power. The gold mines close for a few days and load shedding is implemented. Businesses suffer large losses.
- A death mask of General Koos de la Rey, made by the sculptor Anton van Wouw after his death in 1914, is discovered. DNA tests are used to determine the authenticity of the mask.

Najwa Petersen

- Widespread xenophobic violence breaks out in townships around Johannesburg and Cape Town. Foreigners are attacked and their shops and houses are plundered and burnt down. The violence spreads quickly to other parts of the country. Many people are injured and killed. The army is called in to reinforce the police. African countries help to evacuate their citizens from South Africa and other refugees are housed in temporary camps.
- Judge Chris Nicholson finds that Jacob Zuma, the ANC's candidate for the party's presidency, was wrongfully accused on 18 charges of corruption, money laundering, tax evasion, fraud and extortion, and he alleges that there was political interference in the case against Zuma.
- In September President Thabo Mbeki is forced to resign by the ruling ANC. He is replaced by Kgalema Motlanthe.
- Najwa Petersen, Abdoer Emjedi and Waheed Hassen are found guilty of the murder of theatre legend Taliep Petersen, Najwa's husband.
- A new political party, Cope (Congress of the People), is established under the leadership of Mosiuoa Lekota and Mbhazima Shilowa, as a breakaway group of the ANC.
- For the first time in the history of the Helgaard Steyn Prize for Literature the prize money of R150 000 is shared by Marlene van Niekerk (for *Agaat*) and Hermann Giliomee (for *Die Afrikaners*).

2009
- The court of appeal through Judge Louis Harmse rejects the Nicholson ruling of 2008 and decides unanimously in favour of the National Prosecuting Authority. Jacob Zuma can now again be prosecuted on the previous charges and must also pay the costs of the lawsuit. In April the NPA decides it will not pursue charges against Zuma.
- Giniel de Villiers becomes the first South African to win the demanding Dakar Rally. It is the seventh time he has competed. In 2008 this rally is cancelled because of threats by terrorist organisations, and in 2009 it takes place in South America rather than North Africa.
- The governing ANC party achieves 65,9% (national) in the election and therefore just misses a two-thirds majority. The DA achieves victory in the Western Cape with 51,5%. Nationally, Cope achieves the second-highest number of votes. Most smaller parties fare very badly.
- In May Jacob Zuma is inaugurated as South Africa's fourth president.

Important South African inventions

Invention	Person	Year
Appletiser	Edmond Lombardi	1966
Baracuda (automated swimming pool cleaner)	Paul Lambourn, Michael Moore, Henk van der Meijden and Alex Wadman	1976
Bentley Belt	Mona Bentley	1965
Chutney, Mrs. Ball's-	Amelia Ball	1918
Boxing gloves, shock-absorbing	A. Stanford	1992
CAT scanner	Allan Cormick	1957
Computicket system	Percy Tucker	1975
Harbour blocks (for breakwaters)	Eric Merrifield	1966
Flamingo and Dart cars	Bob van Niekerk, Willie Meissner and Verster de Wit	1950s
Kreepy Krauly (automated swimming pool cleaner)	Ferdinand Chauvier	1974
Optoscan (for retinal examinations)	Bernard Woolf	1978
Pratley Putty	George M. Pratley	1948

Harbour blocks

PART 2
GENERAL

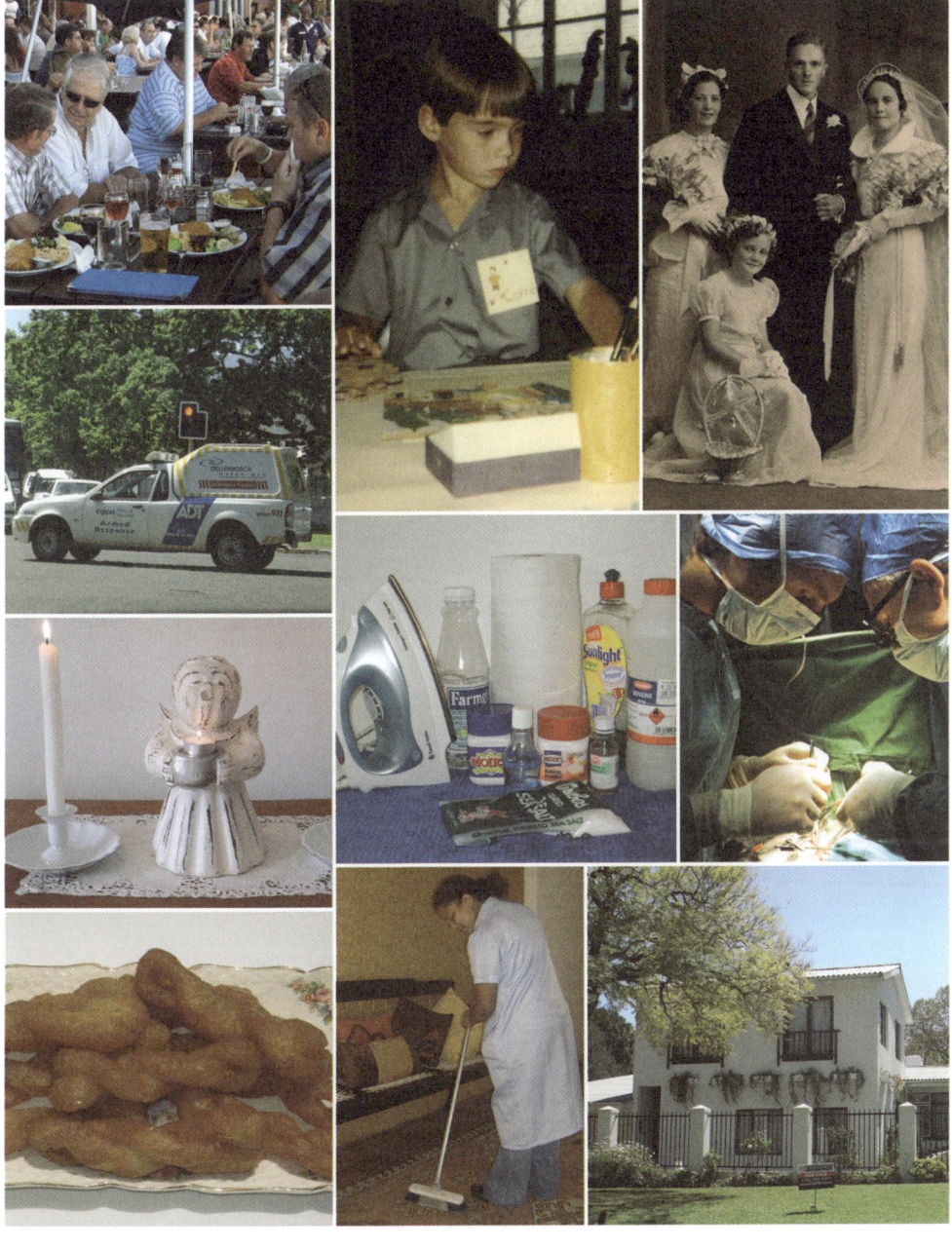

1. LIFESTYLE

Tips for happiness

- Happiness is a choice. You create your own happiness through the way in which you think about your life and circumstances.

- Be thankful. Every day write down three things for which you are grateful.

- You cannot change the world, but you can change the way you view it.

- Live one day at a time and live it as well as you can.

- Don't worry about things that may never happen. And don't worry about things you cannot change.

- Don't concentrate on things that scare you, but rather think about how these problems can be solved or lessened and do something about it.

- If you give love and praise, you will also receive it.

- Believe in yourself, think positively and act in a positive manner. Surround yourself with positive people. If you think and act in a positive way, you will get positive results. If you act negatively and aggressively, you will attract negative and aggressive things. Put negative thoughts out of your head immediately.

- Find the humour in situations and tell other people funny stories. Find things to laugh about.

- Make time to do things you enjoy. Spoil yourself every now and then.

- Concentrate on making time for things that are important to you. Sometimes you should think of yourself and say "no" to a task.

- Do not isolate yourself from people for too long. Do something fun with a friend even if you don't really feel like it.

- Faith and friends are among the most important things that make people happy. Spend time with friends and strengthen your faith.

- Be more social. Become more involved with family, friends and hobbies.

- Lower your expectations. Do not set unreachable goals for yourself.

- Find ways to mean something to others. The greatest joy in life is to stand by others and help them. Care for the people in your community and offer help where necessary. Cherish your family and friends. Be good to people without expecting anything in return. For instance, give someone a compliment, or buy someone flowers without writing your name on the card. Give an unexpected present. Be considerate – allow someone else to drive ahead of you or to take the only parking place. Tell your domestic helper or another staff member how much he or she means to you.

- Be yourself and don't try to imitate others. Don't constantly compare yourself to others. Do not covet other people's lives or possessions. Be content with and grateful for what you have.

- Be more active and exercise.

- You should always have a dream or goal in mind. For example, if you have always wanted to write a story for a magazine, do it. Always seek new dreams and ideals. Don't be discouraged by negative results, be positive and work creatively on your goals. Be determined and strive for success in everything you do.

- Organise your house or tasks so that you have less stress. Tidy your living area and keep your workplace neat. This creates favourable working conditions and makes you feel good.

- Develop your personality. Greet and smile at people more and chat with strangers at the supermarket, hospital or any other place.

- Don't brood on bad things that happened in the past. Make peace with the past. Break away from bitterness. Talk to a friend or psychologist.

- Find joy in small things - a beautiful sunset, a playful kitten or the smile of a stranger.

- Forgive people and don't hold grudges. Everyone makes mistakes.

- Praise people and write thank you notes.

- Maintain a good relationship with your colleagues.

- Become involved with a charity organisation.

One of the best things in life is the happiness that reflects back to you when you have made someone's heart happy. – Henry Ward Beecher.

Developing a good self-image and self-confidence

- Believe in yourself and your abilities. Always think positively.

- Focus on your strong points and develop them. Work on your weaknesses and try to improve where you can.

- Do not link your self-confidence to things or money. You must develop confidence in yourself.

- Reflect upon that which you have achieved that day.

- Be kind to other people and give them compliments. You will be so busy that you'll forget your insecurities.

- Make sure you stand up straight and with confidence; make eye contact with people and act in a confident manner.

- Before you attempt anything demanding, visualise what a great success it will be.

- Do things you've never done alone before. Go to the movies or take a new course on your own.

- Do the difficult or unpleasant things you have been putting off. You will feel good when it's finished. The more things you achieve, the more your self-confidence will grow.

- Prepare well for everything so that you can make a success of it.

- Don't be overly sensitive and don't mind negative criticism.

- Do not allow negative experiences to discourage you.

Friendships

Everyone has a deep-seated need for friendship. It is wonderful to know there are people who care about you; however, friendship cannot be forced. Friendships develop between people who have similar views on things. Friends laugh, cry and just hang out with each other.

How to make and keep friends

- To meet new people, you need to get out. Join a hiking club, book club or any other society.

- Whenever you are introduced to someone, remember the person's name.

- Introduce yourself to people if you are among strangers.

- Whenever you speak to people, call them by their name.

- Make eye contact and listen closely if someone is talking to you.

- Ask questions that cannot be answered with a simple "yes" or "no" to encourage conversation.

- Concentrate on the person and don't talk a lot about yourself.

- Be open and smile often.

- Talk clearly and in a friendly way.

- Compliment the person sincerely if you mean it.

- Be positive and enthusiastic. It should be pleasant for people to be around you. Accommodate other people's opinions and use humour in conversation.

- Invite someone for something, but set a date and time immediately. Vague invitations don't mean anything.

- Accept all invitations, even if you are not keen to go. It is an opportunity to make new friends.

- Do not be afraid to invite people to do something simple; sometimes sandwiches and a relaxed chat are nicer than a formal dinner.

- Discover the things you have in common, although friends who don't always think the same as you can enrich you and teach you new ways of looking at things.

- Be trustworthy and loyal.

- Be available for friends in good and bad times.

- Support and praise a friend, and do not criticise or bring up past failures.

- Offer your help whenever it is needed.

- Admit when you have made a mistake and ask for forgiveness.

- Encourage your friends, even if their goals differ from yours.

- Sometimes you should be a good listener without offering an opinion or preaching.

- Be honest whenever your advice or opinion is sought – even if it's not what the other person wants to hear.

- Do not neglect friends. Make contact regularly with phone calls, emails and visits.

- Do things together. Go walking, jog, attend a concert, or have a meal or a cup of tea together regularly.

- Do not be jealous of a friend's success; just be happy for him/her.

- Everyone has faults. Accept your friend's faults and habits even if it irritates you.

- Accept it graciously if a friend can no longer make a date and don't complain about it. Sometimes it is necessary to cancel or move an appointment.

- Do no neglect your old friends. You can keep your old friends even if you make new friends.

- If there is conflict, talk about it and try to repair the relationship.

Stress

Events that cause the most stress

- Death of a spouse/partner
- Divorce
- Death of a family member
- Weddings
- Leaving your job
- Retirement
- Pregnancy
- Sexual problems
- Arrival of a new family member
- Death of a close friend

Symptoms of stress

- Loss of enjoyment in life
- Loss of creativity
- The feeling that you have lost control of your life
- Changes in behaviour
- More absenteeism from work
- Increase in the use of alcohol or tranquilisers
- Reduced immunity to illnesses
- Insomnia
- Chronic fatigue
- Restlessness
- Weight loss or gain
- A stomach ulcer
- Tense muscles

Ways to relieve stress

- Eat a healthy and balanced diet. Low blood sugar worsens stress. Eat smaller meals more frequently to keep your blood sugar stable. Fruit, vegetables, unrefined carbohydrates, nuts, seeds, fish and herbal teas all have calming properties.

- Do the important things first. If you don't get round to everything, it is not such a big problem. You cannot always do everything you would like to. Do the most difficult things early in the morning when you still have plenty of energy.

- Whenever you start feeling tense, do something about it immediately. Take a few days' leave and do something fun. If you can't take leave, go for a walk, exercise or spoil yourself by going for a massage or something similar.

- Take a little time off during the workday. Have a quick cup of tea with a friend or go to the gym.

- Do not begin a new task until you have finished the previous one.

- You are not the only one who can do things well – learn to delegate.

- Don't brood on things that bother you. Find a solution or talk about it.

- Get enough sleep and rest. Try to go to sleep at about the same time every night and don't drink coffee or tea or exercise late in the evening.

- Sometimes turn off your TV, cellphone or computer and relax by listening to good music or reading.

- Do not always have music or the TV turned on. You are much more relaxed when it is quiet and you are not constantly bombarded by noise.

- Practise a hobby like painting, music or gardening.

- Exercise. Go for a walk or participate in sport. It is a natural way to tackle stress.

- Regularly go on holiday, even if it's just for a weekend. You cannot deliver good work if you are tired and stressed.

- Try to take a less busy route to work.

- Spend time with people with whom you can relax, and do not have too much contact with people who make you despondent and depressed.

- Spend plenty of time in nature. Go for a walk by the sea or in the veld.

- Be active by doing something relaxing, such as meditation or yoga.

> **Tips for handling a panic attack**
> - Take a deep breath and hold your breath for as long as possible. Concentrate only on your breathing and breathe out slowly through your mouth.
> - Count backwards from 20 to one.
> - Take a moment to calm down and control your thoughts, and try to consciously relax.
> - Stretch your whole body. Then consciously relax all your muscles. Start with your feet and work your way up. If possible, go for a short walk.
> - Talk to someone.
> - Remember that an anxiety attack always passes.

Symptoms of post-traumatic stress

- You feel vulnerable, afraid, helpless, depressed, ashamed and sad.
- You cannot believe what has happened to you, and you feel isolated.
- You are confused and struggle to concentrate.
- You cannot make decisions or handle problems.
- You experience feelings of rage and you think about revenge.
- You withdraw from people, are over-sensitive and quickly become irritated.
- You are not interested in anything.
- You are restless, cannot sleep and have nightmares.
- You experience physical problems such as headaches, trembling, nausea and other health problems.
- You cannot stop reliving the event over and over.
- You don't want to go to work and don't want to participate in activities which you previously enjoyed.

Behaviour during post-traumatic stress

- Realise that your reaction is normal and that it will improve with time.
- Do not think that the event is your fault, and do not blame yourself.
- Talk to other people about the event and accept help from people.
- Do not isolate yourself. Do fun things with friends and learn relaxation techniques such as meditation or yoga.

- Try to continue with your normal life.
- Do not use alcohol or tranquillisers to deaden your feelings.

> Reactions normally lessen after a few weeks, but if they last longer than six weeks, professional help should be sought.

How to support someone during a crisis

- It is important to visit the person. Take a small present along, like flowers or something to eat.
- Let the person talk and listen with empathy.
- Do not try to come up with reasons or solutions.
- Help with practical things such as housework and childcare.
- If you do not know what to say, just be there and listen.
- A hug also offers comfort.
- If it is a single person, invite the person along to functions with you.
- Keep up your support by, even months after the event, taking round some food, phoning and sending SMSes.

> *Whenever you give someone your time, you give them a part of your life which you will never get back. Your time is your life. This is why your time is the greatest gift you can give anyone.* – Rick Warren

Breaking bad habits:
- Start immediately.
- Concentrate on one day at a time.
- Find a good habit to replace the bad habit.
- If you falter, don't be discouraged. Just start again immediately.
- Reward yourself for successes.

Tips for public speaking

- Believe you are the best person to convey the information in question.

- Find out beforehand how long your speech should be. Rather make a speech that is too short than too long.

- Do thorough research and have the correct facts on hand. Write everything down.

- If you want to hand out notes, make sure you have enough copies.

- Check all the equipment you will need to use.

- Ensure that your speech has a beginning, a middle and an end.

- Start your speech with something humorous or unexpected. Use quotes if you have appropriate ones, but don't use too many.

- Prepare yourself for all possible questions.

- Learn your speech and practise repeatedly (in the garage, in front of a mirror, in front of the dog), but don't learn it word for word. Make sure that you can pronounce all the words correctly.

- Tell yourself that you are looking forward to the speech or presentation, and that you will make a success of it.

- Make sure you are appropriately dressed.

- Go early and become familiar with the venue where you will be speaking.

- Chat beforehand with people in the audience – it is easier to speak in front of people you know.

- Let your body consciously relax before you start. Don't stand with your hands on your hips or make many gestures.

- If you feel stressed beforehand, take a deep breath and be positive.

- Don't apologise if you are nervous.

- Focus on your message and not on the audience.

- A data projector is an excellent aid. If it cannot be used, take cards with keywords as your speaking aid.

- Keep eye contact with the audience. Move your eyes slowly over the whole audience. Do not focus on one person.

- Don't check your watch openly.

- Speak clearly, concisely and to the point.
- Do not speak too quickly. Use short and simple words.
- Make sure there are small pauses so people can take in what you say.
- Keep talking if you make a mistake, and don't apologise.
- Don't try to change your speech if it looks like some people are not interested.
- Keep facts interesting by adding humorous parts.

Good table manners

Tips for good table manners

- Sit up straight with your feet under your chair.
- Don't ride on your chair.
- Don't sit with your hands in your pockets.
- Wait and see if anyone is going to say grace before your start eating.
- The handles of knives and forks are held in the palms.
- Dessert spoons and soup spoons are held like a pen.
- Taste before you put salt on your food.
- Serve chutney or other sauces on the side of your plate; use your knife to put it on the food on your fork.

Still eating

Finished eating

- Put your knife and fork in an upside-down V on your plate while you eat.
- Break bread and rolls and butter them little by little.
- Take small bites so that you can answer a quick question.
- Take pips and bones out of your mouth with your hand.
- Fruit should be eaten with a knife and fork at the table.
- Cheese and biscuits are eaten without butter before or after dessert.
- Put your napkin on your chair if you need to leave the table during the meal.
- After the meal, put your napkin to the left of your plate. If you have finished eating, put your knife and fork neatly in the middle of plate with the handles facing you and the knife's blade turned to the middle of the plate.
- Hold a cup with just one hand by the handle.
- Stir tea and coffee gently, and put the teaspoon in the saucer.

Things you may not do at the table

- If you are invited out for a meal, don't order the most expensive dish on the menu.
- Do not start eating before the host or hostess begin to eat.
- Do not eat before everyone at the table has been served.
- Do not play with your food.
- No elbows on the table until everyone has finished eating.
- You may only eat with your hands if it is an informal or outdoor meal, if your hostess suggests it, or if there is a dish of water on the table with which to rinse your fingers.
- Ask to be excused and sneeze or blow your nose in the bathroom.
- Do not stretch over the table; ask if you want to be passed something.
- Do not make irritating movements, such drumming your fingers on the table.
- Do not eat only with your fork. Only mince, rice and food that do not need to be cut may be eaten with a turned-over fork.

2. THE SCHOOL AND WORKPLACE

Study tips

It is important to have a suitable study area. If the area is also used by other people, work out a schedule so you know when you can use it. Do not allow other people to disturb you. If you study better with music on, keep the volume low. Make sure the chair and desk are comfortable. The area must have good lighting and not be too hot or too cold. There should always be an open window for fresh air. Make sure that all books, stationery and other necessities are to hand.

- Don't postpone studying until just before the exam. Study a little bit every day.

- Make a study timetable and keep to it.

- Do not sit in front of the TV or computer and become distracted so that you spend more time on that than planned.

- If you don't understand something, discuss it immediately with the relevant teacher.

- First read all of the information on the subject to make sure you understand the background.

- Make summaries, write down keywords and make sketches. A summary of a subject should preferably not be longer than an A4 page.

- Do not study for longer than 45 minutes without a break of 15 minutes. After this break you will be able to concentrate better.

- Do revision after you have completed a section. Repeat the facts.

- Do not concentrate on other people's conversations in the house. After the exam you can be updated on everyone's "stories". Keep your cellphone turned off and only focus on your studies.

- Check newspapers and other publications for study guides and try exam papers from previous years.

- Eat healthy food and eat often. Exercise or do something outside, for example go for a walk or a short ride on your bike.

Exams

- You won't be afraid of an exam if you have prepared well.

- Make sure that you know exactly what to study.

- Set up a timetable for exam preparation. Make allowances for the fact that you may write exams on different subjects on consecutive days.

- Learn all the work and don't leave out certain parts.

- Get enough sleep and eat healthily.

- Do not drink too much coffee. It peps you up for a short time, but will also make you anxious and nervous.

- Avoid stimulants and "stay awake" pills.

- Get together everything you will need for the exam the preceding night.

- Go to sleep early the night before you write the exam.

- Get up in good time and have a decent breakfast.

- Relax for a bit before the exam by listening to restful music or going for a short walk.

- Take a bottle of water along to the exam venue, if it is permitted.

- Arrive at the exam venue in plenty of time.

- On the morning of the exam, don't talk to friends about the work. They might just make you nervous.

- Be positive and decide you will do well.

- Be calm and relaxed when you are given the question paper.

- Read the question paper and instructions through once, before you start writing.

- Read the question twice before answering it.

- Don't worry if you can't answer a question. Carry on with other questions in the meantime and go back to the questions you left out.

- Don't be upset if you feel you didn't do well in an exam. Just decide that it will go better with the other papers.

- Try to write the exam even if you are feeling a bit unwell. If you miss an exam without a medical certificate to justify it, there could be serious consequences.

In 2007 Phyllis Turner was awarded a masters degree from Adelaide University in Australia at the age of 94.

How parents can help during exam time

- Do not put too much pressure on your child. Encourage him or her to do as well as possible, but do not have unrealistic expectations.

- Make sure that there are healthy food and snacks in the house. It is important that learners or students eat plenty of fresh fruit and vegetables. Low GI food types that release glucose slowly and therefore keeps blood sugar levels stable – like oats, nuts and wholewheat bread – keep you full for longer and improve your ability to concentrate.

- Give your child a good vitamin supplement, with especially vitamin B, and do not allow the use of stimulants or "stay awake" pills. They can appear to have a good effect in the beginning, but later will cause side effects such as restlessness, insomnia, headaches and an inability to concentrate.

- The whole family should be considerate and not cause disturbances. Younger children should rather be taken on an excursion so the learner can study in quiet surroundings.

- Keep the atmosphere in the house happy and relaxed. Do not get involved in an argument with someone else in front of the child. Your child will feel the tension and it will break his or her concentration.

- Put up your child's exam timetable somewhere so he or she knows you are interested and you can check that he or she is not studying for the wrong subject.

- Do not force the child to follow certain study methods. Suggest that he or she keeps to a study timetable, but the child should study how it best suits him or her.

- Encourage the person to take breaks and have a chat or take a short walk.

- Do not call or send SMSes straight after the exam, but ask relaxed questions about the question paper. The learner must not feel tense, as there may be other papers that still need to be tackled.

CVs

Example of a covering letter with a CV

> **Guidelines for a covering letter**
> - Make an effort to find out what the name of the person is to whom the letter should be addressed.
> - The letter must not be longer than one page.
> - Say you are prepared to work hard and that you feel you would be an asset to the company.

1 Brand Street
Welkom
9459
16 May 2009

The Manager
Alpha Bank
P.O. Box 12
Bloemfontein
9300

Dear Mr Stander

APPLICATION FOR POSITION AS ACCOUNTANT

With reference to your advertisement in *Die Volkstem* of 13 May 2009, I would like to apply for the position of accountant.

I have six years of experience in all aspects of financial functions, and am currently an accountant at Garden Centre in Bloemfontein North. I am also involved in all human resources issues and the day-to-day activities of the company.

I deal with people on all levels and see inter-personal relations as one of my strong points.

I am prepared to work hard and believe I would be an asset to Alpha Bank.

My curriculum vitae is attached.

Please contact me if you require any further information.

Yours faithfully,
(Signature)

Jan Louw (mr)

Examples of CVs

> **Guidelines for writing a CV**
> - Use white paper.
> - Do not decorate the CV. Keep it neat and simple.
> - Keep your CV short and concise. Do not make spelling mistakes.
> - Always attach a covering letter.
> - Do not attach copies of certificates unless they are specifically requested.
> - Name your most recent experience and achievements first.
> - If an abridged CV is required, under personal details put only your name and surname, age, language proficiency and contact details.
> - Ask your references beforehand if they are prepared to be a reference, and which contact details you may provide.
> - Number the pages.

Matriculant:

Henri Odendaal	
PERSONAL DETAILS	
Name:	Henri Odendaal
Age:	19
Date of birth:	23 March 1990
ID number:	9003233064076
Sex:	Male
Languages:	English (first language) Afrikaans
Marital status:	Single
Nationality:	South African
Driver's licence:	Code EB
Home address:	5 Church Street Panorama 2571
Email:	henriodendaal@mtek.co.za
Cellphone:	084 366 3478

Work experience

I did holiday work (programming) at Top Programming in Parow (2006-present).
I worked as a waiter at the Spur in Bellville (2005-present).
I provided after-school help for primary school learners (2006-present).

Academic qualifications

School: Tygerberg High School, Parow

Highest grade: Grade 12 with full exemption in 2008

Subjects and symbols (final exams 2008):

English (First language) HG	B
Afrikaans (Second language) HG	C
Mathematics HG	B
Computer applications technology	B
Accounting HG	B
Information technology HG	A

Leadership roles and prizes

Class representative (2005, 2006, 2008)
Prize for best student in mathematics (grade 10)
Captain of the second rugby team (2007)
Captain of the first rugby team (2008)
Deputy head boy (2008)
Prize for the best student in information technology (grade 12)

References

1. Mr Jan de Beer, Headmaster of Tygerberg High School
   Telephone: 021 687 9984

2. Mr Koos du Toit, my supervisor at Top Programming in Parow
   Telephone: 021 687 7062

Advanced CV:

CURRICULUM VITAE	
Jan Louw	
PERSONAL DETAILS	
Name:	Jan Hendrik Louw
Age:	32
Date of birth:	26 February 1976
ID number:	7603233064071
Sex:	Male
Languages:	English (first language) Afrikaans (excellent) Xhosa (very good)
Marital status:	Single
Nationality:	South African
Driver's licence:	Code EB
Address:	16 Brand Street Welkom 9459
Email:	janlouw@pan.co.za
Cellphone:	083 777 1324

Employment

1. Employer:	Garden Centre
Nature of work:	Accountant
Period:	January 2005 – present
Job description:	I am responsible for the financial management and accounting of the company. I am also responsible for the administration of all human resource issues and for the day-to-day activities of the company.

2. Employer: **Welkom Trust Company**

Nature of work: Accountant

Period: January 2000 – December 2004

Responsibilities: I was responsible for the financial management of the company.

Work experience
The implementation and maintenance of:
Computer systems, salary systems, disciplinary procedures and information systems.

The administration of:
Cash books, journals, petty cash, bank reconciliations, debtors, creditors, all taxes and the financing of assets.

The preparation of:
Management statements, financial statements, budgets, agendas for meetings and minutes.

Liaison with:
Clients, financial institutions, debtors and creditors.

Academic qualifications

Tertiary: University of Stellenbosch
BCom (1997)
MCom (1999)

Secondary: Welkom High School
Grade 12 with full exemption in 1994

Courses completed
Tax
Communication skills
Business management
MS Word
MS Excel
Pastel 6
VIP Payroll

References

1. Dr J. Coetzee (Financial director of Welkom Trust Company)
   Telephone: 057 278 1298

2. Mr J. Fourie (Manager of Garden Centre Ltd)
   Telephone: 057 379 1006

Example of an acceptance letter

5 Church Street
Panorama
2571
20 May 2009

Mr J. du Toit
Top Computers
P.O. Box 1660
Cape Town
8000

Dear Mr du Toit

ACCEPTANCE OF POSITION

I refer to your letter of (date) wherein you offered me the position of (position). I would like to accept the position as of 1 June 2009.

I thank you for the confidence you have placed in me and assure you I will give you and your company my best service.

Yours faithfully

(Signature)
Henri Odendaal

The personal interview

Tips for behaviour at a personal job interview

- Do not ask too many questions over the telephone if someone telephones to invite you to an interview.

- Accept any appointment time for the interview, even if you need to cancel another appointment.

- Ensure you have enough time, and do not leave in a rush.

- Find out as much as possible about the company and the products or services they offer.

- Write down questions that may be asked and what your answers would be, and practise.

- Look professional. Dress neatly and be well groomed.

- Women should not wear too much make-up or jewellery or low-cut clothes.

- Find out exactly where the company is so that you don't have to look for it on the day of the interview.

- Take an extra CV, a notebook and pen along.

- Arrive about 15 minutes before the interview, and announce yourself at reception five minutes early.

- Remember to turn off your cellphone.

- Be friendly and polite to the receptionist or secretary.

- Introduce yourself and give a firm handshake.

- Only sit when a seat is offered to you.

- Don't put anything down on the desk. Put everything neatly down next to your chair.

- Sit up straight and do not fold your arms. Avoid using too many hand gestures and nervous movements. Fold your hands in your lap.

- Be friendly and try to relax.

- Even if the interviewer is young, your language must be professional. Do not use colloquialisms.

- If you are asked to talk about yourself, start with your academic training, then your professional experiences and last, general topics (like hobbies) in which you are interested. Give details about your personal circumstances only if you are asked and only offer information that could influence your job situation, such as the fact that you are a single parent.

- Rather don't accept anything to eat or drink. You can accept a glass of water. It gives you a chance to think while you take a sip of water.

- Do not smoke.

- Make eye contact with all the interviewers.

- Never interrupt the interviewer.

- Do not talk too much and come across as a know-it-all.

- Do not call the interviewer by his/her first name.

- Be positive and think before you answer a question. Make sure you understand the question before you answer. Keep your answers short.

- If you are asked something you don't know, answer calmly that you do not know.

- Do not talk about salary too quickly. Be honest about your current salary, but if you feel your salary is below average, you can say you feel you should be earning more.

- Never speak badly of a previous employer.

- Thank the interviewer for his/her time and greet him/her with a handshake.

- After the interview, write a short note to thank the person for the opportunity.

Possible questions and answers at an interview

Tell me about yourself.
Tell a little about your background and family (very shortly), but also say you enjoy a challenge and take pride in your work. Don't give out personal information.

What are your strong points?
I work well in a team and prefer work that will present a challenge to me.

Why do you want to change jobs?
I have always wanted to work for this company. I believe I will be an asset because I meet all the requirements.

Where do you want to be in five years?
I hope that by then I will have learnt a great deal about the business and possibly have advanced to a managerial position.

How would you set up a business plan for this department?
I would first of all do thorough research before compiling a new business plan.

What are your weak points?
If I believe in something, it is sometimes difficult to convince me that I am wrong.

Questions you can ask:

- What will my responsibilities be?
- Will I be working on my own or be part of a team?
- To whom will I report?
- Are there opportunities for advancement in the company?
- How do promotions take place?
- Will I need to travel, and if so, how often?
- Does the company have any training programmes?
- Can you tell me what the next step in the selection process is?
- When can I expect to hear whether or not I have been successful?

> **While you are looking for work:**
> - Improve your skills.
> - Consider doing an internship, even without pay.
> - Become a flexi-worker or a temporary worker.
> - Do any work just to get your foot in the door.

Tips for the interviewer

- Make sure you have all the details about the applicant with you.

- Be friendly and try to put the person at ease.

- Ask relevant questions, but don't try to corner the person. Don't ask too many personal questions. Questions should focus on academic training, experience and ideas about work situations.

- Take note of the applicant's appearance, posture and use of language.

- Evaluate his/her personality and view on life.

- Test the applicant's skills, for instance about a specific computer programme.

- Explain the nature of the work and what his/her responsibilities would be.

- Inform him/her about the benefits offered by the company, and also about possibilities for promotion.

- Thank the person for coming to the interview and say you will inform him/her about the outcome.

- Accompany him/her to the door.

Success in the workplace

Tips for employees

- Happiness at work depends mainly on you.

- Success does not come overnight, but you should consistently do good work.

- Dress neatly and appropriately.

- Always be on time for work, meetings and appointments.

- Keep to the prescribed working hours.

- Do not try to change systems at the company during your first month.

- Make friends and win the confidence of management and your colleagues. Avoid confrontations.

- Plan what you are going to do and when you will do it, and keep to that schedule.

- Immediately write down important information and appointments.

- Be positive and work as quickly and thoroughly as possible.

- Offer to do extra tasks.

- Be willing to work overtime. Do not take your whole lunch hour if there is urgent work to be done.

- Answer inquiries, telephone calls and emails as quickly as possible.

- Keep your desk neat and organised. File documents as soon as you are finished with them. Keep a bin next to your desk and immediately throw away unnecessary post, out-of-date documents and paper. Do not put too many personal things like plants or photos on your desk.

- Be trustworthy and always do what you promised.

- Do not do private things in work hours. Friends shouldn't visit you at work and no personal telephone calls should be made from work, except in an emergency.

- Do not talk too much about your previous workplace.

- Try to improve your weak points and learn new skills. Be humble and honest.

- Learn from the people around you. Ask questions, but be careful not to ask unnecessary questions.

- Do research yourself to find solutions to problems.

- Take the initiative and make suggestions.

- Do not gossip, and treat everyone in the workplace with respect.

- At work, do not talk about sensitive matters like politics, problems at home, religion, health problems and sex. Also do not talk constantly about looking for a better job; your loyalty could be questioned.

- Do not go to your boss with problems until you have looked for solutions yourself. Suggest the solutions to your boss.

- Do not apologise for a failed project, but admit it did not go well and explain that you will approach it differently the next time.

- Do not publicly criticise your employer or colleagues.

- Do not become emotional. If you lose your temper at work, people will lose respect for you. Inappropriate language should be avoided.

- If you are upset and angry after reading a letter or document, immediately write down your response but don't send it. Wait at least half an hour, then read it again and make sure it is not emotional.

- Earn more qualifications. Apply for a course. Improve your presentation skills and written communication. Learn more about other cultures.

- Always be well prepared for meetings and other occasions.

- Attend conferences and keep in touch with people working in the same field as you.

- Find out what goes on in the other divisions of your company. It is necessary if you want to have a top position in the company one day.

- Read a lot and take note of what is happening in your industry.

- Talk to your boss if you have problems at work.

- Remember that salary increases are not a right, but should be earned – unless your contract states otherwise.

- Take part in social activities so that you can get to know your colleagues, but act in a responsible manner.

- Do not change employer too often. Only change if the new job offers better career opportunities.

> **Sick leave according to the Department of Labour**
> - If you work five days a week, you are entitled to 30 days paid sick leave over a period of three years. If you work six days a week, it is 36 days.
> - You must have a doctor's certificate if you are sick longer than two days.
> - If you are sick more than twice in eight weeks, you also need a doctor's certificate.
> - You may only stay away from work if you are really too sick to work.
> - Inform your immediate head and call him/her yourself, if possible.
> - In the event of serious illness, sick leave can usually be extended. You can also apply for unpaid sick leave or you can take your annual leave.

How to get on well with your boss

- Find out how your boss would like feedback – personally, by email or telephonically.

- Find out the following: does your boss want full information, a short report or all the documentation on a project?

- Do not take up too much of your boss's time. You are only a part of the team.

- If you go to your boss with a problem, give possible solutions.

- Keep your boss informed. It should not be necessary for him/her to ask for information.

- Do not go over the head of your direct boss, and if is unavoidable, keep your direct boss informed.

- Choose the right time for discussions, requests or questions.

- Always be loyal and honest.

How to handle clients/customers

- Be friendly, make eye contact, smile and greet the client in a friendly manner.

- Introduce yourself.

- Ask how you can help.

- If it is a professional situation, call the person by his/her title, for instance, "Mrs Nel".

- Do not take the anger of clients personally. Remain calm and friendly.

How to resign from your job

- Do not discuss your work options and plans with your colleagues.

- Do not use work time and work resources to look for another job. Continue to do your job well and fulfil your responsibilities to the end so your boss will remember good things about you.

- Do not resign from your job before you have another job. Apply for other jobs while you have a job and don't have to worry about finances. Do not resign until you have a written offer from the new company.

- You should preferably resign on the first day of a calendar month.

- Keep to the required resignation period.

- Complete unfinished projects and offer to help train the new person.

- If there is a possibility you might be fired, look for other work and resign. You are entitled to a certificate of service and you can ask that it does not specify the reasons for your dismissal.

- Do not resign in the hope that your boss will offer you a big raise to keep you. If he does so, think carefully about it and, if you decide to accept it, get it in writing first before you refuse the other offer.

- Give a short, polite resignation letter to your direct boss in person. He/she will then be able to decide how you should inform your colleagues about your resignation.

- It is not polite to tell or show everyone at work that you are happy to be leaving.

- Negotiate about outstanding payments such as commissions or leave pay.

- If your current boss makes you a better offer, think about it carefully and get it in writing before you refuse your other offer.

- Do not talk badly of your colleagues, boss or the organisation before or after you have left.

Normal minimum resignation periods
If you have worked for less than six months: one week.
If you have worked for between six months and a year: two weeks.
If you have worked longer than a year: four weeks.
Some contracts demand a longer resignation period.

Tips for managers

- Be aware of everything that happens in the workplace.
- Create a relaxed atmosphere in the workplace.
- Delegate responsibilities. The business must be able to function even if you are not there.
- Strive to improve relationships between colleagues by organising social activities and outings.
- Keep contact with the staff informal. Be approachable to everyone.
- Get to know your staff and their values and inform them of your values.
- Be humane and friendly to your staff and they will support you in difficult times.
- If someone needs time off for an important personal matter, give your permission. If you respect other people's values, they will give you their best service.
- Be available when a staff member wants to speak to your about any problems (work or personal problems). Show you are willing to listen.
- Praise people often if they have really earned it. Emphasise the good qualities of members of your staff.
- Accept responsibility for the staff and do not blame someone else if something does not go according to plan. You are in control and will be praised or blamed for the successes or failures of your team.
- Always treat everyone with respect.
- If necessary, confront a person immediately so that it is not necessary for someone else to point it out to you.
- Do not discipline someone in public. If someone has transgressed, stay calm and discuss it quietly in private with that person.
- Help the staff understand that everyone makes mistakes sometimes.
- Sometimes give your staff demanding projects. If the workers succeed, it boosts their self-confidence and self-esteem.
- Give clear instructions and make sure that everyone understands.
- Reward successful projects by taking people out for a meal or giving them some other reward.
- Staff work better in small groups.

- Do not get too close to certain members of staff.
- Involve members of staff in decision-making and give them responsibilities.
- Measure staff members' progress and achievements and discuss problems with them.
- Talk about "our" success, not "my" success.
- Always ask for feedback after a project.
- Leaders also make mistakes, so don't be afraid to admit it if you have made a mistake.
- Always end a meeting or discussion with something positive like: "You are doing very good work."

Tips for successful delegation

- Do not decide that you will be able to do the task quicker and better, and then do it yourself.
- Visualise the completed task so you know exactly what you expect from a staff member.
- Let the person write down your instructions and repeat them, so you are sure he/she knows what you expect.
- Write down the instructions yourself as well, especially if the person is forgetful or there is a language barrier.
- Set a date and time by when the task must be finished. Tell the person they must inform you if there are problems with making the deadline.
- Don't be a perfectionist. If the work is not perfect, thank the person and tell him/her how you would like it done in the future. It is a waste of time to redo all acceptable tasks yourself just because you want it perfect.
- Focus on the results of the task, but let the person do the task his/her own way. It will stimulate productivity and creativity.
- Make a list of all the tasks you have delegated, as well as the dates on which they should be completed.
- Ask regularly for feedback about the task so problems can be quickly solved.
- Acknowledge good work and thank the person, even if it just a small improvement on previous work.
- Give tips about how the task could be done better in the future.

Tips for success for entrepreneurs
- You must have certain basic characteristics to be a good entrepreneur, but most skills can be learned.

- You must be positive, have tenacity and a great desire to succeed.
- Don't be impatient to get started. You must have knowledge of how a business functions. Read, learn and investigate every possible topic about the type of business you want to start.
- Keep your family and life partner informed of your decisions. Change can cause tension and it is easier if everyone who will be affected is supportive.
- You must get on well with people. Good service and good relationships with clients are great ways of marketing your business.
- You must be a hard worker.
- First, do thorough research and learn everything you possibly can about the business you want to start. You cannot start something if you know nothing about it.
- Write a comprehensive business plan before you approach a bank or institution for financial support. You must convince them that your product or service will be a success. Be prepared for any questions about the business.
- Your product must be of good quality and fill a gap in the market. You must offer something better than your competitors who provide similar products or services.
- You may have big dreams, but you must start small. Increase your capital before you appoint a lot of people or rent big offices. Keep your start-up costs as low as possible. Limit your expenses to a minimum.
- You must be prepared to adapt your product or service to changing circumstances and to offer new products or services.
- Don't be discouraged by setbacks. Analyse why you have failed, work on it and learn from it. Believe in what you are doing and find solutions. Success does not always come easily.
- Don't try to do everything yourself; rather delegate.
- Maintain a good balance between work, leisure and family. Everyone needs to rest sometimes. If you work too hard and lose perspective, your family will also suffer.
- Be honest, friendly and trustworthy.
- Get a striking logo and use it on your products, business cards, letters, brochures and website.
- Explain to interested people what makes your product better than and different from similar products.
- Offer good value for money. Clients choose which products or services they want to use.
- Advertise in the local newspapers and use a public relations agency, which will be cheaper than regularly advertising in newspapers yourself.
- Consider a website. Clients want to have 24-hour access to information and will sometimes visit the website before they visit the shop or office.

3. MARRIAGES

1938

1975

2009

Marriages

Two types of marriages are legally recognised in South Africa: **civil marriages** and **common law marriages**. The legal aspects of common law marriages differ from those of civil marriages. A new law was approved in 1998 to protect women's rights in common law marriages. Most common law marriages in South Africa are African, Muslim and Hindu marriages.

More information about common law marriages is available from the Department of Home Affairs: **www.services.gov.za**.

Often a couple marry according to their tradition and then marry according to civil requirements.

Civil marriages

There are protections and restrictions on a civil marriage. Each partner has certain rights and accepts certain responsibilities. Both spouses have equal rights. It is advisable to get legal advice and marriage counselling before getting married. A marriage must be conducted by a qualified official – magistrates, special justices of the peace, commissioners and ministers appointed by the Minister of Home Affairs, are all marriage officers.

The wedding ceremony

The wedding ceremony must take place in a place of worship, public office or a house. The doors must be open during the ceremony and at least two witnesses must be present. In the event of serious illness or injury the ceremony can take place in a hospital or other facility.

The couple must have the following documents available: identity documents, divorce papers if they were previously married and divorced, a death certificate if one of them is a widow or widower, and written permission if one of them is a minor.

The couple, the wedding officer and two witnesses sign the marriage register. A marriage certificate will be issued to the couple free of charge.

The wedding officer will register the marriage at the nearest office of the Department of Home Affairs.

People who may not marry

- Minors without the required permission.

- People who are already married. Bigamy is a punishable offence in South Africa.

- People who are closely related. See the list from the Department of Home Affairs below.

A man may not marry his:	A woman may not marry her:
Mother	Father
Daughter	Son
Father's mother	Father's father
Mother's mother	Mother's father
Son's daughter	Son's son
Daughter's daughter	Daughter's son
Sister	Brother
Wife's mother	Husband's father
Wife's daughter	Husband's son
Father's wife	Mother's husband
Son's wife	Daughter's husband
Father's father's wife	Father's mother's husband
Mother's father's wife	Mother's mother's husband
Wife's father's mother	Husband's father's father
Wife's mother's mother	Husband's mother's father
Wife's son's daughter	Husband's son's son
Wife's daughter's daughter	Husband's daughter's son
Son's son's wife	Son's daughter's husband
Daughter's son's wife	Daughter's daughter's husband
Father's sister	Father's brother
Mother's sister	Mother's brother
Brother's daughter	Brother's son
Brother's daughter's daughter	Brother's son's son
Sister's daughter	Sister's son
Sister's daughter's daughter	Sister's son's son
Sister's son's daughter	Sister's daughter's son

Permission for marriages between minors

- If both parents are living and neither has sole custody of the minor, both parents must give their written permission to the marriage.

- If the minor was born out of wedlock, only the mother's written permission is necessary.

- If one parent has sole custody, only that parent's written permission is necessary.

- If the minor is in the care of a legal guardian, only the written permission of the guardian is necessary.

- When a parent whose written permission is required cannot be traced or is legally unfit, a request for permission to marry can be directed to the Commissioner of Child Welfare.

- If permission for a marriage is refused, the minor can apply to the high court for permission. The judge will only give permission if it is in the best interests of the minor and if it is found that permission has been unreasonably withheld.

- Even if permission to marry is granted to boys under the age of 18 and girls under 15, approval must still be given by the Minister of Home Affairs. The application form is available from the Department of Home Affairs: **www.home-affairs.gov.za**.

- The minister can annul a marriage that took place under the above circumstances without his/her permission.

- A marriage concluded without the necessary permission is seen as valid until declared invalid by the high court. The parents or guardians can, before the minor turns 21 and within six weeks of finding out about the marriage, apply for the annulment of the marriage The minor can apply for the annulment of the marriage before he or she turns 21 or within three months after he or she turns 21.

In South Africa people of the same sex have been allowed to marry since November 2006.

Marriage contracts

Marriage contracts are important documents and must be regarded in a serious light. They protect the interests of both parties in the event of divorce, death or debt. In South Africa there are three types of marriage contracts: in community of property, out of community of property without accrual and out of community of property with accrual. Marriage contracts must be drawn up before the wedding date and be registered at a deeds office.

In community of property

At the time of the marriage all personal property and assets become part of the joint property, regardless of whether it was acquired before or after the marriage. When one party wants to make an important transaction, for instance a property transaction, he/she needs the written permission of the other party. Both have equal say over the assets and all profits and debts are shared. This contract is very risky for people who have their own businesses or accrue debt, because if a business fails, both the husband and the wife's assets can be sold to cover debts.

Out of community of property without accrual

Each party retains ownership of his or her own assets acquired before or after the marriage. One person can also not be held responsible for the other's debts. All assets in the wife's name are protected in the event that a business venture in the husband's name must be sold to cover debt. In the event of only one party contributing financially to the marriage and acquiring all the assets, the other party could walk away empty-handed if the marriage ends.

Out of community of property with accrual

For as long as the couple are married, it works as in the above section. Each party retains control over his/her property and is responsible for his/her own debt. A person can specify beforehand that certain assets acquired before the marriage are excluded from the accrual. When the couple get a divorce, assets acquired during the marriage are equally divided between them.

- A marriage contract ranks above a will and determines what a person's assets are.
- It is difficult and expensive to change a marriage contract after a marriage, as permission must be sought from the high court.
- If a contract only specifies "out of community of property", it is accepted that it is with accrual.

Duties of the wedding party

Bridesmaid(s)

- She helps with the general planning of the wedding.
- The first bridesmaid (maid of honour) organises the kitchen tea. Other bridesmaids, close family members or good friends of the bride can help her.

- She helps the bride dress on the wedding day and looks after the bride's dress, veil and bouquet during the ceremony.
- She holds the bouquet when the rings are exchanged.
- She is a witness when the marriage register is signed.
- She helps with presents for the guests and with table decorations.

> - A bridesmaid is there to support the bride and must be a good friend or family member of the bride.
> - Flower girls walk down the aisle in front of the bride and bridesmaids – and when they walk out.

Best man (men)
- Arranges the stag party and makes sure the bridegroom gets home safely.
- Makes sure that the bridegroom arrives at the church on time.
- Takes the wedding rings to church.
- Accompanies the maid of honour when she walks down the aisle.
- Makes sure that the wedding gifts are safe.

Guidelines on who pays for what

Below are the traditional guidelines. These days the bride and bridegroom often pay for many of these expenses themselves.

The bride and her family:
- Wedding invitations and thank you letters.
- The reception venue and all food (including the wedding cake).
- The photographer and the videographer.
- Flowers for the wedding party, the church and the reception venue.
- The bride's entire outfit.
- In some cases, the accommodation for the bride's guests.
- The bridegroom's ring and possibly a gift.
- Gifts for people who help with arrangements and also for the wedding party.
- The church, minister, organist and all decorations at the ceremony.
- Transport to the ceremony and reception.

The bridegroom and his family
- A wedding ring for the bride.
- The marriage licence.
- Bouquets for the bride and her party and all corsages.
- Ties for the men in the party. Suits for the men in the party. Suits may be hired.
- The hiring of a bridal car.

- The bridegroom's wedding suit or evening suit.
- Gifts for the bride's party (the bride chooses these).
- The honeymoon. The bride can help to pay for this.
- Transport costs and accommodation for the wedding night.
- A gift for the bride (usually jewellery, like a gold chain).
- All drinks at the reception.
- Their own accommodation and accommodation for the best man if necessary.

> On the morning of the wedding, the bridegroom should send the bride a bouquet of flowers with a nice message.

Tips for lowering expenses

- Start early with the planning of the wedding, so that you can compare quotations.
- Do not have an unnecessarily large wedding party.
- Choose the right date. Weddings on Saturdays and between December and February are more expensive than at other times.
- A morning wedding is much cheaper than an evening wedding. The catering, alcohol and music will all cost less.
- Get quotations to determine if the bride and bridegroom's outfits can be made or hired at a lower price.
- Use flowers that are in season.
- A buffet costs less than a meal that is served to guests.
- Put tap water with lots of ice, lemon or cherries in pretty jugs on the tables. The lemon slices or cherries can also be frozen in ice cubes.
- Cooldrinks, wine and sparkling wine can be on the house, while a cash bar is offered.

Timeline for wedding planning

12 months before the wedding
- Decide on a big or small wedding and if it will be formal or informal.
- Decide in or near which town or city the wedding will take place.
- Set up a budget and decide who will pay for what.
- Choose a few possible dates.
- Choose the reception venue and book it if it is a popular place.
- If the honeymoon will be abroad, apply for passports and visas.

6 months before the wedding
- Go for marriage counselling.
- Write a guest list.
- Ask the people who will be in the wedding party.
- Decide who will be the master of ceremonies and decide on the order of the service.

- Book the minister and organist or other musicians.
- Book the photographer and videographer, and make sure they are people with whom you get on well.
- Book the venue, usually a church, where the ceremony will take place, if it differs from the reception venue.
- Organise a dressmaker or designer for the wedding dress and the bridesmaids' dresses. If you plan to buy or hire a dress, start looking for it.
- Let the guests know the proposed date of the wedding, so they can start making arrangements to attend. A telephone call or email will suffice at this stage.
- Book a caterer if one is not included with the reception venue and decide on a menu. Pay a deposit.
- Choose and book a florist or someone who will do the flowers. Pay a deposit.
- Decide on and organise the wedding cake if you are having one. Nowadays traditional wedding cakes are not as popular. Chocolate or sponge cake (which can also be decorated with fresh flowers) that can be served as dessert, is very popular. Festive heaps of cupcakes or other individual cakes are also very fashionable.
- Decide on the design of the invitations. Make sure the guests will know what the dress code is. Draw a road map if necessary.
- Decide if you want to have a wedding registry at a shop.

3 months before the wedding
- If equipment like tables or chairs must be hired, book them.
- Buy the wedding rings.
- Order or make the invitations.
- Book accommodation for the wedding night.
- The bridegroom must plan the honeymoon and pay a deposit.
- Decide on and buy presents for the wedding party, the bride and the bridegroom.
- See an attorney about the legal aspects and marriage contracts.
- Change your policies and insurance to include your future spouse.
- Write a new will.
- Book a make-up artist and hairdresser for the wedding day.
- Finalise the menu, flowers, music and running order for the ceremony with all the relevant people.
- Decide on the speeches and toasts and ask people to speak.

2 months before the wedding
- Post the invitations and keep a list of all the guests who are attending the wedding.
- Order the alcohol not being provided by the caterer.
- Go to your hairdresser and decide on a hairstyle. Practise the make-up.

- Decide on the order of the speeches and confirm it with the involved people.
- If you choose to have them, have programmes printed for the ceremony.
- Confirm the menu, number of guests, time and place with the caterer.

1 month before the wedding
- Decide on the table seating and make place cards.
- Get a garter, something old, something new, something borrowed and something blue (according to tradition).
- Attend the kitchen tea or stag party.
- Make sure that your wedding dress fits perfectly and fetch it.
- Decide on and organise the transport of the bride, bridegroom and wedding party.
- Find out what the rules are about confetti or something similar at the venue where the ceremony will take place.

1 week before the wedding
- Confirm the order of the ceremony with the minister, musicians, photographer, caterer and manager of the reception venue.
- Confirm the delivery time of the flowers with the relevant person.
- Give a list of the photos that you would like to the photographer.
- Confirm all travel arrangements and reservations for the honeymoon.
- Pay all outstanding bills.
- Organise someone to collect the wedding presents from the reception venue and keep them safe.
- Rehearse the whole ceremony with everyone involved.
- Start to pack for the honeymoon.

After the wedding
- Get a copy of the marriage certificate and the page in the marriage register.
- Within four weeks, send personal thank-you notes and, if possible, include a photo.
- Have the wedding dress dry-cleaned.

- If you don't get married on a Saturday, you could organise a discount – don't be embarrassed to ask for one.
- Check quotations thoroughly before you sign them and keep everything in writing.
- The bride must try on her wedding dress with the right shoes and underwear.

Seating arrangements at the reception

- A head table is preferable because it allows all the guests to see the bridal couple and it is also handier for the speeches and toasts.
- The traditional seating, which of course can be changed, is as follows: the bride sits on the groom's right. The bride's father sits on her right and the bride's mother sits next to the groom. The groom's mother sits next to the bride's father and the bride's mother sits next to the groom's father. The best man and maid of honour sit at the end of the table.

- If one of the sets of parents is divorced and don't want to sit together, they can sit at other tables and good friends or family can take their places at the head table.
- Make sure that guests who are divorced or don't get on, don't sit at the same table.
- Put a table plan, or preferably two, at the entrance to the venue.

> If the guests all leave at once, it is a good idea for the bridal couple and their parents to form a line so they can greet everyone, wish them well and have a personal word. The sequence of this line is usually the following: the bride's mother, the bride's father, the groom's mother and father, the bride and groom.

Speeches and toasts

Speeches and toasts are important. They should take place between the starters and main course. Good jokes and personal anecdotes about the couple are special, but should not embarrass the couple or guests. Speeches should be light and cheerful and a few jokes are appropriate. Toasts should be short. It is not necessary to have many speeches. A toast is proposed to both divorced parents because they are the parents of the bride or groom.

The master of ceremonies
The master of ceremonies welcomes the guests to make make them feel at home, and informs them about the procedures at the reception. He introduces the speakers, proposes the first toast to the bride and thanks everyone who had a hand in the planning of the wedding.

The best man
The best man proposes a toast to the bride and groom and can also say grace.

The bridegroom
In his speech, the groom should compliment the bride and, if he would like to, say he loves her. He thanks everyone who helped with the wedding and names them. He thanks the parents of the bride for their daughter. He also thanks his parents and makes them feel important. He then thanks the guests for their attendance and gifts and proposes a toast to the wedding party.

Traditional etiquette for thank-you notes

- Guests who give gifts before the wedding should be thanked within two weeks in the bride-to-be's maiden name.

- Guest who give gifts at the wedding or afterwards should be thanked within four weeks.

- Only a handwritten thank-you note is acceptable – not an SMS, email or printed card. It is a good idea to include a photo with the thank-you cards.
- A separate thank-you note should be sent for each gift. If a person has given a gift at the kitchen tea and at the wedding, the person must get two thank-you notes.
- In the note, say what the gift is and how much you are looking forward to using it.
- If money is given do not name the amount, but say what you plan to use it for.

Wedding etiquette

- If you do not want children at the reception, the invitation must state that it is a reception for adults. Don't use the words "no children".
- Indicate on the invitations if there will be a cash bar.
- It is in bad taste to ask for money. A guest should not be told what gift to give. If guests ask, various options can be named.
- Make sure there is enough sparkling wine and wine on the tables.
- It is bad manners for a guest to miss the church service and only attend the reception.
- Guests' attire (formal, semi-formal, casual, etc.) should be indicated in the invitation. Guests choose their attire according to the request on the invitation.

Divorces

A divorce can be settled in the high court or the central divorce court of a specific district. Only advocates or attorneys who are suitably qualified can represent a client in the high court. It is much cheaper and quicker to settle a divorce in a central divorce court.

Important information and guidelines

- Try to reach an agreement with your spouse at the start. A lot of money can be saved in legal fees.
- Do your best to maintain a good relationship with your ex. It makes it much easier for the children, as well as for everyone involved in any future negotiations.
- Consult a lawyer at least once to check the legal requirements of a settlement with your spouse.
- Be careful with your choice of lawyer. He/she must be telephonically available, you should feel relaxed in his/her presence and you must also know what his/her services will cost.

- You will need legal help if you plan to negotiate for a portion of your spouse's assets if you are married out of community of property.
- If you are married in community of property or out of community of property with accrual, you are entitled to a share of the shared assets.
- Be very careful when signing a divorce settlement – do not allow your rights to be compromised. Specify everything very clearly in the settlement, especially financial and future financial expenses.
- Except in exceptional circumstances, the children usually stay with the mother. If the father seeks custody of the children, a family advocate must show that the mother is not a fit parent.
- According to law, the father of the children has financial responsibilities to them that he must fulfil.
- Finalise everything during the divorce. Do not, for example, keep a jointly owned property unless it is unavoidable.
- According to the Pension Act of 2007, a claim can be laid to part of the spouse's pension money. The pension fund must be informed before the divorce and it must be specified in the settlement.
- Do not threaten to get a divorce if you are not prepared to go through with it. An unnecessary amount of money is wasted by stopping the process and later starting again.

The central divorce court

- The central divorce court is usually in the magistrate building. You can find out where it is at your nearest magistrate's court.
- The divorce court only works with divorces and custody matters.
- Only the party who has instituted divorce proceedings need appear in court.
- The clerk of the court will help you fill in the forms and explain the procedure.
- A bailiff will serve the defendant with the divorce papers.
- Take the signed papers, your marriage certificate, your identity number and the settlement to the clerk of the court.
- A court date will be determined.
- In court you will be asked under oath to testify that your marriage is irreparably broken down and that you will answer all questions truthfully.
- If everything goes smoothly, the marriage will be declared dissolved and you will be given a document in which your separation and the dissolution of your marriage becomes a court order.

4. WILLS

WILL & TESTAMENT

This is the last will and testament of

……………………………………………… (Full name and surname)

………………………………………………….. (Identity number)

Unmarried and currently residing at ……………………………………

I hereby revoke all wills and codicils previously made by me and declare this to be my Last Will & Testament.

I bequeath my whole estate to my parents; ………………………….. (full name of father) and ……………………………………. (full name of mother) (née ……………….) in equal parts, and in the event that one has already died, then to the longest-living of them, and in the event of the absence of both, to my *ab intestato* heirs.

If during the distribution of my estate the need or desire arises that any assets are converted to cash, the absolute power is hereby given to my executor to sell the assets in the manner of his choosing, including public auction, public application or private agreement.

As executor of my estate, I name …………………………….. with the power of assumption and substitution. I hereby direct that he be exempted from furnishing security to the Master of the High Court.

SIGNED BY ………………….. **THIS** ……… **DAY OF** ………… **20..**

In the presence of the undersigned witnesses, who were all present at once and in each other's presence signed this document.

WITNESSES:

1. ……………………..

……………………..
TESTATOR

2. ……………………..

General information about wills

A will determines who inherits what from your estate when you die. The **estate** consists of your **personal property**, **possessions**, **money** and any **other assets** you own. If you have a valid will, everything is divided according to your wishes. A will should be **short**, **businesslike** and **clear**. If you die intestate (without a valid will), everything is divided among your closest family members according to inheritance law. It is advisable to consult a **lawyer** when drafting a will.

To be valid, a will must be drafted correctly. You must appoint an **executor** who will make sure that everything is divided according to your wishes and that all outstanding bills are paid. The best person to name as executor is a **family member**. The executor can then appoint an accountant, lawyer, bank or other appropriate person or institution to help. The family stays in control and can replace the agent if the work is not done properly. **Executor's fees** can be negotiated. If a professional executor is named from the beginning, that person is in control and the family can do nothing if the executor does not do his work well. If you do not appoint an executor, the court will do so.

The executor usually pays the **administration fee** first (the fee that is paid to finalise the estate) and settles all the debt from the estate, before the rest can be divided among the heirs.

It is important for the next of kin to respect the person's wishes regarding **organ donation** and **cremation**, and it's therefore advisable to specify this in the will.

A will is only valid after the testator's death. Before the testator's death, the will can be replaced or amended at any time. The most recent will is therefore the legal will.

- It is recommended that married couples set up two separate wills, even if they are married in community of property.
- The testator is the person who makes the will.
- A codicil is an addendum to add something to a will or change something. It must fulfil the same criteria as the will. It does not have to be signed by the same witnesses as the original will.
- If a person does not change his/her will within three months after a divorce, the former spouse will benefit according to the terms of the will.
- If a divorced person dies within three months of a divorce, the inheritance of the former spouse is cancelled.

Criteria for a valid will

- Any person over the age of 15 who is of sound mind and can realise the consequences of his/her actions, can draw up a will.
- All wills must be in writing. They can be handwritten, typed or printed.
- The testator must sign the will on every page and at the end.
- The testator must sign the will in the presence of at least two witnesses.
- Any person over the age of 14 years who is of sound mind and able to recognise the consequences of his/her actions can witness the document.
- The witnesses must sign the will in the presence of the testator and of each other.
- A beneficiary of the will may not sign the will as he/she will not be allowed to draw any benefit from the will. Your legal representative can inform you about any exceptions to this rule.
- If a person cannot sign, he/she can make a mark, for example a thumbprint or an X. Another person can also sign on his/her behalf. A Commissioner of Oaths must be present when it is done. The Commissioner of Oaths must also sign each page of the will, and therefore certify that he/she is satisfied with the identity of the testator and that the will is a reflection of the testator's wishes. The commissioner must sign a certificate.

Division of assets if a person dies intestate

- The assets of a married person are divided equally between the spouse and their children.
- If there is no spouse, the assets are divided among other family members.
- If there are no family members, the assets go to the state.

Circumstances according to which a nominated heir may not inherit

- If the heir has tried to influence the testator or has deliberately caused his/her death.
- If the heir has hidden a will.
- If the heir has tried to defraud a legitimate heir of his/her inheritance.
- A divorced spouse may not inherit for three months after the divorce. If the testator has not removed the divorced spouse from the will after three months, the person again qualifies to inherit.

Example of a simple will

WILL & TESTAMENT

This is the last will and testament of

.... (Full name and surname)

.... (Identity number)

Unmarried and currently residing at ....

I hereby revoke all wills and codicils previously made by me and declare this to be my Last Will & Testament.

I bequeath my whole estate to my parents; .... (full name of father) and .... (full name of mother) (née ....) in equal parts, and in the event that one has already died, then to the longest-living of them, and in the event of the absence of both, to my *ab intestato* heirs.

If during the distribution of my estate the need or desire arises that any assets are converted to cash, the absolute power is hereby given to my executor to sell the assets in the manner of his choosing, including public auction, public application or private agreement.

As executor of my estate, I name .... with the power of assumption and substitution. I hereby direct that he be exempted from furnishing security to the Master of the High Court.

SIGNED BY .... **THIS** .... **DAY OF** .... **20..**

In the presence of the undersigned witnesses, who were all present at once and in each other's presence signed this document.

WITNESSES:

1. ....

....
TESTATOR

2. ....

A living will

In South Africa living wills are still relatively unknown, and there is currently no law regarding their validity.

In a living will the writer makes his or her wishes known for when he/she is dying and cannot make his/her wishes known anymore. Some people want to be kept alive as long as possible, while others choose to die rather than be kept alive by machines. The next of kin are usually asked to give doctors guidelines. It means that these people must decide whether the person should live or die. It places a tremendous responsibility on them and often they differ among themselves on the right decision to make. In writing a living will, everyone takes cognisance of the terminally ill person's wishes, and it frees the next of kin of a large part of the responsibility for these difficult decisions.

The living will must be drawn up while the person is still of sound mind. Three copies of the will must be signed in the presence of two witnesses. The patient's doctor must be given a copy after all the patient's wishes have been discussed with him/her so that there are no misunderstandings later. Two copies must be kept in safekeeping by a responsible person. One copy must be given to the hospital if necessary. Family and friends must also be informed about the patient's wishes in this regard. A living will must be regularly revised.

Regardless of the instructions in a living will, the onus rests with the doctors to decide on the prognosis of a serious illness.

Example of a living will

LIVING WILL

I .... (Full name and surname)

.... (Identity number)

DECLARE THAT

If I am no longer in a state to make decisions myself about my future, the following declaration serves as an instruction of my wishes.

If there is no reasonable prospect for my future recovery (body and mind), and my condition is likely to cause me prolonged distress and pain or will render me incapable of a rational existence, I do not wish to be kept alive by artificial means.

I request that only drugs and intravenous fluids as may be required to keep me free from pain or distress be administered even if the moment of death is hastened.

WITNESSES:

1. ....

2. ....

....
SIGNATORY

5. SAFETY AND SECURITY

Home security

- A wall around the property is not a good option. It hides the view from the street and gives criminals the chance to break in unseen. A metal security fence with remote-controlled gates and an intercom is a good choice.

- Join a neighbourhood watch.

- Dense trees and shrubs in the garden or on the pavement offer hiding places to criminals.

- Do not leave ladders or other tools lying around the property. They may be used by criminals.

- Make sure the property is well lit. Sensor lights are very effective.

- Secure all windows with burglar bars, including bathroom and toilet windows and windows on higher floors. Burglar bars must be installed with one-way screws or rivets.

- Make sure that all outside doors are fitted with security gates.

- Make at least two sets of spare keys for the house and leave them with a family member or friend. Do not write your home address on the key rings.

- Do not attach information to house keys that indicates what door the key is for. Rather write down the codes and information and keep it in a safe place.

- If house keys are lost or stolen, it is better to change the locks.

- Secure outside doors by installing strong locks. The hinges should not be accessible from the outside. The more levers locks have, the more secure they are.

- Removable mortise locks that can be used in the keyholes of existing locks are very effective.

- Make sure that sliding doors cannot be lifted off the rails.

- Keep outside doors and security gates locked at all times.

- There should be peep-holes in solid doors.

- Invest in a good alarm system.

- Keep emergency numbers next to your telephone and on your cellphone.

- Put bolts on the trapdoors in the ceiling.

- Do not open the door or security door for strangers.

- Do not hide house keys in the house. Make sure that everyone who lives in the house has a key.

- Do not sleep with open windows if good burglar bars are not installed.

- A big dog can deter burglars.

- Be aware that attacks can happen. Never confront burglars.

- Call for help as quickly as you can.

Holiday arrangements

- Install timers that turn on the house's lights and TV in the evening and turn them off later.

- Ask a neighbour to open the front curtains from time to time.

- Make sure that ladders and garden equipment are locked away.

- Cancel all newspapers and postal deliveries. The post office or post depot will hold your post until a given date.

- Make sure that the alarm system is in good working order and let your security company know that you are going on holiday and who will have keys for your house.

- Valuable possessions must not be visible from outside the house.

- Duplicate keys must be locked away.

- Make sure that all valuable items are locked away and make copies of all important documents.

- Ask a trustworthy person to keep an eye on the house or ask someone to stay in your house.

- Make sure that all windows, doors and security gates are locked before you leave. Garages and storage rooms must also be locked.

- Outside lights should preferably come on and switch off at different times.

Safety in the street and in shops

- Keep your handbag close against you.
- Carry your wallet somewhere it is not visible – not in your back pocket.
- Do not put your handbag or purse on a counter and walk or turn away.
- Do not leave handbags or other possessions in a supermarket trolley.
- Stay away from deserted or dark areas.
- As far as possible, leave valuable possessions at home.
- If you are attacked or robbed, do not offer resistance or look at the person – your life is worth more than money.

Safety in a vehicle

- Ensure that you car is always in a good condition.
- Make sure that the car has enough fuel and that your cellphone is charged.
- Do not leave valuable items like packages, cellphones, handbags and laptops in a visible place in the vehicle. Lock them in the boot.
- Keep all doors and windows locked.
- Always park in a well-lit, safe place.
- Avoid driving in the dark as much as possible.
- Do not pick up hitch-hikers.
- If you are followed, drive to the nearest police station.
- Be very careful if someone approaches your car and do not open your window.
- Be careful if people at a stationary vehicle ask for help. Make sure that it is not a trap.
- Keep a list of emergency numbers in your car.
- Do not attach your car's registration number to your car keys. If your keys are lost, it would be easy for a criminal to steal your car.
- Make sure you always have spare keys for your car.

Vehicle hijackings

Preventative action against vehicle hijackings

- Know your surroundings and be on the lookout for suspicious-looking people. Do not hesitate to report suspicious-looking people near your residence to the police (10111) or the neighbourhood watch.

- Do not drive in or out of your property if you spot suspicious-looking people or vehicles near your property. Wait until they have gone.

- Do not reverse out of your property if it can be helped. It is easy for criminals to slip in through a gate behind a vehicle.

- Lock the vehicle's doors and windows before you drive off.

- Driveways and gates must be clearly lit and there should not be bushes or shrubs that can provide hiding places.

- Do not take the same route to and from your house every day.

- Your vehicle's mirrors should be adjusted so that you can see around your vehicle.

- Do not sit in a vehicle while waiting for someone. Rather meet each other on a property.

- Be on the lookout for suspicious-looking people at a stop sign or red traffic light.

- Stop about 4m from the vehicle in front of you at a stop street or traffic light so there is space if you need to get away quickly.

- If you suspect that you are being followed, do not stop at your house. Drive around the block or to the nearest police station and phone the police or neighbourhood watch.

- Be careful when anyone asks you for help alongside the road, a strange person approaches your vehicle or a vehicle hits you from behind.

What to do in a hijacking

- If you have to choose, remember a life is always more important than a vehicle.

- Be submissive and do not offer any resistance, look at the attackers or argue with them.

- Keep your hands where the attackers can see them and give them the keys to the vehicle.

- If there are children in the vehicle, ask if you can take them out.

- If the hijackers force you to drive, try to avoid driving to a remote place. Pretend you have lost control of the vehicle and rather cause a small collision by hitting the vehicle in front of you or driving into a pole or tree.

- Call the police as soon as it is safe.

- Go for psychological counselling after the attack.

> - Most hijackers are men between the ages of 16 and 28.
> - Hijackers are usually well dressed and move in groups of two to five people.
> - Vehicle hijackers could be travelling on foot or in a vehicle.
> - Most victims are attacked between 06:00 and 08:00 and between 17:00 and 19:00 in front of a gate or driveway.
> - Any vehicle, old or new, could be hijacked.

Banking safety

Credit cards

- Always sign the back of a new credit card immediately with permanent ink.

- Do not let your credit card out of your sight. Walk to the card machine in the shop or restaurant.

- Keep your card in a safe place.

- Report a lost card immediately.

- Always protect your PIN and do not write it down.

- Check your statements regularly, go through your slips and make sure all your transactions are accounted for.

- Keep a record of your credit card number, expiry date and the security code on the back of the card, and keep it in a safe place.

Cheques

- Never sign a blank cheque.

- Do not use ink that can be erased.

- Start writing at the left margin and do not leave spaces where other words or figures can be filled in.

- Do not keep signed cheques in your handbag, car or chequebook.

- Do not post cheques.

- If people pay you by cheque, ask for their identity number and ask them to write their identity number on the back of the cheque in your presence so you can ensure it is correct.

- Keep a record of your series of cheque numbers and account number.

> **In the event of theft of a credit card or cheque book:**
> - Call your bank's toll-free number and immediately cancel the card or chequebook.
> - Report the theft to the police and get a case number.
> - Close your cheque account and cancel all the cheque numbers in the lost chequebook.

Safety at an ATM (automatic teller machine)

- Keep your PIN a secret and do not write in on your card or keep it in your purse.

- Do not use an ATM in the dark. Take someone along if you must use it at night, and then choose a well-lit ATM.

- Choose an ATM in a very visible place, preferably in the middle of a business centre.

- Be aware of suspicious-looking people or vehicles near the ATM.

- Make sure that there are no devices in the card slot.

- If there are any problems with the ATM or your card is swallowed, report it to the bank immediately. If the ATM is not working properly, cancel the transaction and retrieve your card. Do not try to force your card into the slot.

- Do not accept help or advice from people at the ATM. Rather go to another ATM.

- Always sign your new card as soon as you receive it.

- Never lend your card to anyone.

- Take your card out of your purse before you get to the ATM.

- Do not type in your PIN before the instruction to do so appears on the screen.

- Make sure that no one can see your PIN when you type it in.

- Put the cash away immediately – do not walk with it in your hand.

- Always take your slip.

- Make sure that you are not followed.

- If a criminal demands your cash, do not offer resistance. As soon as it is safe, call the police.

Internet banking services

- Internet banking services are fast, convenient and available at all hours. Be careful of fraud.

- Do not go directly from an email to a bank's website. Close the email and type in your bank's website address.

- Always type in your bank's website address anew. Follow all the steps of your bank's security system and do not make use of any screen short cuts.

- Use all of your bank's security systems.

- Use unusual passwords and change your password regularly.

- Do not store your password on a website.

- Do not write down your PIN.

Internet shopping

- Buy from well-known dealers. If the dealer is unfamiliar, first phone them.

- Trustworthy dealers usually allow that products be sent back or exchanged.

- There should be two symbols in the right-hand corner of the web page to show that the site is secure. Look for a symbol of a key or a closed lock. There are also logos that indicate that the dealer is trustworthy.

- Rather use a credit card than a debit card to pay.

- The website address of the page should begin with "https" and not with "http".

Cellphones

- Change the pre-set PIN on the cellphone.

- Do not talk on your cellphone while walking in the street. It makes you an easy target for thieves.

- Do not put your cellphone down on a counter, a restaurant table or the seat of your car.

- Keep a record of your cellphone's make and model, the IMEI number of the cellphone and your SIM card number, and keep it in a safe place.

- The IMEI number can be found by typing *#06# on your cellphone.

When your cellphone is stolen:
- Call your cellphone number – if the thief answers, you can use his/her voice or background noises to try to identify the thief.
- Report the theft immediately to your service provider so that the cellphone contract can be cancelled.
- Inform everyone when your cellphone number has changed.
- Report the theft immediately at the nearest police station, provide all the cellphone's details and get written proof of a case number.
- In 2005 a law was proposed that will make it mandatory to report cellphone thefts to the police. You can therefore be prosecuted if you neglect to report it.
- If you do not report the theft and the cellphone is used in illegal activities, for instance a bomb threat or robbery, you could be held responsible for it. (This law had not yet been finalised in 2009.)
- According to new legislation, from 1 July 2009 people have 18 months to register SIM cards with service providers. Parents or guardians of children under 16 will be held responsible for the registration. The cellphone number, full name and surname, ID or passport and proof of physical address is necessary for registration. When buying a SIM card this information is also necessary.

Identity documents, passports and driver's licences

- Make two copies of each of these documents (all pages containing information) and have them certified.

- As far as possible, keep the certified copies of the documents with you, and keep the originals in a safe place. There are times when you will need the originals.

- If the originals are lost, the copies will make the replacement easier and can be used as identification until the original documents are replaced.

In the event of theft:
- Immediately report the theft to the police and get a case number.
- pply to the Department of Home Affairs for a temporary identity document (or passport) if it has been stolen. Here certified copies are very useful.
- It is illegal to drive without a driver's licence; you should therefore apply immediately for a temporary one.

Safety for children

Emergency numbers:

SA Police: 10111
Bureau for missing children: 086 164 7746
Missing Children: 072 647 7464

Tips for parents

- Make sure you always know where your children are.

- Get to know your child's friends and their parents.

- Always keep your child in your sight in public places.

- Do not leave your child alone in a parked car.

- Children must not be left alone at home.

- Do not let your children wait for you at school, a shopping centre or any other place for a long time. Make sure they always wait for you in a safe place.

- Teach your children to always take the same, safe route so that you know where to look for them if necessary.

- Teach your children to never get in a stranger's car, even if the person knows the child's name. Children should also be taught not to accept gifts like sweets or money from strangers.

- Children should be taught to report any unusual or upsetting behaviour by strangers as well as people they know.

- Children must know what constitutes unacceptable behaviour towards them, and that they must immediately tell someone about it.

- Children should be taught to scream long and loudly if someone tries to force them into a direction or a car.

- Name tags on children's clothes should not be visible. Children trust people who call them by their name.

- Children should never give personal information about themselves, their parents or their families to strangers.

- All children must know how to use a telephone and know the telephone numbers of their parents, family and friends, as well as emergency numbers.

- Regularly take photos of your children so you always have a recent photo to provide if necessary.

Missing children

- Stay calm.

- Quickly make sure that the child really is missing.

- Search at home, school, neighbours and friends.

- Rather don't ask other children to help you look as they could also go missing.

- Immediately report it to the nearest police station. It is not necessary to wait 24 hours. Take along a recent photo of the child.

- Provide a full description of the child. Also give information about the clothes the child was wearing when he/she went missing.

- Make sure that you get a reference number, as well as the name and telephone number of the police officer who is going to handle the case.

- A reliable person must be at home to answer the telephone.

- Contact **Missing Children SA** at **info@missingchildren.co.za** or **072 647 7464** to mobilise a search in the area.

Behaviour when a lost child is found

- Calm the child.

- Find out what the parents' contact details are and contact them.

- If the child is found on the street, take him/her to the nearest police station.

- If the child is found in a shopping centre, take him/her to the security office.

- Have someone remain at the place where the child was found, so the parents can be informed if they come looking for him/her.

- Always take the name and contact details of the person to whom the child is handed over.

6. HOUSES

Advantages of buying a house

- It is an emotional advantage to own your own home.
- When you rent a house, in reality you are paying off someone else's mortgage.
- The longer you wait, the higher house prices will be and the harder it becomes to buy a house.
- The value of the house will rise in the long term.
- When you need to take out a loan, the house can serve as security.
- If you pay extra money into your mortgage every month, you can pay it off quicker and thus have far fewer financial obligations.
- You can start small and when you sell at a profit, buy a better house. In this manner you can build equity.
- After about five years the payments on the mortgage are usually less than what it would cost to rent a similar house.
- You cannot suddenly be given notice, have the rent dramatically raised or have the rules changed.
- You can renovate the house as you wish.
- When you retire and own a house that is paid off, it is a great asset.
- Fixed property is a much lower risk than other investments, such as stocks.

Disadvantages of buying a house

- The initial costs, such as legal costs and transfer duty, can be thousands.
- You are personally responsible for the maintenance of the house.
- Depending on the conditions of your mortgage, you could experience financial problems if the interest rate rises drastically.
- If you have to move, it can sometimes take a long time to sell the house.

Tips for buying a house

- Make sure that you can afford to buy a house. Draw up a budget and find out beforehand from a bank what amount you qualify for and what your payments will be.

- Look in different neighbourhoods and buy in the best location. It is a better investment to buy a small house in a good neighbourhood than a larger house in a bad neighbourhood.

- Take note if other houses in the area are being renovated or are dilapidated.

- Make a list of everything you would like in a house. Be prepared to give up certain things.

- Look at show houses so you have a good idea what you can get for your money.

- Decide how much money you have for potential renovations, for instance new carpets or tiles.

- Look closely at possible construction faults, roof leaks, worn woodwork, electrical wiring and the condition of installed equipment such as geysers and toilets.

- Make an offer conditional on a full inspection by an engineer or independent inspector.

- The sale must be conditional on beetle and electrical certificates.

- Determine what the house's resale value will be in a few years. Agents will be able to help you come up with a good estimate.

- Ask the municipality if any large-scale building work, like roads, railway lines or factories, are being planned in or near the neighbourhood in the next few years, and discuss the advantages and disadvantages of this with an informed person in the property business.

Home loans and the new Credit Act of 2007

Previously the amount approved for a home loan was calculated on a third of your salary. According to the new Credit Act, the loan amount is now calculated on your disposable income after all other expenses have been deducted from your salary.

Information and documents required by banks when applying for a home loan

- A copy of your identity document or passport.
- Three months' bank statements.

- All bank account details.

- Proof of your residential and postal addresses, as well as phone numbers.

- A salary slip or proof of income.

- If you earn commission, you must show proof of income earned over the past six months.

- If you work for yourself, you must have a letter from your accountant stating your income and your company's turnover.

- You need to fill in a form detailing your assets and debts.

- All your debt, as well as credit facilities such as credit cards and store accounts, must be declared. All the credit available to you is deducted from your annual income, even if you do not have that much debt.

- All expenses, such as household costs, transport, extramural activities of children, domestic help and entertainment, must be declared. The amounts must be realistic.

> To qualify for a larger home loan, reduce your shop and credit card accounts before you apply for the loan. The amount of credit for which you qualify is taken into account and not the actual amount you owe.

Advantages of renting a house

- You do not need a large amount of money for a deposit or transfer costs.

- You do not have expenses such as insurance and property tax.

- You are not responsible for the maintenance of the house.

- If the neighbourhood develops a crime problem, you can give notice and quickly move away.

- Interest rate changes do not touch you directly, although the owner of the house could raise the rent when interest rates go up.

- You will have more money for other things, because the payments on a house would probably be significantly higher than the rental you would pay.

- You can wisely invest the difference between the rental and mortgage payments.

- You do not increase your debt.

Tips for tenants

- Take your last three months of salary slips or proof of income along to the lessor or leasing agency. Show proof of your credit-worthiness.

- Get references from previous landlords, colleagues or employers.

- Read the rental contract thoroughly and note all restrictions, for instance a limit on pets.

- If repair work needs to be done to the house, discuss it with the landlord and get the agreement in writing.

- Keep copies of all correspondence with the landlord, and get all verbal agreements in writing.

- Contact the landlord if there are problems.

- Make sure that you know exactly what your responsibilities are regarding the house and garden.

Tips for landlords

- Tenants can be found through an agency. Commission is paid to the agent and all the administration is handled by them.

- You can find tenants and handle everything yourself.

- It is better to let out the house for a long term.

- Advertise in the local press and specify you are looking for long-term tenants, as well as any other relevant and important information.

- Advertise at least three months before the property will be available. It gives the tenant time to give notice at the place where he/she is currently living.

- Make a list of potential tenants and interview them.

- It is difficult to evict bad tenants. Be very careful with your choice of tenants.

- Show the property to the potential tenants and discuss repair work or changes that will be made.

- Be wary of tenants with many pets that could disturb the neighbours.

- Specify the maximum number of people who may live permanently in the house.

- Discuss what costs, excluding the rent, the tenants will be responsible for.

- Make sure that the tenant can afford the rent by checking salary slips and the last three months' bank statements.

- The tenant must also supply a few references, especially the details of previous landlords.

- Take a deposit of a full month's rent.

- The rent must be paid in advance.

- Draw up a rental contract setting out all the conditions in writing. Also attach an addendum specifying all the loose goods in the house. Ensure that the rental contract is signed as quickly as possible.

- Inspect the house with the tenant the week before he/she moves in and write down everything that still needs to be fixed. If the tenant requests changes that will raise the value of the property, try to oblige him/her.

- Rental income must be declared to the Receiver, but you can claim back the interest on the mortgage, repair work, maintenance, wear and tear, municipal accounts and other expenses.

- If you have good tenants, accommodate them where you can and do not raise the rent by the full amount stipulated in the contract every year. Maintain a good relationship with the tenant.

- Before you enter the rented house, you must arrange it with the tenant.

- Inspect the house every now and then with the tenant. Discuss things that are bothering you in a friendly way and address matters that are bothering the tenant.

- The tenant is responsible for all routine repair work inside and outside the house. Municipal accounts are usually paid by the tenant and the tax is usually paid by the landlord.

- In some cases it is better that the landlord arranges a garden service – it is big bonus when the tenant takes good care of the garden him/herself.

- Check the house thoroughly for damage before a long-term contract is extended. The tenant must repair everything before you sign a new contract.

- You cannot evict a tenant yourself. You can apply for a court order to evict the tenant if he has broken the contract.

- If there is damage to the house when the tenant moves out, you can discuss it with him/her and deduct it from the deposit (as stipulated in the contract). Another option is for the tenant to pay someone to do the repair work.

> **Problems with a rental situation:**
> The Rental Housing Tribunal: **086 010 6166**

Example of a simple rental contract

RENTAL CONTRACT

RENTAL AGREEMENT BETWEEN

....

IDENTITY NUMBER: ....

(Hereafter referred to as the **LANDLORD**)

and

....

IDENTITY NUMBER: ....

(Hereafter referred to as the **TENANT**)

1. The landlord rents the following property to the tenant:

   .... (Erf number:............)

2. The rental period begins on .... and ends on ....

3. If the tenant wants to lengthen the term, the landlord must be notified in writing before ....

4. The rent is R................... per month and is payable in advance on the first day of each month. The rental will increase by ...% on .... every year. If the tenant fails to pay this amount on the first day of every month, the landlord reserves the right to use the full deposit as payment for rent. If the rent is not paid by the tenth of the month, legal steps will be taken.

5. The tenant is responsible for the electricity, water and refuse removal payments on receipt of the accounts.

6. Any damage or breakages noted at the time of occupying the property must be reported within the first seven days of occupation by the tenant, whereafter such damage or breakage will be for the tenant's account. All keys for doors and security doors must be counted and all baths and washbasins should have plugs. All items provided with the house must stay in the house and remain in a good condition. (See addendum for list.)

7. No shelves, nails, screws, glue or any other apparatus may be introduced the house without the permission of the landlord. After the rental period has finished, the walls must be left in their original condition. (All screws must be removed and the holes filled.)

8. The tenant undertakes to maintain the property in the same clean and good condition as it was when it was occupied. If carpets or walls are dirtied, the tenant is responsible for cleaning or painting these with the same quality products as were originally used in the house. Any damage to doors, windows, walls, cupboards, etc., must be repaired or replaced by the tenant to their original condition.

9. The landlord is responsible for municipal tax and the maintenance of the infrastructure and equipment in the house that form part of the fixed property, for instance the geyser, power points, etc., but this does not include any damage inflicted by the tenant.

10. The tenant undertakes to keep the garden neat and to water it regularly (as possible).

11. The tenant agrees to take the neighbours into account at all times and never to create a disturbance such as, for example, to make a racket late in the evening.

12. The tenant will use the property only for residential purposes and there will never be more than six people living in the house for a period longer than one month.

13. No vehicles, caravans or trailers may be parked in front of the house, on the pavement or in the driveway. Guests may park for a short period in the street or in the driveway. The cars of guests may also be parked behind the security gates next to the garage.

14. The landlord is not responsible for any damage or injuries caused by accidents, fires, storms or any other incidents to the residents of the house or their possessions while on the property.

15. A deposit of R......... will be kept as collateral against damage, unpaid rent or other costs for which the tenant is responsible. It is repayable when the house is vacated and cleaned, and all municipal accounts associated with the property are paid.

16. The landlord maintains the right to make an inspection of the property at any reasonable time, and if there is any damage caused by the tenant, the tenant will be obliged to repair it on his own account within seven days.

17. If any of these conditions are not fulfilled by the tenant, legal steps can be taken by the landlord and the tenant will be responsible for all legal costs incurred in this regard between lawyer and client, including the debt collection commission to which this lawyer may be entitled.

SIGNED by ………………………….. **on** ………………………… 2009

AS WITNESSES:

1. ………………………………..

2. ……………………………….

…………………………………
LANDLORD

SIGNED by………………………….. on ………………………………….. 2009

AS WITNESSES:

1. …………………………….

2. …………………………….

……………………………….
TENANT

Tips on selling a house quickly

Use an experienced and trustworthy estate agent. Advertise in the publication with the biggest circulation and property section, as well as the publication in which the most big estate agencies advertise.

Outside

- First impressions are important. Make sure the garden is neat. Plant new shrubs and flowers. Keep the lawn neat.

- Make sure that the intercom, doorbell, taps and outside lights are in a good working condition.

- The veranda, front door, windows and window sills must be clean. A fresh coat of paint or varnish on the front door and window frames is a good idea.

- The post box must be neat and the house number clear and obvious.

- Make sure that driveways, pavement and paving are clean.

- Repair cracks in walls and paint where necessary.

- Do not park old cars or other vehicles in front or on the property.

- Keep the garage doors closed.

- Organise the garage and storerooms and throw away all rubbish.

- No rubbish should be lying around on the property.

- The swimming pool must be sparkling clean.

- There shouldn't be dogs on the property that may bother potential buyers. Not everyone loves animals.

Inside

- Replace all broken items such as light bulbs, broken window panes and curtain rails.

- Paint walls in neutral colours.

- Wash curtains, lampshades and loose furnishings.

- Remove all damaged or unnecessary furniture.

- Replace old carpets or have them cleaned.

- Clean shelves and organise them.

- Put pretty candles and clean towels in the bathrooms.

- Remove all personal photos.

- Do not leave pets' dishes or the cat's litter box in the house.

- Open all curtains and blinds so that the house looks clean and light.

- Make sure that all toilets, taps and showers are in a good working condition.

- Have fresh flowers in the house – and in the bathrooms.

- Make sure that the beds are neatly made and replace old duvets.

- Make sure that there is no old fruit or vegetables in the kitchen.

- Remove all loose items from the kitchen counters.

- There should be no cooking smells in the house, but the smell of fresh coffee or herbs is pleasant.

- Remove any items, such as light fittings, that you do not want to sell with the house.

- If it is a cloudy day or in the evening, switch on lights in all the rooms.

- Ask the neighbour to house the pets for a short period. A house full of pets does not make a good impression.

- Don't tell anecdotes about the house.
- Don't come across as desperate.
- On show days, lock valuable possessions away.
- Do not be at home on show days.

Building and renovating a house

It is always safer to use a builder who is registered with a society like the National Home Builders' Registration Council (NHBRC).

- Choose a trustworthy contractor. Ask for references.

- Get different quotations that include the building specifications, the materials that will be used and the timeline.

- Be wary of quotations that are too low. The contractor could later insist on extra money to finish the work or just disappear before the work is completed.

- Have a written contract that includes the contractor's full details, a description of the work that must be done, specifications of the material that must be used, the total costs, a payment schedule, date when the work will start and finish, the removal of rubble and any other agreements.

- Most contractors have insurance against injuries on the site. Inquire about this and ask to see a certificate.

- If a building permit is necessary, let the contract accept responsibility for it. If the building work does not pass the inspection, he is responsible and you do not have additional expenses.

- If you need to take out a loan for the building work, it is advisable to make the contract conditional on the approval of the loan.

- Inspect the building work thoroughly before the final payment is made and the final certificate signed.

7. IMPORTANT REGULATIONS AND CONTRACTS FOR DOMESTIC WORKERS

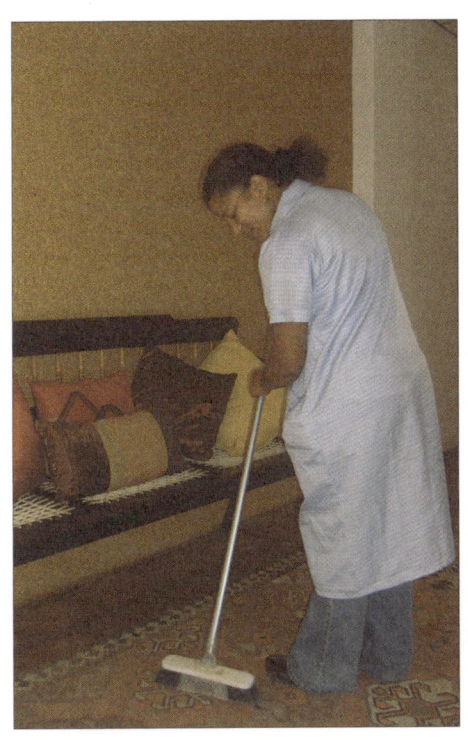

Workers to whom regulations apply

- The regulations are valid with or without a written contract.
- No one under the age of 15 may be taken into service.

- All domestic workers in South Africa.
- People who are taken into service through employment agencies.
- Independent contractors.
- A gardener at a private home.
- A person who looks after children or a sick person in a private home.
- A vehicle driver for a private household.

Minimum wages

- It is illegal to pay a person less than the prescribed minimum wages.
- Domestic workers are paid according to the hours, or part of an hour, that are worked. If the worker works for seven and a half hours, eight hours are paid for.
- If a person works for less than four hours a day, he or she must be paid for at least four hours of work.
- If a domestic worker works for longer than five hours at a time, he or she is entitled to a one hour lunch break.
- Domestic workers who work for less than 27 hours a week have a minimum wage that is slightly higher than workers who work full-time.
- Minimum wage is determined according to two districts (A and B), which are demarcated along municipal borders. Phone the nearest office of the Department of Labour to find out in which district your town or city falls. The minimum wages of the two districts differ slightly. In 2009 the minimum wage for people working more than 27 hours a week was R6,88 an hour in the A districts and R5,63 in the B districts. For workers working less than 27 hours a week, the minimum wage was R8,12 an hour in the A districts and R6,65 an hour in the B districts. The minimum wage is adjusted every year. Information on minimum wages can be obtained from the Department of Labour: **www.labour.gov.za**.
- Workers may not work more than 45 hours a week. If the worker works more than five days a week, it may not be for more than eight hours a day.
- Overtime pay is set at one and a half times the usual hourly rate. Workers may not work more than 15 hours a week overtime.
- No one may be obliged to work on Sundays. Any work on a Sunday is voluntary.

- If Sundays do not count as part of a worker's normal working hours, work on a Sunday must be paid at double the usual hourly rate. If Sundays are part of the normal working hours, the worker must be paid one and a half times the hourly rate.
- A worker may only work on a public holiday if that is the agreement. If the worker does not work, the normal hourly rate for the public holiday is paid. If the worker does work on that day, double the hourly rate must be paid.
- If a worker is expected to work between 18:00 and 06:00, overnight facilities or transport must be available. An extra allowance, as agreed between employer and employee, must be paid per shift. Everything must be set out in writing.

Example of a simple service contract

(To avoid misunderstandings, it is better to draw up a service contract that covers all the regulations.)

SERVICE CONTRACT (DOMESTIC WORKER)

Agreed between

....
(employer)

Address of employer:

....

....

....

and

....
(employee)

1. Acceptance of service: This contract will begin on .... and will continue until the service is ended.

2. Workplace: (e.g. residence and address) ....

....

3. Job description: (e.g. domestic worker, gardener, childminder)

....

4. Responsibilities: (just a few examples)
Tidy the house
Vacuum carpets
Clean toilets, baths, showers and floors
Wash the floor tiles
Look after the baby
Make breakfast

5. Working hours: Normal working hours on Mondays to Fridays will be:
.... to .... with a lunch break from .... to ....

Overtime will only be worked when there is a previous agreement. Overtime will be paid at one and half times the normal rate.

6. Wages: The employee's wages will be paid in cash on the last working day of every week and the weekly wages as agreed will be: R ....

The employee is, as agreed, also entitled to the following allowances: (examples)

Transport allowance	R ....
Accommodation allowance	R ....
Subtotal:	**R ....**

7. The following deductions have been agreed on:

Savings	R ....
Pension fund	R ....
Total wages:	**R ....**

8. Other services, conditions or benefits

....

....

9. General

Any alterations to this written agreement will only be valid if they are accepted and signed by both parties.

Signed by .... on this day of .... 20.........

Employer ....

Employee ....

The payment of wages

Payment can be made in cash, a cheque or direct deposit into a bank account. A cash payment must be made at the workplace during working hours. The worker must be given a salary slip, which must be kept for three years. The following details must appear on the salary slip:

- The employer's name and address
- The employee's name and job title/job grade
- The time period for which the payment is made
- The employee's salary scale and overtime rate
- The number of normal hours worked in the period
- The number of overtime hours worked
- The number of hours worked on Sundays or public holidays
- The full salary of the worker
- Details of any additional compensation
- Details of all deductions
- The precise amount that the worker is paid.

Permissible deductions

- Medical insurance
- Savings
- Pension fund
- Membership fees for a union
- Payments to a financial institution
- Rent
- Repayment of a loan or advance. This repayment may not exceed 10% of the total salary.
- An amount of no more than 10% of the salary may be deducted for accommodation if the room is watertight and in a good condition, equipped with a window and door that can lock, a toilet and bath or shower or access to a bathroom.

Non-permissible deductions

- An amount greater than the salary
- Payment for breakage of or damage to goods

- Meals that are provided during the day
- Clothes
- Equipment needed for work.

Leave and sick leave

- An employee is entitled to three weeks' paid leave for every 12 months of service. If there are public holidays during the holiday period, the employee must be given the same number of days extra leave.
- Sick leave is granted in a three-year cycle.
- It is calculated against the number of working days in a six-week period. An employee who works two days a week is therefore entitled to 12 days sick leave in a three-year cycle.
- During the first six months of service, the employee qualifies for one day of sick leave for every 26 days worked.
- When a person is sick for more than two consecutive days or more than twice in an eight-week period, a medical certificate must be provided.
- An employee is entitled to four months' unpaid maternity leave. No person may be dismissed because of pregnancy.

Termination of service

- The employer and employee must give written notice of the termination of service.
- If he/she has been employed for less than six months, one week's notice must be given. Thereafter, four weeks' notice must be given.
- Leave that has not been used must be paid out.
- Workers who lived on the premises can stay for one extra month (the notice month) or can pay for longer accommodation.
- An employee is entitled to a certificate of service at the termination of employment. The names of the employer and employee, period of service, type of work, salary paid and any training the worker has undergone must be indicated on the certificate. The reason for leaving the job should only be indicated if the employee chooses to do so.

8. FOOD AND DRINK

Traditional recipes

Bobotie

Ingredients
2 onions, chopped
25ml oil
1kg lean mince
2 thick slices of bread, soaked in milk, taken out and squeezed
125ml seedless raisins
25ml chutney
12,5ml smooth apricot jam
25ml lemon juice or vinegar
10ml salt
2ml pepper
6 fresh lemon or bay leaves
12 almonds, halved or flaked (optional)
15ml curry powder
5ml turmeric
2 eggs
250ml milk

Method
1. Sauté the onions in the oil.
2. Add the mince and fry until just brown. Take off the stove.
3. Add the other ingredients, except the lemon leaves, eggs, milk and almonds, and mix well.
4. Spoon the mince mixture into a greased, shallow oven dish.
5. Lightly roll up the lemon leaves and push them into the meat here and there. Sprinkle the almonds on top.
6. Beat the eggs and milk and pour carefully over the mixture.
7. Bake for about 50 minutes in an oven pre-heated to 180°C.

Ginger beer

Ingredients
7,750l lukewarm water
400ml raisins
1kg sugar
40g whole ginger, crushed
12,5ml tartaric acid

Method
1. Mix all the ingredients and allow the mixture to stand until the raisins float to the top.
2. Drain through a cloth and pour the mixture into bottles with corks.
3. Allow to stand for another two days before using.
4. Keep in the fridge.

Chicken pie

Ingredients
1 chicken (or 10 chicken thighs and/or breasts)
1 onion
400ml water
4 cloves
2 bay leaves
6 black peppercorns
salt and pepper to taste
250ml white wine
25ml lemon juice
12,5ml sago, soaked overnight in 125ml water
1 egg yolk, beaten
2 hard-boiled eggs, cut in slices (optional)
puff pastry
egg yolk and milk

Method
1. Cook the chicken, onion, water, cloves, bay leaves, peppercorns and salt until the chicken is tender. De-bone the chicken and cut into pieces.
2. Pour the liquid through a sieve and pour it back into the pot.
3. Put the chicken back in the pot and add the white wine and lemon juice.
4. Cook the mixture over a low heat and thicken with the sago and egg yolk.
5. Spoon the chicken into a greased oven dish and place the slices of eggs in between.
6. Cover with chilled puff pastry. Brush the pastry with a mixture of egg yolk and water. Prick the pastry with a fork.
7. Bake in a pre-heated oven at 220°C until golden.

Curried offal

Ingredients
1 sheep's offal, cleaned
750ml water
2 onions, chopped
12,5ml butter or margarine
12 new potatoes, peeled
10ml salt
40ml vinegar
12,5ml mild curry powder
8ml turmeric
15ml sugar
cornflour (optional)

Method
1. Cook the offal in the water until soft.
2. Sauté the onion in the butter.

3. Add the rest of the ingredients, except the cornflour, and cook until the potatoes are soft.
4. Thicken the sauce with the cornflour if necessary.

Pickled fish

Ingredients
1kg white fish, in portions
salt and pepper to taste
oil
3 onions, sliced
125ml water
750ml brown vinegar
25ml mild curry powder
12,5ml turmeric
25ml apricot jam

Method
1. Season the fish with salt and pepper and fry in oil until just cooked.
2. Allow the rest of the ingredients to simmer for 20 minutes.
3. Spoon the fish and warm sauce into a dish in layers.
4. Keep the pickled fish in the fridge for two days before serving.

Koeksisters

Ingredients
Syrup
1kg sugar
500ml water
12,5ml golden syrup
2ml fine ginger
5ml cream of tartar
2 sticks cinnamon

Dough
1kg cake flour
20ml baking powder
3ml salt
65ml butter or margarine
2 eggs
200ml milk and water, mixed
oil for deep frying

Method
1. Mix all the syrup ingredients and heat while stirring.
2. Allow the syrup to boil for five minutes and then remove the cinnamon.
3. Cool the syrup until ice cold, and keep it cold.
4. Sift together the dry ingredients for the dough.

5. Rub the butter lightly into the flour mixture.
6. Beat the eggs, then add the milk mixture and beat again.
7. Make a soft dough, and then let it stand for about two hours.
8. Roll out the dough to 1cm thick, cut into strips and plait or twist.
9. Fry the dough plaits in hot oil until light brown. Turn with a fork. Drain for a few seconds on a paper towel and then plunge them into the cold syrup. Submerge in the syrup for a few seconds and then let the excess syrup drip off.

Mealie pap (Mealie porridge)

Ingredients
1,1 l water
6ml salt
500ml mealie meal

Method
1. Boil the water and salt in a deep saucepan.
2. Slowly pour the mealie meal into the boiling water without stirring or using the lid – the mealie meal should form a heap in the water.
3. Use a spoon to make a well in the mealie meal so that the water can bubble through.
4. Lower the heat, put the lid on and let it steam for five minutes.
5. Stir the porridge with a fork until it is crumbly. Let it steam again and stir.
6. Repeat step five until the porridge is cooked and crumbly (about 30 minutes).

Milk tart

Ingredients
150ml butter or margarine
250ml cake flour
4ml salt
1 litre milk
2 sticks cinnamon
250ml sugar
4 eggs, separated
puff pastry

Method
1. Line a tart dish with the pastry.
2. Melt the butter in a saucepan, add the flour and salt and stir until smooth.
3. Gradually stir in the milk. Add the cinnamon.
4. Let the mixture cook slowly while stirring continuously, until it is thick and cooked.
5. Remove the mixture from the stove and let it cool slightly.
6. Remove the cinnamon and stir in the sugar and beaten egg yolks.
7. Beat the egg whites until stiff but not dry and fold into the mixture.
8. Pour the filling into the lined tart dish.
8. Bake for about 10 minutes in an oven pre-heated to 200°C and then lower the temperature to 180°C. Bake for another 30 minutes or until the filling is stiff.

Pumpkin fritters

Ingredients
500ml cooked pumpkin (orange)
2 eggs, beaten
125ml cake flour
12,5ml baking powder
12,5ml sugar
pinch of salt
oil
cinnamon and sugar

Method
1. Mix the first six ingredients.
2. Pour about 1cm of oil into a frying pan and heat.
3. Fry spoonfuls of the pumpkin mixture in the oil and drain.
4. Put the pumpkin fritters in a dish and sprinkle with cinnamon and sugar.
5. Serve hot.

Griddle cake

Ingredients
500ml cake flour
4ml cream of tartar
2,5ml salt
3ml bicarbonate of soda
50ml butter or margarine
300ml bicarbonate of soda
300ml buttermilk

Method
1. Sift the flour, cream of tartar and salt.
2. Lightly rub in the butter.
3. Dissolve the bicarbonate of soda into the buttermilk and add to the flour mixture.
4. Press the dough flat with your hands, and cut into squares.
5. Slowly roast the griddle cake for about 30 minutes on a greased grill over the coals. Turn over carefully.
6. Serve with butter, jam and cheese.

Onion in a sour sauce (*slaphakskeentjies*)

Ingredients
1kg small onions
750ml boiling water
7ml salt

Sauce

125ml sugar
250ml water
250ml white vinegar
4ml salt
2 eggs, beaten
25ml cornflour
25ml butter or margarine

Method
1. Boil the onions in the boiling water with salt until soft but firm.
2. Drain the onions.
3. Heat the sugar, 125ml water, vinegar and salt until boiling point.
4. Pour it slowly over the beaten eggs, beating constantly.
5. Pour the mixture back into the saucepan and cook slowly while stirring constantly.
6. Mix the cornflour with a little water and stir in slowly. Add the butter. Stir until the sauce is smooth and clear.
7. Pour the warm egg sauce over the cooked onions and allow to cool.

Braised snoek

Ingredients

750ml cooked snoek
3 onions, sliced into rings
30ml oil
15ml butter or margarine
2 tomatoes, cubed
6 potatoes, thinly sliced
Salt and black pepper

Method
1. Flake the snoek and put aside.
2. Fry the onions in the oil and butter.
3. Add the tomatoes and fry for a while.
4. Add the potatoes, put the lid on and simmer slowly. Add a little water if necessary.
5. Add the snoek and season with salt and pepper.
6. Serve hot.

Sweet potatoes

Ingredients

250ml brown sugar or honey
125ml butter or margarine
50ml fresh orange juice or 25ml lemon juice
2ml salt

1kg sweet potatoes, peeled and thinly sliced
1 stick of cinnamon
water (optional)

Method
1. Stir the brown sugar, butter, orange juice and salt in a saucepan over low heat until the sugar has melted.
2. Add the sweet potatoes and cinnamon and simmer until shiny and cooked. Add water as necessary.
3. Stir as little as possible and turn carefully until the sweet potatoes are golden brown.

Kebabs

Ingredients
2kg leg of mutton, cubed
1kg leg of pork, cubed
salt and pepper
2 large onions, cut in rings
25ml oil
125ml dried apricots, soaked
250ml water
500ml vinegar
25ml mild curry powder
25ml brown sugar
12,5ml turmeric
25ml chutney
2ml fine ginger
lemon leaves, crushed

Method
1. Place the cubes of meat in a dish and sprinkle with salt and pepper.
2. Fry the onions in oil until light brown.
3. Cook the rest of the ingredients for 10 minutes and allow to cool.
4. Pour the cooled sauce over the meat and marinate for two to three days in the fridge.
5. Thread the meat and apricot on kebab sticks.
6. Braai over slow coals.

Bean salad

Ingredients
500ml dry sugar beans
25ml sugar
25ml vinegar
5ml salt
25ml cornflour

Method
1. Soak the beans overnight and pour off the water.
2. Boil the beans in just enough water to cover them.
3. Mix the sugar, vinegar and salt.
4. Mix the cornflour with a little water, add the vinegar mixture, and stir in the cooked beans.
5. Slowly boil for 10 minutes and allow to cool.

Sugar bread

Ingredients
6 eggs, separated
250ml castor sugar
250ml sifted cake flour
2ml salt
12,5ml lemon juice
icing sugar, to sprinkle over for decoration

Method
1. Beat the egg whites and add the castor sugar very gradually.
2. Beat the egg yolks well and slowly beat them into the egg white mixture, a little at a time.
3. Lightly fold in the flour and salt.
4. Fold in the lemon juice.
5. Pour the mixture into a deep cake tin lined with waxed paper. Knock the pan lightly to get the air out.
6. Bake for about 50 minutes in a pre-heated oven of 180°C.
7. Let the cake cool for a little while in the tin before turning it out onto a wire rack to cool completely.
8. Sprinkle with icing sugar.

Herbs and spices used in food

Name	Use in food
Angelica	Cake decoration, jam, stewed fruit
Anise	Rusks, biscuits, bread, stewed apples, red cabbage
Basil	Salads, tomato, egg, cheese and fish dishes
Bay leaf	Meat, fish, soup, casseroles
Borage	Salad, cabbage, peas, beans, cake decoration
Capers	Seafood dishes, salad, sauces
Caraway seeds	Potatoes, bread, cake, cabbage, cottage cheese
Cardamom	Curry dishes, pilaf, Danish baking, puddings

Name	Use in food
Celery seed	Casseroles, coleslaw, herb bread, pickles
Chervil	Salad, soup, sauces, casseroles, omelettes
Chilli	Sauces, curry and Mexican dishes
Chives	Salads, soup, omelettes, salad dressing, garnish
Cinnamon	Baking, puddings, chutney, pork and lamb dishes
Cloves	Meat dishes, casseroles, pickles, rice, stewed fruit, apple tart, puddings, fruit cake, baking
Coriander	Curry and rice dishes, casseroles, baked dishes, soup, meat dishes
Cumin	Curry dishes, pickles, cabbage, chutney
Curry powder	Curry dishes, casseroles, soup, chutney, mayonnaise
Dill	Vegetables, salad, fish dishes, pickles
Fennel	Fish and veal dishes, beetroot salad
Ginger	Baking, curry and Thai dishes, ginger beer
Horseradish	Beef
Juniper berry	Venison, casseroles, pates
Lovage	Soup, salad, sauces
Marjoram	Meat and tomato dishes, soup, potato dishes, green beans
Mint	Mutton (roast), sauces, cream cheese, potatoes, peas, tomatoes, punch, herbal mint tea
Mixed spice	Baking, pickles, jam, stewed fruit
Mustard	Pickles, chutney, meat, fish and cheese dishes, mayonnaise, ham, potato salad, sauces
Nutmeg	Baking, milk puddings, potatoes, spinach
Oregano	Pizza, tomato dishes, salad, salad dressing, baby marrows
Paprika	Curry, goulash, meat and fish dishes, sauces, garnish
Parsley	Soup, sauces, butter, meat and fish dishes, omelettes, cheese dishes, salads, garnish
Pepper	Meat dishes, salad, vegetables, soup, sauces
Pimento	Chutney, marinades, baking, stewed fruit, mince

Name	Use in food
Poppy seed	Bread, baking
Red pepper	Sauces, shellfish, cheese and egg dishes
Rosemary	Meat dishes, fish, soup
Saffron	Paella, sauces, soup, fish and chicken dishes
Sage	Pork and cheese dishes, sausage, herb jelly
Savory	Meat and fish dishes, green beans, soup
Sesame seeds	Bread, biscuits, salad, cereals, cream cheese, vegetables, fruit salad
Tarragon	Fish and poultry dishes, salad, vinegar
Thyme	Sausage, lamb and pork dishes, cream cheese, Benedictine liqueur, sauces, soup, egg dishes
Turmeric	Curry, rice and fish dishes, chutney, pickles
Vanilla	Cakes, puddings, ice cream
Watercress	Salads, soup

Wine

Wine was produced as early as 6 000BC in Georgia and Iran. In South Africa the first wine was produced in the Cape in 1659, seven years after Jan van Riebeeck had arrived. Governor Simon van der Stel later ordered that vineyards be planted in the Cape on a large scale. South Africa is today one of the biggest wine producers and exporters in the world.

Well-known white cultivars

Chardonnay
A French cultivar is used for the famous white wines from Burgundy in France. It was planted for the first time in South Africa in 1985. The wine can have a citrus or subtropical character or a woody and buttery flavour.

Chenin blanc
This French cultivar is the most popular and most planted cultivar in South Africa. Dry and off-dry white wine, as well as sherry and port, are made of this.

Colombar(d)
A French cultivar that was originally used for making cognac. In South Africa brandy, sherry, dry wine and semi-sweet white wine are made of this, and it is also sometimes used in blends.

Crouchen blanc (SA or Paarl riesling)
It is primarily planted in coastal areas and used to make a dry white wine.

Gewürztraminer
This is a cultivar that is not commonly planted. It comes from France and Germany, but may have originated in Austria. The wine has a unique spicy aroma. Off-dry or semi-sweet wine is made from this cultivar. In South Africa it is mostly planted in the Tulbagh area.

Muscat d'Alexandrie (muscat romain)
It is one of the oldest cultivars in the world, and may have originated in the ancient Egyptian port city of Alexandria. In South Africa we know it as hanepoot. It is a popular table grape and is used to make sweet wine and semi-sweet wine, as well as *moskonfyt* and raisins.

Sauvignon blanc
A famous French cultivar, originally from Bordeaux in France. The dry white wine has a fruity character that is reminiscent of grass, asparagus or gooseberries.

Sémillon
This is one of the oldest Cape cultivars, and for a long time was also the most popular. Dry white wine with aromas of lime, citrus and butter, as well as sherry, are made from this grape.

Weisser riesling (Rhine riesling)
A German cultivar that makes outstanding wine that ages well. In South Africa the white wine made from this cultivar is usually dry or off dry.

Well-known red cultivars

Cabernet sauvignon
This French cultivar is regarded as the best red wine cultivar in the world. The best South African red wines with good potential for ageing are made of this cultivar. The wine has a blackberry, cigar or woody aroma. It is often blended with merlot and cabernet franc.

Cinsaut (hermitage)
Cinsaut has been produced at the Cape since 1850. It is a French cultivar that makes a light red wine and is also used in blends.

Merlot
This French cultivar makes a dark red wine that is reminiscent of blackberries and chocolate.

Pinotage
Pinotage is the only cultivar to be developed in South Africa. It is a cross of cinsaut and pinot noir. The flavour reminds one of plums, bananas or mulberries and black berries. Ageing in wood can add a cedar, coffee or chocolate flavour.

Shiraz
Assumptions that this cultivar originated Iran have been proven wrong as vine experts have determined that it is a French cultivar. The wine has a smoky, spicy character.

Tinta barocca
This is a Portuguese cultivar used for making port and sweet wine.

- The red colour of wine comes from contact with the red grape skins during fermentation.
- Wine must always be clear.
- If red wine is brownish, the time for drinking it has passed.

Wine glasses

1. Liqueur, 2. Sherry, 3. Port, 4. White wine, 5. Red wine, 6. Brandy, 7. Champagne/Sparkling wine

Temperatures at which wine should be served

Sparkling wine	Very cold	6–8°C
White wine	Cold	10–12°C
Red wine	European room temperature	18°C
Light red wine	Cool	12–14°C
Red nouveau	Cold	10–12°C
Late harvest wine	Very cold	6–8°C
Sweet wine	Cold	10–12°C
Sherry	Cooled	12–14°C
Muscadel	Very cold	6–8°C

- In the past people clinked their glasses to drive away evil spirits.
- Champagne is only produced in the Champagne region of France. In South Africa the appellation sparkling wine or Méthode Cap Classique is used.
- The legal limit for the blood alcohol level of a vehicle driver is 0,05g alcohol per 100ml blood.
- Wine bottles must lie on their sides to keep the corks moist. They can also be stored upside down in cardboard boxes.
- South Africa's first wine route was started in 1971 in Stellenbosch by Frans Malan from the Simonsig wine estate.
- South Africa is the seventh largest producer of wine in the world.

The correct way to open sparkling wine

- Wrap the neck and cork of the bottle in a napkin.
- Hold the bottle by the neck with your right hand at a 45° angle to the floor and keep your left hand under the bottle.
- Hold the cork and turn the bottle.
- Place pressure on the cork so that it comes out slowly and does not shoot out.
- The bubbles will escape if it is poured too soon.
- Tall, straight glasses keep the sparkle for longer.

Toast etiquette

- The host must propose the first toast.
- Tap lightly on the glass to get everyone's attention. If the guests do not pay attention, stand up and tap the glass again.
- Speak concisely, clearly and sincerely.

- Guests stand up and clink their glasses. Clink your glass with the people nearest to you, make eye contact with them and lift your glass in the direction of the person to whom the toast was proposed.
- Do not clink you own glass if the toast was proposed to you.

Wine and food

Type of food	Appropriate wine
Soup	
Minestrone	Red wine, pinotage
Cream soup	Chardonnay
Fish soup	Dry white wine, blanc de noir
Seafood	
Crab	Off-dry chenin blanc, weisser riesling
Oysters and mussels	Sauvignon blanc, dry sparkling wine, blanc de noir
Sea fish	Sauvignon blanc, blanc fumé, chardonnay, pinot gris, dry chenin blanc
Freshwater fish	Weisser riesling, off-dry muscadel, blanc de noir
Meat	
Beef, pie or casserole	Red wine, shiraz, tinta barocca, cabernet sauvignon
Beef, roasted beef	Cabernet sauvignon, Bordeaux blends
Boerewors	Fruity and spicy red wine
Duck	Semi-sweet white wine, weisser riesling, late harvest, Bordeaux blends, pinot noir
Chicken	Dry or off-dry white wine, chenin blanc, blanc de noir, zinfandel, pinot noir
Veal	Dry white wine, blanc de noir, light red wine
Lamb	Shiraz, pinotage, pinot noir, merlot, cabernet franc
Liver, kidneys, offal	Pinotage, shiraz, tinta barocca
Curry	Fruity, off-dry wines, gewürztraminer, chenin blanc, colombar, blanc de noir, sparkling wine
Pork	Dry or off-dry white wine, chenin blanc, weisser riesling, light red wine, merlot, pinot noir

Type of food	Appropriate wine
Game	Cabernet franc, merlot, pinot noir, red zinfandel, pinotage
Pizza and pasta	
Pizza and pasta	Merlot, red zinfandel
Fruit, sweets	
Chocolate	Noble late harvest wine, raisiny muscadel, port, cabernet sauvignon, merlot
Tart, custard, cheesecake	Sweet wine, noble late harvest
Cheese	
Blue cheese	Noble late harvest, port
Goat cheese	Sauvignon blanc, off-dry chenin blanc
Brie, camembert	Blanc fumé, pinot gris, colombar, chardonnay
Cheddar, mature	Shiraz, zinfandel
Cheddar, young	Cabernet sauvignon, port
Gouda	Shiraz, zinfandel
Gruyère	Shiraz, zinfandel
Fruit, fresh	Special late harvest, noble late harvest

- Wine glasses are held by the stem so the wine stays cold and the glass stays clean.
- Red wine glasses are larger than white wine glasses.
- Wine glasses that curve towards the top hold the flavour of the wine better.
- Dry wines are drunk before sweet wines, and white wine is drunk before red wine.
- A white wine glass must be filled to two-thirds and a red wine glass must be filled to about half way.

9. HOUSEHOLD TIPS

Stain removal (for washable fabrics only)

- Treat stains as quickly as possible.
- Wipe or scrape off as much of the substance as possible.
- Soak washable fabrics overnight in cold water and soap.
- First test the stain removal method on an inconspicuous part of the fabric.
- Open windows and doors when using solvents such as benzine.

Antiperspirant	Rub the stain with white vinegar. Soak stains in methylated spirits.
Ballpoint pen ink	– Rub with methylated spirits and then wash as usual. – Place cotton wool on the stain and rub on the reverse side of the fabric with nail polish remover.
Battery acid	Soak immediately in a solution of bicarbonate of soda or baking powder (50ml/250ml water)
Beer	Rub the stain with 10ml borax dissolved in 250ml water, or wash in warm soapy water mixed with a little white vinegar.
Beetroot	– Rinse immediately in cold water and wash in warm water. If the stain has already dried, soak it in a borax solution (25g/500ml water). – Leave to soak overnight in cold water. Rub undiluted, liquid washing liquid on the stain and rinse.
Blood	– Soak in cold water and then wash with washing powder. – Soak in a solution of 1 litre water, 15ml salt and 15ml ammonia.
Cacao	Rinse in cold water and wash in hot water. Old stains can be soaked overnight in glycerine.
Candle wax	Scrape off as much wax as possible. Place absorbent paper over and under the mark and press with a hot iron. Repeat as necessary. If the wax is off, but leaves a grease spot, benzine or carbon tetrachloride can be rubbed on the stain.
Carbon paper	Rub with methylated spirits or alcohol.
Chewing gum	– Put an ice cube on it to make it harden, then scrape off as much as possible. Place absorbent paper over and under it

	and press with a hot iron. Any grease spot left behind can be removed with benzine. – Scrape off as much as possible and rub with turpentine.
Chocolate	Rub with glycerine, ammonia or a borax solution.
Coca-Cola	– Rinse with cold water, clean the back with dishwashing liquid and rinse again with cold water. – Rub with methylated spirits mixed with a little white vinegar, and rinse.
Coffee	– Soak in a weak ammonia solution. – Soak in a little glycerine. – Soak in a solution of one teaspoon of borax in 500ml hot water.
Colourant	Sponge off with methylated spirits mixed with a little ammonia.
Curry	– Soak in vinegar and rinse with lukewarm water. – Rub with glycerine and wash as usual.
Egg	– Soak in cold water and washing powder. – Bleach with 75ml water to which 5ml ammonia and 10ml peroxide have been added.
Fat	– Place absorbent paper on top and under the stain and iron with a hot iron. – Rub with eucalyptus oil and wash as usual. – Wash the item of clothing and let it dry. Spray insecticide or hairspray on the stain, let it stand overnight and wash again. – Rub the stain with dishwashing liquid.
Fruit	Sprinkle salt on the stain and let it stand for a while before it is washed.
Glue	Scrape off as much of the glue as possible. Then rub with acetone or non-oily nail polish remover.
Grass	Sponge off with methylated spirits and wash as usual.
Grease	Scrape off as much as possible. Iron between two layers of absorbent paper. Wash in warm water.
Hairspray	Soak in glycerine and then wash.
Ice cream	Rub the stain with dishwashing liquid.

Ink	– White fabrics can be covered with a mixture of salt and lemon juice and then held over steam. – Spray hair spray on the stain, allow to dry and then brush lightly with a solution of water and vinegar. – Rub both sides of the fabric with white toothpaste, let stand for a while and then rinse.
Ink, mark	– Soak white linen for a short while in a solution of chlorate of lime and water. – Soak it for a few minutes in ammonia and rinse well.
Ink, red	Soak in a borax solution.
Iodine	Soak in a weak ammonia solution. For white fabrics, use a weak solution of bleach.
Jam	Soak in a warm borax solution.
Lipstick	– Rub off stubborn lipstick stains with carbon tetrachloride or bleach the fabric with hydrogen peroxide. – Rub with eucalyptus oil.
Mascara	Rub with dishwashing liquid, then with ammonia and rinse.
Mayonnaise	Wash in lukewarm water to which a little ammonia has been added.
Mercurochrome	– Soak in a weak hydrogen peroxide solution to which a few drops of ammonia have been added.
Milk	Soak old stains in glycerine for 10 minutes and then wash in warm soapy water.
Mould	Soak in a weak solution of vinegar and water, and then wash in warm soapy water.
Mud	Brush it off when dry and rub with methylated spirits or a weak borax solution.
Mulberries	Rub the stain with mulberry leaves and wash as usual.
Mustard	Rub with glycerine and wash in warm water.
Nail polish	Sponge off with nail polish remover (acetone) and then wash in hot water.
Nicotine	– Sponge off with methylated spirits. – Rub with lemon juice and bleach in the sun.

Oil	Rub with eucalyptus oil.
Paint	Treat water-based paint with water and oil-based paint with turpentine. Wash as usual.
Perfume	Rub with glycerine and was as usual.
Pencil	Rub with methylated spirits.
Red wine	Cover immediately with salt – it will absorb the wine. Wash as usual.
Rust	– Cover with a thick layer of cream of tartar and allow to soak for a few minutes in very hot water. – Dissolve a teaspoon of salt in a dessert spoon of lemon juice. Hold the stain over boiling water and rub it with the mixture. First rinse in hot and then in cold water. – Rub the stain with water in which a little cream of tartar has been dissolved.
Sauce (on table cloth)	Rub borax on the wet stain and let dry before brushing out the borax.
Scorch marks	– Soak the marks in glycerine and wash as usual. – Rub with a solution of one part hydrogen peroxide to ten parts water.
Shoe polish	Rub with methylated spirits or turpentine and sponge off with hot water.
Soot (on a carpet)	Cover with salt, let stand for a while, and vacuum.
Sweat	– Dissolve aspirin tablets in a little water and rub the stains with it. – Sponge off with a weak water and vinegar solution. – Soak in a mixture of water and lemon juice.
Tar	– Scrape off as much as possible and then rub with carbon tetrachloride. – Rub with methylated spirits. – Rub with eucalyptus oil or glycerine.
Tea	The same as coffee stains.
Toffee	Soak in hot water. Then rub with a mixture of white vinegar and methylated spirits.
Tomato juice	Rinse off with cold water, rub in glycerine and wash well.

Tomato sauce	– Rinse with cold water and wash in dishwashing liquid. – Rub with methylated spirits when the stain is dry and wash afterwards.
Turmeric	Soak in diluted ammonia or white spirits, and then wash as usual.
Urine	– Soak in lukewarm water and white vinegar. – Soak in a weak ammonia solution. – Soak in a solution of water and bicarbonate of soda.
Varnish	– Sponge off with methylated spirits or turpentine and wash in warm water. – Rub both sides of the fabric with a solution of equal parts benzine and turpentine and then wash in warm water.
Vinegar	Soak is a weak borax solution, rinse and wash as usual.

Cleaning tips

Bath and basin	– A mixture of peroxide and Epsom salts removes rust stains from an enamel bath. – Rub with a soft cloth and furniture oil. – Yellow stains can be removed with a mixture of lemon juice and salt. – Stains from a dripping tap can be removed with a paste of peroxide and borax. The stains can also be rubbed with a mixture of 150ml white vinegar and 25g salt.
Bottles and flasks	A solution of salt and vinegar removes sharp odours.
Cake tins	Scrub rusting tins with vinegar.
Candlesticks	Wash in soapy water to which a few drops of ammonia have been added.
Carpets	– Remove stains with one part white vinegar to three parts water. – Red wine stains can be removed with soda water. – Carpets can be cleaned with equal parts methylated spirits, benzine and water – Greasy spots on carpets can be removed by rubbing in dry bicarbonate of soda. Brush it out after 15 minutes.
Copper	– Polish copper with a lemon dipped in salt. – Rub with a paraffin cloth.

	– Verdigris can be removed with a toothpaste and vinegar. – A mixture of table salt and vinegar can remove scorch marks on copper.
Cutlery	Immediately place all used cutlery in a container of hot water when food is being prepared.
Fireplace	Put damp tea leaves in the fireplace before cleaning to avoid dust.
Floors	Sprinkle damp tea leaves on very dusty floors before sweeping.
Fridge	– Unpleasant odours can be removed by washing the fridge with vinegar or a solution of bicarbonate of soda.
Glassware	– Remove water stains by filling with water and lemon juice and leaving to stand overnight. To make glassware shine, put a little lemon juice in the rinse water. – Fill with hot water in which a few denture cleaning tablets have been dissolved. Allow to stand for 30 minutes and then rinse well. – Rub scratches on glass with a cloth and white toothpaste. Rinse in hot water.
Grater	Use an old toothbrush to clean a grater.
Iron	Fill the iron with a water and vinegar solution and steam until clean.
Kettle	– To remove build-up, boil three tablespoons of cream of tartar in water. – Boil vinegar and water in the kettle to remove build-up.
Marble	To remove stains, sprinkle with powdered borax. Rinse after a few minutes with hot water.
Microwave oven	To remove stubborn odours, boil three parts water and one part lemon juice or vinegar for 10 minutes on a low heat. Wipe microwave with a damp cloth.
Mirrors	– Clean with a cloth dipped in a mixture of 25ml vinegar and 20ml lukewarm water. – Use weak tea to keep mirrors shiny and clean. – Add a little methylated spirits to water with which mirrors are cleaned.
Oven	Place a dish of ammonia in a warm oven that has been turned off and then clean with dishwashing liquid. A

container of ammonia can also be left overnight in a cold oven.

Tupperware
– Remove coffee and tea stains by scouring lightly with bicarbonate of soda.
– Stains can be removed by rubbing with baking powder and salt.

Porcelain
– Use a damp cloth dipped in bicarbonate of soda to remove coffee and tea stains.
Rub coffee and tea stains with fine table salt.

Pots and pans
– To remove burnt food, boil with a mixture of water and vinegar and let it stand overnight.
– Stainless steel pots will become shiny if they are left for at least four hours in hot water with washing powder.

Cane chairs
Clean with warm soapy water to which a little methylated spirits has been added.

Rubbish bins
– Sprinkle borax in a rubbish bin to remove bad odours.
– Put cat litter in the bottom of your rubbish bin to remove bad odours.

Silver
Silver can be cleaned by rubbing with half a lemon and then rinsing.

Stainless steel
Rub with baby oil or a mixture of one part vinegar to two parts hot water.

Taps
Rub taps with half a potato and then rinse.

Tiles
Glazed tiles can be cleaned with water to which a little ammonia has been added.

Toilet
– Pour three cups of vinegar in the toilet, and allow to stand for a few hours. Brush and rinse.
– Chlorine or swimming pool acid removes stains from a toilet.

Vacuum bag
Throw in wet tea leaves and shake out well.

Vacuum flask
– To remove stains, put three tablespoons of bicarbonate of soda in boiling water and allow to stand for 15 minutes.
– To remove stains, fill with hot water in which a teaspoon of baking powder has been dissolved and allow to stand overnight.
– Boiling water with two tablespoons of vinegar will remove bad odours.

Kitchen sink	Pour a mixture of one cup of salt, one cup of bicarbonate of soda and boiling water down a blocked sink.
Windows	– Use an old T-shirt to clean windows. It does not smear. – Add vinegar to water with which windows are being washed. – Use weak tea to clean windows. – Hot vinegar or acetone can be used to remove paint spots from windows.
Wood	– Varnished wood can be cleaned with cold tea. – Make your own furniture polish with a mixture of half lemon oil and half white vinegar. Apply with a spray bottle.

Cooking tips

Apples	Apples peel more easily if they are soaked in boiling water first. Make a few cuts in apple peels before they are baked. This prevents the peel from bursting. Sprinkle lemon juice over peeled apples and bananas to prevent them from discolouring.
Avocados	Sprinkle lemon juice over peeled avocados to prevent them from discolouring.
Bacon	Make small cuts in the bacon's rind before it is fried and it won't curl up.
Bananas	Bananas ripen quickly in a paper bag in a warm, dark place.
Beetroot	The skins of cooked beetroot comes off easily if they are left in cold water for a little while. To prevent beetroot from boiling over, add a little oil or butter to the water.
Biscuits	– Biscuits stay fresh for longer if there is a layer of sugar in the bottom of the container. – A piece of blotting paper in the cake tin keeps biscuits fresh and crisp.
Bread	– Put a packet of salt in the bread tin to keep the bread fresher for longer. – Sprinkle water over old bread and heat for a little while in a hot oven to refresh it. – To improve the texture of brown bread, use equal parts white and brown flour.
Cabbage	Add a little lemon juice to the water in which cabbage is cooking to lessen the smell.

Cocoa	A pinch of cinnamon gives a lovely flavour to cocoa.
Cake	– Always turn out a hot cake on to a wire rack. The hot cake "sweats" and becomes damp on a plate. – A cake cuts neatly with a knife that has been dipped in boiling water and dried. – If a cake sticks to the pan, leave the tin in cold water for a few minutes. It can also be held over a saucepan for a few minutes. – Sugar and butter mix more easily if a little lemon juice is added. – Add a little baking powder to butter icing that is too soft.
Carrots	Soak wilted carrots in sugar water to refresh them.
Cauliflower	– Cauliflower stays white if half a cup of milk is added to the water in which it is boiled. – Add a little lemon juice to the boiling water in which cauliflower is cooked to keep it white.
Cheese	– A little sugar in the container prevents cheese from going mouldy quickly. – Wrap cheese in a vinegar cloth to prevent it from going mouldy in the fridge. – A little mustard added to cheese dishes improves the flavour.
Chicken	Sprinkle lemon juice over chicken before it is cooked to make it juicy and soft.
Coffee	Keep coffee in the fridge to keep it fresh.
Cottage cheese	Cottage cheese keeps longer if the container is stored upside down.
Cream	– Cream will whip much better if a little cream of tartar is added to it. – Cream must be ice cold before it is whipped. – An egg white added to cream makes it go further and helps it whip better. – Add a few spoonfuls of ice-cold water or milk to cream that is too thick to be whipped.
Custard	– A little butter in custard stops a skin from forming on top. – Sprinkle a little sugar on top of custard to stop a skin from forming. – To stop custard from burning, rub a little margarine or oil on the bottom of the pan.

Dates	Cut dates with a knife or scissors dipped in flour.
Dough	– Place cling film over dough that is rising to prevent a crust from forming. – A few drops of lemon juice improves the texture of all pastry crusts.
Eggs	– Eggs will not stick to a pan if a little salt or flour is sprinkled over the oil in the pan. – Smear your fingertips with a little margarine or butter to easily remove bits of eggshell from hard-boiled eggs. – Soak boiled eggs in cold water before shelling them. – Place a teaspoon in the saucepan in which eggs are boiling to prevent them from cracking.
Egg white	Egg whites will stiffen faster if a pinch of salt is added while whisking them.
Fish	– A little vinegar added to the oil in which fish is fried stops the fish from breaking apart. – Lemon juice in the water in which fish is boiled keeps the fish firm.
Grapes	The grape skins remove easily if they are left in boiling water for two minutes and then plunged into cold water.
Green beans	Soak wilted green beans in boiling water.
Honey	– Add a little lemon juice to honey to prevent it from crystallising. – Place a jar with honey that has crystallised in the sun or in a container of hot water.
Jelly	– Add a little lemon juice or a pinch of bicarbonate of soda to make jelly set quicker. – Only cooked pineapple should be used in jelly, otherwise it will not set. – Jelly can be cut with a knife that has been dipped in water.
Lemons	– Soak lemons in hot water before they are squeezed. – Make a hole in a lemon if just a little juice is needed. It can then be used again.
Lettuce	– Lettuce stays fresh for longer in a paper bag in the fridge (not a plastic bag). – Wilted lettuce leaves refresh in a dish of ice cold water (not with ice cubes). – Put wilted lettuce in cold water. Add a teaspoon of bicarbonate of soda and allow to stand for two hours.

	– Rinse wilted lettuce in lukewarm water and plunge into ice water. Add half a glass of vinegar and a little sugar to the water. – Lettuce stays fresh for a long time if it is kept in sugar water.
Macaroni	Add a little oil to the water in which macaroni is being boiled; this prevents it from boiling over.
Margarine	– A little oil in the pan stops margarine (or butter) from going brown quickly. – Cut a block of margarine (or butter) with a knife that has first been dipped in water. – Hard margarine (or butter) can be placed in a container on top of a pot of boiling water to soften.
Meat	– Pour lemon juice over meat to tenderise it. – A little vinegar in the oil in which crumbed meat is being fried prevents it from burning quickly. – Add ice cubes to greasy meat sauces. The fat will stick to the ice cubes and can then easily be spooned off. – Add a little milk to meat that has burnt and then cook again for a little while. – Salt and vinegar stops meat from spoiling quickly.
Milk	Add a little oil to the saucepan in which milk is boiling. It stops milk from sticking to the bottom of the saucepan.
Offal	A little bicarbonate of soda in the saucepan helps with the gamy smell of offal.
Onions	– Rub your hands in vinegar before you peel onions. This reduces the odour. – A little brown vinegar in the pan in which onions are frying helps them brown quickly. – Peel onions under running water to stop your eyes from burning. – Lemon juice removes the onion smell from your hands.
Pancakes	– A little vinegar or white wine added to pancake batter prevents the pancakes from being tough. – Rub a pan to which pancakes are sticking with dry salt. Do not wash the pan afterwards.
Peas	Peas will shell easily if they are first soaked in boiling water.
Potato chips	– For tastier potato chips, let them sit for 10 minutes in cold water before they are fried.

Potatoes	– A little vinegar in the oil in which potatoes will be fried makes them crispier.
– Add lemon juice to the water when potatoes are cooked in their skins. The potatoes will stay white and the saucepan will not stain.
– A tablespoon of milk in the water in which potatoes are boiled will prevent them from discolouring.
– The skins of boiled potatoes are easy to remove if they have been left for a little while in salt water.
– A pinch of baking powder added to mashed potatoes makes them light and soft.
– To prevent potatoes from going green, keep them in a dark place.
Pumpkin	– To keep cut pumpkin fresh, remove the seeds and sprinkle a layer of bicarbonate of soda on the inside.
– Rub your hands with margarine to avoid staining them when you peel pumpkin.
– Sprinkle sugar over the cut side of the pumpkin to keep it fresh if it has to be stored.
Rice	– Add a little lemon juice to the water in which rice is being cook to make the rice white.
– Place a slice of bread on top of rice that has burnt and let it stand for a few minutes.
Salt	– Add a raw potato to soup or a stew that is too salty.
– Add a few grains of rice to a salt shaker to keep the salt dry and loose.
Sausage	Dip sausages in boiling water before they are fried. This will prevent the sausages from bursting.
Soup	– Boil a few slices of raw potato in soup that is too salty.
– Add a tablespoon of peanut butter to creamed soup that has burned.
Sweet potato	– Place peeled sweet potatoes in salted water to avoid discolouration.
– Add a pinch of turmeric for a lovely brown colour when sweet potatoes are cooked with white sugar.
Tinned food	Use the sauce from tinned vegetables in soup.
Tomatoes	– Put tomatoes in empty egg cartons to prevent them from bruising.
– Tomatoes will keep longer if they are placed in boiling water for a minute and then kept in the fridge.

- The skins of tomatoes will come off easily if the tomatoes are first soaked in boiling water for a few minutes and then placed in cold water.
- Green tomatoes ripen nicely in a brown paper bag in a dark place.

Vegetables Vegetables stay fresh for longer if they are wrapped in wax paper before they are stored in the fridge.

Watermelon Place a piece of wax paper on the cut side of a watermelon to keep it fresh for longer.

White sauce Put a piece of wet wax paper over white sauce to prevent it from forming a skin on top.

General

Ants Sprinkle powdered soap in the holes leading to the ants' nest.

Beads Dab a little nail polish on the end of the string on which beads are threaded to harden it.

Brackish water Borax softens brackish water.

Brooms Soak a new broom in salt water before using it; it will last longer.

Buttons Strengthen buttons by dabbing a little colourless nail polish on the cotton on the reverse side.

Candles Candles burn more slowly and evenly if they are first kept in the fridge for a few hours.

Car windows
- Rub the glass with half a potato so that rainwater runs off quickly.
- Prevent windows from fogging up by rubbing on a mixture of equal parts methylated spirits and glycerine and then wiping dry.
- Use half a lemon to wipe marks off car windows, then wash as usual.

Cast iron pots Put newspapers in cast iron pots to prevent them from rusting.

Cigarette smoke A dish of vinegar will absorb the smell of cigarette smoke.

Cotton thread Pull cotton thread through candle wax to make it easier to thread the needle.

Drawers	Rub a drawer that is difficult to open with candle wax.
Flowers	– Pick flowers early in the morning or after sunset. – Add one teaspoon of bleach and one teaspoon of sugar to the water to make the flowers last longer. – A little bicarbonate of soda or salt in the water keeps flowers fresh. – Put a little camphor in the water to keep flowers fresh. – Flowers that are too heavy for their stalks can be slipped into plastic straws.
Garage	– Fasten a tyre to the wall to prevent bumps. – Hang a ball on a rope from a beam and then park in such a way that the car's windscreen touches the ball.
Glasses	When two glasses stick together, place the bottom one in a container of hot water and pour cold water in the top glass.
Glue	– Remove the glue from labels with white spirits. – Use paraffin to remove tough glue from Tupperware and glassware.
Hinges	– Spray insecticide on squeaky hinges if oil is not available.
Hot-water bottles	– A hot-water bottle will stay warm for longer if a teaspoon of salt is added to the water. – Add a little glycerine to the water in a new hot-water bottle. The hot-water bottle will last longer.
Jars with screw tops	– Place the lid in boiling water and then screw off. – Make a hole in the lid and then screw it off.
Keys	A little powder helps keys turn smoothly in a lock.
Moles	– Soak a cloth in paraffin and put in the mole hole. – Put a mothball in an eggshell, put it in the mole hole and wet it.
Nails	Use sticky putty to hold small nails in place before hammering them in.
Nail polish	Nail polish dries quickly if nails are held into cold water. Keep nail polish in the fridge to prevent it from hardening.
Paint	Put wet newspaper in the corners of windows that must be painted.

Paint rollers	Pull on men's long socks like gloves so your hands and arms are not splattered with paint when you are using a paint roller.
Paint smells	Vanilla essence helps remove paint smells from rooms.
Paint tins	Store paint tins upside down so that the skin that forms is at the bottom of the tin.
Paintbrushes	Paintbrushes that have gone hard can be boiled in vinegar for half an hour and then washed with dishwashing liquid.
Roses	Snip off the ends of the stems of drooping roses and put them in boiling water for a little while.
Scissors	Sharpen scissors by cutting sandpaper with them.
Screws	If a screw keeps falling out before it can be screwed in, put a bit of sticky putty or chewing gum in the hole.
Shells	Soak shells in vinegar for 10 hours before you make holes in them and they will not break.
Shoe polish	A few drops of vinegar softens shoe polish.
Soap	Put small pieces of soap in a stocking and tie to an outside tap. It's useful to wash your hands with when you have been working outside.
Spectacles	Rub spectacles with a glycerine cloth to clean them and prevent them from fogging up.
Sponges	Soak slimy sponges in vinegar water.
Sticky tape	Fold the end of a roll of sticky tape into a point to make it easy to find the next time.
Tar stains	Use liquid polish to remove tar stains from a vehicle's paintwork.
Vacuum cleaner	A little cinnamon, ginger or mixed spices in the vacuum cleaner's bag gives the house a lovely aroma.
Zips	Zips that stick can be rubbed with candle wax.

10. MEDICAL

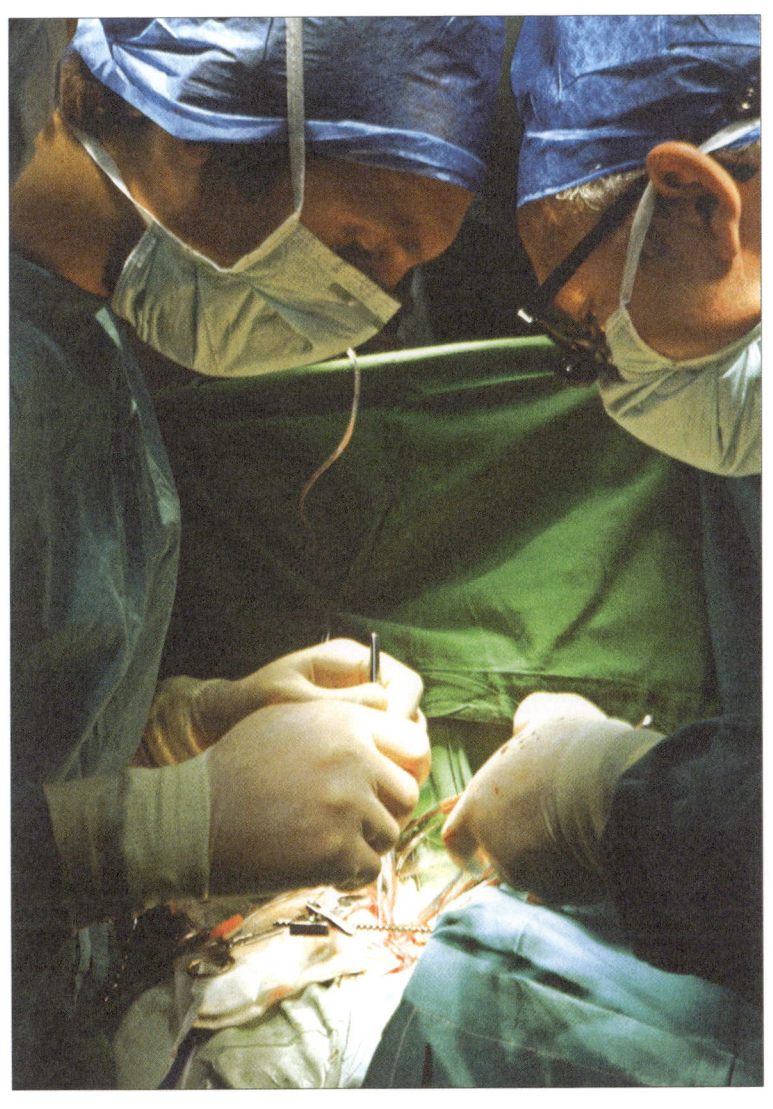

Traditional remedies and natural medicines

(See also **Important medicinal herbs page 438**)

Traditional remedies were once used in South Africa as a matter of custom, and as result of the great distances to the nearest doctors. Many remedies were adopted from indigenous cultures. Traditional remedies are still used on a limited scale. All remedies must be used carefully and at your own risk. If there is any doubt, a doctor should first be consulted.

Alcohol
- Drink plenty of water before drinking alcohol. It lessens the effects of the alcohol.
- If you feel the effects the next day, drink a little bicarbonate of soda dissolved in half a cup of hot water.

Arthritis
- Dissolve half a teaspoon of cream of tartar in a glass of water and drink every morning on an empty stomach.
- Every morning and evening drink a cup of rooibos tea with two teaspoons of honey and two teaspoons of lemon juice or apple cider vinegar.
- Mix the juice of a lemon with two teaspoons of honey and drink every evening. Don't drink anything after that before you go to sleep.
- Allow guava leaves to steep like a tea and drink it three times a day.

Asthma
- Put fresh peppermint leaves in a gauze bag and put in hot bathwater. The steam relieves the symptoms of asthma.
- Boil fresh sage twigs in water until it looks like strong tea. Take one cup of this and boil with two cups of sugar until it becomes a syrup. Add a small bottle of *borsdruppels* and half a cup of lemon juice and mix well. Drink one tablespoon three times a day.
- Mix one teaspoon of honey with half a teaspoon of cinnamon. Take before bedtime.
- Mix half a teaspoon of salt with half a teaspoon of baking powder and a little water. Follow with a teaspoon of honey.
- Eat a knife point of powdered cinnamon.
- Cut one unpeeled pineapple in cubes and pour a bottle of gin and a packet of cream of tartar over it. Allow to steep for 24 hours. Sieve through a cloth and drink one teaspoon three times a day.
- Mix one glass of boiled milk, one teaspoon of sugar, one teaspoon of butter and half a teaspoon of powdered cinnamon. Drink in the evening.
- Mix two parts olive oil and one part gin. Take one tablespoon after every meal.

– Drink the juice of a lemon with a tablespoon of honey.

Baby, bottom Vaseline helps with nappy rash.

Baby, teeth – Rub a little glycerine on sore or itching gums for relief.

Bedsores
– A sheepskin on the bed prevents bedsores.
– Prevent bedsores by rubbing the skin with methylated spirits or Prep.

Bee sting
– Dab with a little vinegar or lemon juice to relieve the pain.
– Sponge with bicarbonate of soda dissolved in water.
– Put ammonia on it.

Bladder infections – Cranberry juice prevents and heals urinary tract infections.

Bleeding, teeth – Rinse out the mouth with hot water in which alum has been dissolved.

Blood clots – Drink a little cinnamon dissolved in hot water every day to thin the blood.

Blood pressure, high
– Mix one cup of boiled water, the juice of half a lemon and one teaspoon of honey. Drink on an empty stomach.
– Drink a spoonful of the vinegar of bottled beetroot every day.
– Drink one tablespoon of vinegar mixed with 125ml water.
– Drink rooibos tea with a teaspoon of honey and a teaspoon of apple cider vinegar three times a day.
– Add the juice of half a grapefruit to a glass of lemonade and drink any time.
– Eat one clove of garlic every day.
– Boil loquat leaves and drink the juice three times a day.
– Make a tea of rosemary leaves and drink it three times a day.

Blood pressure, low
– Mix one part whiskey with three parts honey and drink every evening before bedtime.
– Eat plenty of liquorice.
– Eat a pinch of salt.

Boils Put clean geranium flowers on the boil. Repeat twice a day.

Bruises	To prevent a bruise from forming when you have bumped against something, immediately rub the spot with butter or margarine.
Contusions	Cover with a vinegar cloth dipped in a little eucalyptus oil.
Burns	Hold the burn in ice water at once for immediate relief.
Chest, phlegmy	– Chew two or three cloves three times a day. – Mix one teaspoon of honey and a knife point of bicarbonate of soda and take three times a day. – Mix a tablespoon of olive oil, a tablespoon of honey and a tablespoon of vinegar. Take three times a day.
Chickenpox	Cornflour helps to relieve the itch.
Colds	Drink the juice of one lemon twice a day to prevent colds.
Constipation	– Drink one or two glasses of water on an empty stomach. – Eat half a cup of natural yoghurt before bedtime.
Cough	– Finely chopped sage leaves mixed with lemon and honey bring relief.

	– Mix three tablespoons of buchu brandy, one teaspoon of honey, one teaspoon of sugar and one teaspoon of finely chopped ginger. Take as necessary. – Take one teaspoon of honey with a few drops of vinegar three times a day. – Make a tea from buchu leaves and drink every now and then. – Mix one tablespoon of lemon juice, two tablespoons of honey and two tablespoons of glycerine. Use as necessary. – Add a little honey to brandy and use as necessary.
Depression	Drink tea made of boiling water and the roots of St John's wort.
Elbows, rough	– Rub with half a lemon on which a little sugar has been sprinkled.
Eczema	Put the twigs of a wild dagga plant in bathwater.
Eyes, tired	Put cucumber slices on the eyes and lie still for about 10 minutes.
Feet, burning	Soak feet in salt water.
Feet, sweaty	– Sprinkle a little borax in your socks and shoes. – Put a little wormwood in your shoes. – Sprinkle bicarbonate of soda in your shoes and let it stand overnight.
Feet, tired	Soak your feet for 10 minutes in warm salt water, then rinse them in cold water.
Fever blister	Put a little vanilla essence on the fever blister a couple of times a day.
Flu	– Drink hot water with lemon and honey. – Mix one glass of boiled water, one teaspoon of Jamaican ginger, one teaspoon sugar and the juice of one lemon. Drink it as hot as possible before bedtime.
Hair	Hairspray washes out easily if a little cream of tartar is added to the rinse water.
Hair, dandruff	– Mix half a teaspoon of flowers of sulphur and one teaspoon of olive oil and rub into hair. Then wash as normal. Repeat for a month. – Rinse hair with one tea-spoon of bicarbonate of soda or Epsom salts dissolved in 500ml water.

Hair, falling out	Drink one Bob Martins tablet every morning.
Hair, shiny	Rinse hair in rosemary water.
Halitosis	– Mix half a teaspoon of vanilla essence with a quarter of a glass of milk, heat it slightly and drink. It helps especially for garlic breath. – Chew fresh mint, parsley or celery. – Boil whole pieces of cinnamon and a cup of water and use as a mouthwash. – Rinse your mouth with *lewensessens* (essence of life).
Hands	Mix equal parts glycerine and lemon juice to make a hand cream.
Hay fever (and sinus)	– Make a solution of 750ml cooled boiled water, one teaspoon of salt and one teaspoon of bicarbonate of soda. Sniff it in the morning and evening.
Headache	– Drink a large amount of water. – Make a tea of fresh rosemary leaves and sweeten it with honey.
Hiccups	– Take a deep breath and hold for 30 seconds. – Place a brown paper bag over the nose and mouth and then inhale and exhale into the paper bag. – Eat one teaspoon of sugar mixed with a little vinegar. – Eat half a teaspoon of finely chopped ginger twice a day. – Mix one teaspoon of milk with a little grated nutmeg and drink. – Press your forefingers in your ears and close your nostrils with your thumbs. Swallow quickly a few times.
Hoarseness	Mix one teaspoon of honey, one teaspoon of finely chopped ginger, one teaspoon of sugar and three teaspoons of buchu vinegar. Drink one teaspoon of this mixture.
Insect bite	Put a vinegar cloth on it to relieve the pain.
Insomnia	– Put a sprig of lavender under your pillow. – Drink warm milk with honey before you go to sleep.
Jaundice	Steep ground coriander seed in boiling water and drink one teaspoon a day.

Medicine, bad tasting	Rub an ice cube over the tongue and the medicine will not taste as bad.
Mosquito bite	Put cotton wool soaked in strong Epsom salts and warm water on the bite.
Mouth, bad taste	Chew parsley.
Muscles, injured	Put a cloth that has been dipped in vinegar on the injured muscle.
Nails, brittle	Soak in warm lemon juice.
Nails, stained	Smear white toothpaste on a nail brush and scrub the nails.
Nausea	Drink water with bicarbonate of soda and lemon juice.
Sinusitis	Dissolve a quarter teaspoon of salt and a quarter teaspoon of bicarbonate of soda in half a cup of cooled boiled water, and sniff it up the nose. Hold the head upside down over a bath or basin so that the solution can run out again. Do this mornings and evenings.
Splinter	Place an ice cube on the spot to numb it and then the splinter can easily be removed.
Sticking plaster	To pull sticking plasters off easily, first soak the body part with the plaster on in warm water.
Stomach	Mint tea helps with stomach cramps and rosemary tea helps with poor digestion.
Stress	Make tea of a few sprigs of catnip and sweeten it with a little honey.
Sunburn	– Sponge with methylated spirits. – Rub on a thin mixture of bicarbonate of soda and water.
Teeth	Bicarbonate of soda mixed with a little lemon juice removes stains on teeth.
Thorns	To remove a thorn or splinter, first place an ice cube on it to numb the skin.
Throat, sore	– Gargle with a solution of salt and lemon juice. – Mix honey with a little lemon juice and eat it slowly.
Toothache	Put a clove on the tooth and bite down on it.

Travel sickness	– Take a pinch of ginger or *witdulsies* before the trip.	
	– Drink a little pure lemon juice before the trip.	
Blister	Beat an egg white and smear it on the blister.	
Weight	Regularly drink boiled water with lemon to lose weight.	

Important medicinal herbs

Herbs often have the same medicinal benefits as prescribed medicine, but must be taken regularly and take longer to show results. The results are worth the trouble, however. Herbs also can have side effects, although these are far less severe than that of conventional medicine. Always use well-known herbs or consult an expert. People who are suffering from a chronic disease should not suddenly stop taking their conventional medication. A doctor must first be consulted.

Herb	Botanical name (Alternative name)	Uses
Aloe	*Aloe vera*	Anti-inflammatory, relieves fever and muscle pain
Angelica	*Angelica sinensis* (*Dong Quai*)	Relieves problems with female reproductive organs; relieves PMS and symptoms of menopause; general tonic; improves blood circulation
Astragalus	*Astragalus membranosus* (*Huang Qi*)	Prevents and relieves infections like cold and flu
Bromelain / Pineapple enzyme		Anti-inflammatory
Buchu	*Agathosma betulina*	Relieves arthritis; relieves bloating; relieves bladder infections and kidney stones
Calendula	*Calendula officinalis*	Antiseptic and anti-inflammatory; relieves skin irritations, skin infections, bruises, mouth ulcers and haemorrhoids; leaves on wounds promote healing; improves blood circulation
Cat's claw	*Uncaria tomentosa*	Anti-inflammatory; improves immunity; suppresses the spread of cancer; prevents heart attacks, strokes and thrombosis
Chamomile	*Matricaria chamonilla*	Relieves colic, indigestion and stomach flu; tranquilliser; promotes the healing of wounds

Herb	Botanical name (Alternative name)	Uses
Chaste Tree berry	*Vitus agnus castus*	Prevents breast lumps and breast cancer; relieves hot flushes; calming
Comfrey	*Symphytum officinale*	Anti-inflammatory; relieves bone and muscle injuries, insect bites and skin irritations (rub on as a paste with bicarbonate of soda and goldenseal); must not be drunk
Cranberry juice	*Vaccinium macrocarpon*	Relieves bladder and kidney infections
Dandelion	*Taraxacum officinale*	Dehydrator
Echinacea (Purple coneflower)	*Echinacea purpurea / angustifolia / pallida*	Improves immunity; prevents and heals infections like flu and tonsillitis and bladder infections; effective for acne, boils and insect bites (rub on and ingest)
Elder flower	*Sambucus nigra*	Stimulates the immune system; relieves fever; use externally on bruises and wounds
Eucalyptus oil		Relieves sore muscles and joints (ointment); relieves congested chest and nose (ointment)
Fennel	*Foeniculum vulgare*	Provides natural plant oestrogen and progesterone
Feverfew	*Chrysanthemum parthenium*	Relieves pain and fever; relieves migraines
Garlic	*Allium sativum*	Protects against heart diseases; controls blood sugar; protects against radiation therapy; antipyretic and analgesic; eases infections of the alimentary canal. (Do not take too much garlic with medication that thins the blood such as Disprin or Warfarin.)
Ginger	*Gingiber officinalis*	Anti-inflammatory; improves blood circulation; relieves pain and fever
Ginkgo tree (Maidenhair Tree)	*Ginkgo biloba*	Relieves depression and improves memory; improves blood circulation; relieves leg cramps
Ginseng	*Panax quinquefolium*	Raises energy levels; general tonic to relieve fatigue; lowers cholesterol and blood pressure
Goldenseal	*Hydrastis canadensis*	Anti-inflammatory; prevents infections of the mucous membrane

Herb	Botanical name (Alternative name)	Uses
Hawthorn Berry	*Crateagus oxyacantha*	Lowers blood pressure and cholesterol; prevents fluid retention
Kava	*Piper methysticum*	Tranquilliser; muscle relaxant
Liquorice	*Glycyrrhiza alba*	Relieves respiratory infections and sore throats; protects liver against infections
Meadowsweet	*Spiraea salicifolia*	Anti-inflammatory
Milk thistle	*Sonchus oleraceus*	Repairs and renews liver cells; protects liver against toxins
Red pepper	*Rosa roxburghii*	Raises energy levels and metabolism; anti-inflammatory; detoxifies the body; raises energy levels and improves stamina
Sage	*Salvia officinalis*	Relieves sore throats; good mouthwash; relieves hot flushes
Saw Palmetto	*Serenoa repens*	Protects prostate against an excess of testosterone
Small-leaved lime blossom	*Tilla cordata*	Improves immunity; relieves colds, flu and coughs
St John's wort	*Hypericum perforatum*	Very effective against depression; controls infections; relieves skin problems such as wounds, sores, bruises and sunburn; relieves digestion problems; relieves anaemia and arthritis. (Do not use with digoxin, teofilline, HIV medication, the Pill, anti-epileptic medication or anti-depressants)
Tea tree oil	*Melaleuca alternifolia*	Relieves all skin problems e.g. acne, fungal infections, eczema and boils; rubbed on the chest it relieves colds and coughs
Thyme	*Thynus vulgaris*	Good for gargling or as a mouthwash to relieve sore throat
Turmeric	*Curcuma longa*	Anti-inflammatory
Valerian root	*Valeriana officinalis*	Good tranquilliser and sleeping draught. (Do not take with prescription tranquillisers or sleeping pills.)

Herb	Botanical name (Alternative name)	Uses
White willow bark	*Salix alba*	Anti-inflammatory pain reliever; relieves sore muscles and joints
Wild cherry bark	*Prunus serotina*	Relieves coughs, bronchitis and whooping cough
Wild yam	*Dioscorea villosa*	Provides progesterone, which prevents and relieves osteoporosis; relieves problems of the female reproductive organs

Sage

Fennel

Immunisation programme for children

Age	Immunisation
0–2 weeks	BCG – Vaccine for tuberculosis OPV – First drops against polio
6 weeks	OPV – Second drops against polio RV – First vaccine liquid against the Rotavirus DtaP-IPV/HIB injection against diphtheria, polio, pertussis (whooping cough), tetanus and *haemophilus influenzae* type b (Hib) Hep B – hepatitis B injection PCV7 – First injection (prevents infections of the respiratory system)
10 weeks	DtaP-IPV/HIB – Second injection Hep B – second injection
14 weeks	RV – Second vaccine liquid against the Rotavirus DtaP-IPV/HIB – Third injection Hep B – Third injection PCV7 – Second injection
9 months	First injection against measles PCV7 – Third injection
18 months	DtaP-IPV/HIB – Fourth injection Second injection against measles
6 years	TD – injection against tetanus and Injection against diphtheria (lower dosage)
12 years	Same as at 6 years

Vaccine against the Rotavirus (RV) must <u>not</u> be given after the age of 24 weeks.

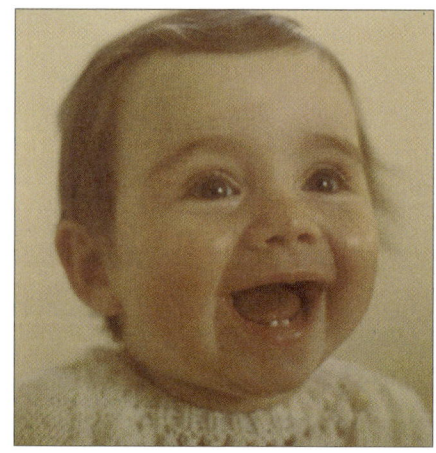

First aid

Bleeding
- Raise the wounded body part, place a sterile or clean bandage on the wound and apply firm pressure.
- Do not remove the first bandage, but place more bandages over it if the blood is seeping through.
- If direct pressure on a wound does not stop the bleeding, apply pressure to an artery between the wound and the heart.
- Get immediate medical help if the bleeding doesn't stop.

Blue bottle sting
- Do not scratch the sting or rub it with sand. Rinse in seawater and wet it well with vinegar, brandy or petrol.
- The skin can later be washed with soap and hot water and a soothing cream can be applied.
- Seek medical help if the person shows signs of anxiety.

Burns
- Immediately put ice on minor burns, or hold it under cold running water.
- Remove watches or tight clothes around the burn and bind it with a clean cloth (one that won't fray).
- Get immediate medical help in the event of serious burns.
- Throw water over a person if his clothes are on fire, or wrap him in a blanket.
- Do not remove clothes that are sticking to the wounds.
- Dress open wounds with a dry, clean cloth (one that won't fray).

Choking
- Remove the obstruction if it is visible.
- Let the person bend over and smack him hard between the shoulder blades.
- If this does not help, put your arms around the person from behind. Place one hand just under the breastbone and the other hand over this hand. Now push a few times quickly and hard with thrusting movements **(see Heimlich manoeuvre p. 447)**.
- If the person is unconscious, place your one hand over the other in the middle of the abdomen. Exert quick pressure in and up.
- Artificial respiration (see below) must be applied if the person stops breathing.
- A baby is held with legs apart over your arm with the head lower than the body. Support the head by holding the jaw with your bottom hand. Now smack carefully but firmly a few times between the shoulder blades.

Dislocation of joints
- Support the injured joint with an elastic bandage, keep it still and put ice or cold cloths on it.
- Let the person lie down and seek medical help.
- With shoulder dislocation, the forearm must be supported with a triangle shoulder bandage tied around the neck. Any strong fabric or a scarf can be used for this.

Drowning
- If the person is not breathing, immediately start mouth-to-mouth resuscitation. It can be done while he is still in the water.
- Do not try to pump water out of the lungs.
- Lie the person down with his head in a lower position so the water can drain from his lungs.
- If there is no pulse or heartbeat, start cardiopulmonary resuscitation **(see page 447)**.
- Cover the person with blankets.
- Seek medical help.

Electric shock
- Do not touch the person before the electrical current is broken.
- Turn off the power or pull out the plug. If this is not possible, stand in a dry place and pull the person away from the source of electricity with for example a piece of dry wood. Do not use anything damp.
- Start cardiopulmonary resuscitation **(see page 447)** if the person is unconscious or cannot breathe.
- Place the person in the recovery position **(see page 446)** when he starts breathing and treat him for shock and burns until medical help arrives.

Epilepsy
- Only treat the person if he is unconscious. If the person does not lose consciousness, stay calm and make him feel safe.
- Do not move the person unless he is in danger.
- Place him in the recovery position **(see page 446)**
- Loosen all tight clothes.
- Do not hold the patient down.
- Do not force hard objects between the teeth.
- Do not leave until the person has completely recovered.

Fainting
- When someone feels dizzy, he must sit with his head between his knees.
- A person who is unconscious but breathing normally must lie on his back with his legs raised so his feet are higher than his chest.
- Loosen tight clothes around the neck and upper body.

Heart attack
- Keep the person still and in a sitting position. Try to calm and reassure him.
- Give the person four aspirin tablets if he can take aspirin – it could dissolve a blood clot in time.
- If the person stops breathing or is unconscious, someone with the necessary knowledge should start cardiopulmonary resuscitation **(see page 447)**.
- Call a doctor or an ambulance.

Insect stings
- Do not pull out the sting, but scrape it out with a knife, needle or fingernail.
- Wash the sting with soap and water and put ice or a cold compress on it.

Nose bleed
- After a blow or knock to the head a nose bleed could indicate a skull fracture.
- Let the person sit up straight and slightly forward with his mouth open.
- Hold the nostrils closed while breathing through the mouth.
- Let go of the nostrils, but the nose must not be blown.
- Seek medical help if the bleeding has not stopped after 20 minutes.

Poisoning
- Determine which poison has been ingested.
- Consult the container for advice.
- Call the nearest poison centre or hospital for advice.
- Remove any mucus from the mouth and start artificial respiration if necessary **(see page 446)**.
- Keep the person warm.
- Seek medical help.
- Pas kunsmatige asemhaling toe indien nodig.
- Kry mediese hulp.

First aid for poison in the eyes
1. Immediately rinse the eyes with water or any other non-damaging fluid.
2. Wipe any poison off the face.
3. Seek medical help.

Antivenin is a serum that is made of the anti-bodies of animals that have been injected with the poison.

Scorpion sting
- Put ice or something cold on the sting.
- Keep the stung limb still and bind the whole limb with a tight elastic bandage.
- Seek medical help.

Seizure (due to fever)
- Stay calm and let the person lie on his stomach with his head to one side.
- Loosen tight clothes and put the head slightly back.
- Do not force anything between the teeth.
- Try to lower the fever by covering him with a wet sheet or sponging him off.
- When he regains consciousness, he can have some water and take something to lower the fever, like paracetamol.
- Call an ambulance if the episode lasts longer than five minutes.
- If it is a first seizure, a doctor must be consulted to determine the cause of the seizure.

Shock
- If the person is not unconscious, normal water can be given, but not fluids like coffee, tea or strong alcohol. There is no need to give sugar water. If the person is diabetic, sugar water could even be dangerous.
- Make the person lie on his back with his legs raised off the ground (on a cushion or low table).
- Loosen all tight clothes.
- Wrap the person in a blanket.
- Seek medical help.

Snake bite
- Keep the person very still and try to calm him.
- Do not give fluids.
- Do not give an antivenin unless it is urgently necessary or the snake has been identified.
- Most snakebites are on the legs. Raise the affected leg.
- Keep the bite cold with wet cloths (not ice).
- Do not cut the bite, try to suck out the poison or rub something into the bite.
- Put an elastic bandage around the limb between the bite and the heart, but don't try to stop the blood flow. If an elastic bandage is not available, use any material. If there is too much swelling, loosen the bandage a little.
- If necessary, start artificial respiration.
- Seek medical help.

Artificial respiration (mouth-to-mouth resuscitation)
- Immediately call a doctor or ambulance if possible.
- Lay the person on his back on a hard surface.
- Remove any foreign objects from the mouth and airways with your fingers.
- If there doesn't appear to be a neck injury, push the person's head back by placing one hand under the neck and pressing with one hand on the forehead so the chin is lifted.
- Close the person's nostrils with the thumb and forefinger of the hand resting on the forehead. Take a deep breath and place your mouth over the open mouth of the person. Now blow air into the person's mouth. Stop blowing when the chest has inflated.
- Listen whether air is leaving the person's lungs and if the chest is moving.
- Carry on by blowing quickly four times and taking a deep breath in between. Repeat until the person begins to breathe on his own.

Recovery position
- Note: Do not put a person in the recovery position if you suspect a fracture of the back or neck.
- Turn the person's head towards you, tilt the head back and pull the chin forward to open the airway.
- Place the arm nearest you next to the patient and tuck it under his buttock.

- Lay the other arm over the chest and cross the furthest leg over the nearest at the ankle.
- Support the head and pull the person by his clothes (at the top hip) towards you so he rests against your knees.
- Bend the top arm and leg to support the body, so the person cannot roll onto his face.
- Again make sure that the head is tilted back and that the airway is open.

Cardiopulmonary resuscitation (CPR)
- This must be taught by an expert and practised regularly.
- Open the airway and look and listen if the person is still breathing. Feel the pulse.
- If the person is breathing, place him in the recovery position **(see page 446)**. If he is no longer breathing, place him on a hard surface and perform mouth-to-mouth resuscitation.
- If respiration does not begin and no heartbeat is detected, apply cardiac compression by placing one hand on top of the other on the bottom of the breastbone. Do not press on the person's ribs. There must be around 80 compressions per minute with two breaths between every 15 compressions.
- If a helper is available, one person can perform mouth-to-mouth resuscitation while the other person does the cardiac compressions.

Heimlich manoeuvre (for choking)
- Place your arms around the person's middle from behind.
- Make a fist with one hand (with the thumb outside the fist) and place the thumb part against the person's abdomen, under the ribs and just above the navel.
- Hold your fist tightly with the other hand and press with quick upwards movements in the person's abdomen.
- Repeat the movements until the object that has caused the obstruction is coughed up.

Essential items for a first aid kit

- Disinfectant such as Dettol or Savlon. Merthiolate in a spray bottle also works well for any open wound
- Antiseptic ointment such as Betadine or Bactroban
- Plasters in different sizes or a roll that you can cut yourself

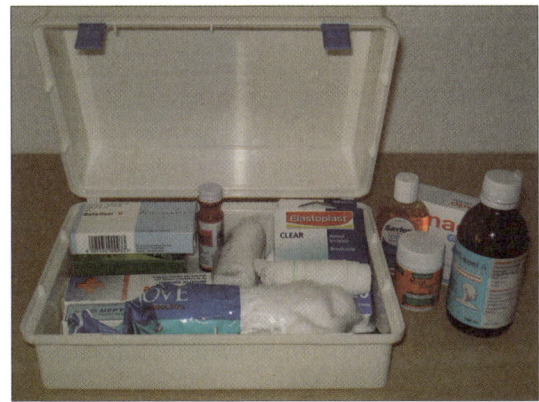

- Gauze to apply directly to a wound
- Bandages in widths of 75mm and 100mm, and safety pins
- Anthisan ointment for insect bites and stings
- Antihistamine pills such as Clarityne
- Painkillers such as Panado or Disprin
- Anti-inflammatory pills such as Cataflam
- Imodium pills for diarrhoea
- Buscopan for stomach cramps
- Valoid for nausea
- Gaviscon for heartburn
- Rehidrat sachets for dehydration
- Viral Choice and Medikeel for colds and sore throats
- Tweezers and scissors
- Thermometer
- Pair of latex gloves

Depression

**The Support Group for Depression and Anxiety:
0800 567 567 (toll free)**

Someone who is depressed feels despondent, melancholy and lethargic. Endogenous (manic) depression is caused by a chemical imbalance in the brain, and must receive medical treatment. Reactive (clinical) depression occurs after a bad experience such as the death of a loved one, financial loss or the break-up of a relationship. Depression is a serious and common illness. If the person does not improve quickly, seek medical help.

Symptoms of depression

- Long-term despondency and moroseness.

- The inability to appreciate things that are usually enjoyable.

- A lack of energy and ongoing fatigue. You get a headache from the smallest problem and start taking more painkillers.

- No interest in things happening in the future or in plans, for instance holidays.

- Isolation from family and friends.

- Inability to concentrate. You forget what you wanted to buy at a shop, forget what you wanted to say and can't focus on one task.

- A change in normal sleeping patterns. Insomnia, sleepiness or an unwillingness to wake up in the mornings. You wake up in the middle of the night and cannot fall asleep again.

- Constant anxiety, irritability or anger. Small things that you used to cope with quite well now suddenly upset you.

- Noticeable weight loss or gain. You suddenly eat excessively or don't want to eat for days.

- Feelings of guilt or worthlessness. You feel you are not good enough or, for example, are a bad mother.

- Thoughts about death and suicide.

- Whenever a person shows about five of these symptoms for longer than two weeks, medical help should be sought.

- Young children do not complain about depression, but show it in ways like wetting the bed, crying, moodiness, anger and isolation.

Factors that cause or worsen depression

- The death of a loved one or the anniversary of the date the person died.

- Physical, verbal or sexual abuse that destroys your self-image and affects your feelings of self-worth.

- Major disappointments such as poor academic results, the end of a relationship or even something that seems less important, like being left out of a sports team.

- Worry about finances or unemployment.

- A traumatic experience or stressful time.

- Some people become depressed during cold, dark winter months.

- The end of a holiday and holidays like Christmas and New Year that you spend alone.

- Unrealistic expectations that you cannot fulfil.

- A chemical imbalance in your brain.

Ways to tackle depression

- Accept that life is not always fun, but it will improve again.

- Talk about your feelings and find out what makes you feel negative.

- Seek positive companionship and laugh at yourself. Don't isolate yourself.
- Exercise, take part in sport, or go for a short walk every day.
- Live one day at a time and don't worry about things that may never happen.
- Keep busy. Force yourself to do something useful. Work in the garden, do needlework or brush the dog.
- Think about everything you have to be thankful for. Do not allow negative thoughts.
- Try to forget about yourself and do something every day for other people, even if you don't feel like it.
- Many people find religion a source of strength.
- Seek medical and professional help if necessary.

Things to be grateful for:
- Being part of a family.
- Friends and family.
- A place to live and a warm bed.
- Financial independence.
- Your general good health.
- Food and clothing.

Coping with a depressed person

- Learn as much as possible about depression. Ask about the diagnosis and details about medication when consulting doctors or psychologists.
- Don't feel ashamed of your friend or family member who is suffering from depression – you may have negative experiences with people who are not informed about depression.
- Acknowledge the courage of the depressed person to cope with his condition.
- Ask the person if he is thinking about harming himself.
- Encourage the person and emphasise that seeking treatment shows courage and strength.
- Involve the person in your activities and hobbies. Try to get him involved in something he was interested in or enjoyed before he became depressed.
- Do not become upset if the person is sometimes insensitive, aggressive or ungrateful. These are feelings he cannot control and under normal circumstances he would not have acted in such a manner. Forgive him for this.

- Be sensitive, listen and give the person a chance to talk about his feelings. Do not try to force the person to be happy or tell him to "pull himself together". He is not lazy or pretending – he really has problems.

HIV/Aids

Exposure to the HIV virus

- You can be exposed to HIV through unprotected sex, rape, blood contact or a needle prick.

- Realise your risk and act immediately. You must start using anti-retrovirals as soon as possible so the virus does not infect you.

- Call the toll-free Aids helpline on **0800 012 322** for advice and information about the nearest clinic.

- Immediately make a doctor's appointment or go to the nearest clinic or emergency room at a hospital.

- Do not wait until you know the HIV status of the other person that's involved – immediately start with anti-retrovirals.

- Use the dosage exactly as prescribed for 28 days.

- You may experience side effects, but you can take medication for these.

- If you do not have medical aid, you can go to a state hospital or HIV clinic.

- You must have a blood test immediately, but even if the first test is negative, you could still be HIV positive. After three months you must have another blood test. Only then can you determine your status with certainty.

- Go for counselling.

HIV-positive

- Improve your immune system by eating healthily. Take a vitamin supplement. Fresh garlic can also improve your immunity, although it will of course not heal you.

- You must stay on your medication and take it correctly or it will not be effective.

- You can never have unprotected sex. You cannot even have unprotected sex with another HIV-positive person, as there are different types of HIV infection.

- Make sure you lead a healthy life in order to avoid illnesses that will compromise your weakened immune system.

- No one may disclose your HIV status without your permission.
- No employer may dismiss a worker because of his HIV status.

Organ donation

- All persons under seventy who do not suffer from cancer, hepatitis, diabetes or HIV/Aids can be organ donors.

- Register as an organ donor by calling **0800 22 66 11** (toll free) or register at: **www.odf.org.za**.

- You will be given a donor card and two red stickers to stick on your ID and your driver's licence.

- The heart, cardiac valves, lungs, liver, kidneys, pancreas, corneas, skin and bone can be used.

- You can determine which organs you wish to donate.

- Your family must be informed of your decision, as they will have to give their permission if you are no longer living.

- The organs are removed after two independent doctors have declared the donor brain dead.

- You can change your mind at any time. Just cut up your donor card, remove the stickers from your ID and licence and tell your family of your decision.

- There is no cost involved for the organ donor or his family.

- No compensation is paid for organs. Trade in organs or tissue is illegal.

- The recipient is not told who the donor was. The information is confidential. Recipients may write thank-you notes, which are then given to the donor's family.

- Parts of the liver, a kidney or bone marrow can be donated by a living person.

A bracelet or neck chain that identifies you as an organ donor can be bought from **Medic Alert**.

Cot death

Cot death is not an illness. It is a diagnosis of healthy babies who die in their sleep for no apparent reason. There is always a police investigation after a cot death. Babies cannot be tested ahead of the time to see whether they are susceptible to cot death.

Risk factors

- If parents have already lost a baby to cot death, the chances are slightly higher that another baby could die.
- A mother under the age of 20, who smoked or used drugs during her first pregnancy.
- Mothers with bad or no pre-natal care.
- Premature babies.
- A mother or carer who smokes.
- A baby who has previously become limp and blue because he could not breathe properly.
- Boys have a slightly higher risk than girls.
- Babies who sleep on their stomachs.

Precautionary measures

- Don't smoke during pregnancy, and do not allow anyone to smoke near your baby or in the house.
- Equip the baby's bed with a firm mattress and no pillow. Do not leave soft toys in the baby's bed or cot.
- Breastfeeding may lower the risks.
- More cot deaths happen in winter because of overheating. Do not make the room too hot or dress the baby too warmly.

Cot death is the most common cause of death in babies between one and six months.

Abortion

When you have fallen pregnant without planning it, you can have an abortion.

Before you make the decision, think about your beliefs and values and those of the other people in your life. Determine how much support you will enjoy from your life partner, friends and family. Evaluate the financial and social aspects, and take your lifestyle and circumstances into account. Think about your feelings about motherhood and the responsibility it would place on you. Take into account what other people's reactions will be to your decision.

Abortion is a difficult decision with which you will have to live your whole life. Ask for other people's opinions, talk to a doctor, psychologist or staff at a hospital, family planning clinic or abortion clinic.

In South Africa abortions are performed in family planning clinics, hospitals and abortion clinics.

Abortions are performed up to the twentieth week of pregnancy, but the procedure is safer and easier if it is done as early as possible.

You can decide of you want an abortion in hospital or a clinic, if you want anaesthesia or want to be awake, and if you want a medical or surgical abortion. Your health and the stage of your pregnancy will also be taken into account.

The different procedures during abortions

Medical abortion. Two types of medication are taken by mouth. The one medication is taken two days after the other. It causes contractions of the uterus and the foetus is expelled. It is done as early as possible and not after the eighth week of pregnancy. The medication causes birth defects, and the person must therefore be prepared to have a surgical abortion if the foetus is not expelled. The person must go for a check-up 10–12 days later. Not everyone can have medical abortions, but a full medical examination will determine if the person does qualify.

Surgical abortion. The foetus is removed from the uterus with a suction apparatus. It is done under local or general anaesthesia. It can be done after the eighth week of pregnancy. A follow-up examination is necessary.

- Abortions were legalised in South Africa in 1997.
- South Africa is the only country in Africa where abortions are legal.
- Abortions are performed for free at state hospitals.
- At clinics, abortions are done up to 12 weeks, and at state hospitals and Marie Stopes clinics they are performed up to 20 weeks.
- Since 2007, 12-year-olds can, under certain circumstances, have abortions without their parents' permission.

Medical specialists

anaesthetist: anaesthetises the patient

cardiologist: specialises in heart conditions

dentist: takes care of the teeth

dermatologist: specialises in skin conditions

endocrinologist: studies hormonal problems

gastroenterologist: specialises in stomach conditions

geneticist: diagnoses and predicts hereditary conditions

geriatrist: specialises in illnesses of elderly people

gynaecologist: specialises in the female reproductive organs

haematologist: specialises in the area of blood and related conditions

homoeopath: believes that healing must take place by stimulating the body's own defence system with natural medicine

internist: specialises in conditions of the internal organs

neurologist: treats conditions of the nervous system and brain

neurosurgeon: operates on the nervous system and brain

oncologist: specialises in tumours (also cancer)

ophthalmologist, optometrist: specialises in eye conditions

orthodontist: specialises in the repair of irregularly growing teeth and other dental conditions

orthopaedist: specialises in bones

otolaryngologist, ear, nose and throat specialist: specialises in conditions of the ear, nose and throat

pathologist: investigates the cause of diseases by performing analyses (as well as post-mortem examinations)

paediatrician: specialises in the treatment of children

physiotherapist: specialises in sports medicine and physical therapy

plastic surgeon: specialises in the improvement of disfigured or injured body parts, as well as cosmetic improvements

psychiatrist: specialises in mental illnesses and emotional problems

radiologist: works with x-rays and ultrasound

surgeon: diagnoses and operates in the event of a wide variety of illnesses

urologist: specialises in conditions of the kidneys and urinary tract

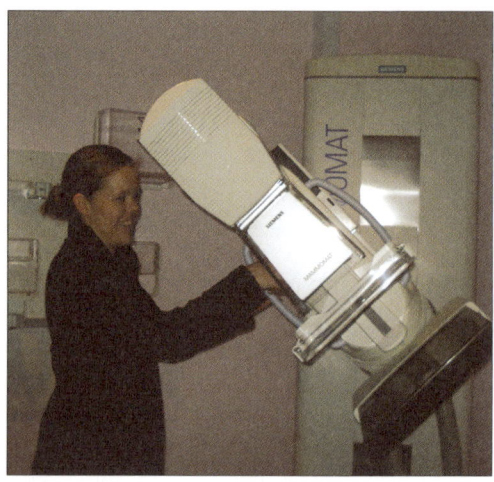
Radiologist

Operations and procedures

amniocentesis: viewing a foetus and amniotic fluid with the help of an instrument that is inserted in the uterus through the abdomen

amputation: removal of a limb or part of a limb

anaesthesiology: administration of an opiate that deadens pain or causes unconsciousness

angiography: radiography of the blood vessels after a dye has been injected

angioplasty: replacement or removal of an artery

arthroscopy: a camera is inserted into the interior of the body through a small incision

biopsy: removal of a piece of tissue from a living organ for analysis

blepharotomy: plastic surgery procedure where the eyelids or bags under the eyes are repaired

Caesarean section: removal of a baby from the uterus through an incision in the abdomen

chemotherapy: use of chemicals in especially the treatment of cancer

cholelithotomy: an operation to remove gallstones

cholecystectomy: an operation to remove the gall bladder

colectomy: removal of the colon

colonoscopy: examination of the abdominal organs with an instrument inserted through the anus

dialysis: removal of toxins from the blood when the kidneys are not functioning normally

echocardiography: an examination of the heart using ultrasound (sonar)

embolectomy: surgical removal of a blood clot

epidural anaesthesia: injection of an anaesthetic in the lumbar region of the back to numb the lower body (without causing unconsciousness)

fetoscopy: viewing of the foetus with an instrument (fetoscope) that is inserted through the abdominal wall into the uterus

gastrectomy: removal of the stomach or part thereof

gastroscopy: investigation of the interior of the stomach by inserting a tube-shaped instrument through the mouth and oesophagus

gastrostomy: incision in the stomach through the abdomen for artificial feeding

glossectomy: cutting off or removal of the tongue

hepatectomy: partial or complete removal of the liver

hysterectomy: removal of the uterus

induction of birth: artificial stimulation of labour

laparoscopy: examination of the abdominal organs with an instrument inserted though an incision in the abdomen

laringectomy: surgical removal of the larynx

lipectomy: surgical removal of fat

lobectomy: removal of one lobe of an organ, like the lung

lumbar puncture: harvesting of spinal fluid with the help of a hollow needle between the vertebrae, for analysis

mammogram: X-ray examination of the breasts

mammoplasty: operation to reduce, enlarge or repair the breasts

microsurgery: delicate operation performed with the help of a special microscope

nefrectomy: surgical removal of a kidney

nail avulsion: surgical removal of a nail

oophorectomy: surgical removal of one or both ovaries

pancreatectomy: surgical removal of the pancreas

percussion: diagnosis by tapping on the chest or abdomen with the fingers

plastic surgery: operation to repair or build up skin or tissue

pneumonectomy: removal of a lung

prognosis: prediction of the possible course of a disease

prostatectomy: removal of the prostate

psychotherapy: treatment of mental illnesses and emotional problems by a psychologist or a psychiatrist

radiotherapy: treatment of diseases with a radioactive ray or a radioactive substance such as radium or cobalt (especially for cancer)

sigmoidoscopy: investigation of the large intestine from the rectum through the colon using an endoscope

splenectomy: removal of the spleen

thyroidectomy: surgical removal of the thyroid or a part thereof

thrombectomy: surgical removal of a blood clot from an artery

venography: X-rays of the veins made visible by injecting a radiopaque dye

Medical emergency numbers

Store ICE and at least three different people's names and contact numbers on your cellphone. Store the letters ICE before their names. ICE stands for *in case of an emergency*. If you are injured in a motor accident or other event, your family or next of kin can be traced.

Ambulance	**10177**
Police	**10111**
Emergency number from a cellphone	**112**

Note that the following telephone numbers could change:

AA (Alcholics Anonymous) (Check in the telephone directory – many cities and towns have their own branches)	021 418 0020
ADD (hyperactivity)	011 483 2470
Aids Helpline	080 001 2322
Allsa (Allergy Society of SA)	021 447 9019
Arda (Alzheimer's and Related Dementias Association)	021 447 9019
Arthritis Society	086 130 3030
Blindness (SA National Council for the Blind)	021 715 3563
Blood transfusions (SA National Blood Service)	0800 119 031
Cancer – Cansa (Cansa Society of SA) **Reach for Recovery (breast cancer)**	0800 22 66 22 021 480 6153 011 646 5628
CHOC (gives help and support to children and their families)	086 111 3500
Childline	0800 555 555
Contraception emergency line (Not-2-late)	080 024 6432
Cot death	021 863 8566
Cystic Fibrosis Association	011 867 5538
Depression (SA Depression and Anxiety Group)	011 783 1474/6
Diabetes Helpline	080 012 1555

Drug Abuse
    De Novo
    Ramot
    Stepping stones
    SANCADD
	
	021 988 1138
	021 939 2033
	021 783 4230
	011 482 1070

Epilepsy (Sanel – SA National Epilepsy League)	021 447 3014 011 816 2040
Gambling Helpline	0800 006 008

Headache Clinic	021 6860093
	011 484 0933
Heart Foundation of SA	086 022 3222
Multiple Sclerosis Helpline	086 045 6772
Nicus (Nutrition Information Centre of the University of Stellenbosch)	021 938 1408
Organ Donor Foundation	0800 22 66 11
Osteoporosis Helpline	086 170 8090
Parkinson's Society	011 787 7892
Poison Information Centre (Tygerberg Hospital)	021 931 6129
Reach for a Dream Foundation	021 555 3013
	011 781 0133
Sea Rescue – NSRI (National Sea Rescue Institute)	021 405 3500
Smoking – Quitline (stop smoking)	011 720 3145
Stroke Helpline	086 110 1066
Suicide Helpline	080 056 7567
Tuberculosis – Santa (South African National TB Association)	021 696 5128
	012 386 2112
	031 208 8474

11. USEFUL INFORMATION

Greetings and useful words and phrases in English, Afrikaans, Xhosa, Zulu, Northern Sotho and Tswana

Greeting terms

English	Afrikaans	Xhosa	Zulu	Northern Sotho	Tswana
Good afternoon (one person)	Goeiemiddag	Molo	Sawubona	Dumela	Dumela
Good afternoon (a group)	Goeiemiddag	Molweni	Sanibona	Dumelang	Dumelang
Good morning (one person)	Goeiemôre	Molo	Sawubona	Dumela	Dumela
Good morning (a group)	Goeiemôre	Molweni	Sanibona	Dumelang	Dumelang
Good evening (one person)	Goeienaand	Molo	Sawubona	Dumela	Dumela
Good evening (a group)	Goeienaand	Molweni	Sanibona	Dumelang	Dumelang
Good night (one person)	Goeienag	Ulale kakuhle	Ulale kahle	Ga e boroko	O robale sentle
Good night (a group)	Goeienag	Nilale kakuhle	Nilale kahle	Le robale gabotse	Lo robaleng sentle
Hello (one person)	Hallo	Molo	Sawubona	Dumela	Dumela
Hello (a group)	Hallo	Molweni	Sanibona	Dumelang	Dumelang

Useful words

English	Afrikaans	Xhosa	Zulu	Northern Sotho	Tswana
bus	bus	ibhasi	ibhasi	pese	bese
call	roep	biza	biza	bit?a	bitsa
car	motor	imoto	imoto	mmotoro	mmotorokara
come	kom	za	za	tla	tla
drink	drink	sela	phuza	nwa	nwa
eat	eet	tya	dla	ja	ja
food	kos	ukutya	ukudla	dijo	dijo
help	help	nceda	siza	thu?a	thusa

English	Afrikaans	Xhosa	Zulu	Northern Sotho	Tswana
how?	hoe?	njani?	kanjani?	bjang?	jang?
listen	luister	mamela	lalela	theet?a	ulwelela
no	nee	hayi	cha	aowa	nnyaa
now	nou	ngoku	manje	bjale	gona jaanong
pain	pyn	intlungu	ubuhlungu	bohloko	botlhoko
please	asseblief	nceda	ake/siza	hle	tsweetswee
stop	stop	yima	ma	ema	ema
taxi	taxi	iteksi	ithekisi	tekisi	thekisi
thank you	dankie	enkosi	ngiyabonga	ke a leboga	ke a leboga
train	trein	uloliwe	isitimela	setimela	setimela
water	water	amanzi	amanzi	meetse	metsi
when?	wanneer?	nini?	nini?	neng?	leng?
yes	ja	ewe	yebo	ee	ee

Phrases

E	How are you?
A	Hoe gaan dit met jou?
X	Unjani?
Z	Unjani?
N	O kae?
T	O kae?

E	Fine, thank you
A	Dit gaan goed, dankie
X	Ndiphilile, enkosi
Z	Ngisaphila
N	Re gona
T	e tsogile sentle

E	Who's there?
A	Wie is daar?
X	Ngubani olapho?
Z	Kukhona ubani?
N	Ke mang moo?
T	Ke mang?

E	What do you want?
A	Wat wil jy hê?
X	Ufanani?
Z	Ufunani?
N	O nyaka eng?
T	O batla eng?

E	Can I help?
A	Kan ek help?
X	Ndinganceda?
Z	Ngingasiza na?
N	Nka thuša?
T	A nka thusa?

E	Come here
A	Kom hier
X	Yiza apha
Z	Woza lapha
N	Etla mo
T	Etla kwano

E	Come in
A	Kom binne
X	Ngena
Z	Ngena
N	Ka gare
T	Tsena

E	Follow me
A	Volg my
X	Ndilandele
Z	Ngilandele
N	Ntšhale morago
T	Ntshale morago

E	What is your name?		E	Where are you going?
A	Wat is jou naam?		A	Waar gaan jy heen?
X	Ungubani igama lakho?		X	Uyaphi?
Z	Ubani igama lakho?		Z	Uyaphi?
N	Leina la gago ke mang?		N	O ya kae?
T	Leina la gago ke mang?		T	O ya kae?
E	My name is …		E	I am going to …
A	My naam is …		A	Ek gaan … toe
X	Igama lam ngu…		X	Ndiya e …
Z	Igama lami ngingu…		Z	Ngiya …
N	Leina laka ke …		N	Ke ya …
T	Leina la me ke …		T	Ke ya …
E	What is your surname?		E	Do you understand?
A	Wat is jou van?		A	Verstaan jy?
X	Ungubani ifani yakho?		X	Uyaqonda na?
Z	Ungubani isibongo sakho?		Z	Uyezwa na?
N	O wa ga mang?		N	Na o a kwišiša?
T	Sefane sa gago ke mang?		T	A o a tlhaloganya?
E	My surname is …		E	I don't understand
A	My van is …		A	Ek verstaan nie
X	Ifani yam ndingu…		X	Andiqondi
Z	Isibongo sami ngingu…		Z	Angizwa
N	Ke wa ga …		N	Ga ke kwešiše
T	Sefane sa me ke …		T	Ga ke tlhaloganye
E	How old are you?		E	Wait just a minute
A	Hoe oud is jy?		A	Wag net 'n minuut
X	Umdala kangakanani?		X	Khawume kancinane
Z	Uneminyaka emingaki?		Z	Yima kancane
N	O na le mengwaga ye mekae?		N	Ema gannyane
T	O na le mengwaga e mekae?		T	Ema go le gonnye
E	I am … years old		E	What is the time?
A	Ek is … jaar oud		A	Hoe laat is dit?
X	Ndine … minyaka ubudala		X	Ngubani ixesha?
Z	Ngineminyaka eyi-… ubudala		Z	Sekuyisikhathi sini?
N	Ke na le mengwaga ye …		N	Ke nako mang?
T	Ke na le dingwaga tse …		T	Ke nako mang?
E	Where do you live?		E	It is late
A	Waar woon jy?		A	Dit is laat
X	Uhlala phi?		X	Kusemva kwexesha
Z	Uhlalaphi?		Z	Isikhathi sesishayile
N	O dula kae?		N	Nako e ile
T	O nna kae?		T	Nako e ile
E	I live in …		E	I must go now
A	Ek woon in …		A	Ek moet nou gaan
X	Ndihlala …		X	Mandihambe ngoku
Z	Ngihlala …		Z	Sekufanele ngihambe manje
N	Ke dula …		N	Ke swanetše go tloga bjalo
T	Ke nna kwa …		T	Ke tshwanetse go tsamaya jaanong

E	I am busy		E	May I have some water?
A	Ek is besig		A	Kan ek water kry?
X	Ndixakekile		X	Ndingafumana amanzi?
Z	Ngibambekile		Z	Ngicela amanzi?
N	Ke swaregile		N	Ke kgopela meetse a go nwa?
T	Ke sa dira		T	A nka fiwa metsi?
E	I am sorry		E	How much does it cost?
A	Ek is jammer		A	Hoeveel kos dit?
X	Ngxesi		X	Ixabisa malini?
Z	Ngiyadabuka		Z	Kubiza malini?
N	Ke kgopela tshwarelo		N	Ke bokae?
T	Intshwarele		T	Se ja bokae?
E	I know		E	It costs …
A	Ek weet		A	Dit kos …
X	Ndiyazi		X	Ixabisa …
Z	Ngiyazi		Z	Kubiza …
N	Ke a tseba		N	E bitša …
T	Ke a itse		T	Se ja …
E	I do not know		E	Where can I phone?
A	Ek weet nie		A	Waar kan ek bel?
X	Andazi		X	Ndingafona phi?
Z	Angazi		Z	Ngigalushaya kuphi ucingo?
N	Ga ke tsebe		N	Nka letša mogala kae?
T	Ga ke itse		T	Ke kgona go letsa mogala kae?
E	What is it?		E	Are you sick?
A	Wat is dit?		A	Is jy siek?
X	Yintoni?		X	Uyagula?
Z	Yini?		Z	Uyagula?
N	Ke eng?		N	A o a lwala?
T	Ke eng?		T	A o a lwala?
E	What happened?		E	I am sick
A	Wat het gebeur?		A	Ek is siek
X	Kwenzekani?		X	Ndiyagula
Z	Kwenzenjani?		Z	Ngiyagula
N	Go diregile eng?		N	Ke a lwala
T	Go diragetse eng?		T	Ke a lwala
E	I am hungry		E	I want to consult the doctor
A	Ek is honger		A	Ek wil die dokter spreek
X	Ndilambile		X	Ndifuna ukubonana nogqirha
Z	Ngilambile		Z	Ngifuma ukuya kwadokotela
N	Ke swerwe ke tlala		N	Ke nyaka go bona ngaka
T	Ke tshwerwe ke tlala		T	Ke batla go bona ngaka
E	I am thirsty		E	Call the doctor
A	Ek is dors		A	Ontbied die dokter
X	Ndinxaniwe		X	Biza ugqirha
Z	Ngomile		Z	Biza udokotela
N	Ke swerwe ke lenyora		N	Bitša ngaka
T	Ke tshwerwe ke lenyora		T	Bitsa ngaka

E	How are you feeling?		E	Please call the police
A	Hoe voel jy?		A	Ontbied asseblief die polisie
X	Uziva njani?		X	Nceda ubize amapolisa
Z	Uzizwa unjani?		Z	Ngicela ubize amaphoyisa
N	O ikwa bjang?		N	Anke o bitše maphodisa
T	O ikutlwa jang?		T	A o ke o bitse mopodisa
E	I am feeling well		E	You are under arrest
A	Ek voel goed		A	Jy is onder arres
X	Ndiphilile		X	Ubanjiwe
Z	Ngiphila kahle		Z	Uboshiwe
N	Ke ikwa bokaone		N	O swerwe
T	Ke ikutlwa sentle		T	O tshwerwe
E	I am not feeling well		E	Call an ambulance
A	Ek voel nie goed nie		A	Skakel 'n ambulans
X	Andiziva mnandi		X	Fonela iambulensi
Z	Angiphili neze		Z	Shayela iambulense ucingo
N	Ga ke ikwe gabotse		N	Leletša ambulanse
T	Ga ke ikutlwe sentle		T	Letsetsa emelense mogala
E	Where does it hurt?		E	Who is speaking?
A	Waar is dit seer?		A	Wie praat?
X	Kubuhlungu ndawoni?		X	Ngubani othethayo?
Z	Kubuhlungu kuphi?		Z	Ubani okhulumayo?
N	O kwa bohloko kae?		N	Ke mang yo a bolelago?
T	Go botlhoko kae?		T	Ke mang yo o buang?
E	Go to the hospital		E	I will call him
A	Gaan hospitaal toe		A	Ek sal hom gaan roep
X	Ukuya esibhedlele		X	Ndiza kumbiza
Z	Iya esibhedlela		Z	Ngiyombiza
N	Eya sepetlele		N	Ke tla ya go mmitša
T	Eya sepetlele		T	Ke tla ya go mmitsa
E	There has been an accident		E	I am lost
A	Daar was 'n ongeluk		A	Ek het verdwaal
X	Bekukho ingozi		X	Ndilahlekile
Z	Kuvele ingozi		Z	Ngedukile
N	Go diregile kotsi		N	Ke timetše
T	Go ne go na le kotsi		T	Ke timetse
E	Are you hurt?		E	How do I find …?
A	Het jy seergekry?		A	Hoe kom ek by …?
X	Ingaba wenzakele?		X	Ugandibonisa indlela eya …?
Z	Ulimele na?		Z	Ngibuza indlela eya …?
N	A o gobetše?		N	A o ka mpontšha tsela ye e yago …?
T	A o utlwile botlhoko?		T	A o kgona go ntshupetsa go ya …?
E	Do not move			
A	Moenie beweeg nie			
X	Ungashukumi			
Z	Unganyakazi			
N	O se šuthe			
T	O se ke wa tshikinyega			

Change of name

- If you want to change your name, you must fill in a form (BI-85 form) at the Department of Home Affairs. A small fee is payable.

- If an illegitimate child wants to take the surname of her mother's next husband, permission must be obtained from the new spouse (BI-193 form).

- If you want to change your surname, a good reason is necessary. A BI-196 form from the Department of Home Affairs must be filled in. It must be approved by the director-general of Home Affairs and published in the Government Gazette.

- A woman who marries and wants to take either her husband's surname or a combination of their names (her maiden name and his) need only inform the Department of Home Affairs of this in writing.

- All the relevant forms are also available on the Internet: **www.home-affairs.gov.za**.

Adoptions

People who can legally adopt children:

- A couple who are legally married.

- The spouse of the natural parent of the child.

- A man and woman who are in a lifelong cohabiting relationship.

- Two people of the same sex who are in a lifelong cohabiting relationship.

- Single people who have the permission of the Minister of Social Development.

Procedures

- Apply to a social worker or adoption agency.

- They will determine if you are an appropriate adoptive parent, and ensure that the process is handled legally.

- If a suitable child is found, the Child Court in the district where the child lives must legally approve the adoption.

- The Commissioner of Child Welfare will determine if you are able to maintain and educate the child, and if the child's race, religion and culture are compatible with your own.

- After these procedures an adoption order is issued.

- Adoptions can be cancelled within two years in the following circumstances:
    - If the adoption is not in the best interests in the child.
    - If the child has mental problems of which the adoptive parents were not aware.
    - If the adoptive parents were persuaded under false pretences to adopt the child.

It is illegal to pay compensation for the adoption of a child.

The Small Claims Court

If someone owes you money, you sue the person through the Small Claims Court. You can only institute a claim as an individual, not on behalf of a company. You can sue an individual, company or municipality, but not the national government. The amount you claim may not be more than R7 000. The biggest advantage of the Small Claims Court is that you do not have to pay high legal fees. There are more than 140 small claims courts in South Africa.

Procedures:

- Contact the magistrate's office and find out where the nearest Small Claims Court is.

- Contact the person or organisation and make your case. If you do not receive satisfactory feedback, make your claim in writing in a letter of demand that you can obtain from the clerk of the court. The person or organisation has three weeks to respond.

- Deliver your demand in person and obtain proof that the person in question has received it or send it by registered post and keep the proof from the post office. You must ask at the post office that the pink card is posted to you – it is the proof that the registered letter was received by the person.

- If you do not receive a satisfactory reaction, go to the Small Claims Court again. Take the letter and proof of receipt along, as well as any other documents or contracts pertaining to the matter. Also take the address and contact details of the involved person or organisation.

- You will not need a lawyer. The clerk of the Small Claims Court will draft a summons that you can hand over yourself. You must ensure that you obtain a proof of receipt. You can also contact the bailiff in the district where the person or organisation is situated to do it for you. There will be a cost attached to this, which you can claim back if you win the case.

- The Clerk of the Court will set a date and time for the hearing. You and the defendant will appear on the relevant date before the Commissioner for Small Claims so that each can state his case.

- If your opponent is willing to pay the claim, make sure you obtain written proof of the payment and immediately inform the Clerk of the Court.

- If there is going to be a court case, make sure that you have all your evidence and documents available. Also take any witnesses to the court. The court case will be informal and simple.

- No lawyers are permitted at the Small Claims Court. You can consult a lawyer before the case at your own cost.

- If the ruling of the Commissioner is in your favour, your opponent must pay immediately. If he doesn't have the money, arrangements will be made so he can pay it in instalments. If you lose the case, you must pay your opponent's costs. It is usually a small amount that only includes the bailiff's fees.

- Judgement will be handed down even if the defendant does not show up at the hearing.

- You cannot appeal unless there has been definite irregularities.

Cases that are not handled by the Small Claims Court:

- Claims of more than R7 000
- Claims against the state
- Claims at the dissolution of a marriage
- Claims regarding defamation and malicious persecution
- Claims regarding unlawful detention and imprisonment
- Claims regarding seduction and breach of promise
- Claims regarding the validity of a will
- Claims regarding the transfer of rights.

- A person under 21 must be supported by a parent or legal guardian.
- If your claim is more than R7 000, you can reduce it to R7 000 so it can be handled in the Small Claims Court and you can save on costs.

Tips for saving water

- Read your house's water meter before and after a two-hour period in which no water has been used. If the reading is not the same, there is a water leak somewhere.

- Make sure that no taps drip and replace washers when necessary.

- Keep drinking water in the fridge so that you don't need to run the tap until the water becomes cold.

Cut-off sprinkler on a garden hose

- When you run a tap to get hot water, collect the cold water in a container and use it for something else.

- Do not defrost food under a running tap. Defrost it overnight or use a microwave.

- Fill the kettle with only as much water as is needed.

- Fill the dishwasher before turning it on. Wash small amounts of dishes by hand.

- Use all the water you can in the garden rather than letting it run down the drain.

- A shower uses far less water than a bath. Take short showers and use as little water as possible in your bath.

- Turn off the shower while you're washing and turn it on again to rinse yourself.

- Put a two litre plastic bottle full of water in big toilet cisterns so less water is used when flushing.

- Repair toilets that do not stop running.

- Avoid flushing the toilet unnecessarily.

- Do not let the tap run while you are brushing your teeth. Run a basin of water with which to shave.

- Wash your car on the grass and use a bucket instead of running water.

- Put a cut-off sprinkler on the garden hose.

- Do not leave a garden hose running.

- Install an irrigation system that turns itself on and off. Monitor the automatic settings regularly.

- Water the garden early in the morning or late in the afternoon.

- Make sure that plants are being watered and not the driveway or the street.

- Sweep driveways and pathways instead of hosing them down.

- Use a fountain that circulates water.

- Make a water-friendly garden with plenty of rocks and indigenous plants.

- Cover beds with bark or other mulches to keep the ground damp for longer.

- Do not use your swimming pool pump constantly, and make sure it is not leaking water.

Tips for saving electricity

- Turn off all unnecessary lights in the house and turn the light off whenever you leave a room.

- Use candles whenever you are not working, reading or writing in the evening.

- Use energy saving light bulbs (CFLs). They last much longer and use 80% less electricity than normal light bulbs.

- Geysers are one of the biggest consumers of electricity. Power and money can be saved by switching your geyser off and turning it on again half an hour before hot water is needed.

- Install a geyser blanket.

- Turn the geyser's thermostat down to 60°C.

- Install the geyser as closely as possible to the places where the hot water will be needed.

- Consider a gas geyser.

- Shower rather than taking a bath. Far less water is used in this way and the geyser uses less power to heat it.

- Ensure that hot water taps do not drip.

- Do not iron articles that do not really need it, and iron everything in one go.

- Consider a gas stove.

- A conventional oven uses a lot more power than a microwave oven, so try to cook as much food as possible in the microwave oven.

- Do not defrost food in the microwave oven. Take frozen food out of the freezer ahead of time and leave it in the fridge to defrost.

- Open the oven door as seldom as possible.

- Do not make toast in the oven.

- When the oven is turned on, put as much food as possible in it. Plan meals so that everything can be made in the oven at the same time. In order for the heat to circulate dishes should not touch each other or the sides of the oven.

- Use saucepans that are the same size as the stove plate and keep the lids on as much as possible to contain the heat. Saucepan lids should fit tightly.

- Do not use saucepans with buckled bottoms. This wastes heat and the food takes much longer to cook.

- Solid plates and heavy-bottomed saucepans retain heat longer and can be switched off sooner.

- Quickly bring food to the boil and then let it simmer until it is cooked.

- Do not cook food for longer than necessary.

- Use a steamer, which cooks food very quickly.

- Soak dry food like beans and peaches before you cook them. They don't have to be cooked for such a long time.

- When cooking, first boil water in the kettle and then put it on the stove.

- Boil just enough water as needed for coffee and tea and do not boil a full kettle each time.

- Open the doors of fridges and freezers as little and for as short a period as possible.

- Ensure that the doors of fridges and freezers seal properly.

- Regularly dust the panels at the back of the fridge.

- Allow food to cool before putting it in the fridge or freezer.

- Do not place your fridge next to a stove.

- Do not overload your fridge or freezer.

- Make a list of everything in the freezer so that you don't have to hold the door open for a long time to search for a particular item.

- Remove unnecessary packaging from food before you put it in the fridge.

- Containers in the fridge should not touch each other. The cold air must be allowed to circulate.

- Wait until the dishwasher is full before starting the cycle.

- Turn off the dishwasher after the last rinse and before it starts drying the dishes. The dishes can then be dried by hand.

- Check regularly that the dishwasher's filters are clean. Dirty filters impede the operation of the machine and unnecessary power is used.

- Only turn on your washing machine if there is enough laundry to fill it.

- Use cold water and a short programme for the washing machine.

- Try as far as possible to dry laundry outside on a line.

- Spin clothes well before putting them in a tumble drier.

- Do not leave your TV, radio, computer or printer turned on when they are not in use.

- As far as possible, use oil or gas heaters with thermostats.

- Close windows and doors when a heater is switched on.

- Close curtains early in the evening to retain as much heat as possible.

- Turn the heater off if you are leaving the room for a long period.

- Do not heat your room with an air conditioner. It uses more power than any other electrical appliance. Use a hot water bottle or an electric blanket to heat your bed. Remember to turn off the blanket when you go to sleep.

- Protect the outside parts of an air conditioning unit from the sun. Install it where it will be exposed to the least possible amount of sun.

- Regularly clean your vacuum cleaner bag.

- Use your swimming pool pump as seldom as possible.

- Do not connect several lights to one light switch.

Power consumption of electrical appliances

Appliance per month	kWh units	Appliance per month	kWh units
CD player	0,3	Computer	10,8
DVD player	0,84	Dishwasher	135
Electric lawnmower	8	Stove: large plate	120
Geyser	300	Stove: small plate	22,5
Light bulb (60W)	9	Swimming pool pump	60
Light bulb (100W)	15	Television (51cm)	14,4
Hi-fi system	5,4	Two-plate stove	210
Cassette player	2,2	Heater (two bars)	130
Kettle	32,4	Heater (three bars)	200
Air conditioner	600	Heater (fan)	200
DSTV decoder	10,1	Heater (oil)	200
Microwave oven	58,5	Video machine	2,1
Oven: grill	16,5	Fridge	64,4
Oven: baking	19	Fridge with freezer	107,3

Tips for power failures

- Always keep a torch with strong batteries to hand.

- Ensure that candles and matches are always available.

- Buy a gas stove.

- Buy gas lamps or lanterns with rechargeable batteries.

- Ensure that your cellphone's batteries are always charged.

- Ensure that your car always has sufficient fuel.

- Always have enough cash with you.

- Disconnect electric garage doors and security gates so that they can be opened manually.

- If you know when there will be a power failure, boil water and keep it in vacuum flasks. Ensure there is food that can be eaten cold.

- Always keep a supply of non-perishable food in the house.

Gas
- Do not use rusted gas bottles.
- When gas is used, make sure there is always an open window.
- Ensure that all gas taps are tightly closed after use.
- Do not light a match if there is a smell of gas.
- Buy gas bottles and accessories with the SABS mark at a reputable dealer.
- Fill gas bottles only at reputable dealers. If it is overfilled it could explode.
- Reputable dealers will ensure that gas bottles do not leak.

Generators
- Ensure that the generator is installed by a qualified person.
- Generators must be situated outside.
- Where indoor generators are used, exhaust gasses must be able to escape to the outside.
- A generator must have a switch that cuts the electricity supply when Eskom power is restored.

Firearms

Criteria which a person must fulfil to apply for a firearm licence:

- The person must be 21 years or older.
- A background check must be passed.
- The person may not have a criminal record.
- The person must be familiar with the law.
- A valid training certificate must be obtained from an accredited instructor.

Obtaining a firearm licence

- Take the training certificate to your nearest police station and apply for a competency certificate.
- When you have received the competency certificate, fill out an application form for the licence and pay the prescribed fee.
- You must take your original identity document as well as four unobscured colour passport photos.
- You must also take a health certificate from your doctor.
- You must provide two references (a spouse, employer or friend).
- You must sign a form to prove that you are aware of the law that applies to firearms.
- You must declare any previous convictions.
- You must provide a short motivation and indicate what the firearm will be used for.
- An interview will be conducted with you and your fingerprints will be taken.
- You will be given a proof of receipt certificate from the firearm officer.
- Your house will be visited to ensure that your safe fits the requirements.
- An interview will also be conducted with your employer or partner to ascertain if you are competent to own a firearm.
- The application will be sent to the Central Firearm Register in Pretoria, with a recommendation on whether the licence should be granted or not.
- You will be contacted if the firearm licence is awarded so you can fetch it.
- If the application is denied, the reasons will be given in writing.
- You can appeal to the Chairperson of the Appeal Board, Private Bag X811, Pretoria, 0001.

- Only one licence for a firearm for self-defence purposes will be awarded to a person.
- A firearm may only be purchased from a registered dealer.
- You may only have 200 rounds of ammunition per firearm.
- A licence for a firearm for self-defence purposes must be renewed every five years.
- If your firearm is stolen or lost, you must immediately report it to the police.
- Someone else may use your firearm if they are older than 21, have a firearm licence and it is used under your supervision.
- When someone inherits a weapon and wishes to keep it, the person must apply for a firearm licence.

Criteria for a safe or device for the safe-keeping of a firearm or ammunition

- It must be made of steel at least 2mm thick.
- It must completely enclose the firearm.
- It must be equipped with an effective locking mechanism.
- It must have a hinge mechanism for the lid that cannot be opened if the pin is removed from the hinge.
- It must be safely and properly fixed to another structure such as a wall or floor.

Tips for consumers

Grocery shopping

- Compare the unit prices on products. It is not always cheapest to buy a big package.

- Always check the date stamp on perishable and preserved products.

- Do not leave food in a warm car. Immediately put it in a cool bag, fridge or freezer.

- Read the labels thoroughly and pay attention to the additives – some can cause allergic reactions.

- Read the instruction on the product thoroughly and follow the directions. Many products must be refrigerated after they are opened.

- Compare a particular brand in different shops before you buy, especially for expensive items.

- Ask about installation and delivery costs. It is advisable to have the delivery date in writing.

- Ask about after-sales service for any expensive product you buy.

- Inquire about the shop's return and exchange policies.

- Keep all receipts, cash register slips, instructions and guarantees until they expire or you are sure there is not a problem with the products or goods.

- "Use before" means that the product may only start going bad after this date. "Best before" means the product will stay fresh until this date, but can be used for a short time afterwards. "Expiry date" means that the product should not be used after that date.
- Tinned products have a date stamp from the manufacturer. It is usually underneath the tin. If you have a complaint, this code can be quoted.

Contracts

- Never sign a contract if you do not understand everything in it. Ask an expert to explain everything to you first.

- Do not sign a contract if the person refuses to allow you to seek expert advice first.

- Ensure that all oral agreements are also written into the contract.

- Do not sign a contract with open spaces. Draw lines through these spaces.

- Always keep a copy of a contract.

Complaint procedures

- Complain as soon as possible after you have encountered a problem. Do not have unrealistic expectations.

- Ensure that you have all the facts before you complain.

- Take along all receipts or slips and speak first to the appropriate supervisor.

- Be friendly, calm and reasonable.

- Say whether you would like your money back or whether you would like the product exchanged.

- If you are not satisfied, ask to speak to the manager of the shop.

- If you are still not satisfied, write to the person at head office who is responsible for customer complaints.

- Write a short, polite and businesslike letter and enclose copies of any relevant documents.

- Make it clear what your problem is and name all the steps you have taken to resolve the problem.

- If you still do not receive a satisfactory reaction, you can contact a consumer journalist, a consumer organisation such as the South African National Consumer Union, an ombudsman or lawyer.

Contacts for complaints

Advertisements:
ASA (Advertising Standards Authority of SA)
☎ 011 781 2006
Email: executive@asasa.org.za

Banking services:
The Ombudsman for Banking Services
☎ 0860 800 900
Email: info@obssa.co.za

Building:
NHBRC (National Home Builders Registration Council)
☎ 021 914 6570
Email: www.nhbrc.org.za

MBS (Master Builders' Society)
☎ 021 685 2625, 011 805 6611
www.mbawc.org.za

CVS (Contractor Validation Services)
☎ 021 914 1474
www.contractorvalidation.com

Competitions:
Competition Commission
☎ 012 394 3200
Email: ccsa@compcom.co.za

Credit information:
The Ombudsman for Credit Information
☎ 086 1662 837
Email: ombud@creditombud.org.za

Dentistry:
The Dental Ombudsman
☎ 011 484 8704
Email: jeffm@sada.co.za

Doctors and dentists:
HPCSA (Health Professions Council of South Africa)
Registrar of the HPCSA
Post Box 205
PRETORIA
0001
Fax: 012 328 4895
(Only written complaints are accepted)

General:
SANCU (The South African National Consumer Union)
☎ 012 428 7122
Email: sancu@sabs.co.za

Office of the Consumer Protector (for any complaints about products or services)
☎ 008 0000 7081
Email: consumer@pgwc.gov.za

Long-term insurance:
Email: info@ombud.co.za

Notes

Notes